SOMEBODY'S GOTTA TELL IT

Other Books by Jack Newfield

A Prophetic Minority

Robert Kennedy: A Memoir

A Populist Manifesto
(with Jeff Greenfield)

Bread and Roses, Too

The Education of Jack Newfield

Cruel and Unusual Justice

The Permanent Government
(with Paul DuBrul)

City for Sale
(with Wayne Barrett)

Only in America:
The Life and Crimes of Don King

SOMEBODY'S GOTTA TELL IT

The Upbeat Memoir of a Working-Class Journalist

JACK NEWFIELD

St. Martin's Press New York

www.stmartins.com

All photographs courtesy of the author

Design by Kathryn Parise

LIBRARY OF CONGRESS CATALOGING-IN-PUBLICATION DATA

Newfield, Jack.
Somebody's gotta tell it : the upbeat memoir of a working-class journalist / Jack Newfield.
p. cm.
ISBN 0-312-26900-5
1. Newfield, Jack. 2. Journalists—United States—Biography. I. Title.
PN4874.N37 A3 2002
070'.92—dc21
[B] 2001048876

First Edition: April 2002

10 9 8 7 6 5 4 3 2 1

To my mother, who gave me everything,
To my father, whom I never got to know,
And to Janie, Rebecca, and Joey

CONTENTS

ACKNOWLEDGMENTS

George Bernard Shaw once said that people who write confessional memoirs are like beggars who display their scabs for money.

This is not the kind of memoir that would irritate Shaw. Intimate public confession is not my temperament. Rather, this is a memoir about being a witness to history. This is a memoir about a political and cultural education by someone who was both a participant and a reporter, a memoir of a poor white kid growing up in a black neighborhood.

This is also a memoir of the glories of a free press and of the newspaper business in New York City, including a strike at the *Daily News*, a staff mutiny at the *Post*, and my years at the *Village Voice* when that weekly was surfing all the waves of the 1960s.

Here are my experiences with a few historic figures—Robert Kennedy, Martin Luther King, and Muhammad Ali, and my friendships with Mario Cuomo, Pete Hamill, Phil Ochs, Tom Hayden, Irving Howe, Mike Tyson, José Torres, Cus D'Amato, Teddy Atlas, Bob Moses, Michael Harrington, Norman Mailer, Dan Wolf, and Allard Lowenstein.

Acknowledgments

This is a tabloid kind of memoir. I choose to define "tabloid" as meaning drama, emotion, conflict, and personality, all elements of my career. I have emphasized the events and people who had some confrontation, excitement, and humor to them. I do *not* define "tabloid" as meaning sex, gossip, or violence.

Memory is fallible and tricky. It can be composite, wishful, or selective. So I have tried to be as accurate as possible. Some dialogue is reconstructed; some from recent interviews. I have also relied on articles or columns I wrote about the experiences I am describing in these pages, to have the benefit of contemporary reporting and, in some cases, lawyering. I have double-checked my memory against clippings in the *Post* library, with the assistance of the chief librarian Laura Harris.

I have looked at hours of videotape of some of the major events described, especially the strike at the *Daily News* and the staff mutiny at the *Post.*

I did keep notes during some crucial episodes, and they have proven invaluable. These notes include my evening with Martin Luther King three weeks before his assassination; my encounters with Muhammad Ali over the years; my decision to resign from the *Daily News* in 1990, rather than cross a union picket line; and my almost daily note-taking during the eight weeks of carnival and mutiny at the *Post* in 1993.

I made notes of my conversations with Walter Sheridan, Professor Robert Blakely, and Frank Ragano about the assassination of President Kennedy.

I also went back and interviewed scores of old friends and colleagues, to help me fill in the potholes of memory with fresh reporting. Among those who were most helpful were: Alan Weitz, Marc Kalech, Nat and Margot Hentoff, Gil Spencer, Wayne Barrett, Todd Gitlin, Mendy Samstein, Pete Hamill, Stuart Marques, Mario Cuomo, Steve Cuozzo, Susan Brownmiller, Sally Kempton, Teddy Atlas, David Schneiderman, José Torres, Juan Gonzales, Karen Phillips, and Geoff Cowan.

The chapters on Robert Kennedy were refreshed by interviews I did in 1997 for a television documentary on RFK's life that was based on my

1969 book about him. Especially illuminating were Arthur Schlesinger, Jr., Peter Edelman, Richard Goodwin, John Siegenthaler, John Lewis, Frank Mankiewicz, Bill vanden Heuvel, Shirley MacLaine, George McGovern, and three of Robert Kennedy's children—Kerry Kennedy Cuomo, Kathleen Kennedy, and Robert Kennedy, Jr.

I want to thank the Osner typewriter store on Amsterdam Avenue for supplying me with twelve manual typewriter ribbons during the course of writing this memoir. In this age of computers, I still find the manual typewriter forces me to rewrite whole pages and slows me down so that I have time to think. I enjoy correcting and improving copy by hand, with a pencil. I can hear a rhythm inside my head with a typewriter that I can't hear with the computer. I know a computer is easier, but harder is better, at least for me. That being the case, I thank Teresa Theophano, Brad Wood, and Michael Connor—all at St. Martin's Press—for their patience and their computer keyboard skills.

My editor, Tim Bent, aided and abetted by his assistant, Julia Pastore, contributed big ideas, fine-tuning, and editing that always improved my prose—and curbed my tendency for making lists.

I thank Stanley Crouch for inspiring the title of this memoir. At my sixtieth birthday party, Stanley took the microphone and for several minutes chanted a blues dirge, repeating over and over the improvised phrase, "Somebody's gotta tell." When this struck me as a potential title for this memoir, I asked Stanley what he meant by it. "What I sang," he told me, "was an attempt to express the fact that the world needs real information. And for the people to receive that real information, somebody has got to go out and discover it and write it. Somebody has gotta tell it. That was you."

A shadow is cast across these pages by some people who died along the way. My father died when I was four years old. His absence is a hole in the middle of my life there was no way to fill. My two close friends—Paul DuBrul, whom I met in college, and Paul Cowan, who worked with me at the *Village Voice*—both passed away before their fiftieth birthday. They were gifted compadres, although opposites in temperament. And Murray Kempton, whom I started reading when I was fifteen. Later in life I got to know Murray as a friend, role model, tutor, and "fellow worker," as he referred to many of us. Several times in writing this memoir, when words or understanding failed me, I just quoted Murray because nobody could say it better.

The famous Greek epigram that was originally inspired by Plato also applies to Murray Kempton: "In whatever direction we go, we meet him on his way back."

If I am not for myself, who is for me?
If I am only for myself, then what am I?

—Rabbi Hillel the Elder,
The Talmud

The tragedy of life doesn't lie in not reaching your goal. The tragedy lies in having no goal to reach. It isn't a calamity to die with dreams unfulfilled, but it is a calamity not to dream. It is not a disaster to be unable to capture your ideal, but it is a disaster to have no ideal to capture. It is not a disgrace not to reach the stars, but it is a disgrace to have no stars to reach for. Not failure, but low aim, is sin.

—Dr. Benjamin E. Mays,
President of Morehouse College and mentor to Martin Luther King, Jr.

The job of the columnist is to comfort the afflicted, and afflict the comfortable.

—H. L. Mencken

The greatest challenge of adulthood is holding on to your idealism after you have lost your innocence.

—Bruce Springsteen

SOMEBODY'S GOTTA TELL IT

CHAPTER 1

A State of Mind Called Brooklyn, 1955

I am a child of the working class, a product of public institutions and public places. I am an American—Brooklyn born. I am proud of these origins. They made me what I am.

I attended public schools, public high school, and the City University—because it was free.

I took public transportation everywhere because my single mother did not own a car. I played in public parks. The public library was my sanctuary of stimulation.

I began to read in the small Tompkins Park Branch five blocks from my house. That's where, while I was in high school, I discovered the Studs Lonigan trilogy by James T. Farrell. That's where I read *The Harder They Fall* and *What Makes Sammy Run?* by Budd Schulberg. That's where I read *A Tree Grows in Brooklyn* by Betty Smith. The first time I ever saw Shakespeare was a free production of *Hamlet* in Central Park by Joseph Papp. It was public theatre.

My adolescence was spent in a small patch of Brooklyn called Bedford-Stuyvesant. It was mostly Jewish and Italian when I was ten years old, predominantly black by the time I was eighteen years old. White flight, and blockbusting scare tactics by real estate speculators, changed it in front of my eyes. It fomented fear of blacks and panic selling of tenements by whites.

The perimeters of my adolescence were Ebbets Field, Tompkins Park, Prospect Park, the Marcy projects on Myrtle Avenue, Boys High, the S & L deli on Dekalb Avenue, the Paramount theater, also on Dekalb, and the Kismet Theatre, which showed a "chapter" every Saturday afternoon—a fifteen-minute soap opera about Flash Gordon, or some other science fiction or cowboy hero.

My Brooklyn was the working-class Brooklyn of the Dodgers, Democrats, unions, optimism, and pluralism. Out of this neighborhood environment I acquired a simple code that would shape my values for the rest of my life:

Play fair and by the rules.
Education is the key to a better life.
Be loyal to your friends.
Never forget where you came from.
Don't be a squealer or a snitch.
Don't be afraid of bullies.
Never cross a picket line.
Help the team win, move the runner along, keep the inning alive.
Never give up.

The seed for this memoir was planted in June of 1999. I was hunched over my Olympia manual typewriter, trying to compose a few pages of remarks for the annual meeting of the Boys High Alumni Association. In a few nights I was to receive an award from that group, and I was having a hard time drafting something that would be adequate to this homecoming evening, that would transport me back to my roots and my adolescence.

I decided to let the free-form reverie of memory float over the year 1955, the year I graduated from high school, the year that now seems to me such a turning point in American history.

I began thinking about my mother, dead since 1991, and how much of her life she sacrificed to raise me, her only child, after my father had died suddenly of a heart attack on the subway when I was four and she was forty-four.

My mother was a nervous woman with anxieties that were probably aggravated by her early, sudden widowhood. She had to go to work as a saleswoman in a downtown Brooklyn department store to put food on the table. I was what they now call a "latch-key child" from fourth grade on. Two nights a week she worked till 9 P.M., standing on her aching feet. Every day, before going to work, she made me a sandwich and left it in the refrigerator. I often didn't eat it, and still feel guilty about that, fifty years later.

We were poor. My mother could not afford to send me to summer camp and wasn't aware of those camps that were free for the "underprivileged." As I've said, we owned no car, and I never learned how to drive. We did not own a television set until I was fourteen. Though I wanted one desperately, my mother had to tell me she could not afford to buy me a guitar. We did not take vacations or travel outside the city. When I told her that I wanted to go to college, she had to inform me that I would not be able to attend college at all, unless my grades were good enough to gain me admission to the City University, which was then tuition-free.

My main memories of my mother are of worry and work. She worked to support me until I was in college. She never stopped worrying about me. Whenever I came home late at night on the subway after putting out my college paper, she would be waiting up, fearful something had happened to me on the subway. She was always pacing or at the window. In turn, I had secret terrors she would die, like my father, and leave me alone in the world.

Her anxieties about me surfaced even on the night I appeared on local television for the first time, early in 1965, when I was twenty-seven, to argue against military escalation in Vietnam. When I got home from the broadcast, my phone was ringing.

"I just watched you, Jackie," my mother was saying. "I have to say two things to you, so please listen, if you ever want to be invited back to go on television."

"What are they?"

"Don't attack the president, and don't slouch."

But talking about my mother in public was too private—and too painful a subject—for me to deal with. She has been gone for ten years now, but I still felt immense guilt that she had to work so hard and had so little joy in her life after my father died. I tried to repay her just by being good and giving her pleasure with my successes. Yet, sitting there in front of my typewriter, I knew I could not say any of this to strangers, particularly on a night I was expected to make a few light remarks of thanks to the Boys High alumni. It would be easier for me to talk about what I felt I owed to my school, and to Brooklyn, than about the much greater debt I owed to my absent mother. I was aware of this, and it made me feel sad.

But there was something about Brooklyn, after the end of World War II—and until the Dodgers left in 1957—that was magical, that fueled a nostalgia industry for fifty years. There was something about the open fire hydrants, the spaldeens, the double-bill movie theaters, the comic books in candy stores, the egg creams, the stickball games with a broomstick handle, that became part of our, and even the nation's, DNA.

There was an optimism after the war, lots of jobs at the Navy Yard, an upward mobility as families began to move off Vernon Avenue, to Flatbush, to Queens, and then to the suburbs. There was a feeling of barriers coming down, symbolized by the arrival of Jackie Robinson in 1947. The Dodgers made us identify with underdogs.

There is something about Brooklyn that has bonded those who grew up there. Pete Hamill and Nick Pileggi grew up in Brooklyn during the same era that I did, and I still marvel at our kinship, at how similar our values, attitudes, and instincts have remained. We almost never disagree about politics, music, film, writers, sports, morals, or other people's characters. We were formed by democratic Brooklyn, by the Brooklyn of working-class pluralism. We were proud of our Irish, Jewish, and Italian ethnic identities, but also shaped by the transcendent values of the old neighborhood. No party platform or political vocabulary has ever been able to bottle the feeling that was in the air of Jackie Robinson's Brooklyn.

My Brooklyn pride runs so deep that even as a teenager I knew which celebrities came from Brooklyn: Lauren Bacall, Jackie Gleason, Vince Lombardi, Lena Horne, Henry Miller, Susan Haywood, Al Capone.

What Lincoln called "the mystic chords of memory" transported me back to my 1955 Boys High graduating class, which was much more than half black. What an education I received from these old classmates—and from quite a few of their parents—in black music, history, culture, and sports.

During my high school years I was being introduced to Billie Holiday singing "Strange Fruit"; to Louis Armstrong; to Ray Charles; to comedians like Moms Mabley and Redd Foxx; to dancer Bojangles Robinson; to Bessie Smith; to Mahalia Jackson; and to pre–Jackie Robinson Negro League baseball stars like Oscar Charlston ("the black Ty Cobb"), Cool Papa Bell, Josh Gibson, and Martin Dihigo, the black Cuban.

From an early age I understood that despite tremendous adversity, poverty, and discrimination, black people had given so much to the American whole that they often set the trends with their creativity. Artists like Miles Davis, Lester Young, and Billie Holiday had a special gift for communicating the deepest sorrow and loneliness of the human condition, and I heard their song.

In 1956 I was invited to see Sam Cooke and the Soul Stirrers perform at a movie theater on Bedford Avenue. The concert changed my taste in music and public performance forever. Sam Cooke was still a teenager, not yet the solo star. But I saw him make churchgoing women swoon. Cooke combined the spiritual and the erotic—and he was handsome in the special Muhammad Ali–Harry Belafonte way. He sang the gospel song, "At the Hem of His Garment," in a way that combined religious ecstasy and carnal sensuality. Right in front of my bulging teenage eyes, in a crowd where I was probably the only white person, Sam was inventing modern crossover music, from the sacred to the secular. At the time I had no way of knowing how privileged I was.

I gained some insight into creativity and equality through my early infatuation with black music. Living in Bed-Stuy, as Bedford Stuyvesant is called, and being guided to black radio stations and record stores, I sometimes got to hear the original version of songs by black artists before the more commercialized "cover" version by a white singer received airplay on AM radio, often greased by corporate payola.

I heard a record of "Hound Dog" by Big Mama Thornton, the blues singer, before Elvis Presley made the song a classic. During the summer of 1954 I heard the Chords' doo-wop harmomy version of "Sh-Boom," before the Crew Cuts—from Toronto—made a schmaltzy cover that sold a million copies.

In 1954, I heard LaVern Baker, who came out of the black church in Chicago, sing "Tweedle Dee," before Georgia Gibbs copied the arrangement and the style, and got the riches from a gold record. But in 1957, Baker recorded "Jim Dandy," and Gibbs again made a cover version, but this time the new youth market was hip enough to buy the real raw thing.

And I heard the exhibitionistic, manic Little Richard version of "Tutti Frutti" before Pat Boone made his pathetic cover version.

While I was still in high school, I was learning who the creators were, and who the copy cats were. Airplay gave me a perspective on fair play.

Only when I got to Hunter College, which was 95 percent white, did I realize how unorthodox and underground my taste was, compared to the television–jukebox–record store–AM radio–top 40 mainstream. My new college friends were listening to show tunes and the *Hit Parade* on TV. They talked about John Raitt, Doris Day, and Theresa Brewer. They teased me about my preference for exotic "Negro music" and "dirty" Negro comedians.

A few years ago my wife and I had dinner with an old friend from the Hunter College newspaper. My wife asked her what I was like in college.

"Jack was blacker than the blacks," she said. "He was always talking about people named 'Moms' and 'Bojangles,' and I never heard of them. It wasn't just civil rights, it was unknown singers and baseball players who never got their chance."

The historian Gerald Early said it best in the first hour of Ken Burns's documentary history of baseball. "When they study our civilization two thousand years from now, there will only be three things that Americans will be known for: the Constitution, baseball, and jazz music. They are the three most beautiful things Americans have ever created."

By 1955 I was already a fan of Early's three great American creations—the Constitution, baseball, and jazz (plus rock 'n' roll). They made me feel American.

During the 1960s segregation, war, and assassination fed feelings of alienation among many people I knew. But my own alienation was always muted whenever I saw Willie Mays or Sandy Koufax or Roberto Clemente play baseball, or whenever I heard jazz or gospel or soul music. These helped immunize me against anti-Americanism. More than that, they inspired me to fight against it. Falling in love with black music prepared a lot of whites like me to join the civil rights movement. B. B. King and Ben E. King were warm-up acts for Martin Luther King. Rock 'n' roll didn't lead to delinquency; it led to democracy.

In 1955 jazz, baseball, and rock 'n' roll were three integrated American subcultures. (The Supreme Court and the U.S. Senate, on the other hand, were still 100 percent segregated, still awaiting the arrival of Thurgood Marshall and Edward Brooke.) I was conditioned to welcome diversity by being a teenage enthusiast of these three American subcultures. And by attending Boys High and growing up in Bed-Stuy when it was becoming a predominantly black neighborhood. And by enlisting in the civil rights movement in 1960. When a generation later New York was being flooded with new immigrants from the Dominican Republic, Korea, Haiti, Mexico, and Pakistan, I automatically thought, "These folks are just like the Irish, the Italians, and the Jews who came through Ellis Island a hundred years ago. They're just like me, Pete, and Nick." I knew instinctively they were going to replenish the city's hybrid vitality with their own shops, music, energy, and businesses—car services, newsstands, groceries, restaurants. I instinctively applied what I had learned from Jackie Robinson (and Roberto Clemente), that there is talent in every community and in every culture. My Brooklyn Dodgers of 1955 were the national frontier of inclusion and integration. In addition to Robinson, there was Hodges, Podres, Campanella, Reese, Gilliam, Furillo, Sinder, Newcombe, and Cuban Sandy Amoros. They had the same core of players for ten years. Nobody retired or was traded. I grew up with this same lineup.

The Dodgers had lost to the Yankees in 1941, 1947, 1949, 1952, and 1953. The Dodgers had lost the pennant on the last pitch of the last inning in both 1950 and 1951, which was when Bobby Thompson, one of the New York Giants, hit his famous home run. The Dodgers always seemed to lose by an inch at the end. So the explosion of jubilation when they finally won in 1955 was evangelical.

The Dodgers were the underdogs who never gave up, the first team to let everybody play.

In 1955 Sugar Ray Robinson and Rocky Marciano won big fights that first electrified my block. Sugar Ray, who was boxing's Shakespeare, shocked all the sportswriters when he regained the middleweight title that December.

For my entire adult life, boxing would remain a guilty pleasure. I would never resolve the paradox of loving both Muhammad Ali, the artist of violence, and Martin Luther King, Jr., the apostle of nonviolence. Even now I loathe boxing each time I see a one-sided mismatch, an unjust decision, an old champ with dementia, or a death in the ring. The fates of Ali, Floyd Patterson, Riddick Bowe, Ray Robinson, Jerry Quarry, and Wilfredo Benitiz make it impossible for me to defend boxing against its abolitionists. I know all those punches to the head did cause brain damage, memory loss, and slurred speech later in life.

But on those rare nights when boxing is done right, there is no sport like it. When two fighters in their prime, evenly matched, compete with all their craft and character, it is something to see. Sugar Ray Robinson is still my standard for perfection, style, and grace in an athlete. My measures for courage are still Ali, Frazier, Holyfield, Carmen Basilio, and Tony Zale. Watching Sugar Shane Mosley, Ray Leonard, Pernell Whitaker, and Roy Jones hit—and avoiding getting hit in return—is to see what is still an art to me; they are scholars of the geometry of angles and distances.

Only some of my friends understand my guilty enjoyment of this sleazy, low-life sport. In the middle of a televised title fight during the 1980s, my phone rang. It was Mario Cuomo, then the governor of New York. "Why are we watching this?" he asked me. When I tried to compose a coherent response, Cuomo laughed and hung up as the bell rang for the next brutal round.

In 1955 I bought the *New York Post* every afternoon to devour the writing of Murray Kempton and Jimmy Cannon. Reading their columns made me want to become a journalist. I would get intoxicated by their use of cadences, by the detail of their reporting, by their ability to create a character in a few words and by their affection for underdogs.

When later I got to know Kempton, I was even more admiring of his deep learning, honesty, radical analysis, biting wit, and the spiritual grace with which he loved all casualties and forgave most sinners. Murray once gave me some valuable counsel. He said, "Always go to the loser's dressing room on election night or after a World Series game. That's where the drama and tragedy will be."

Murray did this famously himself in 1956, the day Don Larsen pitched his perfect World Series game. The next day Murray's column was about Sal Maglie, the losing pitcher, who was forty, had a sore arm, and had pitched well enough to win almost any other game except this one.

Murray had what he called a "losing side consciousness," a feeling for the tragic dignity of the lost cause, like the Brooklyn Dodgers, the loyalist, anti-Franco side in Spain, or Adlai Stevenson's doomed runs for the presidency. "Losing side consciousness" is a precious intellectual and journalistic compass and the sign of a sensibility independent of fashion. I confess I could never see any tragic dignity in the losing dressing rooms of Richard Nixon, J. Edgar Hoover, and Roy Cohn. But I revered Murray so much that I have always felt that this was a defect in me. I envied Murray's forgiving nature and always suspected he knew something I did not. A descendant of Southern aristocracy, Murray said his "losing side consciousness" came from his family's, "Confederate view of everything."

And that mordant wit. Murray would toss off literate quips in casual conversation that it would have taken me a month to think up. "You know, the only form of class consciousness left in America is toadying," he once lamented to me during the Reagan administration. After he won the Pulitzer Prize, he said to me, "The only time prosecutors should ever be allowed to use the RICO statute is to investigate how the Pulitzer Prize is fixed every year in a conspiracy by the big papers." Another time he was recalling how anti-union the *New York Times* editorial page had been. "The only strike they ever supported," he said, "was in Poland. I still have their clips when they came out against the revolt of the Roman slave gladiators. They thought the timing was poor."

One year, the day before the St. Patrick's Day parade, Kempton asked Jim Dwyer, a younger columnist he admired, if he was planning to march with his countrymen in the parade.

"I don't think so," Dwyer replied. "I'm tired of seeing suburban kids throw up on the steps of the Metropolitan Museum."

Without missing a beat, Kempton said, "If they puked on the steps of the Whitney, I'm sure they would exhibit it."

All through college I tried to write just like Jimmy Cannon—tragic, sentimental, lyrical, Irish. I even wrote an homage—a parody of Cannon for an April Fool's edition of the *Hunter Arrow*. It began, as I recall, "You're God, and the smart money doubts your existence. You're old, and your body aches, and tonight at the Garden you have something to prove. You have to pull off one more miracle."

I got to know Cannon during the last year of his life, in 1972, after he had had a stroke and was home-bound. He reminded me of all the great old fighters who had died broke and alone. But I treasure the memory of my afternoon visits, usually with Pete Hamill accompanying me. Cannon once complained, "You guys are no pups out of me! You guys are practically Communists! Stop saying I'm your role model!"

One afternoon Cannon surprised me. I asked him who his favorite writers were, and he had replied, "Hemingway and Rebecca West, the British broad. You gotta read her, kid."

When Cannon suffered his stroke, he lay on the floor of his apartment for two days, until a housekeeper showed up. She called the *New York Post* city desk for help, even though Cannon had not worked for the *Post* for over ten years. That was still the paper the housekeeper associated him with.

I asked Cannon what he had been thinking about during those long desperate hours he was on the floor, alone and unable to move. "I kept thinking I was Billy Conn trying to get up against Joe Louis," he replied.

Beginning in 1955, I started going to the movies as often as my mother could afford. I could lose myself in a movie theater more easily than at a live play. I was dazzled by Marlon Brando in *On the Waterfront* and in *Viva Zapata.* I loved Bogart in *The Harder They Fall*; and Burt Lancaster and Ava Gardner in *The Killers*; I loved the film version of *A Tree Grows in Brooklyn,* since I had read the novel and knew it was set in Williamsburg, a short walk from my house.

I went to see *The Sweet Smell of Success* twice when it came out. The film is partly about the newspaper business and has a jazz music score by Chico Hamilton. And it stars Lancaster. I saw it again recently during a Lancaster retrospective, and it passed the test of time exceptionally well. Now I understand more fully it was partially an attack on Walter Winchell and McCarthyism.

However, the movie that made the strongest impression on me was *Deadline USA.* Written and directed by Richard Brooks, a former reporter, and starring Humphrey Bogart, playing a fearless newspaper editor with a code of honor, the film exposes a mob murder and urban corruption. It made a newspaper city room seem like the most exciting place in the world to be.

In his recent memoir, *A Life in the Twentieth Century,* Arthur Schlesinger, Jr., writes that as a teenager, he went to the movies often, and partly "for instructions in techniques of self presentation." Arthur studied William Powell, Fred Astaire, and Rex Harrison, his models of the "witty, urbane, nonchalant unruffled type." My model in "self presentation" was Bogart, particularly when he played crusading journalists.

Movies had such a hypnotic impact on me—and others of my generation—because they had no competition from the Internet, MTV, cable television, or videos. The Kismet Theatre on Dekalb Avenue was my chat room and VCR. Brando, Lancaster, Bogart, and Ava Gardner left permanent images in my imagination.

Like most moviegoers, I later became dazzled by the great modern mob movies—the first two *Godfather* films, *Goodfellas,* and *Mean Streets.* Knowing some real moviemakers and some real gangsters, I became curious about how they influenced, and looked up to each other.

I have seen killer mobsters become star-struck when they encounter my friend Nick Pileggi because Nick cowrote *Goodfellas* and worked with Scorsese. I know gangsters who watch *The Sopranos* every week and are pleased by how much of their existence is reflected in the show—the terror and the tedium.

In the mid-1990s I became friendly with a famous 1960s' gangster, who had been peripherally involved in the filming of the first *Godfather* movie. This aging capo, who was seventy-six when I met him, told me the producers called him and asked him to arrange for actor James Caan to get access to a young mobster, so he could study his habits, style of dressing, speech, and posture.

"I set it up," my friend told me, "for Caan to spend some time with Carmine 'the Snake' Persico. I knew that Persico spent all his time as a kid in a Brooklyn movie theater watching Richard Widmark. Persico told me he saw Widmark in *Kiss of Death* about ten times.

"I got paid to set Caan up with Persico. It was a joke. Caan could have just watched all them old Richard Widmark movies in Hollywood and saw them white ties on black shirts, which Persico stole from the movie. I made Persico happy. I made Caan happy. And I was selling Hollywood its own shit back to them.

"When the movie came out, what people saw was Caan imitating Persico, who was imitating Widmark."

In 1955 I phoned in the results and box scores from Boys High's basketball games to the city's seven daily newspapers. I was paid $1 a box score.

All through the 1950s, Boys High boasted the best high school basketball teams in the city (and maybe the country), producing future NBA stars like Sihugo Green, Lenny Wilkins, and, later, Connie Hawkins, whose helicopterlike hang time preceded Julius Erving's and Michael Jordan's. The Hawk, as we called him, could swoop and score reverse scoops at fifteen. He could dunk and block shots and rebound with one hand. He was the best high school player in America.

The Hawk was wrongly accused in the Jack Molinas point-shaving scandal of 1961. Manhattan District Attorney Frank Hogan was probing basketball gambling and game fixing at a number of colleges. He sent a detective from his squad out to Iowa, where Connie was a freshman, and had him bring the Hawk back to Manhattan. He was kept in a hotel room for six days without being allowed to contact a lawyer. He was not even allowed to call his mother. Connie Hawkins was an unsophisticated teenager, and didn't even know what a point spread was or what perjury meant. Hogan, who would later become infamous for going after Lenny Bruce, persecuted Connie.

Connie had done nothing wrong. He had fixed no games. He had shaved no points. He had never even played in one college game. All he had done was accept a $200 loan from the fixer—and former NBA player—Jack Molinas to pay for his dorm fees at Iowa. He did nothing in return. He was never indicted, so he could never be vindicated at trial. He was just "named." His name was in the newspapers in a bad context. Iowa asked him to withdraw from college for "academic reasons."

Hogan quietly passed the word to NBA league president Walter Kennedy that Connie was a bad influence. He was blacklisted from the NBA for ten years, until he was thirty and past the kind of playing that only a few of us saw in the Boys High gym and on Brooklyn and Harlem playgrounds.

The memory of this injustice continues to shape my perception of the world. From it I learned that the law is not the same thing as the truth.

In 1955 Martin Luther King, Jr., first entered my awareness, through the columns of Murray Kempton in the *New York Post.* That same year I also read Kempton's columns about the lynching murder of Emmet Till, a fourteen-year-old black boy from Chicago. His killers dumped his mutilated body into the Tallahatchie River in Mississippi. Kempton covered the trial, where Till's obvious killers were acquitted in sixty-seven minutes by an all-white jury. The lynching of Till was the catalyst for the modern civil rights movement, preceding by a few months Rosa Parks and the bus boycott in Montgomery.

Years later Muhammad Ali would confide to me that Till's lynching was the pivotal political experience of his early life. Cassius Clay was thirteen that summer, and followed the news from Mississippi on his TV in Louisville. Two of the early sit-in and voter registration organizers—John Lewis and Bob Moses—would tell me what a traumatic experience the lynching of Till was for them as teenagers in 1955. Lewis, now a congressman, was in Troy, Alabama, and Moses was in Harlem.

In October of 1955 the *Village Voice* was founded by Dan Wolf, Ed Fancher, and Norman Mailer. The very first issue contained an essay by Mike Harrington about Budd Schulberg, Elia Kazan, and *On the Waterfront*. I was soon a faithful reader, under its influence years before I would go to work for the paper in 1964, and remain there for twenty-four years.

While I was at Hunter College I was reading Norman Mailer, Nat Hentoff, Mike Harrington, Jane Jacobs, Seymour Krim, Mary Nichols, Dan Wakefield, Jules Feiffer, and the wonderful theater critic Jerry Tallmer each week.

In the spring of 1960 I wrote an article for the *Hunter Arrow* proposing nonviolent civil disobedience to protest a compulsory civil defense air raid drill. I got the idea to write the article from a similar suggestion David McReynolds had published in the *Village Voice*. The idea for the protest spread to City College, where there was a large student demonstration against this relic of Cold War scare tactics and indoctrination. Protesting air raid drills became a big enough deal that among the artifacts on the cover of Dylan's *Bringing It All Back Home* album in 1965 is a fallout shelter sign. I was even interviewed by a reporter on the *New York Post* who called me "the Trotsky of Tremont." After this description was published, somebody gave me a copy of Trotsky's memoirs and showed me a couple of pages where Trotsky describes how he actually lived in the Tremont area of the Bronx in 1917 for a few months. He was impressed that American workers had stoves and refrigerators. My friends called me "Leon" for a few weeks after the *Post*'s story. Reading the *Voice* helped make me an activist, a believer in nonviolent direct action.

Some of the articles in the *Voice* were amateurish. The layout was awful, resembling the phone book with three jumps. One letter to the editor said simply, "I read your paper every week. Why can't your proofreaders do the same?" Mailer once quit because of all the typos in his column. He had once written the phrase "nuances of growth," and it was published as the "nuisances of growth." The typo gave Norman existential dread.

But the paper had an individualistic, unpredictable quality. Its politics straddled liberalism and radicalism in a confused way, just as would mine for many years. It simultaneously promoted reform, socialism, anarchism, bohemianism, pacifism, populism, and participatory democracy. And it had an alliance with all the emerging political and artistic movements in theater, film, music, and performance art that were percolating in the Village. This engagement gave the *Voice* its insurgent vitality.

My years on the staff of the *Voice* will take up a chapter of this memoir. But my years as a reader were also important. They helped guide me to explore the Village while I was still a sheltered, uninformed college student living in Brooklyn with my mother. Just wandering around the Village on a Sunday afternoon was a form of liberation. Listening to the folksingers in Washington Square Park and browsing the paperback bookstores and record stores provided an education.

The articles—and the Village-oriented advertisements—in the *Voice* became my roadmap to cultural enlightenment. In the fall of 1959 I saw a play about jazz and drug addiction called *The Connection*, by a twenty-seven-year-old playwright named Jack Gelber. It was put on at the Living Theatre, located up a dark flight of stairs at a building at Fourteenth Street and Sixth Avenue. Most of the daily reviewers had panned it. Only the *Voice* gave it a rave. I thought these doomed jazzmen, waiting for their drug connection, were just as interesting as Hickey and his friends in Eugene O'Neill's *The Iceman Cometh*. And the lead performance by Warren Finerty, who looked like Richard Widmark after a long fast, was electrifying. When I got to know a few off-Broadway actors twenty years later, I asked about Finerty and was told he was long dead.

The *Voice* led me to see Lenny Bruce when he was in his fearless prime, before the police and Hogan had driven him crazy. He paced, and improvised, and used dirty words, and punctured society's hypocrisies with monologues that made you think and laugh at the same time. He made Chris Rock and Richard Pryor possible.

I started hearing Miles Davis perform live at the Village Vanguard with his quintet, which included Cannonball Adderly, the young John

Coltrane, and Bill Evans on piano. Miles moved like a dancer and played like Gabriel, especially on songs of loss or sorrow like "My Funny Valentine" and "Kind of Blue." He was Picasso, painting moods with a trumpet and mute.

Essays in the *Voice* led me to poets Dylan Thomas and Hart Crane. But to this day, I regret that the *Voice*'s extensive coverage of painters and the visual arts didn't stir that side of my brain. It's an ignorance I always regretted.

And, of course, the *Voice* introduced me to Norman Mailer, whose influence would grow on me steadily over forty years. In 1960 I read Norman's essay in *Esquire* on the Democratic Party convention in Los Angeles that nominated John Kennedy. Called "Superman Comes to the Supermarket," the piece opened my mind to how journalism could incorporate the techniques of novels, how journalism could be literary, speculative, personal, and intuitive. Norman's article anticipated the Hollywoodization of American politics, the hijacking of politics by marketing and infotainment techniques.

Over the years, Norman's prose would act as a lubricant for my own language, as a drug to stimulate my brain, the same way I would use music to retrieve memory. Whenever my own writing sagged into a slump of dullness or repetition, reading Norman's essays and reporting would restore some verve to my vocabulary and set my imagination free.

Norman has also proved a generous acquaintance over the years. He cooperated with me over a long profile I wrote about him in 1968. He let me bring an ESPN film crew into his home in Provincetown in 1998 to tape an interview about his interest in boxing. That same year I was sitting next to him and his son Michael at a fight in Madison Square Garden, when a young fan approached him and asked Norman for his autograph. The fan looked at the signature and blurted out, "I'm sorry! I thought you was Jake LaMotta."

"I know I'm ugly," Norman said good-naturedly, "but I'm not nearly as ugly as Jake. Ray Robinson did not punch my face a thousand times."

And so I gave my talk at the Boys High alumni dinner, held at the Holiday Inn at Kennedy Airport. I found the event moving. Everyone representing the class of 1955 was black, and virtually everyone seated at the tables representing the classes before 1951 was white.

The biggest reaction to my remarks came when I paid homage to the two street gangs that used to rule the lunchroom in 1955—the Bishops and the Chaplains. The rowdy cheers that greeted my references to these two long-forgotten rivals made me think that though a few zip-gun alumni were now productive members of the middle class, they had not forgotten their outlaw adolesence.

I recalled how the Bishops and Chaplains each had their own distinctive walk. The bouncy strut of the Bishops was known as the "Bishop's bop." When neutrals walked into territory controlled by each of the gangs, they affected the walking style of the local gang, to blend in, to show respect, and to come away unscathed. The Boys High lunchroom sometimes looked like it had been choreographed by Bob Fosse, with Bishops and Chaplains bopping around each other in their contrasting stylized struts.

Another enthusiastic response came when I started talking about an ex-marine geography/math teacher named "Mr. Papke" who scared the hell out of me. I described my mortification when, one day, in front of the whole class, the bombastic Mr. Papke called me "a pimple on the asshole of Western civilization." The insult may have been justified; I flunked the geometry regents exam and was just a C student who needed math remediation to gain admission to Hunter College.

At the close of the evening, several other alumni informed me that Mr. Papke had hurled the same cosmic invective against them for small infractions, like talking in class or submitting incomplete homework assignments.

I learned at the reunion that the conservative writer Norman Podhoretz was also a "famous alumni" of Boys High, about eight years ahead of me. I hadn't known this. One night during a deeply bitter New York City school strike in 1968, pitting a mostly Jewish teachers' union against the black community over control of schools, a belligerent Podhoretz had accosted me at a party and began shouting "You are trying to push our people back into the gas ovens, and I won't let you! You are a self-hating Jew."

I hadn't written anything about the strike and told him he was mistaking me for my *Voice* colleague and friend Nat Hentoff, who was writing about it every week. Norman must have thought I was lying, or putting him on, because he started yelling so loudly that I thought he might have a stroke. That didn't stop me from shouting abuse back at him.

Murray Kempton witnessed this confrontation and later took me aside to explain his theory of why Podhoretz abhorred me so intensely and had persisted in his mistaken identification. "You are Norman's exact opposite," Murray hypothesized. "You're the anti-Podhoretz. Norman grew up among blacks and came to fear and loathe them. You grew up among blacks and came to like them. Your existence makes him uneasy."

Podhoretz's grandparents came from the same part of Eastern Europe as my maternal ancestors—a place called Galicia, which is now part of Hungary. Our ancestors suffered from the same wars, hunger, and pogroms. I am as proud and comfortable being Jewish as I am being an American.

One of my most vivid memories of my childhood is my mother and grandmother crying for joy that day in May of 1948 when Israel became a nation. I was too young to understand the meaning of this event, but I never forgot that it was important. I had only seen my mother cry twice—when my father died and when Roosevelt died. This was the first time I had seen her cry when something good happened.

In the early 1960s Podhoretz was the left-liberal editor of *Commentary*, publishing James Baldwin, Paul Goodman, and Mike Harrington. He even wrote some essays that sounded a little anti-American. In his book *My Love Affair with America*, he attributed this to his "limitless faith in the perfectibility of this country."

Growing up in a neighborhood environment similar to Podhoretz's made me a liberal, but a liberal without a sense of racial guilt—I had a single mom, empty pockets, and went to the same crummy schools that blacks did.

I also can't recall ever being beaten up by black kids, possibly because I was just lucky, possibly because my affiliation with the Boys High basketball team gave me a protected status. Podhoretz must not have been so lucky.

My feelings and political opinions about civil rights and issues involving race stemmed largely from where I grew up and from participating in the civil rights movement, when I lived in the homes of southern blacks like E. W. Steptoe in rural Mississippi.

I came to believe—and still believe—that Dr. King, Bob Moses, Marian Wright Edelman, Fannie Lou Hamer, Julian Bond, Roger Wilkins, Harry Belafonte, and John Lewis are among the small handful of great human beings I have gotten to know during my lifetime.

And that Louis Farrakhan, former Chicago congressman Gus Savage, and Don King are among the lousiest.

The simple folk wisdom of my mother was right: "There is good and bad in every group," she said.

In 1966 I had a tense confrontation with Stokley Carmichael, who was then the leader of SNCC. Our disagreement was over the Student Non-Violent Coordinating Committee's decision to fire all its white staff (who were mostly Jewish) and Stokely's public statements that Zionism was a form of racism.

I had known Stokley since 1961, when he was a brave and witty freedom rider. Now he was calling me a "honkey" who was hiding behind my "white-skin privilege," a phrase then fashionable.

So I finally said to Stokley, "You went to the Bronx High School of Science and Howard University. I went to Boys High and Hunter College. I have no white-skin privilege. But you should, at least, have a little class guilt about me!"

What I realized most deeply while preparing for my speech for the reunion and at the reunion itself was that the Brooklyn of the 1950s had started me on a journey. I never would have suspected that journey would lead me to a church in Selma, Alabama, to hear Martin Luther King, Jr., preach a sermon about voting rights and "the right to protest for right" or to a jail cell in Maryland. Or that along the way I would hang out with Muhammad Ali when he was banished from boxing for refusing induction into the army during the Vietnam War. Or start a close friendship with Robert Kennedy just as he was starting to touch the soul of America's disrespected and dispossessed. On perhaps the worst night that journey, I stood in a Los Angeles hospital hallway with others, all of us watching history slip through our fingers. This same journey would take me to a gym in Catskill, New York, where I first encountered Mike Tyson when he was fourteen years old. I would have a ringside seat to Tyson's rap-opera life of unfulfilled potential, the life of a bipolar Dempsey who couldn't face his inner demons.

The journey would include a friendship with Mario Cuomo, starting when he was an unknown neighborhood lawyer in Queens, through his twelve years as governor of New York, and back into his being a private citizen.

I would take this journey as a journalist—with the *Voice*, and the *Daily News*, where I would resign from a job that I loved, to support a strike by ten unions in 1990, and the *New York Post*. Quitting my job at the News to support the strike may have been the hardest thing I ever had to do, being the only management employee out of two hundred to surrender my job, to walk on a picket line in the November cold. I knew I had to live by the words that I wrote—or I was a phony forever.

And sometimes my journey would be a crusade. For an entire year I wrote articles in the *Village Voice* about the injustice I felt the New York legal system had done Bobby McLaughlin, convicted of committing a murder one night in Marine Park in Brooklyn. During Bobby's sixth year in prison, his foster father, Harold Hohne, and a homicide detective named Tommy Duffy convinced me Bobby was innocent. So I wrote, and wrote, until a judge named Anne Feldman released Bobby on the eve of Independence Day—July 3, 1986.

This experience would deepen my resolve to oppose capital punishment. I came to believe that the mistaken application of the death penalty is the worst thing a government can possibly do.

Injustices need exposure. I named the city's worst landlords and judges; exposed mob domination of labor unions; campaigned for a city program to test children for lead poisoning and delead the slum apartments they were living in.

I wrote about nursing home abuses, campaigned for a law that required sprinkler systems in high-rises after covering a fatal fire, and exposed corrupt local politicians. Over two years I wrote sixteen columns about the drugs being sold openly to teenagers in the clubs owned by

Peter Gatien. Last year Gatien's liquor licence was finally revoked by the state and he was put out of business.

Gradually but inexorably I evolved into a local muckraker, who probed what I felt were injustices and kept writing follow-up articles until something was accomplished. Because I had grown up in Bed-Stuy and listened to Alan Freed, and gone to Freed's shows at the Paramount, I was a fan, and later a friend, of Lloyd Price, who wrote and recorded "Personality" and "Stagger Lee." I would run a campaign in my columns for Lloyd to get voted into the Rock 'n' Roll Hall of Fame. He was finally inducted in 1998—about twenty years too late.

The newspaper business has been my ticket for my journey. No day is boring. I have learned something new every day, met somebody new every day, observed something new every day. It has given me the chance to defend the falsely accused, expose the bogus, champion the powerless, stand up to a few bullies, and meet the occasional hero and artist. It has been my way of giving something back to those who started me on the journey to begin with, in Brooklyn, in 1955—the year the Dodgers won the World Series.

CHAPTER 2

A Child of Jackie Robinson

The deepest root of my belief in racial justice goes back to Jackie Robinson and the summer of 1947, when baseball's color line fell, in the borough of my birth, and I became a witness to a grand event in the annals of American democracy.

I was, as I've said, a fanatical Brooklyn Dodgers fan, and Robinson and that team gave me my first lessons in equal opportunity. Number 42 in Dodger blue opened my youthful eyes to the fact that lots of people believed blacks were inferior. Robinson demolished this genetic myth in a ballpark that was within walking distance of my home.

In 1947 Brooklyn was seven years ahead of the Supreme Court of the United States in rejecting the doctrine of separate but equal and in burying the stereotype of white supremacy. The Dodgers were a full generation ahead of the rest of the country in actually practicing integration.

Jackie Robinson's first game began the second half of the twentieth century in America. And there I was, soaking up this epic story in nine-inning installments every day—on the radio, in the newspapers, and in street-corner replays. It was soon obvious to us all that Jackie was making the whole team better. And by so doing he was turning baseball-berserk Brooklyn into a more unified community, a more exciting place to live. In 1946 the Dodgers lost the pennant on the last day of the season to St. Louis. In 1947 they won the pennant. The difference was Jackie Robinson.

Here was a simple lesson for a ten-year-old: Give everyone a fair shot, and the whole team—or city, or society—will flourish. By the time I was in sixth or seventh grade and had absorbed the sports pages like a sponge, I got the picture.

I read somewhere that the Boston Red Sox had given Jackie a "sham tryout" in April of 1945 at Fenway Park, without ever seriously considering giving him a contract. Tom Yawkey, the Red Sox owner, was biased against blacks, and Boston would become the last team to integrate its roster, in 1959. I calculated that if the Red Sox had signed him, they would not have lost the World Series in seven games in 1946, or lost the American League pennant in a playoff game in 1948, or again lost the pennant on the last day of the season in 1949 to the Yankees. A Brooklyn boy obsessed with baseball standings and statistics could figure out that Boston had lost a World Series and two pennants because it had missed the opportunity to sign Jackie Robinson. Boston's "Curse of the Bambino," for trading away Babe Ruth in 1920, became the curse of Jackie Robinson in 1945.

Inclusion is better than exclusion. That was the headline lesson of Jackie Robinson for me and for most people of my generation with ties to Brooklyn, baseball, or civil rights.

Recently my wife and I were having dinner with Robert Caro and his wife, Ina. Caro is the Pulitzer Prize–winning biographer of Robert Moses and Lyndon Johnson. The conversation touched on Robinson. Suddenly Caro's voice became charged with quiet intensity. "Robinson was one of the great people of the twentieth century, one of the most important," he declared. "You should put aside your memoir and write Robinson's biography."

I mentioned that a Princeton professor named Arnold Rampersad had published a full biography of Robinson two years earlier. Caro, a Princeton graduate himself, interrupted me. "That book was so dry and lifeless, nobody read it! It is as if it was never published! I wish I could take a sabbatical from LBJ and write Robinson myself, but that's not practical. But that's what you should do. Robinson was of such huge historical significance, and you are one of the few people who understand that. You have the passion that Rampersad lacked. A professor should never have done Jackie."

I had known Caro for over twenty-five years, and I could remember him speaking with such pure boyish enthusiasm about only one other figure in history—Al Smith, New York's social reform governor who had grown up in poverty on the Lower East Side.

"Robinson was it," Caro said. "He affected so many people's lives."

Jackie Robinson began to affect my life through Walter Lanier "Red" Barber's broadcasts of the Dodger games and Jimmy Cannon's sports columns, always filled with tabloid emotion and drama. Together, they helped me decode the meaning of the Dodgers having a black rookie in 1947. As that season unfolded, I became increasingly preoccupied by the Dodgers and baseball. My older cousin, Herb, showed me how to keep score. I started a scrapbook with the standings, batting averages, and box scores from each game. I started to clip stories about the Dodgers out of every source I could find.

Just before his death, my other cousin, Nat, recalled for me how he tried to interest me in classical music. Nat played the violin as a hobby. One day when I was nine or ten he insisted I request a song so I could get "some appreciation for the finer things in life." I requested "Take Me Out to the Ballgame."

I still associate Robinson with the rich, poetic, folksy, Deep South radio voice of Red Barber, the play-by-play broadcaster, who was born in Mississippi and grew up in Florida under segregation. I listened to Red on the radio almost every day during the season. I also listened to the pregame show with Marty Glickman and sometimes to the re-creation of the day games at 7 P.M. with artificial crowd noise piped in on tape. Radio gave the imagination freedom to roam and invent.

I listened in my house. I listened in the candy store at the corner of Nostrand and Vernon. I listened in the car radios adults played loud. I listened in the schoolyard or playground if a friend had a portable radio, or on a stoop. When the World Series came, I sometimes watched the small TV screen in the window of an appliance store on Myrtle Avenue.

I loved Red Barber's signature southern colloquialisms. "This lineup is tearing up the pea patch" when the Dodgers were scoring runs. "With two strikes, Preacher Roe is sitting in the catbird seat" when the pitcher had the advantage. "He's eating high on the hog" when a batter had a hitting streak. "The ducks are on the pond" when the bases were loaded.

When the Dodgers' Cookie Lavagette's ninth-inning hit won the game and ruined Bill Bevan's no-hitter in the 1947 World Series, Barber exclaimed, "Well, I'll be a suck-egg mule."

Red was more than just a colorful play-by-play guide. He was a real reporter, who hung out around the batting cage before the game and shared insightful anecdotes with exquisite timing during the broadcast. If a slumping batter changed his bat or his socks, Red found out about it and told us. If a pitcher was learning a new exotic pitch, he let us know. He saved his inside knowledge for just the right moment—when there was a pitching change or when it was deep in the count in a tense situation.

Red was a professional. He did not root for the Dodgers. He was objective. He didn't dumb down the game or pander to civic emotionalism. He let us know how great Stan Musial was, how dangerous Ralph Kiner or Johnny Mize were. He believed in the aristocracy of talent no matter what uniform it was wearing. He would mention the weaknesses of the Dodger players if it was relevant to the moment. If Carl Furillo was a little slow, and therefore vulnerable to the double play or unlikely to score from first, he reminded us of that calculation.

Ultimately, when he took over the franchise, Walter O'Malley would fire Red for being too impartial. Red had been hired by Branch Rickey, who understood that his candor gave the team, and the game, and the broadcast, credibility. O'Malley wanted a shill who did not mention any home team imperfection. O'Malley had been a corporate lawyer who saw baseball as a business; Red Barber was a purist who saw baseball as a sport.

Years later, when I read several of Red's books and saw him interviewed on television, I realized that prior to 1947, he had never had a meal with a black person in his life. The contacts he had with blacks were with those who shined his shoes, or picked up the soiled uniforms off the floor of the clubhouse, or carried his bags onto the train. Yet his was the radio voice that heralded Jackie Robinson into my imagination, that welcomed him, that gave us some hint of the stress Robinson was under, the cruelties he was subjected to—all with its southern accent.

What led this man from Mississippi to play this historic role is a mystery. But I do know that Red's parents forbade him from using the word "nigger" when he was growing up. His mother was an English teacher who instilled in him a love of language. He had a basic American decency inside him, and it flowed like honey out of his microphone in the summer of Jackie Robinson's rookie resolve to neither strike out nor strike back.

Jimmy Cannon also informed and fueled my identification with Robinson through his lyrical columns in the *Post.* And to a lesser extent so did Milton Gross in the *Post* and Dan Parker in the *Daily Mirror.* While I devoured these columns, I was also aware that Jimmy Powers in the *Daily News* was knocking Jackie at every opportunity, predicting he would never hit big-league pitching. Powers clung to his own stereotype of black inferiority and wrote about it in the paper with the biggest circulation in Jackie's hometown.

Cannon, Gross, and Parker gave me a sense of what Robinson—and Branch Rickey—were up against and how high the stakes were that the Dodgers' "experiment" be a success. Early in the season Ben Chapman, the Alabama-born manager of the Phillies and a notorious bigot, went too far in demeaning Robinson. Chapman's insults helped unify the Dodgers around Robinson, including those southern-born teammates who had originally opposed him, like Dixie Walker, Bobby Bragan, Hugh Casey, and Kirby Higbee. When I met Robinson in 1965, he would compare Ben Chapman to Bull Connor as a reverse catalyst, rallying the forces of integration with his harsh excess.

One Dan Parker column made a deep impression on me and, it turns out, on Robinson, too, because he quoted it in his 1972 autobiography, *I Never Had It Made.* Parker, the sports editor of a downscale tabloid known mostly for the accuracy of its racetrack handicappers, wrote:

> Ben Chapman, who during his career with the Yankees, was frequently involved in unpleasant incidents with fans who charged him with shouting anti-Semitic remarks at them from the ballfield, seems to be up to his old tricks of stirring up racial trouble.

> During the recent series between the Phils and the Dodgers, Chapman and three of his players poured a stream of abuse at Jackie Robinson. Jackie, with admirable restraint, ignored the guttersnipe language coming from Phil's dugout, thus stamping himself as the only gentleman among those involved in the incident.

In 1961, when I was a copyboy on the *Mirror*, I got to meet Parker, a tall, natty, polite man who by then had become the leading journalistic crusader against corruption in boxing. He was not as elegant a prose stylist as Cannon or Red Smith, but he was brave and relentless.

Cannon wrote dozens of columns about Robinson, each one of which was filed away in my brain for years to come. He wrote one in April of 1946 during spring training, when Robinson was starting out with the Montreal Royals, that condemned "the sneering bigotry" of the southern fans who watched him.

"I know there are ways to lynch a man without hanging him from a tree," Cannon wrote. He added an assessment of Robinson's skills:

> After watching him for nine innings, this I know. He is a base thief whose taunting leads upset the Dodgers the three times he reached base. Such a judge as George Sisler, now scouting for the Dodgers, believes Robinson will hit a ball a long ways once he is playing for himself, and not for the people sitting in the segregation of the bleacher seats.

On May 27, 1952, Cannon composed one of his deadline masterpieces. They should teach it in journalism schools forever:

> You're Jackie Robinson, an historic athlete. Baseball should be grateful to you. You allowed baseball to prove it isn't a satire on the American dream.
>
> Your presence in the big leagues must not be commemorated as an act of tolerance. You are there because you possess many spectacular skills. No one did you a favor. Who has the right to make freedom a personal gift when it is guaranteed to all of us in the documents by which we live as a people?

> You are similar to the man who goes to the property clerk of the Police Department, and claims a stolen article. We don't honor a cop because of what he finds on a burglar. Why should baseball be praised for honoring the basic laws of the country?
>
> You more than any other player on the team have made the Dodgers what they are. Without you they couldn't have won three pennants. They will not understand how important you are until you are gone . . . You had more ways to beat the other people than any man in your time.
>
> You were expected to accept abuse without retaliation. Remember this is a sport where Ty Cobb was revered for brutal nastiness. Some have condemned you for behaving like a ballplayer who wants to win. Some would have deprived you of your anger.
>
> No one can ever know the pressure you conquered. The other club was a minor opponent.

It was reading Jimmy Cannon that made me first want to become a journalist. From his sentimental columns I could tell that Cannon had grown up poor like me, that he had had only six months of high school, that he had had no big-shot relatives, and that he was self-taught. I could relate to all that. I had no idea, at thirteen or fourteen, how to cross the bridge to Manhattan, let alone how to get on a newspaper. But getting paid to write about sports seemed like the perfect life to me. Later I would discover that Hamill, Gay Talese, Jerry Izaenberg, and Joe Flaherty were also reading Cannon at the same time I was, and finding the same inspiration.

As I continued to read Cannon in college, I came to appreciate his sense of proportion about sports and about life. He had covered World War II and later the Korean War. He knew what death was. He knew what tragedy was. He had seen the corpses of young men. Years later, when I got to know Cannon, when he was a cranky conservative, he explained that he had crusaded for Robinson to come to Brooklyn in 1946, and embraced him in 1947, because he had covered the war. Cannon understood you cannot fight a world war against Hitler and Ayran racial supremacy, and then come home and not let black people play baseball because of the color of their skin. Defeating fascism and ending baseball segregation were both elemental justice to Cannon. Cannon saw Hitler as just another hoodlum bully, the way Brecht did.

Also, growing up poor in Greenwich Village and having only six months of high school gave Cannon a sharp sense of economic class. He instinctively didn't like rich guys like Jim Norris, the sleazy boxing promoter, and stadium owner, or most baseball owners. He saw mobster Frankie Carbo as a "two-bit Hitler." He liked the athletes, in the era when they were still accesible to a columnist like Cannon, before the era of handlers and press agents and sports agents. Cannon recognized excellence and was a close friend to DiMaggio, Louis, and Ray Robinson. As a kid in the Village, Cannon had grown up around Tammany politicians, fighters, and hoodlums; he knew what was real and what was bogus.

With Cannon in mind, I joined something called "the newspaper club" in seventh grade and later the *Red and Black* newspaper at Boys High. By the time I entered high school I knew what I wanted to do with my life.

Early clarity about a profession made up for a lot of my disadvantages. No father to take me to a ballgame or be a role model. Average grades. Lack of social graces. Shyness. No relatives who could open doors for me. No money for college.

But at least I knew that journalism would be my chance to get out of dead-end Bed-Stuy, where most of my black friends were headed for the army or the post office and where some white friends would never go to college.

Life is a search for self-definition. Growing up with no father and no siblings, I think much of my life has involved a search for community. Newspapers are a community. Newspapers are a family.

I credit Jackie Robinson and Jimmy Cannon with leading me toward the first flicker of an idea of becoming not just a sportswriter but a sportswriter who defended underdogs and rebels. In a column on Jackie Robinson written early in 1947, at the peak of Robinson's ostracism and solitude, Cannon called him "the loneliest man I have ever seen in sports."

The image of Robinson as a lonely outsider, as an underdog rebel, struck a chord inside me. I felt like an outsider in my own family. My widowed mother, who was treated badly by all the bullying and eccentric relatives we had to live with, was the lowest person in the pecking order, without a protector. I felt like a pariah in my own house. That was probably one reason I spent most of my time on the street, in the neighborhood. I didn't rebel so much as escape.

Baseball was king on our crowded block in this time before television made basketball the city game. Every kid I knew was a baseball junkie. We had intense street-corner debates on the rival merits of Reese versus Rizzuto, of Campanella versus Berra, or Red Barber versus Mel Allen and versus Russ Hodges, the Giants' announcer, who openly rooted for the team. We even argued over the merits of Schaefer beer, the Dodgers' sponsor, versus Ballantine beer, the Yankees' sponsor, even though few of us had yet tasted beer. The older kids—thirteen, fourteen years old—started betting a dime a day, at six-to-one odds, on which three players would get six hits combined. The odds rose to ten to one if you picked three on the same team to get the six hits.

When I got to high school and knew who the lunchroom bookies were, I still didn't bet, fearful of losing the 50 cents a week and unbalancing my mother's tight budget.

We played stickball in the middle of the street with a sawed-off broomstick handle and a pink "high-bouncer" spaldeen, with three or four or five to a side. Sometimes there was a pitcher and we would debate "underhand" versus "overhand" fast pitching. If there weren't enough players to go around, the batter would throw the ball up himself and hit it.

I was an enthusiastic competitor but a very ordinary athlete. I would usually get picked last for pickup basketball games because I didn't have a shot. I couldn't jump well enough to rebound or block. And no one ever showed me the correct technique for moving my feet on defense.

I was a line-drive hitter in stickball and softball, but I did not hit for distance. I didn't have the powerful wrists and forearms to be a "two-sewer man," which is what we called the home-run hitters in stickball. Sewer covers were how long balls were measured on my block.

My best sport was punchball. I could place the spaldeen between fielders and use my speed to get a double. I was also a defensive specialist in punchball, able to catch line drives barehanded. I did have quick reflexes and could shake off the sting in my fingers, since nobody used a glove.

My home at 31 Vernon Avenue was in the middle of the block, and frequently the ball from our street games would bounce into our front yard. I had a killjoy aunt called Viola who lived in our tenement. Viola became so annoyed by our ballplaying that she placed jagged shards of glass in our yard. She thought they would be an incentive to move the games to another block, but I don't think she would have gotten too upset if one of my friends slashed his hand on the sharp glass reaching for a wayward spaldeen. She would have thought one bloody hand a small price to pay to get us to move our games, and their attendant noise, chatter, and interlopers into our garden, which actually had almost no flowers worth worrying about.

Viola's son (my first cousin) Teddy also lived in the house. He was a straight-A student and Boys High valedictorian who never played ball and never got dirty. He was the impossibly perfect standard—four years older—that I could never equal in grades, deportment, manners, or dress. Teddy died from lung cancer when he was about thirty, and my family never talked about it. I never saw him in the hospital. I have no recollection of his funeral and doubt that I was even there.

The same repressive secrecy shrouded the death of my favorite cousin, Judy Miller, the daughter of Nat and Alice. Judy committed suicide in Mexico at age twenty-two in 1962. I was never informed about a funeral.

Nobody talked about Judy's suicide in my family, where secrets were manufactured by silence and avoidance. I was close to Judy, who loved music and theater, but nobody would speak about her after she died. I have a vague memory that she was having a love affair with a Mexican boy whom her parents disapproved of. And that she had been deeply affected by the suicide of Marilyn Monroe in August of 1962.

The deaths of Judy and Teddy still haunt me, because of my ignorance of them and the absence of memory.

But my teenage years were dominated by baseball, by living in the city that was the 1950s capital of baseball in America, with three winning teams. Between 1947 and 1956 a New York team was in the World Series every season except one: in 1948. We thrilled to Dodgers-Yankees "subway series" in 1947, 1949, 1952, 1953, 1955, and 1956. We thought it was an annual ritual of entitlement. (Then it did not happen for forty-four years, until the Yankees beat the Mets in five games in 2000. I rooted for the Mets but wrote a column celebrating the skills of Paul O'Neill, Orlando Hernandez, and Derek Jeter, keeping the faith with Red Barber's sportsmanship lessons.)

I had grown up hating the Yankees in a childish way because they beat the Dodgers every year. But in the late 1970s, I was able to stop hating the Yankees and appreciate one of their players—Reggie Jackson. Reggie was the bridge I was able to half cross. Because of my appreciation of his talents and his self-proclaimed straw-that-stirs-the-drink maverick personality, the Yankees stopped being just a one-dimensional object of hate and envy. I cheered for Reggie, and this prepared me to respect the professionalism of the Joe Torre–managed dynasty team. Steve Garvey of the Dodgers says that when Reggie hit his third home run in the 1978 World Series game, he secretly clapped, "inside my glove," to acknowledge the feat. That's how I felt about the Yankee team that beat my Mets in the 2000 World Series—reluctant, private applause.

I know I was spoiled growing up in a baseball-mad city at a time when three future Hall of Fame centerfielders were playing every day—Mickey Mantle, Duke Snider, and Willie Mays. I know I will never again see such power and grace every summer day. Despite my devotion to the Dodgers, I did not get to see any games during the 1947 season. I was nine years old and nobody in my family offered to take me to a game.

However, years later I got to know the gentle poet Joel Oppenheimer, who contributed to the *Village Voice* and was one of the regular drinkers at the Lion's Head bar on Sheridan Square. He described what it was like to be present on the day Jackie Robinson broke the color line at Ebbets Field. Joel was then eighteen and a freshman on Easter break from Cornell. He and his father sat in a section that was mostly black. It was the first time he had ever been surrounded by black people. There were none at Cornell and almost none in his Manhattan neighborhood.

"I remember Jackie made a good play in the field," Joel told me one night, "and all the blacks around me started to yell his name, 'Jackie,

Jackie, Jackie!' Suddenly some guy behind me started shouting 'Yonkel, Yonkel, Yonkel,' which was Yiddish for Jackie. He looked like a little Jewish immigrant tailor. It was a tremendously moving moment. It symbolized what Jackie meant to me, to Brooklyn, to New York. He brought everyone of goodwill together."

My grandfather was also an immigrant Jewish tailor whose English was punctuated with Yiddish. He was a short, neat man who wore a vest and was in his seventies in 1947. I tried to get him interested in baseball without success. One day I was listening to a game on the radio and Red Barber was saying "Strike one, strike two, strike three." My grandfather looked up and muttered, "Too many strikes. The unions have gotten too much power."

On July 4, 1948, I got to see my first baseball game at Ebbets Field. The father of a friend took three of us to see the Dodgers play the crosstown rival Giants. We sat in the 60-cent bleacher seats and ate hot dogs and peanuts.

My memory of that spectacular day is bittersweet. I missed not having a father of my own to do this with. The thoughtful kindness of my friend's dad somehow made me more aware of this hole at the center of my existence. This fleeting feeling of loss came back to me when I started taking my daughter, Rebecca, to Mets games in the 1980s, renewing the American ritual I never got to perform with my father. I remember crying in a darkened movie theater when Rebecca and I saw *Field of Dreams* together, as the dead father and the living son play catch with a baseball on the screen.

Walking out of the runway into the sunlight of the ballpark, on that long-ago July 4, I felt like I was entering a cathedral. The colors were so sharp—the green of the grass, the white of the Dodger uniforms, the reddish brown of the earth, the yellows and blues of the shirts in the crowd. I still get this goose-bumpy feeling whenever I walk into a ballpark, and I'm sure there is some kind of subliminal flashback to that first sight of rowdy, intimate, colorful Ebbets Field.

For all the hours I had spent listening to the games on radio, I was not prepared for the carnival atmosphere, the Dodger symphony with trumpet, drum, and cowbell parading around the stands, or the camaraderie of the fans, the passion of the rooting. Those commingled, pungent aromas of mustard, cotton candy, peanuts, and cheap cigars. Most of all I was not prepared for the level of sound 34,000 human throats could manufacture with the proper incitement. And in this first baseball game I ever saw, Jackie Robinson stole home.

These days nobody steals home. It's a lost art. Jackie would do it nineteen times in his career and once more in the 1955 World Series.

One thing you couldn't really tell from listening to the radio was how fast Jackie Robinson could run. You had to see the power in his football stride and the abandon in his eyes. He was a tornado with a temper.

In September I got in to see a second game. We waited for some fans to leave after the first game of a double header and give us their ticket stubs so we could sit in their seats for the second game. A lot of kids did that and it usually worked. On this occasion we ended up sitting behind first base and kept moving down closer to the field, as people left later in the game. We played cat and mouse with the ushers until we were close to the field by the ninth inning.

What I remember about the second game was Robinson getting hit by a pitch. The whole ballpark booed with fury because, by then, all of Brooklyn knew Jackie was a marked man by pitchers who resented his existence. During his rookie season, Jackie was hit by pitchers nine times, which is still a record. And in those days, batters did not wear protective helmets.

There was another reason I identified with Robinson. I read in the *Post* that Hank Greenberg had supported and befriended him. All my relatives said Greenberg was the best Jewish role model in America. He was the vicarious vessel for Jewish immigrant dreams, the Jew-as-athlete who made all Jews feel both more American and more Jewish. Even my mother talked about Greenberg as a god.

My Jewish uncles told me that Greenberg would have broken Babe Ruth's record of sixty home runs in 1938, but anti-Semitic pitchers started walking him with bad pitches when he reached fifty-eight. This was believed by most of the Jewish grown-ups I knew.

Later, when I looked it up, I could see that Greenberg struck out a lot the last week of the season, including on the last day, when Bob Feller struck him out twice. He had his chances.

But it was true that Greenberg was the victim of anti-Jewish slurs and several intentional spikings during his career. And in 1947, when Robinson came up and Greenberg was playing out his final season with the Pirates, he did go out of his way to encourage Robinson. Robinson appreciated the friendship. He later wrote and talked about its importance to him.

The kinship between blacks and Jews would play a big role in my life. And this alliance between Robinson and Greenberg was probably my first awareness of this kinship of hardship.

I loved another thing about Jackie and all these Dodgers. I read in the *Post* and the *Brooklyn Eagle* that many of them, like Reese, Snider, Erskine, and Jackie, all lived in Brooklyn in rented apartments and that they sometimes took the subway to and from the ball games. They were accessible, part of the community. The team that was growing in Brooklyn stayed essentially the same for ten years. There were no trades. Stability and familiarly solidified our loyalty. These Dodgers seemed as much a part of Brooklyn as Coney Island.

When the Dodgers clinched the pennant in 1947, some of the older kids in the neighborhood went to Grand Central Station in Manhattan to be part of a crowd that greeted the team on its arrival from Philadelphia. They later told me they chased Jackie into the subway, which he was taking to get home.

This was a great story, but I wondered if it was true. Was memory playing a trick on me? Would I be concocting another myth based on adolescent exaggeration or romanticized nostalgia? Before writing this chapter, I went through the microfilm of the *New York Post* sports pages for September 1947. I found a story under the byline of Leo Casey. The headline read: "COPS RESCUE JACKIE FROM FANS."

> The fans really went stark raving mad over Jackie Robinson. The rookie first baseman ducked into a phone booth to call his wife. The press of fans against the booth was so heavy that Robbie couldn't get out.
>
> Six cops pushed their way through the mob and pushed them back. Then the bluecoats literally formed a ring around Robinson and escorted him to a nearby Independent Subway station.
>
> More than 200 fans followed the first baseman down into the subway, shouting and begging to pay his fare. More than 100 men and

some women either jumped over the turnstiles or ducked under them to crowd into the train with Jackie. And the cops stayed with him to protect him.

It was only after I entered my teenage years and had seen Jackie perform over many seasons that I came fully to appreciate how Bill "Bojangles" Robinson, the great black tap dancer, described him. "Ty Cobb in Technicolor" was the phrase Bojangles created, like a new step, when he spoke at Ebbets Field on a night that celebrated Jackie at the end of the 1947 season, when he was voted "Rookie of the Year." The allusion to Cobb conjured up speed, aggression, base stealing, and will to win, and placed it in the fist of racial pride.

By the 1949 season a few families on my block had small, black-and-white television sets, so I got see a few games. I also got to hear Red Barber on TV, where his literate understatement and long silences fit in even better than on the radio.

It is still Red Barber's voice that I associate with Jackie Robinson's greatest game. It came on September 30, 1951, in the final game of the regular season, when Jackie was thirty-two and his body was starting to run down.

The Dodgers were playing the Phils in Shibe Park, and the game must not have been on television—even though the pennant would be decided by the outcome of this single game. The Dodgers and Giants were tied for first place. A group of us listened to the game pacing around a portable radio in the schoolyard of PS 54.

By late in the afternoon the Giants had won their game in Boston, putting them a half game ahead of Brooklyn. We needed a win to force a playoff. But in the middle innings the Dodgers were losing 8 to 1, and hope was dying in the schoolyard shadows.

But our resilient heroes rallied back, and tied the game 8 to 8 in the eighth inning. As the game went into extra innings, we hung on to every word Red Barber spoke, looking for some omen, some life raft of optimism. He kept describing the setting sun and the shadows that were making it hard for the hitters to see the ball.

In the twelfth inning the Phils loaded the bases and the Dodgers seemed doomed. Then Eddie Waitkus smashed a low line drive that sounded like the game-winning, season-ending hit. But Robinson dove—perpendicular to the earth—and made the catch, knocking himself out but still hanging on to the ball. It was, I thought, the first miracle ever broadcast live on radio.

My friends and I pretended to have heart attacks as we fell into a pile of joy around the radio.

Jackie had jammed his elbow into his solar plexus and was lying stretched out on in the infield. It sounded like he would have to come out of the game.

Jackie not only remained in the game, he *won* the game. He hit a home run in the fourteenth inning. He saved the season twice in the twilight. I would give anything I have for a tape of Red Barber's call of the catch and then the homer.

Robinson's heroics forced the three-game playoff with the Giants that ended with Bobby Thomson's famous home run, the hit that cost Brooklyn the pennant.

Fifty years later it still pains my heart to write about it. I was watching that third playoff game in the house of my next-door friend Marvin Ort. I had been Bar Mitzvahed that year, and we were both literally praying with Hebrew prayer books for an out when Thomson hit the ball over the left-field fence.

The next day one of the papers published an amazing photo, taken from the outfield. It showed Thomson arriving at home plate, engulfed by his teammates. The only Dodger left on the playing field is Robinson. He had the presence of mind to remain in his position, to make sure Thomson had touched every base, as the Polo Grounds went insane and the other Dodgers walked off the playing field like dead men.

This image of Robinson's competitive focus is the tiny fragment of solace in this memory of sports heartbreak.

In the 1990s I told zealous Red Sox fans Doris Kearns and Richard Goodwin that Thomson's home run hurt almost as much as Robert Kennedy's assassination. "I would rather talk about Dallas than Bill Buckner's error," Richard Goodwin replied, referring to the error that cost the Red Sox the World Series against the Mets in 1986. Goodwin had worked in the White House with JFK. I judged he was only half joking.

In 1960 Jackie Robinson endorsed Richard Nixon for president against

John F. Kennedy. It was an incomprehensible choice to me. How could Robinson, the hero of my boyhood, the pioneer of equality, oppose the first Roman Catholic to become president? It contradicted all the codes of the neighborhood, all laws of logic.

By November of 1960 I understood what JFK meant to the Irish, to Catholics, and to the children of immigrants in America. He was their Jackie Robinson. The Irish had suffered systemic discrimination since the 1840s. Al Smith, the great tribune of labor and social reform in New York, had been rejected for the presidency in 1928 because of anti-Catholic bigotry. And this intolerance gave us Herbert Hoover.

How could the pathfinder against racial prejudice not support the pathfinder against religious prejudice—in the service of a candidate so odious as Nixon? Jackie's defection prepared me to accept that life is always more intricate and paradoxical than you can ever expect.

I met Robinson several times at civil rights rallies but had only one extended conversation with him. It happened in the autumn of 1965, when he was campaigning with liberal Republican John Lindsay for mayor of New York in Manhattan.

I was covering Lindsay for the *Village Voice*, and after the campaign stop was over, I persuaded Robinson to have a cup of coffee with me. I said I wanted to interview him about why he was supporting Lindsay, but I really just wanted to talk to him. Sitting in a Madison Avenue coffee shop, I tried to express what a gigantic influence he had been. I told him that I had participated in the youth march for integrated schools that he had spoken at back in 1959. And I told him I saw him steal home on July 4, 1948.*

I never mentioned his endorsement of Richard Nixon.

What I remember most vividly about that cup of coffee is a story Robinson told me about what happened to him one day in January of

---

*When I met Stan Musial in 1988, I told him that I once saw him go five-for-five against the Dodgers at Ebbets Field when I was a kid and that the Dodger fans had clapped for his achievement as a visiting player.

"*I* remember the game," Musial said. "I bet *you* don't remember that I got all five hits with two strikes."

1962, as he was walking down Madison Avenue, right near where we were sitting. Robinson set his anecdote a few days before the voting for the Hall of Fame was going to be announced, a ballot that would make him the first black ever voted into the Cooperstown shrine.

"I was walking down Madison," Robinson recalled, "and a Negro man stopped me. He was a total stranger. The fellow started shouting at me, 'You're going to make it, you're going to get in, and that's going to be the greatest day of my life.'

"He was speaking of *his* life, not my life," Robinson continued in his high-pitched voice of amazement.

"That I still meant so much to the average Negro years after I stopped playing ball . . ."

Robinson let the thought trail off.

Jackie Robinson, the grandson of slaves, the son of a sharecropper, affected my life by playing baseball, brilliantly, in Brooklyn. His first season became my Passover story, a fable of freedom, to be retold again and again to keep memory alive. For a while I forgot how much more important Robinson was to the generation of blacks born in the 1930s. I let his 1960s Republicanism temporarily blur my understanding of the enormity of his historic impact. My black friends talked more about Dr. King and Malcolm X. My white friends talked more about Robinson.

Then in 1982 I read *A Man's Life* by Roger Wilkins, a writer, a thinker, and an old friend I much admired. Roger, born in a segregated hospital in Kansas City in 1932, helped put Jackie back in historical perspective for me. He wrote: "There were lots of beacons, of course. W. E. B. Du Bois, Martin Luther King, Jr., Malcolm X, Mary McCloud Bethune, Joe Louis, and Adam Clayton Powell were among them. But, Jack Roosevelt Robinson was my main man . . . If it hadn't been for Jackie Robinson I probably wouldn't have gotten a chance to play my game. Jackie changed the way we all think of ourselves."

In 1957 the Dodgers gave me a lesson in cold betrayal. They abandoned Brooklyn for Los Angeles, even though the team was making money in Brooklyn. Owner Walter O'Malley, already quite rich, wanted to be even richer. I already knew O'Malley was a heartless bastard because he had tried to trade Jackie Robinson—*to the Giants!*—after the 1956 season—*for Dick Littlefield!* Jackie retired rather than play for the hated Giants, discarded like a used car. The Dodgers leaving Brooklyn said loyalty meant nothing, that baseball was a cutthroat business.

The thing that consolidated Brooklyn was ripped away overnight. The excitement went out of the street corners because there was nothing left to argue about. We stopped listening to the games. The rhythm of life lost its drummer. I was an orphan with no team to cheer for or care for.

One night some years ago, Pete Hamill and I were having dinner, and we began to joke about collaborating on a parody article that would name "The Ten Worst Human Beings of the Twentieth Century." We decided we would each write down three names on our napkins and see if they matched. Then we traded the napkins. We had each written the same three names in the same exact order.

Hitler
Stalin
Walter O'Malley

Innocence is lost over and over. My faith in the presumption of human kindness and goodness would be eroded when I learned about the Holocaust and Anne Frank, when the four little black girls were killed in the Birmingham church bombing by the Klan, and when President Kennedy was assassinated.

But my first layer of innocence was shed when O'Malley yanked baseball out of Brooklyn for a buck.

In the summer of 1999, I was able to repay a small portion of the debt I owe to Robinson, Reese, and the Dodgers of my boyhood summers.

When Reese passed away in August, I wrote a column in the *Post* urging New York City to build a statue in Brooklyn commemorating Reese and Robinson and their cross-racial friendship. I proposed that such a statue memorialize a moment that occurred early in the 1947 season.

The moment has been described in several books, including Robinson's autobiography. It took place in Cincinnati when Reese and Robinson were being targeted for primitive racial heckling by both fans and opposing players. A lot of the taunting was focused on Reese for being "a traitor to the South." Reese, the captain and veteran leader of the team, had been one of the few southern-born players who declined to sign the petition in spring training that protested Robinson joining the team. (Eddie Stanky also refused, and so did Pete Reiser, who grew up in Missouri.)

As the insults poured down on the two players, Reese walked over and placed his arm around Robinson's shoulder. It was a defiant gesture of solidarity the whole ballpark could see. My column suggested the statue re-create this moment of unity in the face of racist ignorance. I felt such a sculpture in a public space could become a national rallying point of racial reconciliation—and a permanent celebration of the Dodgers' team.

A few days later Mayor Giuliani called me up and said he was going to adopt my suggestion and "make it happen." He said he wanted me to join a committee with the widows of Reese and Robinson and a group of civic big shots to help choose a design and a location.

The mayor's positive response slightly surprised me; we got along well personally, but my columns criticized his policies on police tactics, his meddling in education, and his general harshness toward blacks.

At the close of the conversation Giuliani quipped, "I hope by now you realize that I only take your columns on baseball seriously, never on politics."

Two months later Giuliani held a press conference at City Hall to announce that sufficient funds had been raised privately and that the Reese-Robinson statue would definitely be built in Brooklyn. He gave me more credit than I deserved for the idea (I had gotten it from former *Newsday* sportswriter Stan Isaacs), then insisted I say a few words at the press conference.

I said I would rather not, beforehand in his office, but once the press conference began, the mayor summoned me to the microphone in a room full of friends and colleagues.

"My only function on this committee," I said, "is to make sure the crony of some political boss doesn't get a no-bid contract for the design."

The reporters laughed, but the mayor muttered, "Boy, you never let up, do you?"

Standing up there with Giuliani, Reese's son, Mark, and men who had been friends of Jackie Robinson, I thought about an autographed ball I still owned, signed exactly fifty years ago by all the 1949 Dodgers.

I remember how my daughter Rebecca, when she was about thirteen, asked me what the ball was worth. We went together to a memorabilia store in the Village and I asked the owner for an appraisal.

"Is Jackie's signature on the ball?" was his only question.

"Yes."

"Then it's worth at least $1,500."

I told my daughter that the old baseball was priceless to me and that I would never sell it. Someday she would own it.

On it are the signatures of Robinson and Campanella, surrounded by those of Reese, Snider, Hodges, Furillo, and Branca.

It is the symbol of and the proof that equal opportunity works, that inclusion is always better than exclusion.

CHAPTER 3

The Making of an Activist

On a snowy February night in 1959, I went to see Mike Harrington speak at a socialist loft on University Place with my best friend at Hunter College, Paul DuBrul.

Mike was then the presumed heir to Norman Thomas as the voice of American democratic socialism. But that night he was talking about the civil rights movement and in particular about a march planned for Washington that April to pressure the Eisenhower administration to quicken the tempo of school desegregation.

Mike was a hypnotizing speaker. He made the civil rights movement sound like a combination of a biblical prophecy about to come true and a tabloid drama of danger and courage. I remember him comparing Martin Luther King and his movement to the sanitary squads in Albert Camus's novel *The Plague*.

The speech also gave me a sense of what a social movement was. Mike painted a picture of people in motion, of direction action, of marches and protests, of King as a modern Moses. It gave me a sense of history, of how social change happens, of how ordinary students, sharecroppers, and ministers were writing history.

A few days later, along with Paul DuBrul, I showed up at an office in Harlem, at 312 West 125th Street, to volunteer my stirred soul and racing imagination. The office was the home base for several civil rights and labor groups.

I answered phones, stuffed envelopes, dropped off literature, met with some high school students. Once I got to meet A. Philip Randolph, the president of the sleeping car porters' union, a mentor to Dr. King and Harrington, a revered old lion of American social protest. I was so starstruck I went right out and read Murray Kempton's book about the 1930s—*Part of Our Time*—that contained a chapter on Randolph, who, along with Walter Reuther, is the cohero of the book, held up as moral contrasts to the communists. They "would rather rise with their class, than from it," Kempton wrote.

I also glimpsed the chain-smoking Bayard Rustin in his brisk comings and goings. Rustin was the logistical commander behind the march. He was an ex-communist and current pacifist. He spoke in a clipped accent that suggested Cary Grant. I was told he was very close to King and had even helped behind the scenes with the successful Montgomery bus boycott of 1955–56.

The mild message behind the march was that the Congress and the Eisenhower administration had to do more to integrate public schools. A lot of the talk around that beehive space on 125th Street was that Democratic senators like James Eastland of Mississippi were blocking civil rights legislation and that President Eisenhower had been too timid in using the federal authority against Arkansas governor Orval Faubus, who was resisting school integration.

The office talk made it clear the Supreme Court's unanimous 1954 desegregation decision was being nullified by the stalling southern politicians, who were more determined to resist than the president was to enforce. This was a more practical education in how power really worked than I got in any civics class or political science lecture.

In his speech in the Village loft, Mike Harrington had called the Democratic Party a "coalition between the New Dealers and the slave dealers," and I could see how that was being played out in the closed rooms of Washington, where the southerners had the seniority to control the key committees of Congress and use the filibuster and parliamentary gimmicks to kill civil rights legislation.

There had been an earlier school integration march in October of 1958 that attracted about 10,000 young people. That was about the size of the crowd we anticipated in April 1959. But when our bus arrived near the Lincoln Memorial, the crowd was at least 25,000. It was mostly young and totally integrated. There were waving signs identifying the schools students had come from. There were signs identifying religious denominations that had sent delegations. There were signs and hats identifying the labor unions that came. I remember a lot of signs from the auto workers and Local 1199, the hospital workers' union in New York City. There were signs urging passage of the "Douglas-Javits civil rights bill."

This was my first Washington protest march, and it made an impression as indelible as my first baseball game. It had the same dynamic of community and group solidarity—plus a high purpose.

The night before the march there had been some newspaper stories saying the protest had been infiltrated by communists—probably a smear leaked by J. Edgar Hoover. This upset me since I knew personally how intensely anticommunist the march organizers—Harrington, Rustin, and Philip Randolph—actually were. I heard these democratic socialists lecture about the evils of Stalinism. My own lifelong vehement antagonism to authoritarians of the left came from these three men, later fortified by Irving Howe and Arthur Schlesinger.

The speeches were moderate, considering what was about to come.

This was the first time I ever heard Martin Luther King, who gave the most visionary and uplifting speech of the day. King was then just thirty years old, and he spoke about "voting rights" and the morality of equality in his church cadences and blues repetitions that the world would get know four years later with his "I have a dream" speech. Dr. King touched my soul that day, and he would do that every time I saw him speak after that.

King held out the prospect of "registering three million new Negro voters in the South" as the way to end segregation, which is what would happen.

The other speakers—Daisy Bates of the Arkansas NAACP, Roy Wilkins, Harry Belafonte, and Jackie Robinson—emphasized the need for school integration and a faster pace of implementing the Supreme Court's 1954 decision. A. Philip Randolph also spoke, sounding like God addressing Moses with his voice of thunder.

This was the coalition of the future being born. I felt like I was now in a movement that gave life meaning and gave idealism a channel.

By the winter of 1960, the office on West 125th Street had evolved into the headquarters for an umbrella organization named the Committee to Defend Martin Luther King and the Struggle for Freedom in the South. This was the era before mass marketing and clever acronyms.

The sit-ins were spreading across the South. Martin Luther King was getting arrested, harassed, and even prosecuted on a trumped-up (and eventually dismissed) charge of felony tax fraud. Our main activity that February and March was organizing support picket lines in front of Woolworth department stores in Manhattan, while southern students were getting arrested at segregated Woolworth lunch counters in the South. The point was to boycott Woolworth's in the North until the economic pressure made them integrate in the South. These protests were coordinated out of the 125th Street office on Harlem's main commercial cross street, not far from the Apollo Theatre.

I was back at Hunter College in 1960 after spending part of 1958–59 working at Madison Square Garden as a sports publicity trainee. My ambition, of course, was to become a sportswriter, and my older friend from Bed-Stuy, Stan Fischler, had gotten me a job as an apprentice to Herb Goren, the publicity director of the New York Rangers hockey team. Fischler went on to become a respected hockey writer and television broadcaster, known as "the hockey maven."

But hockey proved to be the only sport that didn't interest me. Goons—tough guys without much scoring or skating skill—were then coming into the league with instructions to intimidate the finesse players on the other teams. The Rangers' coach, Phil Watson, would put a bounty on injuring—or at least taking to the penalty box for fighting—the shooters on opposing teams. My romantic sense of sportsmanship was violated by this tactic of recruiting a thug to neutralize talent.

The Rangers' enforcer was a popular and colorful defenseman named Lou Fontinato. One night he picked a fight with the great scorer for

Detroit, Gordie Howe. But Howe pulled Fontinato's blue shirt over his head and pummeled him with about fifteen brutal uppercut punches to the face.

Fontinato was all bloody; I think he had a broken nose. I was assigned to ride with him in an ambulance from the old Garden at fiftieth Street and Eighth Avenue, to a hospital a few block away. In the back of the ambulance Fontinato came out of his stupor, wiped the blood away from his lips, and muttered: "This fuckin' franchise doesn't give a fuck about me! Look who they're sending to the emergency room with me. A fuckin' nobody, a kid."

I spent as much time as I could hanging out in the Garden's boxing office and dodging my responsibilities for the amiable Goren. I met Sugar Ray Robinson as a hockey truant. And I got to talk to boxing storytellers like Harry Markson and Teddy Brenner. They gave me an education in how the Mafia ruled boxing, owned Sonny Liston, and controlled the welterweight division. Somehow this dose of realism didn't diminish my interest in boxing.

But my daily, up-close exposure to the hockey players was deromanticizing. Many of them were uneducated, homesick Canadians with whom I had nothing in common. All they seemed to talk about was sex and drinking. And what dentist to go to.

So I returned to Hunter College, no longer certain that I wanted to be a sportswriter. I was now more interested in political reporting, because of my new commitment to the civil rights movement. I wanted to write about things that mattered.

On weekends, and sometimes after school when we weren't putting out the twice weekly *Arrow*, Paul DuBrul and I would take the train down to the 125th Street office all through February, March, and April of 1960. We did what we were told. We just wanted to feel part of what was happening in the South.

Most of what I did was support actions for the sit-in activists. After a while we also got assignments and directions from "Snick"—the just-founded Student Non-Violent Coordinating Committee. They were the marines of the movement, in the foxholes at the frontiers of direct action. And most of them were my age or even younger. Their youth created an instinctive kinship.

One of the volunteers at the Committee to Defend King office was the reticent, spiritual, cerebral Bob Moses. He volunteered after he saw the student sit-ins on television. Moses would have a tremendous influence on me and my like-minded network of friends over the coming decade.

In 1960 Bob was already twenty-five years old and teaching math at a top private school in the Bronx—Horace Mann. He had graduated from the elite Stuyvesant High School and Hamilton College and spent two years in a Ph.D. program in philosophy at Harvard. He was forced to leave before he finished because of the death of his mother and a mental breakdown suffered by his father.

From the first day I met him, when he was Rustin's apprentice, I felt Bob was one deep cat. Like Harrington and like many young people in that office, Bob was deeply influenced by Camus. His main topics of conversation were metaphysical philosophy, Zen Buddhism, pacifism, and redemptive suffering. I never had a small-talk conversation with Bob Moses.

After a few months Rustin dispatched Bob, by bus, to work directly for Martin Luther King in Atlanta. But something failed to click between these two secular saints, and Bob went off to rural Mississippi alone, to organize for SNCC, not the Southern Christian Leadership Conference.

The next time I remember seeing Moses was in the winter of 1962. He had come up to New York on a short speaking tour, to report what he had seen and experienced trying to register black voters in the most violent, Klan-dominated, lawless county in Mississippi.

He said there was a town "named Liberty" in Amite County, but there was no liberty for the blacks who wanted to "reddish"—register—to vote, in the nation that cherished liberty and had a cabinet department named justice.

In his quiet, matter-of-fact monotone, Moses described the murder of Herbert Lee, a farmer with nine children, who had attended voter registration classes run by Moses and had sometimes been Moses's driver around Amite County.

Moses recounted how a member of the Mississippi state legislature named E. H. Hurst killed Lee outside the cotton gin in Liberty. Hurst then placed a tire iron under Lee's dead body lying in the street and told the police he had killed Lee in self-defense. The same day the coroner's jury ruled Lee's death was "justifiable homicide." (There was one black witness to Lee's murder, a logger named Louis Allen. He told Justice Department officials that Hurst executed Lee without provocation. In 1963 Allen would be murdered.)

Moses emphasized that neither the FBI nor Attorney General Kennedy had done anything to bring federal charges against Hurst. He spoke for an hour about what it was like to bear nonviolent moral witness alone, behind the enemy lines of segregation, in a place to which even the freedom riders hadn't come. Moses barely mentioned that he had just spent two months in jail and had been badly beaten. But he told us that at Lee's funeral, his widow cried at him, "You killed my husband, you killed my husband."

In 1967, when I became close to Robert Kennedy, I asked him several times about Lee's still-unsolved homicide and why, as attorney general, he had failed to prosecute the known killer of a victim engaged in voter registration. His response was there had never been an autopsy, and there was no forensic evidence, no photos of Lee's body. Louis Allen had lived in Amite County for two years after the murder and was not given federal protection as a witness.

In 1998, when I wrote and coproduced with Charley Stuart a three-hour documentary on Robert Kennedy for the Discovery television network, I made sure it included a reference to the long-forgotten murders of Herbert Lee and Louis Allen, though of course the film overall was very sympathetic to Kennedy: a sound bite of me saying one reason I picketed Robert Kennedy in June of 1963 was that the outlaw who killed Herbert Lee was then still a lawmaker in Mississippi.

In February of 2000 Philip Alden Robinson directed and wrote a first-class television movie based on Bob Moses's first year in rural Amite County. The film contained the scene of Hurst killing Lee in cold blood outside the cotton gin.

Eventually I would get to know Bob Moses. I interviewed him in the Mississippi delta in the summer of 1963. The first lengthy article I wrote after joining the staff of the *Village Voice* was about Moses, published on December 3, 1964.*

---

*The lead on my *Voice* article read: "The biblical Moses was a prophet and liberator who drew

In November of 1965, while I was working on my first book, *A Prophetic Minority*, I spent a week in Amite County. I stayed at the home of the heavily armed farmer E. W. Steptoe, which is where Moses stayed part of the time in 1961. I saw that Steptoe's property was adjacent to E. W. Hurst's property. I even saw Hurst himself one morning along the dirt road.

A Prophetic Minority, published in 1966, contained a whole chapter about Moses in southwest Mississippi and about the homicides of Lee and Allen. Giuliani was right, I never let up.

The headline on the *Voice* article was "THE INVISIBLE MAN LEARNS HIS NAME"—a bow, of course, to Ralph Ellison and James Baldwin.

In March 1960 the King defense committee's office, hectic and disorganized as it was, became the incubator for the landmark Supreme Court decision on free speech—*Times v. Sullivan*—for that was where a full-page advertisement in the *New York Times* was composed and edited. The sit-ins began on February 1 in North Carolina and spread like a freedom fever across the mid-South. Martin King quickly endorsed them, and two weeks after his endorsement, an Alabama grand jury indicted him on felony, perjury, and tax charges. It was a frame-up, but a trial would bankrupt King and his Southern Christian Leadership Conference, and a conviction by an Alabama jury of whites could produce a long prison sentence. Simply having to defend himself against the charges would distract King from participating in this activist hour in history.

I was a fly on the wall as these events began to unfold, stuffing envelopes and listening to the office buzz that became the news the next day.

The advisers around King were clearly frightened by the perjury indictment, so the defense committee was energized to raise money, and the *Times* ad became the vehicle. The difficulty was raising enough money to pay for the full-page advertisement and then getting enough

---

water from a stone. For the past three years Bob Moses, also a prophet and liberator, has been trying to draw justice from the stone of Mississippi. The difference between them is that the Old Testament Moses drew his inspiration from God, and the modern Moses draws his from the housemaids, cotton pickers, and tenant farmers of Mississippi."

respectables to sign it. I called people to obtain in writing their formal permission to use their names in the ad. The ad itself was drafted by Rustin, the executive director of the King defense committee, and a volunteer playwright named John Murray.

"Heed Their Rising Voices" ran the headline on the ad, a phrase borrowed from a *Times* editorial from March 19, 1960, that tepidly supported the student sit-in movement as "something understandable."

The ad contained ten paragraphs of text that seemed just right to me. It said unnamed "Southern violators of the Constitution" were "determined to destroy one man, who more than any other, symbolizes the new spirit now sweeping the south—Rev. Martin Luther King, Jr.":

> Again and again the southern violators have answered Dr. King's peaceful protests with intimidation and violence. They have bombed his home, almost killing his wife and child. They have assaulted his person. They have arrested him seven times for speeding, loitering, and similar offenses.
>
> Now they have charged him with perjury, a felony under which they could imprison him for ten years.

Among the sixty-four names attached to the ad were: Eleanor Roosevelt, Harry Belafonte, Jackie Robinson, Marlon Brando, Dorothy Dandridge, Langston Hughes, John Lewis, Norman Thomas, Lorraine Hansberry, Ossie Davis and Ruby Dee, Rabbi Edward Klein, Mahalia Jackson, Nat King Cole, Marc Blizstein, Sammy Davis, Jr., Sidney Poitier, Nat Hentoff, and Shelley Winters.

It was a spicy stew of Hollywood, Las Vegas, Greenwich Village, and Harlem. The ad ran, full page, on March 29, 1960. Money immediately began to pour in the 125th Street office. I saw the big checks, and some envelopes containing a single crumpled dollar bill, accompanied by the handwritten note of a teenager.

But the ad contained a few minuscule factual errors. King had then been arrested four times, not seven. One paragraph described the police "ringing" the campus of Alabama State University and arresting students as they sang "My Country 'Tis of Thee." The students had actually been singing "The Star Spangled Banner." And the police did not form a complete circle around the campus, so the word "ringing" was technically inaccurate.

These trivial errors could not rationally be described as malicious or libelous. But Montgomery police chief L. B. Sullivan, a hard-line segregationist, sued the *Times* for printing the ad the King defense committee had drafted and paid for. Sullivan filed his suit in state court in Alabama, naming the *Times* and the four Alabama preachers as defendants. Suddenly the *Times* felt as vulnerable as Dr. King felt about the perjury tax charge. It was baseless, but it could hurt them.

Although the ad did not mention even one public official of Alabama by name, Sullivan claimed it libeled all the sovereign officials of Alabama with the vague reference to "southern violators of the Constitution."

This is the same Chief Sullivan who, the following spring, would break his promise to the Justice Department to make sure his police units protected the freedom riders when they arrived at the Montgomery bus terminal. In fact, Sullivan made sure there was no police protection at the bus terminal. And the Klan was waiting there to ambush the riders with pipes and clubs.

One of those who was beaten unconscious that day—while he was trying to get two young women into his Justice Department vehicle—was my friend John Siegenthaler, then the executive assistant to Attorney General Kennedy.

"Sullivan double-crossed Bobby," Siegenthaler later told me. "The police peeled away as soon as those buses reached the Montgomery city limits. These freedom riders were beaten bloody. The police were absent by design."

John lay in the gutter for a half hour before he was taken to the hospital, where he remained for two weeks. Later FBI director Hoover would tell John the FBI knew the names of the Klansmen who assaulted him but that he wouldn't arrest them because they had broken no federal law.

This brutal, unpunished beating of a federal officer would begin to personalize the civil rights issue for Robert Kennedy.

In May 1960 the King defense committee volunteers were confused when the *New York Times* published a statement apologizing to Governor John Patterson of Alabama for any unfair characterizations of his state in the ad. Two weeks after the retraction, Patterson sued the *Times* for $1 million. Patterson also named Dr. King as a defendant and brought the suit in state court. In the fall of 1960 an all-white jury ruled in favor of Sullivan after a three-day trial.

The Alabama Supreme Court—incredibly—upheld the jury verdict in Sullivan's favor, ordering the *Times* to pay him $500,000 for an ad no *Times* reporter or editor saw or touched. Finally, in March of 1964, the Supreme Court of the United States reversed the Alabama high court ruling in a landmark decision written by Justice William Brennan:

> Thus we consider this case against the background of a profound national commitment to the principle that debate on public issues should be uninhibited, robust, and wide-open, and that it may well include vehement, caustic, and sometimes unpleasantly sharp attacks on government and public officials . . . The present advertisement, as an expression of grievance and protest on one of the major public issues of our time, would seem clearly to qualify for the constitutional protection . . .
>
> Erroneous statement is inevitable in free debate and it must be protected if the freedoms of expression are to have the "breathing space" they need to survive.

In his concurring opinion, Justice Hugo Black wrote: "We would, I think, more faithfully interpret the First Amendment by holding that at the very least it leaves the people and the press free to criticize officials and discuss public affairs with impunity . . . an unconditional right to say what one pleases about public affairs is what I consider to be the minimum guarantee of the First Amendment."

As a very marginal volunteer in an obscure office that had produced the *Times* ad defending King, I followed closely the judicial journey of *Times v. Sullivan.* The case became my private seminar on the First Amendment. I went to law school on this case. It made freedom of the press personal rather than an abstract principle. The Alabama Supreme Court decision against the *Times* and King had a big effect on me. It helped me realize how fragile free speech is in this country and how cynical, stupid, and political judges can be. It helped me see that racism can blind jurists to the truth.*

Sullivan dramatized for me just how powerful and entrenched the enemies of integration were. And, most of all, it cured me of thinking civil rights gains would be easy, fun, or cheap grace.

My first civil rights arrest occurred on June 6, 1961. It was mostly an exhilarating experience because it was in Manhattan, not Mississippi. Fifteen of us—mostly members of Yipsel (the Young People's Socialist League)—were arrested for sitting in at the ABC television center building on West Sixty-sixth Street. We came to sit-in that night because of a phone call from Sandra "Casey" Cason (later to marry Tom Hayden) who was in Austin, Texas, working with SNCC. Casey—beautiful, blond, smart, and poetic—had notified SNCC's New York supporters that the Paramount-owned theater in Austin was segregating blacks, forcing them to sit in the balcony, while whites sat downstairs.

Casey figured out that ABC and Paramount were part of the same corporation, and asked for volunteers to get arrested sitting in at ABC's corporate headquarters in Manhattan. The idea was that this would draw media attention and convince the managers of the theater in Austin—a college town—to desegregate.

Starting in the evening of June 5, four SNCC supporters began a sit-in in the office of Leonard Goldenson, the president of ABC television. By most accounts he was a decent, informal, and philanthropic executive. But he was definitely not pleased to find four uninvited young people occupying his reception area with demands for integration.

Sometime during the afternoon, I was summoned to the sit-in location and instructed to picket the rest of the day and be prepared to get arrested if the four people inside were arrested, evicted, or attacked. One

*In 1991 Anthony Lewis published a history of the Sullivan case called *Make No Law*. Writing about the Bill of Rights doesn't get much better than this. Lewis tells a clear narrative story about the libel suit that led to a sea-change in the way freedom of the press is interpreted in this country.

of the four people inside was Lucy Komisar, a Queens college student, who would become a writer specializing in human rights issues.

At about 9 P.M. twenty-five of us were picketing on the sidewalk and singing civil rights songs. Suddenly Lucy's angry father arrived and went upstairs to take his eighteen-year-old daughter home, before there was any violence or arrests. A few minutes later Lucy came down in tears, her father scowling, and drove her home to Valley Stream, Long Island.

At about 9:30 Mike Harrington arrived—with a date—and joined the picket line.

At about midnight the three remaining sit-ins were escorted out of the building by Pinkerton guards. They told us how they had been denied access to a bathroom or food for nineteen hours. This was as harsh as conditions got in Manhattan. Harrington suggested we all sit down on the sidewalk and begin singing, and get arrested in solidarity "with our brothers and sisters fighting racism in Texas."

I sat down on West Sixty-sixth Street and sang "We Shall Not Be Moved." I was sitting between Bob Arnold, a friend from Hunter College, and Richard Roman, of Yipsel (Young Peoples Socialist League).

We were eventually all arrested for "disorderly conduct" at about 1 A.M., and booked at the West Sixty-eighth Street precinct house. I was fingerprinted and my belt and shoelaces were confiscated, so I would not commit suicide. I felt so proud to be initiated into the fraternity of those arrested for civil rights activism.

As we were being booked, *New York Post* photographer Artie Pomerantz took a photo of our ragtag group. The next day it appeared in the *Post*, accompanied by a story by Alfred Hendricks that ran under a three-column headline: "THE WEST 66 ST. SIT-IN HAS ITS WINDUP IN COURT." "A total of ten youths, a man, and four girls were taken into custody. All will be arraigned in Manhattan Adolescent Court, 100 Centre Street." No names were printed.

I was one of the ten youths, and the man was Harrington. His date was one of the four "girls."

When I joined the *Post* thirty years later, I asked Laura Harris, the chief of the *Post* library, to try to find a copy of the picture of my being booked, but no one could ever locate a print. At least I still have the actual disintegrating page from the paper in which it ran.

After we were booked, all the male arrestees were placed in one large holding cell. We had a wonderful night, feeling heroic and singing "We Shall Overcome" and "Oh, Freedom" as loud as we could, trying to make believe we were with SNCC and we were in the Birmingham city jail.

At some point during this high-adrenaline night I had a long talk with Harrington. He told me about his early research on American poverty for *The Other America*, the book that would instigate the Kennedy and Johnson administrations to declare a "war on poverty."

Mike also asked me if I wanted to become his assistant (managing editor) on the democratic socialist newspaper *New America*. The job paid almost nothing, but it would give me the privilege of hanging out with Mike in the backroom of the White Horse tavern on Hudson Street, which was the de facto office for the bimonthly paper. The White Horse is where Dylan Thomas drank himself to death one night, where longshoremen drank alone at the bar, and where college students came to see where Dylan Thomas drained his last glass. How could I refuse?

I didn't regret my decision. Sitting quietly next to Mike at the White Horse, I met Norman Mailer, James Baldwin, Judy Collins, radical writer Paul Jacobs, NAACP labor secretary Herb Hill, Dan Wakefield, most of the editors of *Commonweal* magazine, emissaries from Martin Luther King, and various union organizers and student activists. On many nights Tommy Makem and the Clancy Brothers materialized about midnight and sang Irish ballads and Spanish Civil War songs till last call.

Mike knew how to have fun; I remember more laughter than gloom or angst from those special nights. I was not a drinker and usually left by 2 A.M., when Mike and the Clancys felt the night was just beginning.

We all need mentors and role models. Stephen Sondheim had Oscar Hammerstein. Jimmy Cannon had Damon Runyon. Martin Luther King had Dr. Benjamin Mays and Gandhi. Harry Belafonte had Paul Robeson. Vince Scully had Red Barber to show him how to broadcast a baseball game. Richard Brooks had John Houston to show how to be a writer-director. Aretha Franklin had Sam Cooke to show her how to cross over from sacred gospel music to secular soul music. Spike Lee had Martin

Scorsese as a role model for how to become an independent filmmaker with a personal vision.

And I had Mike Harrington.

An only child without a father, I had a strong need for a mentor, for someone to guide me in my search for knowledge. I needed connections to the world, and Mike, exactly ten years older and far more worldly, offered them.

Mike was a good fit for me. As a kid growing up Irish lower-middle-class in St. Louis, he wanted to be a sportswriter. He knew his baseball. He had been a social worker and might have become a poet. He himself had been mentored by Dorothy Day, editing the *Catholic Worker* newspaper and serving food to the lost souls and derelicts of the Bowery. He had lived in the "voluntary poverty" of the Catholic Worker house on Christie Street, trying to reconcile Christ's teachings with the human suffering he found all around him.

Mike had a boyish, sensitive Irish face and always dressed like a bohemian in workshirts, pea jackets, and wool pullover hats. He was, in fact, a very fine poet and a scholar of Yeats and T. S. Eliot. His literary heroes included Albert Camus, George Orwell, and André Malraux, because "they combined thought with action." His more personal mentors, in addition to Dorothy Day, were Norman Thomas and Max Shachtman, the former secretary to Leon Trotsky, who was almost a cult figure among sectarian factionists in New York in the late 1950s.

I once saw Shachtman speak. He was witty and forceful but something of a crank—on this occasion he was speaking in support of nuclear fallout shelters. Fear of the Soviet Union seemed to be the engine that drove his ideology by the time I encountered "the old man," as he was called.

Shachtman was a terrible influence on Mike, pulling him back into hermetic, European-style sectarianism and preventing him from becoming more of a native American radical, who could employ his considerable speaking and writing skills to attack specific injustices.

Mike was very attractive to women; there were always a couple waiting to go home with him after a talk or a night of drinking. They were always pretty and artistic. His most serious relationship was with Sally

Backer, the daughter of Dorothy Schiff, the owner of the *New York Post.* There were some late-night socialist fantasies about Mike becoming the editor of the *Post.*

Mike always gave panhandlers whatever loose change was in his pocket, even though he assumed they would use it to buy a bottle of cheap wine. Whenever he heard somebody use the word "bum" he corrected them, suggesting a less demeaning reference. "Our ideal was to see Christ in every man," Mike would later write, "including the pathetic, shambling, shivering creature who would wander off the streets with his pants caked with urine, and his face scabbed with blood."

Mike had gone to Holy Cross and spent a year at Yale Law School, but it was his two years among the poorest of the poor at the *Catholic Worker* house, helping the most defeated alcoholics and offering solace to the most depressed casualties of the city, that shaped him the most. And planted the seeds for his 186-page masterpiece of reporting, *The Other America,* which changed the direction of the nation.

When Mike died of cancer in 1989, Pete Hamill would write, "He was, more than any other great man I've met, intensely human; he lost his Catholic faith the first time, after all, because he could not believe in Hell. So he had fun, too."

Part of my education in Mike's saloon seminar was about getting out *New America* twice a month. The two of us did the editing, layout, headline writing, picture cropping, caption writing, book review assigning, and reportorial assigning. Mike wrote the editorials. He also would convince a young cartoonist named Jules Feiffer to let us publish his work for free.

I loved the process. It was like editing the Hunter College paper again.

New America was especially good at covering the civil rights movement. Freedom riders wrote personal accounts of beatings and jailings. James Baldwin gave us a few pieces of his neon prose. We also published a moving letter from Tom Hayden, which described how he celebrated his twenty-first birthday in the Albany, Georgia, jail. The letter demonstrated what a fine, natural writer Tom was.

One afternoon in April 1962 we were facing the printer's deadline for the next issue, and it was time for Mike to bang out the editorial, something I had seen him do in about twenty minutes of white heat. On this day he decided, at the last minute, to make it about the Kennedy administration's misguided policy in a place called Vietnam. It was the first time I can remember ever thinking about that remote Asian country.

Mike's editorial attacked the tyrannical Diem regime for corruption and lack of democracy, and it warned against increased commitment of American troops.

> One has the feeling that the American people may be on the verge of another Korea, that there may be a fundamental commitment to interventionism in Vietnam. And yet, there is hardly any understanding of this nation . . . It is a question of a regime which is basically unpopular, which is firmly given over to dictatorial methods, and which cannot be, under any circumstances, a "defense" against Communism.
>
> The standard apology when America backs a dictator against Communists is that one cannot be finicky, that one must work with what "is," that there is no third choice. And yet, the reports of the German Socialists demonstrate the self-defeating character of such a thesis: these reactionary governments, which will sign anti-Communist pledge cards, are themselves the source of Communism in their society.
>
> At a bare minimum, we believe that it is tragic that America does not possess the information on Vietnam, that we are drifting towards intervention in terrible ignorance of the facts. But more basically, we see Vietnam as a profound confirmation of the point of view that reaction is not a defense against Communist totalitarianism. Time and time again, this nation has chosen a "lesser evil," only to discover this is the way of self-defeat. In Vietnam, the result of this tragic policy may be a bloody, terrible jungle war.

Under the prescient headline "DRIFT TOWARDS INTERVENTIONISM," the article appeared in the May 4 edition of *New America*, which had a print run of only 10,000 copies.

In the fall of 1961 Mike arranged for my first freelance article to be published in *Commonweal*, the liberal Catholic weekly that Mike frequently wrote for and where he was friends with most of the editors. The article described the political campaign in East Harlem, where a Puerto Rican named Carlos Rios had defeated a longtime white clubhouse incumbent named John Merli. I was paid $75 for my first published work in a mainstream publication.

Paul DuBrul and I had been grunt-work, doorbell-ringing volunteers all summer, and when Rios won, I saw it as an example of Hispanic empowerment and grassroots politics ascendant in a northern city. However, Rios quickly became a party-line hack and absentee member of the City Council. But his mediocrity as a politician did not distress me. It was the idea—not the individual—that drew me to East Harlem. Puerto Ricans deserved self-determination, their own representation in a community that was 80 percent Hispanic.

The principle was empowerment. This principle had room for representatives who were disappointing like Carlos Rios. By 1961 I didn't expect much from politicians. My faith was already being invested in ideas. The idea of self-determination included the right to elect hacks who looked like you.

Mike also helped get my second freelance article published in *Commonweal*, in the spring of 1962. This one was about a Young Americans for Freedom rally, featuring Barry Goldwater, held at Madison Square Garden. I had covered the rally for *New America*, and Mike proposed expanding it for *Commonweal*.

Helped by Mike's capacity for analyzing and generalizing, I expanded the reporting to include some grand assertions, such as that in the near future the student radicalism of the left would make a larger impact on the country than the young conservatives—even though they had just proved they could fill the Garden with 18,000 followers.

Early in 1962 I joined SDS—Students for a Democratic Society—which was just being formed. I continued to serve as Mike's apprentice on *New America*, but more and more of my time was being spent in the SDS office on East nineteenth Street.

There I got to know the founding fathers (most were male, white, middle class) of SDS: Al Haber, Bob Ross, and Tom Hayden from the University of Michigan; Todd Gitlin from the Bronx High School of Science and Harvard; Paul Booth, a mature freshman from Swarthmore; Robb Burlage, a funny and ironic Texan who actually understood economics;

Steve Max, a so-called red diaper baby and organizer from New York City; Dick Flacks from Brooklyn College; Tim Jenkins from Howard University; Texan Sandra Cason; Paul Potter and Rennie Davis from Oberlin.

For the first half of 1962 a founding manifesto was being drafted, circulated, critiqued, and then rewritten by Hayden. (He was the best writer among us; he probably should have become a writer instead of a politician.) Tom was then under the influence of Harrington, Camus, C. Wright Mills, Kenneth Keniston, Paul Goodman, and Michigan professor Arnold Kaufman. Every draft of the manifesto reflected this contemporary democratic radical pedigree.

With talk of Camus so much in the air that spring of 1962, I started to make my way through his works. I read *The Rebel* and *Resistance, Rebellion, and Death*, as well as a number of pieces on his recent "absurd" death in an automobile accident. A year later, when the two volumes of his notebooks were published, I read them and underlined passages.

Camus seemed above all to be a moral man, an intellectually honest intellectual. He was an advocate of nonviolence, a poet of loneliness, a voice of reason who never wrote in a shout. His tortured ambivalence about Algeria impressed me more than did the certainties behind Sartre's rationale for revolutionary violence. Camus tried to be neither the victim nor the executioner.

I admired Camus because he remained independent of both the East and West in the Cold War. I admired that he saw history from the point of view of ordinary people, "those silent men, who, throughout the world, endure the life that has been made for them." He was for the powerless everywhere. I admired the fact that he had been active in the French resistance, writing unsigned weekly editorials for *Combat* whose authorship did not become known until after the liberation of Paris. I clipped a copy of his 1957 Nobel Prize acceptance speech in which he said, "The writer's function is not without arduous duties. By definition, he cannot serve today those who make history; he must serve those who are subject to it."

Later in the 1960s, Sartre and Frantz Fanon, the theorist of anticolonial violence, would become more fashionable in New Left circles. But Camus was always my touchstone. His cyclical passage into and out of fashion only made him more appealing to me, more pure.

The final draft of the manifesto said plainly, "As democrats we are in basic opposition to the communist system. The Soviet Union, as a system, rests on the total suppression of organized opposition." Its two central ideas were faith in "participatory democracy" and in "the University as the catalyst of social change." (This was absurd, since southern blacks were clearly the catalyst for social change in 1962.)

In a defining passage, the document proclaimed: "As a social system we seek the establishment of a democracy of individual participation, governed by two central aims: that the individual share in those social decisions determining the quality and direction of his life; that society be organized to encourage independence in men, and provide the media for their common participation."

The statement also blamed both East and West for the Cold War and for the failure to negotiate a nuclear test ban treaty. We were a full year ahead of President Kennedy and his 1963 speech that broke the logjam to nuclear detente.

The bottom line, the essence of it, was that society had to change, that conformity and the status quo had to be pushed aside by direct action.

The SDS had a parent organization—the League of Industrial Democracy (LID)—that controlled our financing. The LID's board included Harrington, Norman Thomas, and Sarah Lawrence college president Harold Taylor. But it also included a large number of older, sectarian Cold War trade unionists, veterans of the 1930 wars with the communists—Harry Fleischman, Murray Gross, and Emanuel Muravchik among them. They didn't like the manifesto one bit, thinking it was pro-communist when it should have been "pro–State Department," as one of them told me.

Their unease might not have caused an explosion if Mike Harrington hadn't shared it so intensely. Mike attended the first major SDS convention in Port Huron, Michigan for two days, then left before it was over. He debated the draft statement fiercely with Hayden in a tense workshop panel.

The personal chemistry between these two went haywire, and I still am mystified by the reason. Hayden and Harrington respected each other and had fundamental similarities: both Irish, both lapsed Catholics, both democratic radicals, both bohemian, both intellectual, both deeply influenced by Albert Camus, both baseball fans, both my friends. Harrington had been a guest at Hayden's wedding in Texas only a few months before, where Tom and Casey had read aloud passages from Camus's writings to each other.

But at Port Huron, they attacked each other harshly over nuances of difference in the criticism of communism. Harrington also felt that the draft was "too antilabor."

After Harrington left Port Huron, the convention incorporated most of his objections in a final rewrite of the seminal statement. The union criticism was muted, the anticommunism was clarified and slightly toughened.

After Mike returned to New York, he spoke to his three Yipsel comrades who had remained behind at the convention—all three devoted followers of Max Shachtman—Tom Kahn, Richard Roman, and Rochelle Horowitz. They never told him that his ideas had moved Hayden, and many others, who wished to meet the LID halfway. They made Mike feel like his passion had been spent and ignored, which was opposite of the truth.

Without having read the final, revised version of the *Port Huron Statement*, Mike himself convened an emergency meeting of the LID board to consider what to do about their disobedient student affiliate.

A week later the LID decided to abort SDS. They summoned Hayden, Haber, and Steve Max to a "hearing" on July 6. At this confrontation, the LID fired those three from the SDS staff, even though they had been democratically elected by the convention. They imposed Richard Roman (my ABC/Paramount cellmate) as their receiver to run the office. They changed the locks on the office, depriving us of access to the mailing list, which meant we couldn't inform members of what was happening to us. And they blocked the distribution of our founding manifesto—our identity. We didn't have enough money to mail it out.

I was stupefied by this authoritarian repression. This is how the bosses reacted when those old men on the LID board started their union—the International Ladies Garment Workers' Union. They had been fired and locked out by their garment industry bosses.

For two weeks Mike Harrington was a different person—cold, factional, acting brutishly on false information. I never saw him behave that way again. He was like a stranger.

For three days after the July 6 debacle we held a round-the-clock marathon meeting in Steve Max's spacious apartment on Riverside Drive, trying to compose some response. I remember listening to a tape recording of the July 6 meeting. It sounded like a communist purge trial to me.

One LID board member seemed to think the *Port Huron Statement* included a direct attack on the LID—a fiction. Another was upset that an "observer" from a Maoist youth group had been seated at Port Huron. In fact, after a long debate, this seventeen-year-old Maoist was approved to be a nonvoting "observer," but he had left before the vote was taken. Mike had even red-baited Steve Max, even though he knew Max had broken with the Communist Party's youth group years earlier, in 1956.

At some point during these sleepless deliberations, one of our number went downtown, picked the lock, and liberated our mailing list.

At another point, Tom Kahn and Richard Roman showed up to argue in support of everything the LID had done to us, even though the convention had elected both of them to the SDS leadership. Hayden called Kahn a traitor and threw a pencil at him. I thought Hayden was about to fight him physically, before Kahn and Roman left Steve's apartment.

Tom Kahn went on to become a fascinating back story—a supporter of the Vietnam War and Richard Nixon, a speechwriter for George Meany, and a special assistant to AFL-CIO president Lane Kirkland. Kahn also became a cruel factional antagonist toward Harrington. He cut him off from funding sources. He gave interviews mocking Mike for associating with Bella Abzug, George McGovern, and the *Village Voice.* In 1972 Kahn, who was gay, even wrote a speech for Meany to deliver to the steelworkers' union convention that ridiculed gays in vulgar, pandering tones. Mike showed me this speech. It was one of the few times I could detect real disgust in his eyes, and I could see why. One part of Meany's speech read, "We listened to the gay-lib people who want to legalize marriage between boys and boys, and between girls and girls . . . We heard from people who look like Jacks, acted like Jills, and had the odor of johns about them."

Tom Kahn would betray Mike, SDS, and himself in one decade. He died of AIDS in the early 1990s.

For two days I was a member of the sleep-deprived, pizza-eating writing committee that drafted an appeal from the LID's decision to suffocate its SDS baby in its cradle. The appeal ran twenty-seven pages, a mishmash of styles and voices. It argued for due process rights, denied that we were soft on communism, pointing out "participatory democracy" was aimed at Russia as much as the United States. It also tried to say that we were just speaking in "the voice of our own generation," trying to break free of all the old sectarian disputes of the past.

During these sessions we were visited by LID board members Harold Taylor and Andrew Norman, who was the youngest member of the board. They told us that Norman Thomas agreed with us; they would try to work out a compromise that would allow the elected staff to go back on salary and permit the distribution of the *Port Huron Statement*, which, at that point, was being suppressed as subversive.

On the third night I slipped out to meet Mike for a cup of coffee. I was still in awe of him. And I was still, in a naive fashion, hoping to paper over the differences to make peace between my peers and my teacher. I didn't even raise the most upsetting thing Mike had done—his personal attack on Steve Max as having hidden pro-Stalinist sympathies. As I've said, Mike knew Steve had broken with the Young Communist League in 1956, which was when Steve's father quit the Communist Party and resigned as city editor of the *Daily Worker*. Steve often cracked me up with his comic routines making fun of the way real communists functioned and thought.

Now, forty years later, I can think of plenty of arguments I should have made to Mike. In 1962 two of his closest friends and political partners were themselves former communists—Bayard Rustin and Paul Jacobs, the colorful writer and organizer from San Francisco.

And some of Mike's intellectual heroes (and mine) had briefly been communists—or young communists—Albert Camus, Murray Kempton, Ignazio Silone, and Richard Wright. Some of the most effective anticommunists were ex-communists who remained on the left.

But my best recollection is that we stuck to the larger, less personal differences, like the actual content of the *Port Huron Statement*. Mike told me that he agreed with "about 90 percent" of what was in the final draft. He admitted that Kahn and Horowitz had misled him, or never told him, about the improvements the convention had made, based on Mike's passionate debating points in the dispute with Hayden.

I sensed Mike was already starting to regret what he had done. I said that 10 percent of political differences wasn't worth the LID's extreme response—even if he was right about all 10 percent of the disagreement, which was mostly about emphasis and omission. Rob Burlage, one of the founding members of SDS, considered Russia to be a bureaucratic relic of no appeal. I said the manifesto had that same "emotional truth" as his own dazzling editorial in *New America* opposing military intervention in Vietnam.

"We are rebelling against the void of the 1950s," I said, "but the LID is living in the 1930s."

We parted on excellent terms personally but without any agreement on how to resolve the current impasse. I now think of this failure as a tragic moment in the history of SDS and in the development of the student radicalism for the rest of the decade.

And in Mike's evolution. Mike could have—*should* have—been the bridge between the generation of 1960s' activists and 1930s' veterans. As a product of the 1950s, as a Norman Thomas–type democratic socialist, he could have been the link between the founders of SDS and the few older radicals we admired, like I. F. Stone, Paul Goodman, Paul Jacobs, Norman Mailer, and, above all, Martin Luther King, whom Mike knew and whom he had done some writing for. He could have played the mediator, but instead he played the prosecutor. Something very deep inside Mike caused him to snap at Port Huron and mug his own protégés.

The closest Mike came to speculating about what might have happened came in an interview he gave years later to Jim Miller, for his fine history of SDS, *Democracy in the Streets.* Mike described his "emotional overresponse" as part of what he perceived to be "an Oedipal assault on the father figure. I'd always been the youngest at everything I'd ever done," Mike continued. "I graduated from college at nineteen; I was the youngest editor of the *Catholic Worker.* My self-image was as a young person . . . Up comes this younger generation. I think that they are ignoring my sincere, honest, and absolutely profound advice. And this struck at my self-image."

In the spring of 1965, at the peak of his popularity over *The Other*

America, Mike had a nervous breakdown that he sketchily described in his book *Fragments of the Century*. Mike had suppressed "issues" involving his mother, his role as good son to his mentors, and feeling threatened by the younger generation of radicals who should have been his protégés. If only he could have felt a little less rigid and embattled.

During the summer of 1962, with critical support from Norman Thomas and Harold Taylor, the LID board relented and retreated. Our desperate "Son of Port Huron" appeal for SDS's right to live made an impact. A compromise was reached.

We got the keys to the office back. The manifesto was sent out to the world. Hayden was reinstated as SDS president. But Steve Max was never restored as the field organizer, an innocent victim of red-baiting.

It had all been needless, tragic overreaction. The LID's repression gave a bad name to the legitimate anticommunism of the democratic left. Cutting this tradition off from the founders of SDS was a huge mistake.

I have always been pleased to have been an original member of SDS in 1962. Rereading my sixty-four-page mimeographed copy of the *Port Huron Statement* today, I find that it holds up quite well, as a system of values, as a call for economic and racial equality. It warns against the growing power of the CIA; proposes a program to "abolish poverty"; warns against supporting foreign dictators and against nuclear proliferation; talks about the dehumanizing effect of vast impersonal bureaucracies; and urges "experiments in decentralization based on a vision of man as master of his machines and his society."

The idea that the campuses would be the catalyst of social change now seems self-important and elitist, of course. But taken as a whole, it still makes more sense and is more farsighted than either the Democratic or Republican Party platforms of 1964. Or even 1984.

When I published my book on Robert Kennedy in 1969, I made sure my charter membership in SDS was part of the short biographical sketch on the back cover. When my marriage announcement appeared in the *New York Times* in 1971—by which point SDS had disintegrated into nihilism and psychosis—I half playfully told my Republican banker father-in-law that I wanted my SDS affiliation to be part of the wedding announcement. And it was.

In 1965 Mike Harrington, recovered from his breakdown, was named the new chairman of the LID at a luncheon. I covered the event for the *Village Voice*—the job Mike had helped me get. In his acceptance remarks, Mike made another public apology for participating in the attempt to crush SDS at its creation. He could never stop seeking atonement.

In 1966 Mike contributed the introduction to my book *A Prophetic Minority* about the origins of SDS, SNCC, and the antiwar movement. Mike wrote:

> Jack Newfield thinks that this handful of radicals constitutes a "prophetic minority" that will stamp its image into these times and eventually affect American history itself. I think Newfield is right . . .
>
> If I may invest a personal relationship with political significance, the heartening thing to me is that Newfield and I have maintained a friendship despite our differences.
>
> We were arrested together in a sit-in in 1961; we were on opposite sides of the generational barricades in a faction fight in Students for a Democratic Society in 1962; and now in 1966, I have the privilege of writing my own opinionated introduction to his excellent book.

It was typical of Mike that he would graciously help promote a book that criticized him for a decision he already apologized for.*

The chimes of freedom were sounding in June of 1963. Thought and action were in alignment. Martin Luther King's campaign of mass demonstrations in Birmingham had won some concessions and branded the image of police dogs and fire hoses turned on children onto the nation's conscience. King and the national civil rights leadership were now planning their August "March on Washington."

President Kennedy finally introduced a major new civil rights bill and spoke to the nation on television, for the first time calling equal rights a moral issue, asking whites if they would willingly change places with blacks in this society.

The assassination of Medgar Evers by a Klan sniper, who shot the NAACP leader in the back, horrified indifferent moderates.

---

*In his last book before his death, *The Long Distance Runner*, Mike again apologized for his attack

And in June of 1963 I threw myself into organizing for a mass sit-in at Baltimore's segregated, privately owned Gwynn Oak amusement park.

Civil rights activists in Maryland had been trying to integrate this popular park for years without success. Now they sent out the word to New York, Philadelphia, and Washington, D.C., asking for volunteers to make the park a national symbol of racial segregation in the North. The owners—David, James, and Arthur Price—refused to sell admission tickets to blacks, saying it was just a business decision, that whites wouldn't come any more if they had to share rides with blacks. A summons had gone out from Baltimore activists, and SNCC, SDS, CORE (Congress of Racial Equality), and a national coalition of clergy set it for the nation's birthday, to draw as many people as possible to the park and submit to nonviolent arrest.

Early on the morning of July 4, four busloads of New York activists set out for Baltimore. At about 11 A.M. we arrived at the Metropolitan Methodist Church in West Baltimore. It was packed with four hundred singing, inspired people. Oh, was music important to the movement!

To my surprise, there were short speeches by a parade of clergy. The protest was much more religious-based than I realized. Students were the soldiers, not the generals here. First Eugene Carson Blake, the leader of the United Presbyterian Church, spoke, emphasizing nonviolence, the need for direct action, and the obligations of religious leaders to join the civil rights movement. Then Monsignor Austin Healy of Baltimore's Catholic Archdiocese spoke, followed by several black ministers and a rabbi. Local CORE chairman Ed Chance also blessed and baptized us for battle.

When we arrived in disciplined fashion at the appointed place of arrest, we were surrounded by about three hundred hostile, mostly teenage hecklers, some waving Confederate flags, some shouting out insults like "jungle bunny" and "nigger lover," and, most memorably, "stick them in the zoo." This was not Manhattan. The eastern shore of Maryland was

---

on SDS. He apologized for his "rude insensitivity to young people struggling to define a new identity. I had treated fledgling radicals trying out their own ideas for the first time as if they were hardened faction fighters whose lives were perversely dedicated to principles I abhorred. I then compounded that stupidity by making an alliance with the old guard of the LID against my former protégés. When I came to my senses, the damage had been done."

a hotbed of racism. George Wallace would do very well in these precincts in the presidential campaigns of 1964 and 1968. The face of white resistance was shouting "white nigger" and spitting at me.

There were plenty of adults and clergy in the group waiting to get arrested. The proportion of dark suits and clerical collars struck me as much as the white hostility on the hillside. Some of the demonstrators went limp, compelling Baltimore County police to carry them, on a very hot day, to the waiting vans a few hundred yards away. I walked to the van, singing "The Star-Spangled Banner" (since it was July 4). There were a lot of TV cameras to record the first mass arrests in Baltimore.

Most of those arrested were white, and this pleased Ed Chance of CORE and the local black ministers. They feared the protest would be smaller and blacker. We were all charged with trespassing on private property.

Once in the van, I saw many folks I knew. It was a reunion. There was Todd Gitlin, the president of SDS, and Mickey Schwerner of CORE—who would be murdered in Mississippi within the year. There was Lee Webb and Richie Rothstein of SDS. There was Sy Posner, a liberal assemblyman from the Bronx, and Theresa DelPozzo of SNCC and the Bronx. There was Danny Kalb, the guitarist with the Blues Project band.

When I got into a holding cell, I met Julian Beck and Judith Malina, the founders of the Living Theatre, where I had seen Jack Gelber's play about jazz and junk, *The Connection*. Later I would learn that among the 283 people arrested that day was John Darnton, then a student at Wisconsin and now a top editor of the *New York Times*.

Sometime that night in the Baltimore jail I made the connection—that it was exactly fifteen years earlier, on July 4, 1948, that I saw my first baseball game and saw Jackie Robinson steal home.

Jackie Robinson had led me to this place of protest. It was July 4, and I felt just as proudly American in a police van as I had at Ebbets Field eating a hot dog and keeping score. Baseball and nonviolent civil disobedience seemed equally consistent with patriotism and citizenship. I had sung "The Star-Spangled Banner" getting arrested and before my first Dodger game.

Who could know that within seven years it would all turn to lunacy? The whites getting evicted from SNCC; Dr. King and Mickey Schwerner getting murdered; SDS turning into vandals and bomb makers; Tom Hayden glorifying the gangsterism of Huey Newton and the Black Panthers; Stokley Carmichael spouting the poison of "Zionism equals racism"; Jerry Rubin calling Sirhan Sirhan a "freedom fighter"; SDS leader Bernadine Dohrn praising Charles Manson. And then three SDS alumni—Ted Gold, Terry Robbins, and Diane Oughton—blowing themselves up while trying to manufacture a bomb in a Greenwich Village townhouse in March of 1970. And three days later Ralph Featherstone, a friendly SNCC veteran whom I knew, died when a bomb he was transporting in his car in Maryland exploded accidentally.

When I was released from the Baltimore jail the next morning, I rushed to find a copy of the *New York Times*. How would they play our mass witness to segregation on private property in the North? They put it on the front page.

Early in the evening of August 28, I was riding in a car filled with SDS and SNCC friends, returning to New York from the vast March of Washington. We had just heard King's "I Have a Dream" speech (and Bob Dylan). We were in a state of grace. King had been a combination of Scripture, Lincoln, and Shakespeare that hot and humid afternoon. The immense, integrated, perfectly behaved multitude was a sight and a thrill I will never forget. It was a community.

Suddenly somebody in the car got an idea: "Let's go back to Gwynn Oak and sit in."

Our integrated group arrived at about 7 P.M., just as a cooling breeze was starting to break the oppressive heat of the day.

But instead of facing arrest, our group was informed that the park had desegregated for the first time that very day. Our group was welcome to pay our admission fee. This historic day ended with me and my friends going on the rides.

At the top of the Ferris wheel, I sang the old spiritual "Oh, Freedom" at the top of my lungs.

Oh, freedom over me
An' before I'll be a slave,
I'll be buried in my grave
And go home to my Lord and be free.

CHAPTER 4

A Guilty Pleasure

I love boxing and I hate it. Boxing has given me a some unforgettable nights of drama and displays of courage. And it is a sport rife with fraud, burlesque, and the risk of death and injury.

At its best boxing is art. Ballet with blood. Some matches prove it can be what Joyce Carol Oates called "America's tragic theater": Ali and Liston; Ali and Frazier; Sugar Ray Leonard and Thomas Hearns. Rocky Marciano and Walcott; Carmen Basilio and Tony DeMarco; Sugar Ray Robinson and Jake LaMotta; Robinson and Basilio; Buster Douglas and Mike Tyson; Aaron Pryor and Alexis Arguello; Archie Moore and Yvon Durelle.

Yet there have also been too many fixed fights, ring deaths, wrong decisions, sadistic mismatches, and fighters cheated out of their pay by promoters. I have never heard of a benefit being held for a promoter, but I have attended my share of charitable events for old fighters.

I can no longer offer an intellectual defense of boxing or romanticize it. Boxing is—and always has been—a corrupt, brutal, and unfair sport.

It always seems on the verge of extinction, except it is too deep in our blood to be abolished, too much a part of human nature.

I view boxing through an economic populist lens and try to apply the values of equity, workplace safety, government regulation, and unionism to the sports slum of sad endings. The fighter is the exploited worker, the promoter the robber baron, and the corporate cable giants—HBO and Showtime—the bankers. The gym is the factory assembly line, the arena the mine shaft, where some workers will die in accidents.

I see boxing as a dangerous craft, more about Marx's concept of surplus value than literary metaphor. There is nothing existential about a punch to the liver. I have seen too many fighters die in the ring, from Benny Paret in 1962, to Beethoven Scottland last year. I always look to see if there is an ambulance in the arena.

I accept the ambivalence of both guilt and pleasure because I know boxing's triumphs and casualties. The best way I feel I can show my respect for the sport is to try to change it and speak out for the boxers. With no pension fund, no union, incompetent regulatory commissions, inadequate medical exams, corrupt rating organizations, and rapacious promoters who make more money than the fighters and never have to disclose their profits, they are often the sport's voiceless victims.

I have seen too many former champions with their brains scrambled, their speech slurred, their memory a blur, and their bank accounts empty. Injured or indigent former fighters need protection.

Parkinson's disease and too many punches have turned Muhammad Ali into a modern Buddha—mute, calm, iconic. When I see Ali these days I bow, I hug him, and I slip away because the sight hurts so much. His family says Muhammad is at peace in his faith and daily prayers, but it is still so deeply disturbing to be with a man once so renowned for his speed and speech and who now is deprived of both.

Sugar Ray Robinson had Alzheimer's disease during the last years of his life. At the end, the boxer whose fights were among the best we ever saw had no memory of performances others cherished their whole lifetimes. It was as if Shakespeare couldn't remember his own plays.

The great Mickey Walker suffered from both Parkinson's and Alzheimer's years before he died in 1981. Joe Louis lost his final years in dementia and paranoia. Floyd Patterson's memory is gone. Riddick Bowe has severe mental problems. The great featherweight Sandy Saddler, afflicted with Alzheimer's and legally blind in one eye, was mugged by a gang of punks and spent his final years in a Bronx nursing home. The last time I saw the welterweight champion Wilfred Beneitiz, he was being fed by his brother and the food was dribbling out of his mouth.

That so many great fighters end up with brain damage can't simply be coincidence. And if this is the fate of the champions, what happens to all the journeymen who never boxed on television, who never made $2,000 for a fight?

I am not alone in my ambivalence. Boxing maintains a love-hate grip on our national imagination. More good movies have been made about boxing than about any other sport, among them *Body and Soul, Champion, The Set-up, Raging Bull, The Harder They Fall, Somebody Up There Likes Me*, the first *Rocky* movie, and *Fat City. On the Waterfront* is about a boxer, Terry Malloy, who took a dive for the mob.

As a topic, boxing has attracted writers of the caliber of Norman Mailer, Budd Schulberg, Jack London, Joyce Carol Oates, David Remnick, George Plimpton, A. J. Liebling, Pete Hamill, Gerald Early, Ishmael Reed, James Ellroy, Leonard Gardner, and Albert Camus, who once wrote a marvelous essay about a club fight in Algeria.

The history of boxing is the mirror image of America's immigrant experience. Every immigrant group, living in slums, seeking an American identity, had fighters as their first heroes. The Irish had John L. Sullivan, Terry McGovern, and Jim Corbett. The Italians had Tony Canzoneri, Willie Pep, and Rocky Marciano. The Jews had Benny Leonard and Barney Ross. The blacks had Jack Johnson, Henry Armstrong, and Joe Louis. More recently Latinos have had José Torres, Salvador Sanchez, Roberto Duran, Julio César Chavez, Alexis Arguello, Wilfredo Gomez, Oscar Dela Hoya, and Felix Trinidad.

Boxing is often the first act of the American dream, before the civil service, the colleges, the professions, and the suburbs open up to allow equal opportunity. One night, one round, or one punch can determine your whole career and your whole life. Billy Conn's life would have been totally different had he hung on to defeat Joe Louis in 1941 and not made the cocky mistake of trying to knock Louis out. Sonny Liston's life and reputation were forever changed when he mysteriously quit on his stool in his first fight with Cassius Clay. Rocky Marciano's life was transformed by that one punch he hit Joe Walcott with in 1952.

Boxing also gave me one of my all-time favorite Subway Moments. One day a couple of years ago I was standing on a subway platform when a young black man—about twenty or twenty-one—approached me.

"Yo, old-timer!"

I almost laughed. I don't think of myself as old or as an old-timer.

"Ain't you almost famous?" he asked, squinting and trying to place my face.

Before I could properly introduce myself, he said, "I know who you are! You're the guy on that Ray Robinson film, right?" He meant a documentary I had made for HBO. I said yes. He then gave me an awkward hug and then a warm embrace.

"I thank you, man, for doing that. My father always said Robinson was the best and that Ali copied his style from Robinson. I never believed him. I thought he was making it up. After I saw your show, I told my pops he was right, now I know what he was talking about. You helped me connect with my pops. Thanks, man."

I still find boxing compelling partly because I find most fighters personally admirable and partly because the spectacle of a great fight can be unforgettable.

Boxing is a great leveler, a bridge across the boundaries of class, race, generation, and politics, and has given me something in common with a vast range of people. Former New York City police commissioner Ray Kelly, in my mind a truly classy law enforcement professional, told me I was his "friend for life" when I gave him a tape of the 1976 George Foreman–Ron Lyle fight. My involvement with boxing has opened the door to friendships with FBI agents, cops, fire marshals, and blue-collar union leaders. Peter King, the conservative Republican congressman from Long Island, has come to my home to watch old fight films of Billy Conn and Mickey Walker and talk the evening away. Peter, the son of a cop, and with a maverick temperament, has become both a friend and a sounding board through talking about the fights. When I need to find out what Republicans are thinking about an issue, Peter will tell me the blunt truth.

For the last fifteen years, whenever there is a big fight on HBO or Pay-Per-View, a crowd of about twenty or twenty-five assembles in my living room to watch, and socialize, and debate. A typical night might include writers Budd Schulberg, Nick Pileggi, and Mark Jacobson; former FBI agents Joe Spinellie and Warren Flagg; boxing insiders Teddy Atlas, Max Kellerman, and Don Elbaum; composer and musician David Amram; Kevin McCabe, whose career shifted from politics to music and who once ran the city morgue; artist Sherman Drexler; reform Teamster union leader Dane Kane; TV interviewer of actors Jim Lipton; Latino political activists Julio Pabon and Ramon Jiminez; former boxing champions José Torres and Tim Witherspoon; and a Very Famous Gangster (now eighty-two years old) who always brings pastries. We all assume he is retired.

Music writer Lisa Robinson is also a regular. Lisa has wanted to write a magazine article about this gathering, which she calls "the fight club," but we discouraged her, trying to protect the privacy of the group and of the Very Famous Gangster, who is usually the center of attention. Even when Matt Dillon, Helen Mirren, Taylor Hackford, or Spike Lee is also present.

The Very Famous Gangster is always deferential. "Which is Jack's favorite chair?" he whispered to my wife the first time he came to one of these gatherings. "I don't want to sit in it."

On the night George Foreman shockingly knocked out Michael Moorer, the whole room went crazy. Except the gangster. He didn't move a muscle. Twenty-three years in prison—for a crime I wrote he did not commit—conditioned him to mask all emotion.

Almost everyone in boxing is a character. Or a colorful storyteller. Or a charming rogue with a heart divided between blarney and larceny. The sport doesn't attract many 9-to-5 kind of guys. Boxing is like the racetrack or the record industry. It's an unstructured place where nonconformists can flourish.

My first direct exposure to the fight racket came in 1959, the year I worked for the Rangers at Madison Square Garden. That's when I learned to respect fighters and resent the gangsters. Undercover managers fronting for Frankie Carbo, like Gabe Genovese and Jimmy White, were pointed out to me in nervous whispers. I saw the manicured retired don,

Frank Costello, get seated in the front row, while old-time fighters were assigned mediocre seats.

Most of the fighters I was able to interact with were honest, unaffected workmen—men like Joey Giardello, Billy Graham, Gasper Ortega, and Dick Tiger from Nigeria. Beau Jack, the former lightweight champ, had a glorious optimism and sweetness. I once saw Rocky Marciano without any entourage, signing autographs. Some of the fighters I've gotten to know have been the nicest of people.* Tony DeMarco, the welterweight champion from Boston's North End, once said to me, "Fighters tend to be friendly and humble because we have had all the anger punched out of us."

Working at the Garden, then located at Fiftieth Street and Eighth Avenue, I was able to observe three boxing aristocrats: Red Smith, the *Herald Tribute* columnist; Hall of Fame trainer Ray Arcel, who had been slugged with a lead pipe by the mob and nearly killed a few years earlier in Boston; and Harry Markson, a cultured man who loved symphonic music and who ran the Garden's boxing department. They did not try to act vulgar or "street" to blend in. They never hid their class. That made an impression on me.

The only fighter I became close friends with was José Torres. In fact, I cared so much about "Chegui" that I found it almost unbearable to watch his fights and came to understand why his mother could never watch him in the ring. I suspect that the emotional turmoil I went through with José kept me from feeling quite the same way about any other fighter. It was easy to love José. He was warmhearted, funny, bright, extroverted, and curious. He was an intellectual who read a lot and published two books after his career was over. José's manager and mentor was Cus D'Amato. Cus had his own theories about boxing, which he described as a test of "character and will" as much as a contest of skill, timing, and quickness. He often said that "boxing is at least 50 percent mental." Cus was highly quotable and ended up influencing as many

---

*My exceptions to this generalization have included Jake LaMotta, Don Jordan, and Rubin "Hurricane" Carter. They were not nice and not pleasant to be around. Sonny Liston was also a criminal thug and strikebreaker who brutalized women. But there can be a tragic interpretation to his life, if you prefer the literary to the literal.

writers—myself included—as fighters. He was also something of a crank, and you sometimes had to filter out some of his more crackpot theories.

I had been following José's career for a couple of years before I ever met him. He was already a hero in Spanish Harlem when I was ringing doorbells for Carlos Rios, who, as I've mentioned, was challenging the old Italian Tammany machine. José was then an undefeated rising star, and young Puerto Ricans were talking about his fast hands and his peek-a-boo technique—the hands-at-the-cheekbones defense that Floyd Patterson used.

In 1964 I started going up to the Gramercy gym on Fourteenth Street, hanging out, watching José train, meeting Pete Hamill—who, along with Norman Mailer, became friends with José before I did—and listening to Cus's motivational speeches. Gradually I became part of José's world, of dance clubs, Latin music, sparring partners, gym sweat, and fun, lots of fun.

One summer evening a group of us went with José to eat at El Quijote, the Spanish restaurant on West Twenty-third Street, part of the Chelsea Hotel, after José had finished training at the Gramercy. Somebody at the table asked José why he had never gotten a shot at the middleweight title, something that should have happened in 1961, when he was a natural 160-pounder. Without any rancor or bitterness, José told the story of why this big early chance never came.

José spent years in the gym sparring with Floyd Patterson and gave Patterson credit as his teacher. Patterson was the heavyweight champion, was about twenty pounds bigger than José, but they had competitive sparring sessions. José once even knocked Patterson down in training and then denied it to the reporters, because he did not want to embarrass his friend.

In 1961 José won three fights in a row by knockout in Boston, where the middleweight champion Paul Pender resided. José was undefeated, and the Boston promoter Sam Silverman offered to match him with Pender in the Boston Garden for the title. Sam wanted Cus to put up $50,000 in escrow, to secure the title shot for José.

Cus did not have the $50,000. (Cus did not care much about money. He often quote Gene Fowler's famous line, "The only thing money is good for is throwing off the back of trains to people." In 1971 Cus would declare bankruptcy, the only manager I know who went broke before his fighters.) So he went to Patterson, who was rich, and who had just regained the heavyweight championship in March of 1961. Cus had developed Floyd, coddled him with cautious matchmaking, and guided him to the title. The papers reported that they were father and son.

But as José told the story that night on Twenty-third Street, Floyd refused when Cus asked him for the ninety-day loan of $50,000 to secure the opportunity of a lifetime for José.

José never held Floyd's refusal against him and they remained friends. But the refusal drove a wedge between Cus and Floyd. Cus was obsessed with loyalty. He believed José would have beaten Pender, become a champion at twenty-five, and then made a lot of money fighting Ray Robinson. He felt Floyd had let them down.

José ended his story by laughing at the irony. Floyd drifted away from Cus, signed on his own to fight Sonny Liston, and was knocked out in the first round. Cus had never wanted Floyd to fight Liston. He knew that Floyd was too small and his chin too fragile.

José became the light heavyweight champion four years later, and for the poor kid from Playa Ponce who used to fight for free in the street all the time, that was good enough. "I always threw the first punch hard in the street," José once told me. "But when I was a professional, I always made the other guy miss, and then I counterpunched. . . . Cus taught me how to face my fear. He taught me how to make fear my ally. The hero and the coward both feel exactly the same emotion we call fear. The only difference is that the hero can discipline and control his fear, and convert it to his use—if he admits he has it and is not ashamed that he feels it."

Those of us who loved José felt he lost the four best years of his fighting prime, at his best weight. During these four years that José should have been middleweight champion he made very little money. When he knocked out former middleweight champion Bobo Olson at the Garden in 1964, he took home only $10,000. That amount might have been even smaller, except Cus accepted no money for his role as a manager. José and Cus never had a written contract between them. Everything was based on a handshake.

Still, Cus didn't always help José's cause. Joey Fariello trained José during some of these lost years, and he would lament to me that José was "losing something" by being idle for such long stretches of time, while Cus attacked everyone in boxing, saw mobsters behind every telephone booth, and boycotted television, which could have made José the biggest box office attraction in New York, with its growing Spanish-speaking immigrant population. José boxed only three times in 1962 and twice in 1963. None of these fights was on television. They were held in places like Utica and Teaneck.

Fariello felt José should have been fighting better opponents, boxers he could learn from and gain confidence from beating. But Cus was the manager and he didn't see the need to fight on television, or take any risks, or expose José to anything that might taint his purity. Looking back now, I believe that some of José's best rounds might have been spent in the Grammercy gym with sparring partners and an audience of thirty.

On March 30, 1965, José, at age twenty-nine, finally got a chance to win the light heavyweight championship from Willie Pastrano. This time José found a friend willing to put up $100,000 as a guarantee—wealthy Brooklyn real estate operator Cain Young. Cain was an imperious landlord whom José called "Mr. Young." But if it hadn't been for Young, my friend might never have become champion. And once you're the champion, your name is in the history books forever. The achievement of one night can never be erased.

José trained with an intense dedication. I remember one day when Mailer, Hamill, and I were at his upstate training camp. José asked Mailer what he thought of Pastrano, whose training site Mailer had also just visited. Norman had been around a lot of fighters, so he knew it was important not to say anything that might undercut José's confidence. "You should be aware of his triple jab," Norman said with some diplomacy. José seemed upset by what he took to be a lack of faith and walked away. (When I later asked Pastrano about Mailer, he replied, "The guy is a nut. He wanted to fight me in the street.")

At the weigh-in for the fight, José got into a dispute with the Garden matchmaker, Teddy Brenner. José was extremely proud of his Puerto Rican heritage, and he had been asking Brenner for weeks to make sure the Puerto Rican national anthem was played along with the American anthem before the fight began.

Brenner told him not to worry about it. But this was important to José. On his own, he had lined up Filippe Rodriguiz, "the Elvis Presley of Puerto Rico," to play "La Boriquena" in the ring with his trio. Brenner said the TV network thought there might not be enough time to play *two* anthems and televise fifteen rounds and a decision. "I won't fight unless you play the anthem," José said. Ethnic pride made him intransigent.

And for the first time ever, the Puerto Rican national anthem was played before a fight at the Garden.

The night of the fight I was too nervous to eat dinner. I wanted so badly for José to win. And I knew Pastrano to be a fast, clever boxer who had never been knocked down in his long career.

But José was in the Zone that night. He was perfect. He won every round. He controlled every minute of every round. He outjabbed Pastrano in the first round. He went back to his corner, skipping with confidence. That night José had timing, accuracy, quickness, anticipation, and mastery of the geometry of distance and angles. He was twenty-one again.

I was sitting in the press row and could hear Cus and José's wife, Ramona, who were sitting near José's corner, yelling out instructions in code. (You can still hear their urgent voices on the film of the fight.) Before the fight Cus had devised a life-size dummy—named "The Willie" in honor of Pastrano—that had the vital organs of the body outlined. Each organ had a number and each punch had a number; these were the numbers Cus and Ramona were screaming at José over the din of the crowd.

In the sixth round, José knocked Pastrano down with a left hook to the liver. Pastrano winced as if stuck with a hot branding iron. He got up but he was done. His legs were momentarily paralyzed.

After the eighth round the doctor asked Pastrano if he knew who he was. "I'm Willie Pastrano and I'm getting my ass kicked," Willie replied. The fight was stopped after the next round.

The instant José realized he was the new champion, he leapt into the air. I was tingling from relief and euphoria.

Norman Mailer was one of the first to charge into the ring, bulling his way past the security, determined to share the moment with his compadre. There was one big hugging, shouting, jumping scrum in the middle of the ring. I could see José, Norman, José's father, three of his brothers, his wild, street-fighting trainer Johnny Manzanett, and his cutman that night, Victor Vallee.

At about 2 A.M. I ended up at Mailer's Brooklyn Heights home overlooking New York harbor and the magical Manhattan skyline. The party was just getting started. Norman had won $500 betting on José and spent probably far more on the victory party. There was a live rock band, open bar, a feast of food, and three hundred jubilant guests.

I never drink, but that night I had a lot of champagne.

At noon, without any sleep, José went to East Harlem to be with his fans. He climbed up on a fire escape at 110th Street and Lexington Avenue, sang a song, and gave a speech in Spanish. When he finished there must have been a few thousand people down below in the street. The police had to stop the traffic.

Years later José told me he had wanted to retire from boxing that day, at the top, and become a writer. "I wish I had done that," José said. "I lost my desire as soon as I became champion. I had no more goals, no incentive to sacrifice for. I think I became a *worse* fighter after I became champion because I lost interest. Sometimes when you lose interest, it's unconscious. But I knew I was losing interest as soon as I became champion."

It was clear to his friends that José did not really enjoy his reign as champion. The driving desire to reach a destination had been satisfied. The demands of fame, the pressures to make personal appearances, and the responsibility and structure imposed on his life ill suited a free spirit like José.

And he was already growing in a new direction. Mailer had talked to him about writing an autobiographical novel. Hamill talked to José about journalism and gave him books to read and ideas to think about. And through me, José became friendly with Robert Kennedy, then the senator from New York. We spent long evenings talking about poverty, jobs, race and class, Vietnam, boxing, courage, Cus, and Hispanic culture. Bobby asked him a million questions and José gave him thoughtful, complex answers. They had lively exchanges. José was a counterpuncher in conversation too.

One night in 1967 rioting broke out in East Harlem. José and I drove around the looted and arson-struck community with Kennedy. We talked about the roots of the rage and what government might do to win back the trust of teenagers and jobless young men so alienated from the mainstream that they would burn down their own block. At one point we came across the city's police commissioner, Howard Leary, asleep in his own car, a few blocks away from the violence. Kennedy woke him up. José laughed until he was almost in tears.

José defended his title three times. He went home to Puerto Rico and knocked out Chic Calderwood in the second round. Calderwood was either so dazed or terrified that he tried to crawl out of the ring when José put him down with a straight right. José also beat Wayne Thornton in an outdoor fight at Shea stadium. He dropped Thornton with a body punch in the first round and then won almost every round. The younger, more instinctive Torres of 1961 would never have let Thornton get out of the first round.

Then José lost his title on a fifteen-round decision to Dick Tiger, the friendly Nigerian I had met at the Garden in 1959. It was an even fight. The decision could have gone either way. José knew he had not fought his best fight. His diminished desire had been a factor, and he lacked the necessary focus.

There was a rematch in May of 1967, and this time José had the incentive of redemption. The fight was harder and faster-paced. I thought José won it. He finished stronger, taking three of the last four rounds. I could see he was giving everything he had. The referee, Harold Valan, who, I thought, scored many big fights badly, gave it to Tiger, 8 rounds to 7. Joe Eppe gave it to José, 8 rounds to 7. The third official, Johnny Dran, scored it 8 to 7 for Tiger. Tiger had won a split decision. The *New York Times* reporter Bob Lipsyte judged the fight in José's favor, 8 to 7 in rounds.

The crowd of 12,500 in the Garden felt the decision was a burglary in progress and started throwing bottles, and then chairs, into the ring. I think I remember a piece of the organ in the mezzanine flying through the air. I put a folding chair over my head for protection and ran to José's dressing room. Johnny Manzanet, a tear in his eye, was gently pulling off José's shoes. "I'm going to become a writer now," José said.

And he did. He wrote a column for the *New York Post.* He wrote articles in the *Village Voice* and *Parade* magazine. He published books about Ali and Tyson.

Over the years many people have asked me if I helped José write his books and articles. Others wondered whether Mailer, or Hamill, or Budd Schulberg served as his ghostwriter. Whether innocent or not, their doubts reflect the stereotype of the dumb ex-fighter or the racial stereotype of the Latino not being literate in English. Plenty of smart, well-meaning people could not accept that a child of extreme poverty who became a boxing champion could evolve into a writer.

The answer is that no one helped José. He can write, and he can think, in two languages—something I can't do.

José is at home with diversity, far more than most people I have known. I've seen him with the Kennedys; translating for me in poor kitchens in the South Bronx; advising young fighters in a gym; going on stage with Tito Puente; dining with movie stars like Shirley MacLaine and Ryan O'Neal; addressing juvenile inmates at Rikers Island jail and urging them to stop lying to themselves; speaking honestly to police officers about fear.

José imploded all the stereotypes, laughing all the way.

Unlike José, Muhammed Ali was not a close friend, and my contacts with him were episodic. I attended most of his early fights, including his debatable decision over Doug Jones in the Garden in 1963; and I was there at his historic upset win over Sonny Liston in 1964, in a half-empty arena in Miami, when Malcolm X, Sam Cooke, and Sugar Ray Robinson were sitting ringside in the small faction of Cassius Clay believers.

I championed Ali's cause with essays in the *Village Voice* when his title was stripped from him in 1967 without due process, because he had refused induction into the army. It was during this period of enforced exile that I first spent time with him, writing a profile and accompanying him as he gave speeches on college campuses. I remember sitting with him in a hotel room while Harold Conrad tried to book him a fight on an Indian reservation. It didn't happen. The government had seen to it that his ostracism was absolute.

I also spent a wonderful day with Ali in 1991, during a nostalgic revisit to his old training camp at Deer Lake, Pennsylvania. Ali had invited a group of journalists who had supported him during his title-stripping license revocation and exile to take the bus ride with him. The group included Dick Schaap, and Tom Hauser, Ali's biographer. That day Schaap interviewed me about the meaning of Ali's significance for the ABC Nightly News.

Ali did me a favor later in 1991 when he encouraged his friend and early Islamic teacher, Jerimiah Shabazz, to appear on camera with me for a documentary film I was making (with Charles Stuart) on Don King for the PBS series *Frontline.* Jerimiah had delivered $50,000 in cash to Ali from King in 1982. The money was King's inducement for Ali to drop a lawsuit he had filed against King for cheating him out of $1.2 million of his earnings from his brutal comeback loss to Larry Holmes. Jerimiah delivered the money to Ali in a hospital room. Ali was then retired and his health was starting to fail.

Jerimiah had been wavering over whether to go public about his bagman role, which he came to regret. Ali, who did not wish to criticize King on national television, urged Jerimiah to tell me the whole, sad story with the camera rolling. It helped make the documentary more poignant and intimate. The scene was later re-created in a HBO film about King, based on my book.

The King documentary premiered on PBS in November of 1991. Ali's great friend, photographer Howard Bingham, was part of a crowd that watched the show at my home. Howard was satisfied with the way everything had worked out—with Jerimiah telling the story on the show and Ali spared from having to do it himself. He was pleased that King's chicanery had been highlighted on national television.

Nonetheless, I was never an intimate friend of Ali's like Schaap or Bud Schulberg was. I was more of a supportive acquaintance, a singer in his choir. Whenever I spent time with Ali, I made notes afterward. From the moment he beat Liston in 1964, I had an instinct that Ali would be a historic figure, an embodiment of the spirit of the times, the essence of the 1960s. Ali represented freedom in a decade that was about freedom.

Ali was all about black pride and black power. He made himself into an emblem of opposition to the Vietnam War and resistance to the draft. He was the anti-establishment Pied Piper with a rock 'n' roll strut. When he refused induction into the army on April 28, 1967, his act of defiance was a watershed in the history of sports—and in the way black athletes thought about themselves.

Ali's plea for conscientious objector status, based on religious beliefs, is now part of folklore. But while it was happening, Ali was the most reviled person in America. He was condemned by members of Congress. FBI director Hoover launched a surveillance campaign against him. My favorite sportswriters Red Smith, Jimmy Cannon, and Jim Murray wrote scathing columns, calling him a coward and a traitor. He was attacked by Joe Louis and Jack Dempsey. Attorney General Ramsey Clark prosecuted Ali even though the local draft board hearing officer had recommended that his CO request be granted, as it was "sincere" and based on religious beliefs.

Every boxing commission in the country—run by political hacks—stripped him of his championship and license to fight, without due process or a hearing of any kind. New York's boxing commission chairman, Ed Dooley, a former congressman, stripped Ali of his title on the same day he declined induction. The New York commission at that time was licensing dozens of fighters convicted of violent crimes. Ali had not yet even been convicted of anything, let alone even charged, but he was immediately made an ex-champion by fiat.

Ali was defended only by a few younger, liberal sportswriters like Jerry Izenberg, Larry Merchant, and Bob Lipsyte. A writers' committee seeking Ali's reinstatement was led by Norman Mailer, George Plimpton, and Pete Hamill. Howard Cosell declined to join this small faction of writers in Ali's corner when asked by Plimpton, although years later Cosell acted as if he had joined.

The only prominent public figure to defend Ali's action was Martin Luther King. King spoke out in Ali's defense several times, despite their differences in views over violence, religion, and the Nation of Islam's preference for separatism over integration. But King understood that Ali was right under the Constitution and right in his opposition to the war.

Ali told me that several people, including some members of the Louisville, Kentucky, elite, came to him offering him "a deal" before he declined induction. He was told "something could be worked out." What they had in mind was a face-saving compromise: He could do some form of National Guard service, which we now know is how President George W. Bush and former vice president Dan Quayle avoided combat during Vietnam.

But Ali would not bend. In 1968 he told me his stand was "about freedom, my freedom, freedom of religion, freedom to be me . . . I'm taking a stand for white people, black people, everyone not rich enough to get out of going—by going to college and getting a deferment."

Ali was convicted of draft resistance by an all-white jury, after twenty minutes of deliberations, on June 19, 1967. The judge, Joe Ingraham, immediately impounded his passport so he could not fight outside the country. For over three years—his prime boxing years, when he was between the ages of twenty-six and twenty-nine—Ali could not get a fight. He had stood up for his principles, given up millions of dollars in earnings, and now his only income came from speeches on college campuses.

The exile was both the making and the breaking of Muhammad Ali. In one sense, it transformed him into a more sympathetic figure—a victim of injustice, a hero to the antiwar generation, an athlete whose idealistic principles made him bigger than sports. But Ali was not some secular saint. He showed a mean streak during the years he was fighting the government over the draft, and it took him a some time to get this venom out of his system. In one fight he taunted and tortured challenger Ernie Terrell because Terrell had addressed him as Cassius Clay. Ali also said some repugnant and untrue things about Joe Frazier. He called Frazier "an ignorant gorilla," an "Uncle Tom," and a "black white hope." These distortions wounded Frazier deeply, and Frazier had grown up in more ghettolike circumstances than Ali, had a blacker skin, and a black trainer. Also Frazier had supported Ali's efforts to get a license and thought he was Ali's friend.

Ali's defiance of the draft, over time, created an image that overshadowed his moments of pettiness. Eventually people came to understand what a sacrifice he had made. But the exile diminished Ali as a fighter in some ways. When he was Cassius Clay, his art had been based on speed and mobility, on his seemingly tireless dancing on the tips of his toes. By the time Ali finally returned to the ring, his legs were gone. He was flat-footed. He couldn't move like he had against Liston. If his comeback career was triumphant it was because of different assets—courage, character, guile, intelligence, and a harder punch, and the regrettable discovery of an ability to take a punch and not go down. Ali beat Foreman in Africa and Frazier in Manila because he could endure punishment and pain. This cost him dearly in his later life. The punishment I watched him intentionally absorb in the gym at Deer Lake, preparing for his fight with Foreman, contributed both to his victory and to his present condition.

Ali was just not ready to fight Frazier in March of 1971. He had had only two tune-up fights, and his legs were not ready to evade the relentless Truth Machine that Frazier was. Ali rested on the ropes during that fight and took punches. Afterward Ali told several friends that he took the fight with Frazier before he was ready because he was expecting to surrender for prison during the spring of 1971. He felt he had to get in this $2.5 million payday with Frazier *before* he would have to start serving his five-year prison sentence for draft evasion.

I watched the Ali-Frazier fight in Madison Square Garden—and their two subsequent rematches—in turmoil. I identified with Ali as the carrier of my politics, as a victim of the establishment, as the first rock 'n' roll heavyweight champion.

But I could not accept the fan formulation of Good versus Evil, of black versus white. The whole country was choosing up sides between Ali and Frazier, reducing both of these remarkable fighters into symbols, weighing them down with external meaning.

I identified with Ali, but I also appreciated Frazier. There was something profoundly working class about his boxing method and values, and this drew me to him. I found my sympathies involuntarily shifting to whoever was behind in the ebb and flow of the three fights. I was basically rooting for Ali, but Frazier kept invading my heart. Joe had his own kind of dignity.

My unease with the rivalry's manufactured polarization taught me a lesson. In the future I would refuse to choose when presented with false choices. I liked both Larry Bird and Magic Johnson. I like both Mark McGwire and Sammy Sosa. I liked both Billie Jean King and Chris Evert.

On June 28, 1971, the Supreme Court reversed Ali's conviction, 8 to 0, ruling that Ali's religious objection to fighting in a war was valid and sincere. The case should never have been brought by the Justice Department.

In 1994 Ali traveled to North Vietnam as a hero. Thousands of Vietnamese greeted him at a rally in Hanoi. They chanted "Thank you!" in English, over and over.

Ali was always engaging, but he was most revealing when he wasn't performing for a crowd or when he was with his closest friends. In these moments of repose, it was easier to get fresh answers. For me those moments came driving around Chicago in 1968, walking around the Deer Lake training camp in the summer of 1974, at a dinner in 1985 in New York, and sitting on the bus going back to Deer Lake in 1991—a new baby on his lap, his fourth wife, Lonnie, at his side.

JN: Who were your heroes growing up and as a young man?

Ali: Rock 'n' roll people. Sam Cooke. Lloyd Price. Chubby Checker. James Brown. Little Richard. I met Lloyd when I was sixteen in Louisville and he went with me to the hospital after the Doug Jones fight. He was with me in Zaire. Sam was with me before the first Liston match. He tried to climb in the ring with me when it was over, but they stopped him. They didn't know who the man was."

JN: Who inspired your act, your public style after you turned pro?

Ali: Gorgeous George, Liberace, and Little Richard. I saw people bought tickets to boo George, to hope he loses. I did the same thing. I wanted people to buy tickets and root against me. George once told me after a radio show, "Always be outrageous."

JN: Did any political event in the 1960s have a major influence on your thinking?

Ali: What I remembered most clearly happened in 1955. The lynching of Emmett Till for whistling at a white woman in Mississippi. He was fourteen and I was thirteen at the time. I heard about Till on TV and knew that could have been me. That lynching opened my eyes to racism and how unfair the legal system is. The people who killed him got off from an all-white jury. That was a long time before I went into a mosque in Miami in 1961 and felt spiritual for the first time.

JN: What was the biggest thrill of your career?

Ali: Easy. Foreman. Got my titles back. In *AFRICA!*

JN: What fighters before your time do you admire the most?

Ali: Jack Johnson and Ray Robinson.

JN: How do you feel about Joe Frazier?

Ali: I love Joe. I feel bad I said all those things against him that hurt his feelings. I was just having fun and trying to sell tickets.

JN: (posed in 1991) Who would have won if Frazier and Mike Tyson met in their prime?

Ali: Joe. By a knockout.

JN: Who hit you the hardest?

Ali: Earnie Shavers in the Garden. But I conned him. I didn't let him know how bad I was hurt. I'm a good actor.

JN: Did you really hit Liston in Lewiston, Maine? Was it a knockout punch? Why did you yell at him to get up, sucker?

Ali: I did hit him, but I can't say how hard. What actually happened was that the whole world blinked at the same moment and missed the punch because it was so fast. [Ali then winked.]

JN: What's your best one-liner on Don King?

Ali: Don's body did four years in prison, *but his hair got the chair!* I gotta admit I stole that line from Dick Schaap. I love Schaap. He took me to meet Ray Robinson in Harlem before the 1960 Olympics. Dick gave me a lot of good lines.

JN: Tell me about your relationship with Malcolm X.

Ali: Malcolm was my friend. I liked him a lot. He made me laugh. He was really funny. And he was so smart. I learned a lot from him. He helped me. At one point Joe Glazer, and I think Joe Louis, wanted to take over my career, and Malcolm helped keep me independent. He assigned Archie Robinson to my camp.

Malcolm was with me all the time just before the Liston fight in Miami. He kept my confidence up. He kept me relaxed. He talked to me a lot. He understood fighters. He was a very wise man.

JN: (asked in 1968) What made you change your name from Cassius Clay?

Ali: It was the smartest thing I ever did. It was the most important thing in my life. It liberated me from the slave name I was given.

I was hurt when people wouldn't accept my new name. Right

after I did it in 1964 I went to see a fight at Madison Square Garden and Harry Markson wouldn't let me get introduced from the ring under my new name, Muhammad Ali. He said I had to be introduced under the name of "Clay" that was on my boxing license. I just walked out of the Garden, I was so angry. The people booed me until I was outside on the street.

The Pope changed his name. The biggest movie stars changed their names and were idolized under their new Hollywood names. Sugar Ray Robinson changed his name. But they don't let me change my name.

JN: Did you ever feel fear or self-doubt at the start of any fight?

Ali: Only one time. In the first minute of the first round in the first fight with Sonny. I thought Liston was the devil. After that I knew I would win every fight.

I have a theory that at the root of Ali's genius is his ability to absorb energy and inspiration from external forces and then filter them through his imagination. Ali drew strength from being black, from being a Muslim, from Allah, from being beautiful, from being a rebel and outsider, from being loved by the poorest of the poor, from Africa, from being booed by bigots, from children in hospitals, from anyone down on their luck, and from believing he was a mortal vessel with a grand destiny. He came to believe he was an existential hero from scripture and history, a man with a divine mission who could not lose a mere fight, the equivalent of a Frederick Douglass or Malcolm X.

In his most desperate moments—blinded against Liston, exhausted against Frazier—Ali drew motivation and resolve and calm from sources deeper and larger than sport. He convinced himself that if he won a fight, a drug addict would become motivated to kick the habit and become sober; a sick child would be cured of a terminal disease; a derelict would turn his life around; a welfare mother would get a job. He had a faith in his own magic. He believed his life affected other lives, that his fate was tied to the fate of the masses.

Just before Ali departed Deer Lake for Africa, in August of 1974, he delivered an improvised oration that was filmed by Leon Gast, who would codirect the film *When We Were Kings* with Taylor Hackford and win an Academy Award twenty-three years later that Taylor should have shared. Here is what Ali said, sitting on a porch and looking into a camera lens:

"I'm fighting for God and my people. I'm not fighting for fame or money. I'm not fighting for me.

"I'm fighting for the black people on welfare, the black people who have no futures, black people who are wineheads and dope addicts. I am a politician for Allah. I wish Lumumba was here to see me. I want to win so I can lead my people."

Every generation has its own champions. The generations of the 1930s and 1940s thought Joe Louis was the greatest. The gangsta rap generation that celebrated Tyson's short rule between 1987 and 1990 was confident he was the greatest. Old men in my youth spoke of Dempsey's eye-of-the-tiger aggression. For my generation Ali will always be the all-time champion.

I was once asked on an ESPN classic TV show who were the two greatest heavyweights of all time. "Muhammad Ali and Cassius Clay," I answered. "The Cassius Clay who defeated Liston and the Ali who beat Frazier and Foreman."

During the summer of 1980 José Torres called me up. He wanted me to accompany him to see "the future heavyweight champion of the world." I said sure, and assumed I was going to see a professional fighter on an undercard somewhere nearby. Instead, José explained, we would be driving up to Catskill, New York, to see a fourteen-year-old kid being trained by Cus D'Amato in the gym above the police station. The kid's name was Mike Tyson.

Cus was then seventy-two years old. He had declared bankruptcy in 1971 and was running the gym mostly for amateur boxers and troubled kids on probation. Tyson had just been paroled out of Tryon Reformatory into Cus's custody. Cus was his legal guardian. He had been a recidivist mugger and served eighteen months in the juvenile justice system. An ex-fighter named Bobby Stewart worked as a counselor at Tryon, boxed a little with Tyson, and brought him to Cus as a prospect. Here was a kid who wanted to learn and who needed an outlet for his anger—like so many other kids who worked at the gym. Tyson lived with Cus and Camille in a big old Victorian mansion with thirteen rooms.

Cus was half genius and half crank, as I've said. He was a genius about psychology, tactics, matchmaking, and training repetition, but he also would never fly or go on an elevator. He was pathologically secretive: Nobody could enter his room, and he kept tape on the door.

I watched Mike spar three rounds that day with headguard and heavy gloves. You did not have to be an expert to see this kid was a prodigy. His hands were faster than most pros I had seen. He looked like he was eighteen, not fourteen, with thick bicep muscles. And he had a meanness, an intention to maim with every punch. It was the hand speed that took your breath away.

I tried to talk to him afterward, but he was sullen. He was expressive, however, with José, hugging him, giggling with him, clowning with him. He seemed to relate to José as an older brother.

Over the next two years I went up to Catskill several times with José to watch Mike's development. He quickly became an amateur sensation, knocking people out in the first round with regularity. Once he boxed in a "smoker" in the Bronx, and there was almost a riot when he scored a first-round knockout over a local favorite. Nobody believed Mike was sixteen, nobody believed he was an amateur. Teddy Atlas, who was training him then, had to calm down the losing bettors by showing them proof of Mike's youth and amateur status.

In the gym Teddy was doing most of the work. Cus, who by then was spending a lot of his time watching *Barney Miller* and *M*A*S*H* on TV, was more the supervising architect. Teddy did the hands-on carpentry and electrical work in the gym, building Tyson into a fighting machine. He spent the long gym hours with all the troubled and lost kids who came to Catskill. Most of them never turned pro, but they all graduated from the gym as better people and better citizens, with better values and attitudes about life.

Teddy Atlas is one of the most interesting and impressive people I have ever known. The son of a successful and popular doctor, he nonetheless had two felony convictions before he was eighteen. He also had a scar the length of his face from a knife fight in the street. Teddy spent his teenage years as a thug and as what he calls "an incompetent thief." He had the reputation as the most feared street fighter on Staten Island. You could not hurt him with a punch or even a garbage can top. He spent years trying to get his father's attention (and approval) by getting into trouble and needing stitches and bail.

When Teddy's father died in 1993, I interviewed mourners at the wake and wrote a column about all the quiet good the doctor had done, all the house calls in the projects, all the times he delivered babies for free, all the twelve-hour days he put in treating the sick and the poor. He was Teddy's real role model, although a lot of people in boxing thought it was Cus.

When Teddy was eighteen, he was arrested for the second time in three days and faced ten years in prison. He had only recently started training under Cus in Catskill. At Teddy's trial, Cus came down to Staten Island and took the witness stand. He gave a performance worthy of George C. Scott, who once played Cus in a television movie. Cus wept on the witness stand. He vouched for the "special character" of young Teddy Atlas. The judge was impressed by Cus's certainty. He released Teddy on probation, under the condition that he live with Cus, and train with Cus, in Catskill, far removed from the streets and bars of Staten Island.

Cus changed Teddy's life. Teddy spent every day and night in the gym. He found a mission in his life. Every week he would drive a bunch of kids in a borrowed station wagon down to Nelson Cuevas's gym in the South Bronx and put on "smokers." Teddy was the matchmaker. The referee was usually drunk. The judging was biased. There was betting on every fight.

Up in Catskill, around the communal dinner table, Teddy started absorbing Cus's theories about boxing and life. These were a homemade gumbo of Freud, Nietzsche, General Patton, and Machiavelli. They made an impression on Teddy, although he could see that Cus didn't always practice what he preached.

The essence of the Atlas philosophy, as refined out of Cus's gumbo, is "Be a professional and never lie to yourself. There is the easy way to do something, and there is the professional way to do it. The professional way is much, much harder. It has no shortcuts. It's based on not bullshitting yourself. On making yourself go beyond where you think you can go. Of taking responsibility for everything you do in your life."

"When I tell a young kid to be a professional," Teddy says, "I know I am telling that kid to go against human nature. Human nature is basically about survival. People will do whatever they have to do to survive. And a lot of survival is about lying, conniving, conning, and cheating. That's what we would all do in a concentration camp, or on a desert island after a shipwreck.

"But," he continues, "in everyday life, in the gym, in a boxing match, people use survival as a copout. They use it to cover up being lazy. They use it to cover up being afraid. They use it to take the path of convenience. They use it as the rationale to say 'No one is perfect.' Of course, none of us is perfect. If we were perfect, we would be God. I happen to be in a business—boxing—where the imperfections are more apparent. You can see them. They show up late in a fight. If you don't do something to correct these imperfections, they can get you hurt real bad."

One major thing Teddy learned from Cus was the difference between the relative world and the absolute world. There is no compromise in the world of the absolute. Sacrifice and obedience to the absolute world is what makes a champion. "The professional lives in the world of the absolute," Teddy says, "where you unconditionally seek the ideal of perfection. There is no room for self-deception in the world of the absolute.

"Yet most people want to live in the relative world because it's much easier," he adds. "People want to make silent contracts with everyone around them. 'If you won't hurt me, I won't hurt you. If you don't punch, I won't punch.' That limits the damage to both of us. Only the pro strives for the whole other standard of perfection. I know that I insist on perfection, on the ideal, and almost nobody can meet that standard. This has caused me problems in my life. I often get disappointed by people. I expect too much. I won't make silent contracts to survive."

There is an amazing segment from a 1982 documentary film made by Michael Marton about Teddy, Cus, and Tyson. The camera captured Tyson at sixteen, suffering an attack of fear and panic before an amateur fight in Colorado Springs. Mike is standing on a terrace, outside the arena, crying on Teddy's shoulder, sobbing that no one will like him anymore if he loses. Teddy hugs him and softly talks him out of this moment of self-doubt. We literally eavesdrop while Teddy transforms Tyson's fear into fire, which was Cus's favorite mantra. Tyson then gathers himself and wins the match on a first-round knockout.

The intimate truth of that moment showed Teddy both how much potential Tyson had as a fighter and how vulnerable he was as a human being. It shows how much of boxing is mental. And how essential the D'Amato method, as refined and purified by Atlas, is to understanding boxing.

Cus D'Amato deserves some of the credit for what Tyson became—and some of the blame. He did take Mike in and sheltered him in Catskill for four years, kept away from all the outside pressures and temptations, out of Brownsville and Bed-Stuy. He talked to Mike every day, and filled his head with sayings, ideas, and positive self-images, giving him confidence. And Cus was the blueprint architect of Tyson's distinctive style—the constant head movement, the gloves held high on defense, the dipping and bending at the knees, the aiming of each punch at a vital organ, the make-the-opponent-submit-to-your-will mentality.

Cus, then in his early seventies, saw Tyson as "his Liston," his legacy, his avenger. Twice he had to help Floyd Patterson out of the ring—after first-round knockouts by Liston in 1962 and 1963. That experience made Cus want to find and develop his own Liston, his own mean, ex-convict with the killer punch.

At the beginning, this was a fairy tale of mutual redemption: Cus and the Ghetto Kid, giving each other a second chance at life.

Cus died in November of 1985. I wrote a piece on Cus and Tyson that ran in a December edition of the *Voice*. Called "Cus's Unfinished Masterpiece," it was the first article on Tyson, then nineteen, in a nonboxing publication:

> On the day Cus died last month, Tyson cried and was inconsolable. The next day Jose Torres drove him to the train that would take him back to Catskill, and spoke to Tyson fighter-to-fighter, brother-to-brother, since Cus had been a father to both of them.
>
> "Who is going to teach now?" Tyson asked. "I was learning every day with Cus."

Torres answered, "Cus had enough time. You know everything already. You know everything Cus could teach you. All you need now is experience, confidence, and desire."

That same night I happened to read my seven-year-old daughter, Rebecca, the end of E. B. White's great children's book *Charlotte's Web.* It was the chapter where the brave old spider dies, consoled by the knowledge that her eggs are rescued and about to be hatched.

My article unwittingly helped to create the myth of Cus and the Kid. I was naive. I was a romantic. I hadn't lived in Catskill. I hadn't spent day after day in the gym, actually seeing what was real.

A few years later I began to learn the carefully hidden truth about Cus and the Kid from Teddy Atlas. Teddy never wavered from the principle of telling the truth no matter what. He once walked away from an $800,000 payday with heavyweight champion Michael Moorer because he got disgusted with Moorer's friends, values, lifestyle, and his lack of commitment to the world of the absolute.

In the fall of 1982, Tyson sexually molested an eleven-year-old girl, the sister of Teddy's wife, Elaine. Teddy responded the way he was then, in his early twenties, just starting the transition from a street thug with uncontrollable rage a professional boxing trainer with a future. He got a gun and put it to Mike Tyson's head. Years later Teddy finally told me the story of that night:

"I went and got a gun from a friend who was a bouncer in a local disco. Then I encountered Tyson getting out of a cab and he was walking toward the gym. I sort of ambushed him and pushed him into the dark alley next to the gym." Teddy continued, "I caught Tyson by surprise. He didn't say anything. I showed him the gun and put it to his ear. I told him that if he ever touched a member of my family again, I would kill him. Then I fired a shot into the air to show Mike the gun was loaded. He was sixteen at this time, and he was really scared. He knew I was capable of pulling the trigger."

I don't doubt that the Teddy Atlas of 1982 was capable of shooting Tyson and throwing his life away. He was not yet the trainer who made citizens out of delinquents and professonals out of prospects. In 1982

Teddy believed that an act of street revenge was an expression of principle.

In the autumn of that year, with Cus preparing Tyson for the 1984 Olympics, Teddy confronted his teacher and told him what Tyson had done to his sister-in-law. He wanted Tyson held accountable, suspended from the gym for a period of time sufficient to teach him a lesson. He demanded that Tyson be punished. If the police found out what Tyson had done, he could have been sent back to prison. Tyson also appealed to Cus with his story, which was that Teddy was a thug and had threatened to kill him with a gun.

Cus chose to side with Tyson. He forced Teddy out of the Catskill gym. Cus had an intermediary "fire" Teddy and ask him to leave Catskill.

Cus could not lose "his Liston," his last chance at another champion. Cus, as Tyson's legal guardian, could have lost him back to the prison system.

This should have been the turning point in Tyson's life. He should have been punished, taught a lesson about abusing women, about rules being equally applied to future champs and working stiffs. Instead, he absorbed the wrong lesson: that rules can be bent, that incidents can be covered up, that he could escape accountability, that someone else would always bail him out because he could punch.

Had Cus kicked Mike out of the gym for three months, Tyson might have learned a lesson about limits and about accepting responsibility. He might not have raped a woman in an Indianapolis hotel room. He might not have bitten off a piece of flesh from Evander Holyfield's ear in a Las Vegas ring.

A few hours before that second Holyfield-Tyson fight, Teddy Atlas was in my backyard at a party. He was telling everyone who would listen—many of them *New York Post* editors and reporters, such as my editor Stuart Marques—that Tyson would get himself disqualified that night if things didn't go his way, if he couldn't knock out Holyfield easily and quickly. "Mike will foul on purpose and get disqualified," Teddy predicted. "It's in his nature. I can tell Mike is planning it if Evander fights back and doesn't submit."

A few seconds after Tyson intentionally bit Holyfield's ears twice and was disqualified, my phone rang. It was Stuart. "Write for tomorrow," he said. "Find that guy Atlas. Get more from him."

The next morning Teddy talked and I took notes for a column that was mostly quotations from a certified prophet.

"It's like what Cus used to say," Teddy began. " 'People born round don't die square.' Tyson was always a mugger looking for a shortcut. He was a meteor, not a star. He was never Godzilla. There was always a falseness about him. He had fractures in his character. Mike never faced his fear. You need self-honesty to face your inner fears. Tyson needed all that scum around him to help him avoid facing what was deep inside him. He was always a bully who needed a posse to back him up."

I asked Teddy what triggered his premonition of a disqualification.

"When he started complaining about Mitch Halpern as the referee," Teddy responded. "He was setting up an alibi about unfair treatment. He already knew from the first fight that Evander would not submit to him, that his intimidation would not work.

"Mike knew this fight was going to be the moment of truth for him. He knew his career had been built on a lot of lies. But there is a certain purity about boxing. No matter how much you lie *before* the fight, *during* the fight you have to come clean."

Teddy then suggested Mike was a "weasel," which was the harshest thing Cus could call a fighter. Weasel was the opposite of "character." In Cus's world, "character" described that rare combination of courage, intelligence, discipline, will, self-honesty, self-respect, and grace under pressure. The best fighters in history had character. They got better in adversity. Tyson lacked this heroic resolve, this foundation of self-respect, this jazzlike ability to improvise in a crisis.

When Archie Moore was forty-three years old, young bull Yvone Durelle knocked him down four times early in the match. But Moore, boxing's Robert Johnson, boxing's hard-luck blues traveler, came back to stop Durelle in the eleventh round and keep his title.

When Ali realized his legs wouldn't let him dance and move for fifteen rounds against Foreman, he improvised the rope-a-dope strategy. He let Foreman punch himself out. He took the blows, whispering into Foreman's ear "Is that all ya got, George?" Then he knocked Foreman out in the eighth round, surprising even his own doubting doctor, Ferdie Pacheco, who had a plane waiting to rush Ali to Lisbon in case he needed brain surgery after the match.

When Rocky Marciano was knocked down, bleeding, and losing to Joe Walcott, he found a way to knock Walcott out with one right-hand punch, in the thirteenth round.

When Ray Robinson's eyes was cut badly by Randy Turpin at the Polo Grounds, he threw more punches, faster punches, and pulled out a TKO victory. The taste of his own blood was a stimulant, not a distraction or a depressant.

When Joe Louis was losing to Billy Conn, he figured out a way to get to Conn in the thirteenth round, never losing his confidence, focus, or patience.

When Ray Leonard's eye was closing during his match against Tommy Hearns, and Angelo Dundee told him, "You're blowing it, son," Leonard discovered an extra reserve of energy and passion and stopped Hearns in the fourteenth round.

Atlas and I agreed that these were all luminous examples of courage in boxing history, of exceptional talent married to steel will and self-respect. This was the thing called "character" that Cus preached.

What happened to Tyson is hardly unique. His fate is not that different from Robert Downey, Jr., Darryl Strawberry, or Doc Gooden. Excess, entitlement, enablers, denial, and emotional instability shorten many artist's prime years. A part of me feels sorry for Tyson, whom I have not seen be really happy since his manager Jimmy Jacobs died in March of 1998. I have seen him give away money to derelicts and old friends. I know he sent a six-figure check to Bobby Stewart in the late 1990s, as a belated reward for taking him to Cus in 1979. When Brian Hamill had a serious medical problem last year, Tyson called him up with encouragement more than once, Brian's brother, Pete, told me.

But Mike Tyson can blame only himself for a series of spectacularly bad choices. He got rid of Teddy Atlas and Kevin Rooney as his trainers, and they both cared about him as a human being, not as a meal ticket.

He turned his career over to the predatory Don King twice—once in 1988 and again when he emerged from prison in 1995. Mike never knew whom to trust. He had no insight into his own life.

In those pre–Don King, pre–Robin Givens days, I mostly saw the sweet side of Mike. He played tenderly with his homing pigeons. He would hug me and put a playful headlock on me. And we talked about the old-time boxing "immortals" like Jack Johnson, Henry Armstrong, Sam Langford, and Stanley Ketchell. Mike had seen hundreds of old-time fights on tapes from the collection owned by the managers, Jim Jacobs and Bill Cayton. His historical knowledge was impressive.

Mike also was developing an interest in the Jewish gangsters from Brownsville, his old neighborhood, who had formed Murder Incorporated in the 1930s. He was amused by their colorful, raplike nicknames, like Tick Tock Tannenbaum, Kid Twist Reles, and Bugsy Siegel.

Tryon Reformatory had listed Mike as "borderline retarded," but that was not my impression. He had done some reading. He knew all about Jack Johnson's life and in particular about his persecution at the hands of the federal government. He knew the story of how the Jewish Brownsville fighter Al "Bummy" Davis had died trying to stop a stickup in a neighborhood saloon. He knew how Stanley Ketchell had been murdered, and Battling Siki too. His historical knowledge did have a morbid streak.

I attended almost all of Mike's early fights during 1985 and 1986, including his frightening thirty-second knockout of Marvis Frazier. During this period I thought of Mike, who turned twenty in June of 1986, as a Samurai, a warrior with a philosophical, inner code of conduct and a reverence for the history of his violent craft. Mike radiated fearless confidence in the ring. He was polite to reporters and respectful toward opponents, except for Mitch Green, who baited him as a homosexual. In those early bouts, he came to the ring wearing black trunks, no socks, and no robe.

Within two years Mike lost this aura. He betrayed his trainer Kevin Rooney, just as he had betrayed Teddy, and switched loyalty to Don King. He started to act like a bully and run around with drug dealers, pimps, and outlaws. His training habits deteriorated. He slipped into a disco, champagne, sexual-predator lifestyle.

I thought it was ironic yet fitting that the fighter I once saw as a modern Samurai would lose his first fight, and his cloak of invincibility, in Japan. He lost to Buster Douglas in Tokyo in 1990.

In my early period of easy and casual access to Tyson, I did get the briefest peeks into his warped psyche. José, Tyson, and I were driving from Albany to New York after one of Tyson's early fights. I was in the backseat and José was asking Mike a lot of questions about Mike's days as a mugger and gang leader on Amboy Street in Brownsville. Mike started to describe how he liked to make women scream in pain during rough sex. I also heard Mike say that he once had an orgasm by making a rival he beat in a street fight beg for his life.

During that two-hour car ride I asked Tyson who his heroes are. He started naming characters in karate movies, gangsta rappers, superheroes from movies, characters from Nintendo games. They were characters from the violent fantasy life of a twelve-year-old.

During my season of access, I could not figure Tyson out at all. I took to describing him to my curious friends as a chameleon. Some days I believed he was smart and had a sharp memory. On other days I felt he had an attention deficit disorder, no impulse control, and that he might be a manic depressive. One minute he could be coltish and affectionate, the next he could be angry and thuggish, and a little later he would seem depressed. Like a politician, he would tell you what he thought you wanted to hear.

After Mike beat Trevor Berbick in 1987 for partial recognition as champion, he became a little harder to reach by phone. But whenever I asked José or others, to get a message to him, he would always call me back and chat about his new life as a celebrity without privacy.

After Mike went with Don King in June of 1988, I never heard from him again. No message got returned, or possibly delivered. Soon José, Rooney, and Steve Lott were cut out of his life. It was as if Tyson vanished into a cult. Anyone who was critical of King was cut off. José had a signed contract to write a book with Mike's cooperation. Suddenly that cooperation stopped, and Mike would no longer talk to the man who had been like a big brother to him since he was fourteen.

José's book, *Fire and Fear*, ends with him going to a gym in Las Vegas in 1989 to see Mike Tyson. Mike had invited José to meet him at the gym. Two bodyguards asked José to leave the gym. Mike's manager, Rory Holloway, told José that Mike left specific instructions that José should be kicked out of the gym if he showed up. When I saw José a few days later back in New York, he told me about the insulting eviction and how much it hurt him.

José made some excuses for Tyson: Cus died too soon. Jimmy Jacobs died too soon. Don King took him over. He got into a bad marriage. He was too young to be so rich and famous. "Bed-Stuy and Brownsville were like concentration camps for Mike," José said. "He lost his humanity there." I was less forgiving.

Ten years later, in 1999, Tyson quit King and sued him for $100 million. The lawsuit claimed King had cheated, manipulated, and robbed Tyson.

One of Tyson's new handlers, music business powerhouse Jeff Wald, called and asked me if I wanted to write a book with Tyson. He told me that Tyson had asked for me. Wald was very nice and flattering. He had until recently been close to King and apologized for spreading King's rumors about my being a racist. Wald said he was sorry. He had heard the inside truth from Tyson about how King had kept him in ignorance of who his real friends were. He asked me to send him—and Tyson—copies of my 1985 *Village Voice* article on Tyson, which I did.

A week later I called Wald and told him I did not have any real interest in writing a book with Tyson. Wald's offer did not really tempt me, but it did make me reflect on Mike's life—on all its wasted potential, all its bad choices, all its self-destructiveness, and all its bad luck.

On the morning of his ear-biting loss to Holyfield, Tyson visited the gravesite of Sonny Liston outside Las Vegas. Mike placed flowers at the headstone that simply said "A Man." Mike's gesture was frighteningly fitting. His identification with Liston was deep and morbid.

Like Liston, Mike was the child of a fractured family and a product of the penal system. Like Liston, he felt misunderstood and rejected for his mistakes. Like Liston, he sometimes said things that suggested self-loathing. Like Liston, he had the gift of the killer punch. And like Liston, he wanted to be feared, but faltered when opponents were immune to intimidation.

Of all the fighters I have been around, Sonny Liston might be the most complicated, repugnant, sinister, tragic, misunderstood, and mysterious. Nobody knew the date of his birth or the date of his death. Ali thought he was the Devil. A lot of people think he threw his first fight with Ali, or the second, or both. His opponents say he punched harder than any man who ever lived. He was owned by the Mafia, but he couldn't keep track of which hoodlums owned which parts of him. He could neither read nor write. He was often drunk, and abused women when he drank too much.

On the nights he knocked out Floyd Patterson and Cleveland Williams he seemed invincible.

Sonny died from a drug overdose in Las Vegas. His close friend, the writer and public relations specialist Harold Conrad, told me and writer Mark Jacobson that he believed that the Vegas gambler and bookmaker Ash Resnick had had Sonny killed. Sonny thought Ash was his best friend, but he was wrong, according to Harold, who really was his friend.

Sonny had a little-noticed gift for making a phrase. He had a kind of bittersweet and ironic blues of the street in his speech. He once said, "The only thing my old man ever gave me was a beating." Another time he said, "A boxing match is like a cowboy movie. There's got to be good guys and bad guys. The good guys are supposed to win. I change that. I win."

I was in Sonny's dressing room in New Jersey after his last fight. He had just stopped Chuck Wepner, putting about seventy stitches in Wepner's face.

"Is Chuck the bravest man you ever saw?" a local reporter asked Sonny.

"Fuck, no," Sonny grunted.

"Well, who is?" the young reporter persisted.

"Wepner's manager," Sonny grunted.

One of Sonny's most famous remarks, first quoted by my old *Village Voice* friend Joe Flaherty, can serve as the epitaph for all the fighters I have known, from champions to sparring partners:

"Some day there's gonna be a blues song just for fighters. It will be for slow guitar, a soft trumpet, and a bell."

My view of boxing is now close to the view of the drug trade as expressed in the film *Traffic*. Boxing is so corrupt, at so many levels, that reforms to protect the fighter seems almost hopeless. It is like trying to keep drugs out of the country. The futility of reform makes Liston's remark blues poetry.

CHAPTER 5

Village Voices

In September of 1964 Dan Wolf, editor in chief of the *Village Voice*, hired me to be a staff writer at a $100-a-week salary. When I came to ask Dan for the job, I had just "flunked" my summer tryout on the *New York Post* as a reporter and night rewriteman. Before that I had been fired as the editor of the *West Side News*, a community weekly for Manhattan's Upper West Side. Before that I had worked for three months on *Women's Wear Daily*, covering the "fur market." Before that I had been fired as a copyboy on the *Daily Mirror* in April of 1961.

Actually, I had lost the *Mirror* job intentionally. I had been ready to quit before I saw the first bulletins come over the AP wire about the invasion of Cuba at the Bay of Pigs, a landing I'd been opposed to. So, along with another copyboy with his own strong feelings about foreign policy, I burned the first few "takes" of the front-page story instead of rushing them out to the editors. I was justifiably fired for insubordination. I was lucky it wasn't for treason.

Dan already knew most of my history as a loser and misfit, but he still decided to take a chance on me. He knew that I had actually done pretty well at the *Post.* I'd gotten several bylines and written some big weekend feature stories. I'd also covered the July 1964 riots in my old Bed-Stuy neighborhood, surviving two scary nights of bottle-throwing and store-looting. I had gotten my tryout through editorial page editors James Wechsler and Murray Kempton, and the only reason I wasn't kept on at the end of August was because an editor named Al Davis disliked Wechsler and used me as a sacrificial lamb in their office politics. Kempton told me later, "You died in the first drive-by crossfire shooting." In fact, a couple years later, when Davis was fired, several *Post* reporters told me that my departure had contributed to his demise, since Wechsler was showing the publisher my stories in the *Voice.*

I didn't really fit the profile of other *Voice* hirees. During my early years at the paper, almost all the other staff writers had famous fathers. Dan had hired Paul Goodman's daughter, Susan; Murray Kempton's daughter Sally; Max Lerner's son, Steve. He also hired Mike Harrington's wife, Stephanie, and printed columns by Nat Hentoff's wife, Margo (whose wit, I always thought, was a match to Dorothy Parker's). A few years later he hired Dwight McDonald's son, Mike, and Kempton's son Mike, who would die in a car crash with his wife in 1971.

All I had going for me in my interview-lunch with Dan was that I had already published a couple of freelance articles in the *Voice* on civil rights and an essay suggesting that John Lindsay run for mayor.

The *Voice* job was a dream come true. I had thought longingly about becoming a journalist throughout high school and college. I had written for my college paper, written press releases for Madison Square Garden, written pamphlets for NCC, written articles for *Commonweal,* and worked for a summer, against deadlines, in the hot, dirty *Post* newsroom on West Street.

Dan recognized me as a late bloomer, like himself, a shy, lower-class, fatherless dreamer, like himself.

For more than five years the *Voice* was my paradise. Dan had made the *Voice* "a writer's paper." This meant the editing was minimal. Dan edited by conversation—Ron Rosenbaum called him a "charismatic listener." I would talk about what subjects I was contemplating writing about, and talk again after I had finished the reporting, and talk again after the article was completed. He didn't rearrange paragraphs; he rearranged assumptions and perceptions.

Dan created an atmosphere where you were not afraid to fail. He wanted me to take risks. He encouraged me to keep branching out, to write about boxing, about anti-Semitism, about Bob Dylan; to review books; to dig deeper into the civil rights movement and to put my doubts about separatism and Black Power into print as soon as I felt them. He helped me find my inner voice and then gave it amplification. When I hear actors talk about what they owe Stella Adler and Lee Strasberg, I think of what Dan meant to me in the 1960s.

Dan taught me to doubt party lines, dogmas, sacred cows, and orthodoxies. He could see the hole in every position, the contradiction in every theory, the phony side to every public figure. He was skeptical of all mass movements—especially those that engaged in what he called "group think." He felt they would all end up being totalitarian.

Dan himself was a critic and a cynic with almost no wholehearted enthusiasms or attachments. He seemed a little misanthropic; he was passionate about nothing. He even seemed detached from his own family. I noticed how he would linger and dawdle in the office, till 7:30 or 8 in the evening, and once I asked him about it. He explained that he liked to get home after son John, who was the baby, was asleep. He told somebody else at the paper that his favorite times were when he came home early from Fire Island on Sunday evening during the summer and his family remained out there, and he could have his empty apartment on Christopher Street to himself.

The gift Dan gave me was an apprenticeship, a period of development, during which I could outgrow feeling like a social misfit, outgrow my innocence, self-doubt, self-censorship, and learn. I learned from listening to Dan, and from listening to his silences. In one of our silence-punctuated conversations during my first year at the *Voice*, Dan told me, "You have the gift of distorting things in the direction of emotional truth. Therefore, you have a special need to appreciate complexity, triple-check every fact, and never forget you might be wrong." This counsel became my credo. Another remark that Dan made to me early on, about himself, was "It's my job to orchestrate the obsessions of my writers."

That was indeed his genius. I thought of him as Duke Ellington, giving all us insecure soloists performance space at the right time, on the right song. That's what made the *Voice* many voices. Dan was never a great supporter of civil rights, or feminism, or gay rights, or underground film, or experimental theater. But he gave all the singers of those songs solos in the spotlight. And in my case, he did it before I was ready to compose my own music.

Dan also liked writers who wrote long and who wrote often. That way he got the most out of them. One of his techniques was to get them to talk, and he got them to talk during the informal salon that took place every Friday afternoon in his office. Here people like Norman Mailer, Mike Harrington, the Reverend Howard Moody of Judson Church, Ed Koch (then the *Voice*'s lawyer), Professor Norman Dorsen of NYU Law School, staffers Mary Nichols, Stephanie Harrington, and Howard Smith would debate at whatever controversy was topical that week.

My first few years on the *Voice*, Dan and I would have lunch at least once a week. I got to learn something about his pre-*Voice* life. He grew up middle class in Manhattan. His father died suddenly of a heart attack, the same way my father had died on the subway one night. Dan never went to college but took philosophy and psychology classes at the New School. And he learned from Norman Mailer, his best friend and chief intellectual stimulant. I found out that the *Voice* had lost money for eight years, until a 114-day daily newspaper strike in 1962–63 turned things around. And Dan lied about his age; he was three years older than he told everybody.

Politically, Dan was a tolerant, passive liberal, which was in keeping with his lack of enthusiasm and passion. He never marched and never signed a petition. In 1960 he endorsed JFK "without reservation" for president. In 1965 he endorsed John Lindsay for mayor as the Republican fusion candidate. He wrote a "no-endorsement" editorial in 1964 when Robert Kennedy was running against Kenneth Keating for the Senate (although he did publish Norman Mailer's exceptionally compelling essay urging a vote for RFK).

However, Dan was a radical, a true original, when it came to journalism. He gave writers complete freedom. He liked to hire and print young writers who were "inspired amateurs," who had not gone to graduate school, who had not worked for a daily paper where their opinions would have been squeezed out of them. He preferred people with strong convictions and a story to tell.

He codified this distinctive philosophy in the introduction to the original *Village Voice Reader*, published in 1962, where he wrote: "The *Village Voice* was originally conceived as a living, breathing attempt to demolish the notion that one needs to be a professional to accomplish something in a field as purportedly technical as journalism. We wanted to jam the gears of creeping automatism."

Dan hired and inspired amateurs. He hired boxing writer Barbara Long, who had been working in a linotype shop. He hired Marlene Nadle, a schoolteacher. And Paul Cowan, who had been a civil rights worker. And Sally Kempton, fresh out of Sarah Lawrence College.

Vivian Gornick had been working as Irving Kristol's secretary at Basic Books when she mailed an article in over the transom about LeRoi Jones insulting white people at the Village Vanguard. Michael Smith read it and showed it to Dan, who put it in the paper. It was a brilliant piece of work. Vivian wasn't paid for it—just encouraged to write some more.

Joe Flaherty was a self-educated high school dropout working on the Brooklyn docks when Dan hired him; Don McNeill was a dropout from the University of Washington who had hitchhiked to the Village; Alan Weitz was a Hunter College dropout when Dan hired him in 1967. Alan started by sorting the mail, but Dan gradually nurtured him into an editor in his own image.

In the late 1950s, Dan gave the highly original literary critic Sy Krim his own column upon his release from a mental hospital, where he'd gone after suffering a nervous breakdown. Krim wrote some of the best pieces of the *Voice*'s early years, including a column describing what it had been like in "the looney bin." He eventually committed suicide.

Dan gave Nat Hentoff his own column in 1958—for no pay. The deal was that Nat, who was by then a well-known jazz critic, could write on any subject he chose, so long as it wasn't jazz. After eight years Nat asked for $20 a week; Dan gave him $10. He "hired" Jules Feiffer as a cartoonist in 1956, giving him absolute freedom—and absolutely no income for years.

I never knew other editors of legend, such as William Shawn or

Harold Ross of *The New Yorker*. But from 1964 to 1970, Dan Wolf was something special. He would sit there puffing on his pipe, listening closely, asking penetrating questions, letting you know you wouldn't be fired if you failed on an assignment, as long as you had tried to stretch yourself and tried something new. He had an eye for talent, an ear for nuance, and a brain for psychological analysis.

I would not see the weaknesses until later.

I flourished during my early years at the *Voice*. Dan let me write about whatever I wanted. I wrote a piece defending Bob Dylan's right to go electric and apolitical at Forest Hills Stadium, feeling that an artist should be free to go in any direction he wants. I reported on Emille Griffith's middleweight title fight with Joey Archer at the Garden. I wrote about folksingers Phil Ochs, Tom Paxton, and Eric Anderson. I covered the 1965 campaign for mayor. And most of all, I wrote about the civil rights movement—profiles of Bob Moses, Fannie Lou Hamer, and Stokely Carmichael; the big march in Selma; the passage of the 1965 voting rights act; and the early signs of battle fatigue and bitterness among organizers in the South.

Writing for the *Voice* made me feel good about myself. For the first time I was a success. I was getting invitations to go on radio and television programs to talk about issues and to write for other publications. I was Dan's favorite son in the *Voice*'s dysfunctional family, where he was the intellectual father we all wished we had. Dan hired Paul Cowan on my recommendation and gave assignments to Cornell dropout Susan Brownmiller, again at my suggestion. He put Susan on staff in 1966.

In April of 1965 I received an invitation to lunch from Carey McWilliams, the editor of the *Nation*. I had read his book, *Factories in the Field*, about California's migrant farm workers in the 1940s. McWilliams was as a serious figure in journalism, an American radical who had commissioned articles on the civil rights movement as early as 1955, who had fought against McCarthyism, and who had published writers I admired deeply—Fred Cook, Dan Wakefield, and Howard Zinn.

Carey asked me to cover the upcoming SDS march in Washington against the Vietnam War. I agreed and, wrote the piece that led to my first book, *A Prophetic Minority*, about the origins of 1960s campus radicalism. But Carey not only wanted me to be a regular contributor, he also wanted me to be a scout for younger writers for the *Nation*, and this, too, I was glad to do.

Carey recognized that the *Nation* was stuck in the past, out of touch with the generation of the 1960s. He himself was a product of the 1930s. Most of the writers and editors were over fifty. Even the *Nation*'s musty office at 333 Sixth Avenue (two blocks from the *Voice*) felt like a relic. An old-fashioned switchboard sat in the outer office, and you had to take a rickety freight elevator up to the fourth floor. I used to joke that I feared getting black lung every time I went up to that office, where dust seemed to drift like snow through the dirty Venetian blinds. There was no music and no smell of pot in the *Nation*'s offices, the way there was at the *Voice*'s office.

In his memoir, *The Education of Carey McWilliams*, Carey described me as a contributor and as a door-opener to a new generation. But the truth was I was never able to form a strong bond with him. He was an aloof and formal man, whose strength was an intransigent radicalism on the big issues like McCarthyism, civil rights, and Vietnam.

My relationship to Dan was very different. In March of 1965 Dan sent me down to Alabama to cover the Selma-to-Montgomery march for voting rights. Earlier, on "Bloody Sunday," a small group of protestors led by John Lewis had been clubbed and beaten by police at the Edmund Pettis Bridge. I reported on this protest as a participant, walking the last ten miles to the state capitol in the midst of forty thousand other marchers.

For most of those ten miles I fell in behind the barefoot, mud-caked Joan Baez, as she sang anthems in her heavenly voice. I think I must have been in a hypnotic trance, because she is my strongest memory of that day—this tanned angel singing "Oh Freedom" in a voice that soared above all others. There were Hollywood movie stars around us, but in my mind, thirty-five years later, Joan Baez still eclipses them all.

Dr. King's speech, as always, was God's trombones, rich with intelligence. He was the only leader with a mass following among both blacks and whites.

This march was the high-water mark of the civil rights movement. It led to the signing of the Voting Rights Act that August. It was the last victory, before the war escalated in Vietnam, Watts rioted, and the movement stalled in the North. I can still remember the thrill of marching down the eight-lane Dexter Avenue, past Dr. King's red-brick Baptist Church, toward the white stone Capitol Building—the place where George Wallace had given his defiant "segregation now, segregation forever" inaugural speech and the place where Jefferson Davis had taken his oath of office as president of the Confederacy during the Civil War. We were marching toward this place of shame singing "America the Beautiful," feeling that history was at last on our side and waving American flags. White and black rocked the cradle of the confederacy with pro-American protest.

In the article for the *Voice* I wrote that marching through the unpaved, rundown black part of Montgomery "was like taking LSD for the soul." (Purely a literary metaphor, since I have never taken LSD.)

I described how a hunched-over elderly black woman ran off her porch and kissed a white marcher. And "a very old man, his cane resting between his legs, sat on his porch steps and wept."

> There were rabbis, junkies, schoolboys, actors, sharecroppers, intellectuals, maids, novelists, folksingers and politicians marching to Montgomery behind James Forman, who hates the oppressor, and Martin Luther King, who loves the oppressed.
>
> There were thousands of high school and college youngsters—that new breed of revolutionary that has somehow grown up inside the bowels of prosperous America. They were the kids who rioted against HUAC [House Un-American Activities Committee], vigiled against the Bomb, invaded Mississippi last summer, and turned Berkeley nearly upside down. They are a new generation of insurgents, nourished not by Marx or Trotsky, but by Camus, Lenny Bruce, Bob Dylan, and SNCC. Their revolt is not against capitalism, but against what they deem to be the values of an enlightened America—Brotherhood Weeks, factories called colleges, desperation called success, and sex twice a week.

My piece ended with a description of the murder of marcher and mother Viola Liuzzo from Detroit, by Klansmen, a few hours after the rally dispersed.

A little over a year later I wrote my first article against civil rights orthodoxy, taking issue with the direction SNCC was taking by firing its white staff and embracing black separatism. I had seen SNCC followers of Stoklcy chanting "Wc want white blood" on a march in Belzoni, Mississippi.

Writing this was very hard to do. I had just come back from Belzoni, and my views were being formed in reaction to what I had witnessed. Some of my white friends who were being forced out of SNCC were not sure if I should commit anything to print so soon. But Dan gently prodded me to write the piece, quoting Yeats's line about making rhetoric out of our quarrels with others and poetry out of quarrels with ourselves. He said my job was "to write the truth, no matter what."

This is what I wrote:

> Black power, the substitute for love, is the new thing that has entered the bruised history of the civil rights movement, existing alongside Dr. King's dream of freedom, and Roy Wilkins's notion of integration.
>
> It is a mixture of agony, dignity, alienation, death wish, and aggression. It is generated by the same inevitable frustration that makes the victim take on the mask of the executioner, or the girl in the television ad scream 'Mother, I'd rather do it myself.'
>
> It may be healthy and purgative for black men. But for a movement seeking majority support in a 90 percent white country, a movement rooted in humanistic values and a chiliastic vision of brotherhood, it would be the final doomed act of a Greek tragedy.
>
> SNCC declaring for separatism seems like the troubled Oedipus gouging out his own eyes.

Last year Mendy Samstein, one of the last and most committed of the whites to leave SNCC, told me that he thought the shift to separatism, the antiwhite rhetoric, and anti-Semitism was one of the turning points of the 1960s, and he wished he had been more openly critical of it at the time. Mendy had grown up on the Lower East Side, attended Orthodox

Jewish schools as a kid, and Brandeis University. He was, he also told me, rediscovering his Jewish identity.

In September of 1968 Dan gave me a nine-month leave of absence from the *Voice* to write my book on Robert Kennedy. When I came back, Nixon was president, the civil rights movement was a ruin, and the Vietnam War was still expanding.

I decided to change my career, to become more of an investigative reporter, to become more local, to focus on specific injustices and to crusade against them. During my leave I had read, for the first time, *How the Other Half Lives* by Jacob Riis and Lincoln Steffens's autobiography, the two seminal works of urban American muckraking. I had already read, and been affected by, Mike Harrington's *The Other America.*

At the end of my leave from the *Voice* I wrote a profile of Ralph Nader for *Life* magazine. During our talks, Nader pointed out that Steffens had two weaknesses as a muckraker: (1) Unlike Riis, he rarely followed up his written exposés with direct action or personal lobbying, and this made his work less likely to influence the political culture or local institutions; and (2) Steffens usually did not return to the cities he had exposed and write followups. I resolved not to duplicate these tactical errors.

Another factor in my transition to muckraking was my feeling of powerlessness about affecting national policy. Localism seemed more manageable than railing against the Vietnam War and Nixon's election. I wanted to dig into New York City—its neighborhoods, its institutions, its history, and its power elite (which I started to call the "permanent government"). I wanted a smaller canvas, so that I could paint a more complex and detailed picture. I thought that if my goal was actually to have an effect on government, as Riis did through both his writing and photography, the best way was through highly focused local campaigns and relentless followups.

I was in this frame of mind in about 1981 when I spoke to a class at the Columbia School of Journalism. A student asked me if my journalistic philosophy was more influenced by Murray Kempton or Jimmy Breslin. "Neither," I replied. "I think I am more influenced by Magic Johnson and Joe Frazier."

I was trying to make a point that Frazier represented discipline, tenacity, courage, and maximizing whatever talent God gives you. And that Magic represented collaboration, seeing the whole game, and submerging the ego to improve the group enterprise.

After the class was over, I was furious at myself for being too flip. I should have just said that the key to good writing is rewriting and reading! I just should have given them my personal canon of people to read: Shakespeare, Abraham Lincoln, Walt Whitman, Mailer, Kempton, Orwell, Dickens, Ralph Ellison, Camus, Rachel Carson, John Hersey, Arthur Miller, Tennessee Williams, Mark Twain, Robert Coles, Garcia Marquez, Octavio Paz, Arthur Schlesinger, Jane Jacobs, Joan Didion, Grace Paley, A. J. Leibling, James Baldwin, Robert Caro, Martin Luther King's speeches, Riis and Steffens, Hamill and Breslin. Reading is to a writer what observation is to an actor. I should have told those Columbia journalism students to read 10,000 words for every 500 they write, because that's what I, as a self-improving late bloomer, was trying to do myself.

As part of my shift from national to municipal reporting, I began to immerse myself in the literature of the city's history and, much too late, finally began to understand the defining history of immigration. I read about the building of the subways and the bridges that enabled the development of Brooklyn. I realized New York City had renewed and reinvented itself many times. I got a sense of the city's changing economy from shipping, to manufacturing, to banking and commerce, to culture and tourism.

I talked to Pete Hamill and Nick Pileggi, who were far ahead of me in their knowledge of New York's history. Both were already experts on the waves of Irish, Italian, and Jewish immigration, on the changing neighborhoods, the changing face of the city's architecture and skyline. They knew the city's secret history—police corruption, the mob, black gangsters in Harlem like Bumpy Johnson, the spread of heroin during the era when "nobody was looking." They knew who killed Albert Anastasia, what secret Lepke told DA Hogan in the death house, and which reporters were on the take.

Nick gave me a copy of Murray Werner's history of Tammany Hall, published in 1928 and out of print. I also read Jane Jacobs's masterwork, *The Economy of Cities*, and later Robert Caro's still-breathtaking Robert Moses biography, *The Power Broker*, which was also a history of the city from 1900 to 1965. I devoured Alfred Kazin's memoir, *A Walker in the City*, which turned me into a walker of the city and gave me a renewed feeling of romance about New York. These books were my spring training for my new urban beat.

My first crusade was against lead poisoning among slum children. And the person who gave me the idea, and gave me an education on the issue, was my Hunter College compadre and future collaborator Paul DuBrul.

In the summer of 1969 Paul was the housing direction for the University Settlement House on the Lower East Side and teaching urban planning at Pratt Institute in Brooklyn. He had been wrestling with the plague of lead poisoning for about a year and had helped form an organization to combat it. Paul invited me to lunch and gave me a folder of scientific-medical material to read. We brainstormed about the best way for me to start writing about the issue, which was then invisible in the media, in politics, and in the city's health and housing bureaucracies. Paul was a radical organizer with tabloid instincts and a deep anger, that came from the fact that he had cystic fibrosis and knew he wouldn't live a full life. (Paul would dic in 1987 at the age of forty-nine, the day before his son Sascha's Bar Mitzvah.)

When we were in college, Paul thought of himself as a doomed James Dean, as Woody Guthrie with his Huntington's disease, as Jack Kennedy fighting off his chronic Addison's disease. Mortality was always a wolf outside his door. He was impatient and direct because he felt he had no time to waste. So he didn't waste time. Paul was the brother I never had. We worked on the college newspaper together, joined the civil rights movement together, became protégés of Mike Harrington together, joined SDS together, supported Robert Kennedy together in 1968—when most of our friends were either backing Gene McCarthy or organizing the protest in Chicago against the Democrats. In 1977 we wrote a book together that was about the "permanent government" of New York City and entitled *The Abuse of Power.* Paul knew cystic fibrosis was slowly killing him. He viewed every particle of pollution in the air personally—because it was personal. It was weakening his lungs and robbing him of time. He saw lead poisoning as an environmental genocide, man-made by slumlords.

"I feel like my anger is keeping me alive," Paul once told me.

My favorite story about Paul took place just after our book was published. Howard Rubenstein kindly purchased two dozen copies to send them out to his clients, some of whom were treated unkindly (not unfairly) in the book. Howard asked Paul and me to inscribe these copies. Paul and I sat side by side, writing inscriptions, and then trading copies so the other could also sign it. I bowed to conformity, writing polite inscriptions to creatures like Roy Cohn and Harry Helmsley. But then I saw what Paul was slashing down with his felt pen. To Lew Rudin, a major developer and landlord, Paul wrote, "Best wishes to a greedy parasite." To Jack Bigel, a former Marxist who became a wealthy pension fund consultant to city unions, Paul wrote, "You are a social climber and a traitor to the working class." To real estate lawyer John Zuccotti, he wrote, "To John, who has murdered whole neighborhoods." The inscription to Charles Luce, the CEO of the Consolidated Edison utility—the city's biggest polluter—was so long and savage I have blocked it out.

At our 1969 lead poisoning lunch, Paul said, "You start writing in September and it will become an issue in the campaign for mayor. All my life I've been saying that 'slums kill,' and this story proves it."

For a month I immersed myself in the science of lead poisoning. I became like a method actor, using sense memory—meeting the parents of victims of the disease, listening to bureaucrats tell me it was impossible to draw a blood sample from a one-year-old, attending a meeting of seventy-five doctors and nurses at Judson Church, and then going by subway with Paul up to the ill-named Tiffany Street in the South Bronx, to meet Brenda Scurry, whose twenty-three-month-old daughter, Janet, had died of lead poisoning that April.

My day with Brenda Scurry became the launching pad for five lead poisoning articles I would write over the next four months. I sat in her kitchen, listening to what was like to be poor, powerless, and unlucky. "I used to live at 113 Teller Avenue," Brenda told me.

> Plaster from the walls started falling all over the place last November. I asked the landlord a couple of times to do something about it, but he never did.
>
> Then in April one morning my daughter wouldn't eat anything. She

> started trembling and couldn't breathe. I got scared and she started to change color. A neighbor called a policeman and we took her to Morrisania Hospital. A doctor looked at her and told me to go home, that she would be okay. They asked me if Janet ever ate paint or plaster, and I told them yes.
>
> I went home but her temperature kept going up and down. After five days they gave her a blood test for lead poisoning. And then she died the next day. The day after she died, the blood test came back positive. Later they sent me a death certificate that said Janet died of natural causes. The doctors did an autopsy, but I still haven't gotten the results. I called the administrative director of the hospital, but I still haven't got the autopsy results. The hospital doesn't want to say it was lead, I guess.
>
> I asked welfare if they would pay for Janet's funeral, but they made me fill out a bunch of forms. So I paid for the funeral with the rent money. Then I asked welfare to pay for the rent. They said I had to fill out some other papers and that it would take a while. Then I got an eviction notice.
>
> I went to central welfare with it, but they still wouldn't give me any money. So I borrowed some money because I didn't want the landlord to put me on the street.

Brenda then told me she had written a letter to a *New York Times* reporter explaining all this. She then showed me the moving letter the reporter had written back. The letter described how touched the reporter was by her plight and how much he wanted to write a story about Brenda and her daughter, but that his editors would not let him because the hospital was officially denying lead poisoning was the cause of death.

I took the subway back to the *Voice* office and that afternoon and evening wrote five thousand words in the white heat of fresh emotion. Dan read it and put it on the front page.

"Lead was a story hard to make visible or dramatic for the television networks," I wrote.

> It didn't involve famous leaders, or exotic militants, or public violence. How do you show a process, how do you show indifference, how do

> you show invisible, institutionalized injustice, in two minutes on Huntley-Brinkely?
>
> How do you induce the news department of a television network to get outraged about nameless black babies eating tenement paint when the public health profession, school teachers, housing experts, scientists, the NAACP, and the politicians haven't given a damn?

Paul kept feeding me scientific studies and policy papers to read. He introduced me to his activist cohorts. One of them got me an interview with Dr. René Dubos, the microbiologist who was the chairman of a citywide conference on lead poisoning and a scientist of unusual eloquence. Dr. Dubos impressed me on first contact as a person of serious purpose and intellectual heft, the way John Cardinal O'Connor would unexpectedly dazzle me with the same qualities when I met him years later.

I had ended my first lead poisoning article with a quotation from Dr. Dubos: "The problem is so well defined, so neatly packaged with both causes and cures known, that if we don't eliminate this social crime, our society deserves all the disasters that have been forecast for it."

Over the next few months I became an agitator on the lead issue. I wrote an op-ed column for the *Times.* I went on radio and TV shows. I proselytized other journalists to write about it. And I spoke to several aides to Mayor Lindsay about it, including Peter Goldmark, press secretary Tom Morgan, and Jeff Greenfield, who had worked for Robert Kennedy was now a junior speechwriter for Lindsay. Jeff even slipped a line into one of Lindsay's campaign speeches about "fighting the menace of lead poisoning in our neighborhoods."

Finally, early in 1970, Mayor Lindsay appropriated $3.4 million to fund these programs administered by the city's health and housing departments. The person Lindsay assigned to coordinate these programs was Ronnie Eldridge. Ronnie had been Robert Kennedy's adviser and Al Lowenstein's campaign manager for Congress in 1966. She is now married to Jimmy Breslin and served two terms on the City Council in the 1990s. When I met with Ronnie, Paul, and Greenfield at City Hall, it was like an evening in my living room. We were all trying to make the city's arthritic bureaucracy move a little.

In 1970–71, the city's new lead program identified 4,500 children with lead levels at or above 60 micrograms per 100 millimeters of whole blood—the definition of "a case." The city created 130 locations in almost every poor neighborhood to give blood tests to children under the age of six. The city also began an education campaign—including public service spots on TV aimed at parents—to get their children screened. This campaign of writing and activism saved some lives.

In 1970 Paul and Ed Rothschild told me national legislation was now needed to bring code enforcement and testing and apartment repairs to other cities. The first politician Paul and I approached was Representative Shirley Chisholm of Brooklyn. We asked her to sponsor the federal legislation, assuming that because she represented Bed-Stuy and because of her "unbossed and unbought" self-promotion she was a logical choice. But she refused. A few weeks later several black activists in Brooklyn told me that Chisholm's key campaign fundraisers owned slum properties and had told her it would cost him too much money to remove lead-based paint.

We then approached Congressman William Fitts Ryan and Senator Edward Kennedy, and they agreed immediately. Kennedy, whom I did not know well at the time, but who had appreciated my book on his brother, started calling me at home every time the Kennedy-Ryan bill cleared another legislative committee hurdle in Washington. The bill became law in 1971, but Richard Nixon refused to allocate any funds, "impounding" the money and preventing it from being appropriated in the budgeting process.

The campaign against lead poisoning became the model for the rest of my career: Pick an issue. Study it. Make yourself an expert so you won't make any stupid factual mistakes. Figure out who the decision makers you want to influence are. Name the guilty men. Make alliances with experts. Combine activism with the writing. Create a constituency for reform. And don't stop till you have achieved some progress or positive results. This is what I meant by the Joe Frazier method. Keep coming forward. Don't get discouraged. Be relentless. Don't stop moving your hands. Break the other guy's will.

Over the next eighteen years at the *Voice*, I would apply the Frazier method to elder abuse and fraud in nursing homes; to lousy judges; to rapacious landlords; to corrupt labor union leaders; and to corrupt Democratic Party bosses who picked the lousy judges. In 1985 and 1986 I waged my most gratifying muckracking campaign. I set out to prove Bobby McLaughlin was in prison for a murder he did not commit. Bobby was a self-described "knucklehead," a tough Irish kid from Marine Park section of Brooklyn.

Bobby's foster father, Harold Hohne, and a homicide detective named Tommy Duffy gave me two shoeboxes full of transcripts about the case and a list of phone numbers of prosecutors, witnesses, and jurors. I spent about a month reading everything before I believed there might be a miscarriage of justice here. I visited Bobby at Greenhaven Prison. Then I started my interviewing. One of the first people I went to see was Milton Mollen, the presiding judge of the Appellate Divison for Brooklyn, Queens, and Long Island. He was a jurist whose religion was equal justice and one of the few human beings I knew who could be objective about himself. According to the files I had read, Milton had sat on the appellate panel that unanimously affirmed Bobby's conviction.

"I want to ask you about a case you sat on five years ago," I said to Milton one night at dinner. "I have some doubts about it."

"You must be referring to the Bobby McLaughlin conviction," Milton said without prompting. "It's been on my mind for years. It's the only case where I think I might have made a mistake."

Milton recused himself in his judicial role and quietly went to see Brooklyn District Attorney Elizabeth Holtzman about reopening the case, or at least holding a hearing on new evidence. The case against Bobby had been based on a single eyewitness's identification. This witness was now refusing to talk to me and had been arrested several times since the trial for auto theft.

Holtzman resisted all suggestions she reopen the case, which surprised me. Bobby's conviction occurred under her predecessor as DA, Eugene Gold. Holtzman had a strong reputation for fairness and support for civil liberties. I had one meeting with her where I made an impassioned plea that there was enough doubt about the conviction, and enough new questions about the one witness against Bobby, that she should open her mind to the possibility of a mistake, as Mollen had done.

Holtzman told me she would not speak to me about the specifics of the matter. Noting she was speaking purely hypothetically, she said I should consider what would happen to a district attorney, who let someone out of prison in a homicide case, and then that person committed a new crime, perhaps a new homicide. She asked me what I thought would happen to the career of that prosecutor.

By early 1986 John Miller started doing a series of hard-hitting reports on the case on the NBC local news. John had a strong identification with law enforcement and would become the chief of public information for the NYPD under William Bratton in 1994. He became convinced of Bobby's innocence in the course of his reporting.

Once a month I had strategy and planning dinners about Bobby's case with Miller, Duffy, ACLU lawyer Richard Emery, and Harold Hohne. I named our group "the cop-commie coalition."

In the spring of 1986 Dick Schaap did a powerful segment on the ABC TV network show *20/20* that was seen nationally. It included a jailhouse interview with Bobby and an interview with a juror who was having second thoughts about his vote to convict.

Finally, in June of 1986, the single witness against Bobby recanted and refused to appear at a hearing on the case that Emery's legal work had convinced Brooklyn judge Anne Feldman to conduct.

On July 3, 1986, Judge Feldman ruled Bobby had been wrongfully convicted and released him on the spot. We all danced out of the courthouse and drove to Harold Hohne's home in Marine Park, Brooklyn. It was like a block party, an early celebration of July 4, and Bobby's independence day.

Playing a role as both reporter and cataylst in getting an innocent man released from prison gave me more satisfaction than anything else I did in journalism. The day Bobby got out, he told me and Emery, "If it wasn't for you guys I would now be ashes in an urn on my mom's mantelpiece."

In 1991 a made-for-television movie about Bobby and his father was aired, based in part on my articles. It featured Martin Sheen as Harold Hohne. It was fairly typical of the formula genre, but it told the story and made viewers think about the death penalty. It showed how the legal system can make mistakes in murder trials—and how hard it is to correct those errors.

In January of 1970 Dan Wolf and Ed Fancher sold the *Village Voice* to City Councilman Carter Burden for $3 million, which was split evenly between Dan and Ed. Burden, the great-grandson of Cornelius Vanderbilt, was worth many millions and was one of the "Beautiful People." His wife, Amanda, was the stepdaughter of William S. Paley, the chairman of the CBS network. They were WASP royalty. (Years later I got to know Amanda Burden as a member of the City Planning Commission. Her judgment, intelligence, and taste were A plus.)

I was twice shocked—that Dan would sell the *Voice* and that the paper was worth $3 million! The sale made Dan financially secure. Both he and Fancher soon bought co-ops at 40 Fifth Avenue, an address Alan Weitz called "the most prestigious German Jewish building in Greenwich Village."

I knew nothing about the sale in advance; like everybody else, I read about it in the paper. The amounts involved did give me a new appreciation for Marx's theory of surplus value, since I was still making $150 a week. Marx was right: The surplus value of my labor was extra profit for the capitalists.

A few weeks after the sale I was talking to Nat Hentoff and Jules Feiffer, both of whom had donated years of free labor to the *Voice*. The paper might not have survived into the 1960s, when it caught the wave of history, if not for the loyalty of these two contributors, who had accepted the trade-off of absolute freedom for no salary. I asked if they had gotten any kind of bonus from Dan, any gesture of gratitude for their work. They had received nothing. It would rankle them for decades.

"I thought Dan might send me a bottle of champagne, at least," Jules said. "But I didn't even get a phone call."

Dan's decision to sell the *Voice* to Burden was a fatal blunder. It set in motion years of instability. It led to Dan himself being forced out as the editor four years later, in a corporate power play and stock transfer. It was one more End to Innocence, vaporizing the warm and fuzzy illusion that we were a family, that Dan was our benevolent father who was pure, who was above any crass financial, commercial interest.

I knew and liked Burden from his staff work for Robert Kennedy and from his helpful role in the lead poisoning effort, but most staffers were stunned that Dan had sold him the paper. There was, people felt, some inherent contradiction that a Vanderbilt heir, and a politician, would own the antiestablishment, independent *Voice.*

In retrospect, I think Dan was always secretly dazzled by old money, although he pretended the opposite. I often heard him talk about the old monied families of New York, mostly the German Jews, but also about the Astors and Rockefellers. I think his usually astute radar defenses were melted by Burden's pedigree.

"Now I understand why Dan hired the children of Murray Kempton, Max Lerner, Paul Goodman, and Dwight MacDonald," Margot Hentoff said to me. "That was a very high-class form of social climbing. Selling the paper to Burden is a somewhat lower form of social climbing."

Margot knew Dan better than the rest of us. She and Nat rented a summer home on Fire Island near Dan's, and she spent a lot of time with Dan during the summers. Margot and Dan were also both becoming more conservative in this post-1969 period.

Reflecting on Dan's attitude toward money and social status a few years after his death in 1996, Margot told me, "Dan came from German Jews who had real money but lost it all in the Depression. Dan resented anyone who had money at one level, because he felt deprived of his rightful, comfortable status by his family misfortune. Dan felt he was a Jewish prince cheated out of his inheritance.

"But at the same time that he resented some people's money," she continued, "he also wanted it. He was a toady to rich people. He ridiculed his writers who had some money behind their backs, like Paul Cowan, but at the same time he kept talking about old German Jewish money. That was his big hang-up. He was really screwed up about money. It was a love-hate kind of thing."

In November of 1971 I went into Dan's office and asked him for a twenty-five dollar raise.

He did not own the paper anymore, so I wasn't asking for any money out of his pocket. And I had married Janie that April and thought that would bolster my modest request. Dan looked at me and said, with hostility, "You don't need a raise. Your wife is rich."

I was dumbfounded. The rejection coming from this father figure I owed so much to hurt to the bone, and I felt rejected, assaulted, abandoned, almost worthless. I was so vulnerable to Dan that I attempted to reason with him. I told him Janie was not rich and that I had no idea how much her family might be worth. We lived on our combined salaries, and Janie was working for the city.

On April 25, 1971, Janie and I had gotten married at her father's home in Sands Point, Long Island. Just before the wedding we had moved from Janie's small apartment at 35 Morton Street in the Village, where we had lived together for three years, to a co-op at 250 West Ninety-fourth Street.

As soon as we had gotten married, Janie started hinting about having children. But I was scared and did not feel ready to become a father. I felt like I didn't know how to be one, probably because I had no recollection of my own father as a role model. It would take me until November 20, 1978, when Rebecca was born, on Robert Kennedy's birthday, before I felt prepared or qualified for fatherhood. Joey, named for Janie's father, was born on May 19, 1981—the birth date of Malcolm X. Parenthood would prove to be the fulfilling and completing life experience everyone assured me it would be.

My recent marriage, our new grown-up apartment, and the hints about raising a family were all in the back of my mind when I sat down to ask Dan for my modest $25-a-week raise.

I tried to explain to Dan that I had no interest in material things. Couldn't he see that from my antiluxury lifestyle? From my lack of talent for business and commerce? From the casual, antifashion, antistyle way I dressed?

But Dan cut me off and told me it was time for me to leave the *Voice*. He said the *Voice* was never meant to be "a parking place for life." It was meant to be a place where young writers started careers but then outgrew when they had matured and needed more money to raise a family.

I was even more dumbfounded by this line of argument. Mary Nichols, who had been at the paper for years, but left to work in the Lindsay administration, was welcomed back at a higher salary than anyone else at a paper, double what I was earning. Also, one of Dan's pet writers, Howard Blum, had married money and was able to move into a co-op in the same Fifth Avenue building into which Dan and Ed had moved, but Dan didn't insult Blum's wife. On top of all that, I knew from his own lips that Dan bitterly resented writers who started at the *Voice* and then did move on, like Sally Kempton and Jane Kramer. He believed they would never maximize their potential because they had left him and that they still needed his handling.

It took me a day or two before I was able to tell my closest friends at the *Voice*—Paul Cowan and Nat Hentoff—what transpired during my humiliating meeting with Dan. They were angry on my behalf, and out of a series of conversations, a plan for some kind of collective response began to emerge. Nat certainly felt exploited and underpaid. So did Paul. So did most freelance writers and critics. And now that we knew the paper was worth at least $3 million, the exploitation no longer seemed justified by pleading poverty or the cry that "we are a family."

On a cold Sunday in November 1970, thirty or so *Voice* writers and contributors assembled in Paul Cowan's living room to discuss what we should do. Among them were Joe Flaherty, film critic Andrew Sarris, Nat and Margot Hentoff, and Jules Feiffer, whom most of us looked up to for his seniority, maturity, and moral authority. Somebody had invited a labor lawyer, who helped keep unionization in the mix of the meandering gripe session.

Staff writer Mary Breasted also showed up. This created a problem. A few of us knew she was having an affair at that time with our owner, Carter Burden. I went into the kitchen with Paul Cowan and Nat Hentoff to talk over whether we should ask her to leave because of this conflict of interest. I wondered whether she was a "spy for management," as I put it. But we decided it would be too divisive to raise the issue openly, that most people didn't know about the affair, and that it might be perceived as "sexist" to confront Mary in front of all her coworkers. So we said nothing and continued with the meeting.

At the end of the evening we agreed that a small delegation would meet with Dan to seek better pay across the board for staff members, freelancers, columnists, and theater, film, and art reviewers. We also agreed to seek "a health and hospitalization plan" and to explore the possibility of unionization.

A drafting committee put these thoughts into writing, and a delegation, which included me, was picked to meet with Dan. The night before the meeting we met at Mary Breasted's apartment. Theater critic Dick

Bruckenfeld said he had seen Dan that day, and Dan had told him that I should not be part of any delegation. He said that would be a personal affront to him, and my participation would make any constructive result impossible. I immediately withdrew from the delegation, though I suspected this was one of Dan's mind games. My role was less important than getting some results.

At the meeting the next day, Dan savagely attacked the weakest, most marginal members of the delegation—sometime freelancer and political radical David Gelber and Ellen Frankfort, the health columnist. Either genuinely angry or feigning anger for tactical advantage, Dan attacked the group, again saying that the *Voice* "is not a parking place for life" and the *Voice* veterans were keeping fresh blood from entering the paper by staying around too long. "Freezing you in means freezing everyone else out," he said. He also asked where all these petitioners were all those years when he and Fancher were losing money on the paper.

When Ellen Frankfort tried to speak, Dan shouted at her, "Who the hell are you? What are you even doing here? I don't even know why I publish your stuff. You are one of the worst writers we have."

A few weeks later Dan agreed to give us across-the-board pay raises and expanded Blue Cross/Blue Shield benefits.

Freelance pieces now received $125, not $75. The salaries of staff writers increased by $100 over the next three years, and more writers were added to the staff. But there was no union, and Dan swore there would never be a union as long as he was in control. I got my raise—but I had lost my father figure.

In the middle of this staff insurgency, the *New York Times* published a Sunday article about what had happened at the *Voice*. In her quotes, Mary Nichols tried to frame the whole conflict as an attempted coup by the New Left. She did not address the economic improvements that had been our main goal. At least she had the sense to know she couldn't attack our demands while she was making by far the most money.

So began an era of demoralizing factionalism at the *Voice*. Dan seemed to derive perverse pleasure in pitting people against each other, like some promoter of cockfights in a garage. The atmosphere in the office became poisoned. After a while there were factions within factions. Writers began to forget the reasons for their feuds, only that they were enemies and wouldn't speak in the elevator. It felt like a combination of high school and Bosnia.

Judy Coburn summed it up well: "The *Voice* is dog eat dog on the long march." "It's like Yeats's description of Ireland," said Richard Goldstein: " 'Great hatred, little room.' "

There was, of course, another rowdy, rock 'n' roll side to the *Voice*. There were a lot of office affairs and one-night stands. There were staffers who did heroin, cocaine, speed, and LSD. There is one frequently retold anecdote from a staff meeting in the mid-1970s that is actually true. A square young intern sat listening to a typical debate about what to cover, and what not to cover, about new trends in gay sexual practices. After the meeting this young intern, scratching his head, approached a senior editor and asked for guidance.

"Now let me get this straight," he said. "We're *against* gentrification, and we're *for* fist-fucking. Do I have this right?"

Writers felt an intense psychic connection to the *Voice*. Most were young and had turned the paper into a surrogate family. There was also just an unusually high concentration of eccentrics, paranoids, hotheads, and potheads who felt it was acceptable to act out. Some writers acted like it was a therapeutic community, not a newspaper.

Meanwhile I tried to understand what happened to Dan Wolf. Superficially at least, I had repaired my relationship with him and, having achieved some emotional detachment, attempted to comprehend him better. I also had frequent conversations with Alan Weitz, who became his last protégé and edited my copy now, and with Margot Hentoff, who had been very close to Dan until he ran a savage review of Nat's first novel, a review written by an outsider nobody had ever heard of and without ever warning anyone in advance it was coming out.

One theory I developed was that Dan, as he grew more conservative, began to feel guilt over his own contributions to the excesses of 1960s. I suspect he felt this guilt most sharply in the area of drugs. The paper had glamorized the counterculture of be-ins and Woodstock and making drug use seem cool and risk-free. It had made Timothy Leary into the guru-huckster of acid. Dan knew that too much drug abuse created casualties and zombies.

I knew this, too, and though I smoked an occasional joint, I didn't make an issue out of all the pro-drug stories in the *Voice*. I regret my silence now, knowing what junk did to Charlie Parker and Billie Holiday. After raising two children in Greenwich Village, after seeing some of my own 1960s' compadres suffer from one too many acid trips and from habitual pot smoking, I regret now that I lacked the independent thinking to mount a dissent.

But I try to keep my own guilt in perspective. I was wrong and freely admit it. Nobody is right all the time, in every news judgment, in every political judgment. RFK wiretapped Martin Luther King. Jackie Robinson endorsed Richard Nixon. Jimmy Cannon despised Muhammad Ali.

A watershed for Dan may have been the death by drowning of writer Don McNeill at age twenty-three in the summer of 1968. Don had become Dan's favored son. Several staff writers told Dan that Don had drowned because he had been tripping on LSD. He had a reputation as a good swimmer.

Don's death hit Dan hard, but this reaction seemed extreme, out of proportion. Drugs and Black Panther gangsterism were only a small part of the 1960s and only a small part of the *Voice*'s coverage of the 1960s. There was much more to that decade of progress, protest, and liberation. I will always be proud of the way the *Voice* supported the civil rights movement, Dr. King, and equal rights for all minorities in every sphere of humankind. I will always be proud of the way we opposed the Vietnam War, reported the birth of feminism from inside the movement, and campaigned for gay liberation even before the 1969 riot at the Stonewall Inn on Christopher Street.

Dan should never have lost his pride in the glory of this writing by young writers he had selected and nurtured. He should have felt pride at the way Mary Nichols kept hammering away at Robert Moses, railing against, for example, the Lower Manhattan Expressway (which was stopped in 1965, allowing the new community of Soho to arise organically). Mary's articles also helped save historic Washington Square Park, a sanctuary of benches, trees, sandboxes, and chess tables, the incubator of the modern folksong revival, where Woody Guthrie and Ramblin' Jack Elliot played for free. Nat Hentoff's columns made it seem as if he had breakfast with Jefferson and Madison every morning. They defended the Bill of the Rights, free speech, freedom of the press and privacy, week after week. Paul Cowan wrote about ordinary people with the sensitivity of a young James Agee. He reported on elderly poor Jews living on the Lower East Side and book burners in West Virginia. When the New Left turned violent, anti-democractic, and anti-American in 1968, many of us condemned the unpleasant truth, even though it angered "our side," which was no longer our side.

During the late 1960s and early 1970s, the *Voice* celebrated and explained the contibutions of the Beatles, Bob Dylan, the Stones, Norman Mailer, Allen Ginsberg, Jimi Hendrix, Janis Joplin, *Easy Rider, Bonnie and Clyde, The Godfather, The Battle of Algiers*, Martin Scorsese, Robert DeNiro, and *Mean Streets.* As Ron Rosenbaum, another writer Dan hired, recently wrote, "I'm a child of pop culture, whose emotional life is a creation of rock 'n' roll as much as Dickens and Shakespeare. I don't think pop culture and high culture are necessarily in conflict; the rare great moments in the history of culture are the ones in which high culture was pop culture."

The *Voice* had even published fine pieces about the dark side of the Lower East Side's "love community" and the real price of joining the drug culture. (Don McNeill wrote some brilliantly critical pieces about the consequences of dope in the hippie culture.) But Dan let himself feel guilt over his contributions to the drug culture. As he grew more conservative, more hostile to everything the 1960s had brought to American life, his guilt became even more disproportionate to what he had actually published. He lost sight of the balance between the good parts and the bad parts. He was like someone who had devoted most of his life to a cause and then loses his faith in it. And he had nothing to replace this lost faith with.

Another symptom of Dan's drift away from liberal pluralism was on the subject of race. Right after the school strike of 1968, organized by the predominantly Jewish teachers' union, a few black militant leaders expressed anti-Semitism. Dan and Ed Koch, by then a congressman, had both become less sympathetic to the movement for black equality after this. They used this vile fringe anti-Semitism as a rationale to pull back from broad support for civil rights. Both fiercely opposed the attempt to build low-income housing projects in Jewish Forest Hills, Queens, in

1971–72. Although Dan published my anti-Rockefeller coverage of the massacre of thirty-nine prison inmates at Attica Prison in September of 1971, he didn't like it and he didn't agree with it. Many well-intentioned liberal Americans revised their feelings about race after 1968. And Dan Wolf was one of them.

In June of 1974 Clay Felker made a deal with Carter Burden and became the owner of the *Village Voice*. It was a complicated stock transaction that was either a sale or a merger, depending on who was doing the explaining.

Dan was as shocked by this sale as we had been by his sale to Burden four years earlier. Within a few weeks Felker had fired him.

A new layer of factionalism was created, based on degrees of loyalty to Dan after his firing. Who called him first? Who had lunch with him most frequently? Who would be the first to quit the Felkerized *Voice*? Who sucked up to Felker the most?

This new layer of antagonism came to overlay all the old anthropological layers of conflict, based on unionization, whether pornographers were protected by free speech, who got the most space on covers, Arts versus Politics. We were one big unhappy family—the Sopranos without bodybags.

I was one of the few *Voice* writers who had experience writing for Felker at *New York* magazine. I had published a piece on John Lindsay in 1966 when *New York* was still a supplement inside the Sunday *Herald Tribune*. And in October of 1972, I had published my first installment of the "ten worst judges" for Felker in *New York* magazine.

Part of Clay's strength as an editor was that he surrounded himself with some first-rate associates, fine line and text editors, like Jack Messell and Sheldon Zalaznick. Clay was comfortable delegating authority to them. They were like the brass section in the Basie band. They made the thing swing.

The background to the "ten worst judges" piece was a series of judge-raking exposés I had written for the *Voice* early in 1972, exposing one judge's lenient favoritism toward mobsters and drug dealers and another judge's racist attitude toward blacks. Felker, whose skill was taking ideas out of the air and packaging them in an attention-grabbing way, invited me to lunch. He suggested that I do a piece naming New York's "ten worst judges" and printing all of their pictures with the text. I did two months of fresh reporting, finding cops, court officers, and court stenographers my best sources.

It caused a sensation when it came out. People went nuts. My lawyer, Martin Garbus, called me up one day and said, "I have good news and bad news for you. The good news is the bar association is starting an investigation because of your article. The bad news is they are investigating you, not the judges."

The probe lasted a year, and in the end the bar association issued a report supporting my findings on five of the seven judges they investigated. The legal establishment's overreaction to the piece convinced me I should do it regularly, to accustom judges to journalistic scrutiny. Since 1972 I have done it ten times, including three times in the *Post,* where my exposés have played on the front page each time. In thirty years only four judges have sued me, and each suit was thrown out before trial.

I managed to get along with Felker for a while. He gave front-page display to most of my articles on nursing home swindler and elder abuser Bernard Bergman. (This series led to a special prosecutor being appointed by Governor Hugh Carey and to Bergman going to prison.) But I gradually came to realize that Felker was simply not suited to edit the *Voice.* His sensibility was alien to the paper's liberal-libertarian-bohemian values and history. Felker was an uptown, upscale editor who invented *New York* magazine in his own image. Creating *New York* was as big an idea, and as big an accomplishment, as Dan's creation of the *Voice.*

Felker did not know what to do with the *Voice,* or, rather, he only knew how to replicate *New York magazine.* Articles about real estate in the Hamptons, or costly new restaurants, or service articles for the upper middle class, didn't fit in the *Voice.* Felker's formula for a magazine was a mixing work by some good writers like Breslin, Tom Wolfe, Richard Reeves, Nick Pileggi, Peter Maas, and Gloria Steinem with celebrity profiles; trend-spotting; gossip; consumerism; eye-catching, original graphics designed by Milton Glaser; and articles that ended with a recipe.

We could not let Felker colonize the *Voice* with such a formula. We would not let him turn it into a conquered province of glitz. At a staff meeting I pompously said Felker was General Westmoreland, Hentoff was Ho Chi Minh, and I was General Giap.

Clay was still editing *New York* magazine uptown on Second Avenue and then rushing down to the *Voice* on Monday afternoon, a few hours before deadline, changing everything, not listening to anyone, writing flashy cover lines that promised the reader more than the story would deliver. Every week there was a blowup between Felker and the editors. Felker did not like the left-of-center politics of most of the writers. And he felt physically uncomfortable around the paper's two most authentic bohemians—bearded poet Joel Oppenheimer and madcap lesbian critic Jill Johnston, who had a large following. Felker ranted about how he would not longer permit Joel and Jill to write their copy in all lowercase letters without punctuation. There were months of negotiations till a compromise was reached—they would use periods, but not capitalization or paragraphs.

Clay could also be a bully. He once shouted at editor Karen Durbin, "You're a visual idiot!" "This page is SHIT!" he once screamed at Richard Goldstein, right on the Monday deadline. "Bullshit!" Goldstein yelled back just as forcefully. "I'm not going to change it now. And I'm not going to feel guilty about it."

Clay's temperament and management style were all wrong for the *Voice*. He acted like a Hollywood executive producer who drops in on the location set once a week and then orders drastic changes in the script based on market research. He was the opposite of the quieter, slower-paced writer's paper, where the articles evolved out of the writer's personal experiences and had an emotional authenticity, and no necessary connection to the latest sitcom or the disco song of the week.

But at first nobody quit. One reason was that during his first month, Clay gave everyone raises. He raised the base weekly staff salary to $300 and the base freelance fee to $200. Then one evening in April 1975, a crisis erupted. The cover story that week was a wonderful piece of reporting by Judy Coburn, a freelancer who had come out of the radical movements on the 1960s. She had spent a lot of time in Vietnam, and her article explored the politics behind Operation Babylift, the massive airlift of Vietnamese infants out of Saigon, which was about to fall to the real Ho Chi Minh and General Giap.

Felker rushed into the *Voice* at about 6 P.M.—late even for him—and quickly read Judy's article. "This is communist propaganda!" he thundered.

The fight was on. Felker wanted her to take out some sections and add something about the fate of an American aid package to Vietnam that was a matter of pure conjecture. Judy refused. When Karen Durbin, Judy's editor, backed up her writer, Felker roared, "Why can't I get my way? *I AM THE EDITOR*!" Calming himself, he said he was insisting on changes because "it's a matter of truth and integrity in journalism."

Alan Weitz, Dan's protégé, whom Felker had made an associate editor, spoke up. "How can you talk about truth and integrity in journalism?" he asked quietly. "Every week in *New York* magazine there is some exaggeration. You've always made stories out to be more than they are. Now you are trying to do the same thing to the *Voice*."

Felker was enraged. "Why am I being thwarted? Why can't I get my way?" he screamed.

"Because you don't know how to be civil," Weitz replied. The whole room wanted to applaud Alan's precision and guts. Two weeks later Alan resigned from the *Voice*.

My worst experience with Felker did not come till August 1976, when the time had arrived for the *Voice* to choose among Daniel Moynihan, Bella Abzug, Paul O'Dwyer, and Ramsey Clark in the four-way Democratic primary for the Senate. By that time Felker had given up trying to control the paper and appointed Tom Morgan, who was both civil and had integrity, to be the new editor. Tom began a series of open-ended talks about the Senate endorsement among a group that included Hentoff, Paul Cowan, Pete Hamill—who was then writing pieces for the *Voice*—and me.

I was conflicted. I loved O'Dwyer but didn't think he had a real chance to win. I didn't love Bella, but she was right on the issues, and she was electable. And I did not want Moynihan to win. Nat liked both O'Dwyer and Ramsey Clark. Pete loved O'Dwyer. Paul was undecided. I couldn't tell whom Tom preferred.

Finally a compromise was reached: The paper would endorse Bella.

But it would also praise O'Dwyer, who was one of the civic saints in the history of New York. O'Dwyer had run guns to Israel in 1948, marched for civil rights in the 1950s, backed labor, defended the indigent for free, and made sure he talked to Protestants every time he visited Northern Ireland. Paul was the only person in the world who could make Jimmy Breslin obey a moral imperative as defined by somebody other than "JB, Number One."

Tom assigned me to write the consensus editorial, which I did, outlining all the reasons to vote for Bella and all the reasons to admire O'Dwyer as the salt of the city.

But Felker killed the editorial. He said Bella was a communist. The *Voice* therefore published no endorsement. And Tom Morgan quit as editor two weeks later.*

By late spring 1975 the *Voice* was deteriorating. Ron Rosenbaum began organizing a new union effort, enlisting support from Cowan and Hentoff. In early May Ron quit the paper. He walked up to Felker, tore his paycheck into pieces, and scattered them on the floor. "There is no amount of money that can make me work for the piece of shit you have turned this paper into," he told Felker. Then he turned and walked out of the building.

Felker turned to Ken Auletta, sitting next to him, and asked, "Who was that?"

Although Felker was still treating me nicely—promoting my stories, asking my advice—I found the chaos all around me depressing. The paper was losing its identity, and staff morale was at a low ebb. That July Alan Weitz came to say Dan Wolf was thinking about starting a rival paper, a new weekly that would be "*The Real Village Voice*" to compete with Felker's Vichy *Voice*. Was I willing to quit and join this new effort?

Alan's visit led to a series of meetings among Hentoff, Paul Cowan, and me. Alan said he would be the day-to-day editor of this new paper and that Dan would act in some as-yet-undefined supervisory capacity,

*In the end, Moynihan won the primary, beating Bella by a mere 9,000 votes, and went on to serve for twenty-four years in the Senate. He turned out to be better than I would have imagined. He was ahead of his time on challenging CIA secrecy, on forcing a national discussion about the disintegration of the black family. Bella would have been wonderful, too, but in a more radical way.

an editor emeritus of some sort. My questions to Alan about financing elicited only vague answers. Alan said that others were also committed to this new venture. But when I did some checking, I found there were divisions even within this group of Dan's loyalists. Not everyone agreed over who would be in charge.

And Dan did not seem really committed to starting a competing paper. His energy and interest had waned during the last few years he was at the *Voice*. He was now sixty. He communicated through intermediaries, sending out mixed messages about what exactly his role might be.

Nat, Paul, and I were dissatisfied enough with Felker to meet with Dan to try to work out our differences. I wanted to hear directly from Dan if he had the energy to lead this effort. If the answer was yes, I was prepared to quit the *Voice* and join it. Alan arranged a lunch for Friday, August 11, 1975, at Gene's Restaurant. Present were Dan, Fancher, Alan, the Hentoffs, Cowan and his wife, Rachael, and me and Janie.

To the astonishment of everyone at the table, Dan almost immediately launched into a bitter personal attack on me, accusing me of treachery and disloyalty. I could see the stricken look in the eyes of Alan Weitz. "I know you met last night with Felker behind my back" was Dan's opening remark. "I did meet with Felker last night," I replied. "The reason was that Karen Durbin and I went to see him to save Nat's job. He was going to fire Nat, and we talked him out of it." Dan said that I was lying and that he could never trust me again. He then went on to make a series of cruel remarks about me and Paul and Nat, with our wives sitting at the table in disbelief.

"The attack on your meeting with Felker," Margot Hentoff recalled, "was just a pretext to blow everything up and kill the new paper. Nat and I came to the lunch thinking we were going to join the new paper. But Dan came to torpedo the project. I told Dan at the lunch that you were telling him the absolute truth, that Felker was about to fire Nat and you had saved his job. But the truth didn't matter. Dan hated all of us. He hated us for not quitting when Felker fired him. Dan was just a very cruel person. He liked me because he thought I was just like him. But I wasn't."

"I was very optimistic going into that lunch," recalled Alan Weitz. "I saw my dream of a new *Voice* about to come true. The purpose of the lunch, I thought, was to pin down that you, Nat, and Paul were going to quit and that would send a message to everybody . . . You and Nat were essential to us going forward. But Dan was always ambivalent. He wanted to stick it to Felker with the new paper, but he didn't really want to do the work. Or take the risk of failing."

In November of 1975 a group of ten or twelve of Dan's loyalists met to talk about going ahead with the new paper (without us). Alan recalled that at this meeting Howard Blum declared that he wanted to be the editor of any new paper instead of Alan. "I just sat there in pain," Alan told me.

> I waited for Dan to speak, to defend me, to tell Blum that I was going to be the editor. I was heartbroken. Then Lucien Truscott said he should be the editor. I kept waiting for Dan to silence this debate. But he just got up and left the meeting without saying anything to support me. He said he had another appointment. I was so traumatized I can't remember anything else that went on during that meeting, after Dan left the room.
>
> The worst part of all of this is that I had a relapse on heroin. I started using again when Dan dropped the offer of a retainer, the promise of paying me $300 a week while I worked on the new paper and didn't have a job for six months. The relapse got worse after the meeting when Dan didn't defend me and say I would be the editor. I didn't talk to Dan for three years after that night.

A little over a year later Rupert Murdoch bought the *Voice*. Felker was out. A few days after that, on January 11, 1977, my phone rang. It was Michael Kramer, an acquaintance who was then the owner of and editor for the journalism review named *(More)*. "Jack, I want you to be the first to know that I am the new editor of the *Village Voice*," he said. "And I want you to be my political editor. I want you to run the politics of the paper."

I responded by telling him that the *Voice* already had a splendid editor named Marianne Partridge and that I would be loyal to her till death. He was making a mistake if he thought he could get me to displace a popular editor by offering me a little bit of power. I think I may also have threatened violence. I later discovered what I had said shook up Kramer enough to get him to call Marianne immediately and walk over to her apartment for a talk.

I only knew two people who knew Murdoch, and I called both of them. The first was James Wechsler, the *Post*'s editorial page editor and columnist who had given me my try-out in 1964. I advised Jimmy that Murdoch (who, as owner of the *Post*, was his boss) was about to make a mistake in firing Marianne, and that if he could contact Murdoch and alert him, he would be doing all of us a big favor. Marianne Partridge had only been the editor for a few months, but most of us had already been impressed with her talent, judgment, energy, and humor, and her operatic half-Italian personality. I would do anything to save her job, including sacrifice my own.

Then I called Alex Cockburn, the Oxford-educated *Voice* press critic whom I correctly assumed had Murdoch's home phone number. While Alex tried to get us an immediate audience with Murdoch, I called *Voice* staffers, alerting them that we had a Pearl Harbor–Mayday–Paul Revere kind of crisis on our hands. I reached Karen Durbin and Margot Hentoff, told them what was happening, and suggested people start assembling at my house on Charlton Street for emergency strategic planning.

Alex called me back at about 7:30 to say he had reached Murdoch and that he and I were expected at Murdoch's apartment on Fifth Avenue at 9 P.M. Alex had conveyed the message that hiring Kramer and firing Marianne would not be wise move. Alex and I agreed to meet in the lobby of the Plaza Hotel at 8:45, then walk over to Murdoch's together, so we would have a few minutes to think about what we might say that might change the mind of such a powerful and decisive executive. We rang the bell, and Murdoch opened the door with these words: "Relax, fellows. We're back to square one. Marianne will remain the editor. Have a drink, please."

The next twenty minutes were the only extended time I have ever spent with Murdoch, in my life, although I worked for him for more than fifteen years at the *Voice* and the *Post*. He was charming and witty, telling us a few stories about his own radical youth at Oxford, where he said he was known as "Red Rupert."

Apparently my negative reaction and Marianne's calm resolve combined to give Kramer second thoughts about ruling a rebellious, picketing, or absent staff. I also think Wechsler reached Murdoch and gave him some sound advice.

When Alex and I returned to my home there were about twenty *Voice* writers and editors assembled there in a state of high anxiety, including Marianne. The celebration began as soon as Alex and I reported Murdoch's decision to rescind Marianne's dismissal.

During Marianne's two years as editor, the *Voice* enjoyed one of its most vital cycles. She hired an eclectic group of excellent writers—including Michael Daly, Denis Hamill, Mark Jacobson, and Wayne Barrett. Marianne also beat back attempts at censorship by the ideological Thought Police on the staff. She preserved the paper's traditions of libertarianism and pluralism. She stood up for Hentoff and Feiffer when some staffers took offense at their work. She also resisted efforts to censor certain language and to boycott "politically incorrect" films. She was not very political, believing that readers should make up their own minds, and there should not be one political line for judging culture. Those two years were the most fun I would have at the *Voice*, except for my early apprenticeship under Dan Wolf.

I think Marianne and I bonded immediately as friends, partly because I was the only person at the *Voice* who knew about the raffish racetrack world she had grown up in. Marianne's father, John Partridge (who died when she was twenty), trained racehorses for Jim Norris, including big-stakes winners Jamie K and Nell K. Marianne knew that Norris was the wealthy front man for Frankie Carbo's corrupt control of boxing during the 1950s. As a teenager, she had met Carbo—a hitman for Murder Incorporated—and played cards with Carbo's mistress, Viola. She knew that Viola was on Norris's payroll for reasons unrelated to her job skills. The first time we had lunch, I was able to connect some of the dots in her memory bank, telling her about some of the fighters Norris and Carbo had exploited.

Marianne had come from *Rolling Stone,* where none of the young music writers had ever heard of Norris or Carbo. She and I were able to talk about horses like Native Dancer, and racetracks like Belmont and Hialeah, where she had hung out as a child, at early-morning workouts, in the paddock, and sometimes in the winner's circle, holding her dad's hand.

When Marianne's father died, Norris coldly cut her mother dead and never spoke to her again. Norris also failed to pay her mother some money that was owed involving horses in which John Partridge had an ownership interest. When Norris finally tried to pay this debt a year later, her mother would not accept the cash-stuffed envelope, delivered by a retainer, even though the family needed the money. Marianne was sent by her mother to return the money herself to Norris's mansion on Long Island.

What I liked about Marianne—beyond her editing skills and hiring decisions—was her deep working-class consciousness. She saw Jim Norris as the emblem of the corrupt rich, as an enabler of hoodlums and fixers who himself lived like the Great Gatsby, in a Long Island mansion. Whenever I wrote articles exposing gangsters, judges, politicians, or real estate developers, I suspect Marianne saw these miscreants as stand-ins for Jim Norris, who hadn't treated her father right.

"Until I met you," Marianne told me last year, "I thought my childhood might have been a fantasy, a dream life. I had observed these mobsters, and crooked jockeys, and decadent rich people, as a child and had never been able to talk about them with anybody I met in journalism. Young writers at the *Voice* and *Rolling Stone* were ignorant of that whole low-rent subculture. I wondered if my memories were true. Then we met at the *Voice*, and you knew about these people. You verified that Norris, and Carbo, and that whole world really existed, that I wasn't crazy."

Early in 1984 the *Voice* organized a roast-celebration to mark my twentieth anniversary with the paper. One of the speakers was Pete Hamill, who told a story of his meeting with Mayor Ed Koch and making the mistake of mentioning the *Voice*. "Koch said, 'They should burn down the *Village Voice* with Newfield in it!' " Pete recounted to the four hundred people at the Village Gate. They roared with laughter.

I understood why Koch felt that way. He was the popular mayor and the *Voice* was his only consistent critic. His feelings were made more

With my mother at my Bar Mitzvah in February 1951.

With Robert Kennedy on the Lower East Side in 1967. (PHOTO: FRED MCDARRAH)

Sitting under a tree with Mayor John Lindsay at Gracie Mansion in 1967. (PHOTO: JANIE EISENBERG)

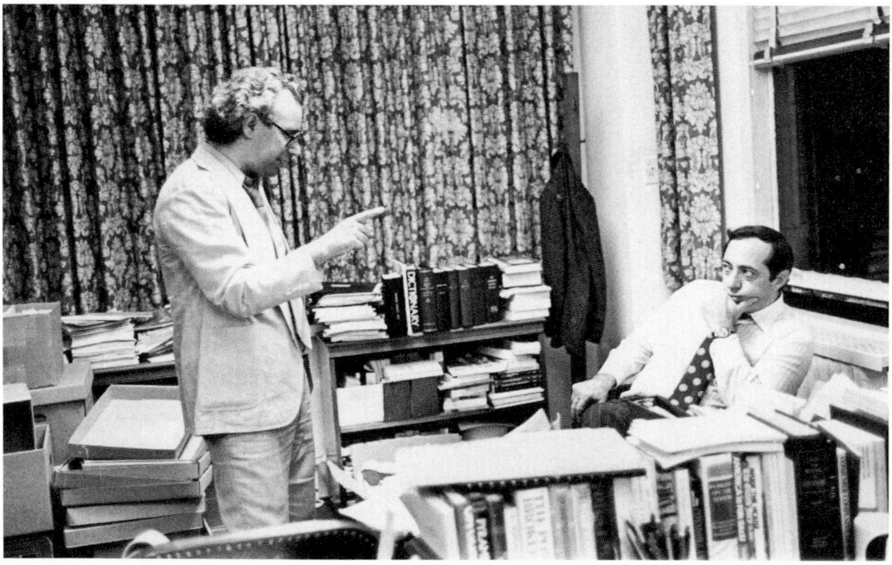

Debating with Mario Cuomo in his law office in Brooklyn in 1972, before he got into politics. (PHOTO: JANIE EISENBERG)

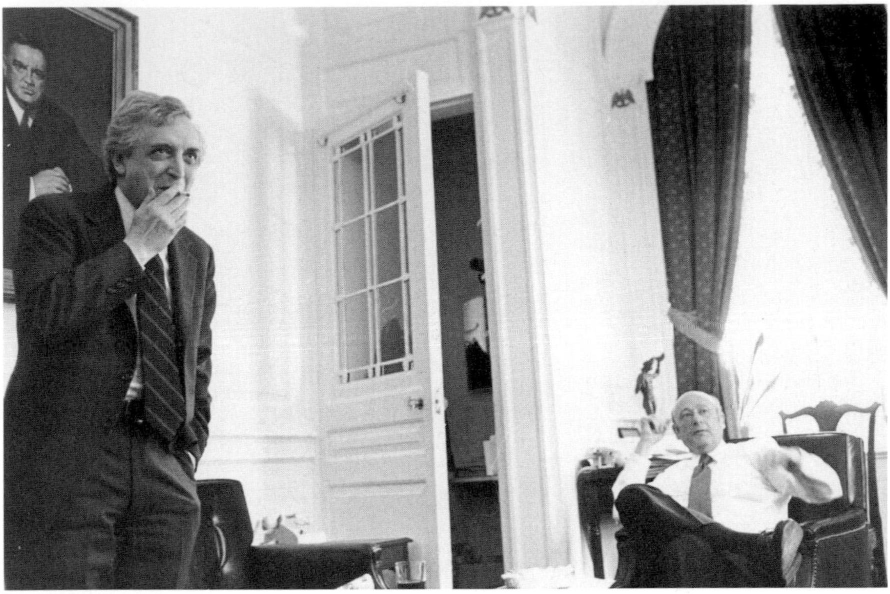

Dan Wolf (left) and Ed Koch in City Hall in 1978. (PHOTO: JANIE EISENBERG)

My two journalistic heroes: Murray Kempton and I. F. Stone, circa 1978. (PHOTO: JANIE EISENBERG)

With two of my favorite people: (left to right) Nat Hentoff and Studs Terkel, circa 1979. (PHOTO: JANIE EISENBERG)

With Bobby McLaughlin on July 3, 1986, at his father's home in Brooklyn, about an hour after he was released from prison.

With Dennis Rivera the day I quit the *Daily News* to support the strike.

Saying a few words to 15,000 union activists at a rally supporting the strike at the *Daily News* the day after I resigned. From left, labor leaders George MacDonald, Cleveland Robinson, Jim Butler, and Jim Bell.

At the *Daily News* staff reunion party at my house honoring Gil Spencer. Front row (left to right): Joe Kovach, Stu Marques (behind Jimmy Breslin), Jimmy Breslin, Joanne Wasserman, Jerry Capeci, and Adam Nagourney. Vie Zeigel and Bill Gallo are behind Adam. I am at the top of the stairs with Don Singleton, Gil Spencer, Arthur Browne, and the late Lars Erik Nelson. (PHOTO: JANIE EISENBERG)

Standing between mayoral rivals Rudy Giuliani and David Dinkins at a "Save the *Post*" rally I organized with Jim Nolan in 1993.

Muhammad Ali whispering a joke in my ear at a party at Gracie Mansion in 1991.

Anita Hill presenting me with an Emmy in 1992 for cowriting a PBS documentary on Don King.

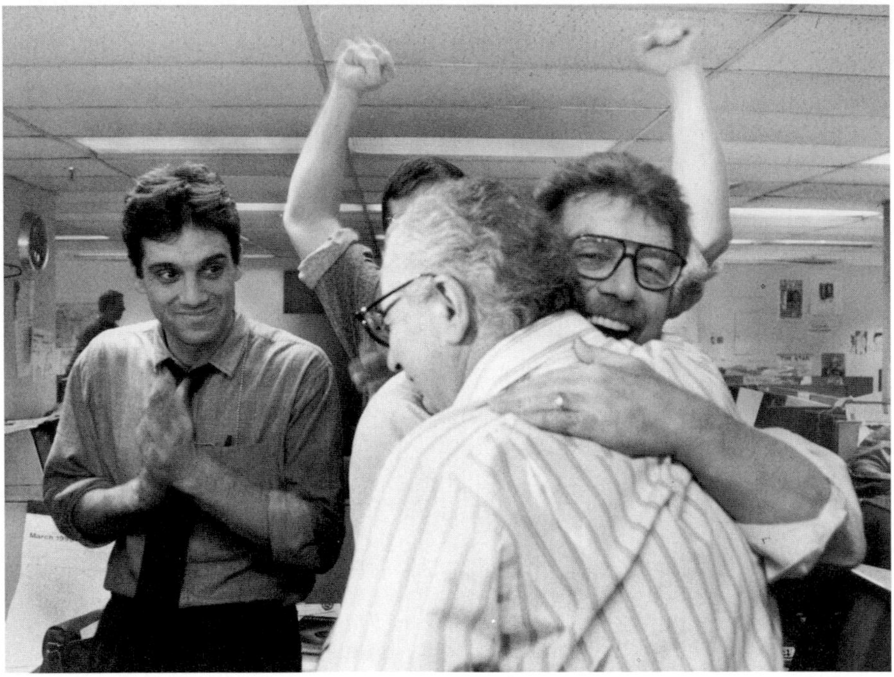

Pete Hamill embracing me on the day he returned to work at the *Post* in 1993 following our mutiny edition of the paper. To the left is Charley Carillo, smiling and clapping. Bill Hoffman's clenched fists are over our heads.

Picture taken at Budd Schulberg's eighty-seventh birthday party on March 24, 2001 (Schulberg seated at center). I am flanked by fighters Archie McBride and José Torres, Bert Sugar, and artist Leroy Neiman. Next to Budd is former fighter Roger Donahue. It was Roger who spoke the famous line later used in Schulberg's film *On the Waterfront*, "I coulda been a contender." (PHOTO: JANIE EISENBERG)

complex by the fact that he had once been, as I've said, the lawyer for the *Voice*. My mentor, Dan Wolf, was at Koch's side in City Hall, advising him. And I was telling interviewers that I owed my career to Dan, and that if it hadn't been for him I would not now be able to write so effectively about the defects of the Koch administration. There was an almost Shakespearean symmetry to it all.

Along with Wayne Barrett and Joe Conason, I was making the case against Koch in the *Voice* with regularity. Our indictment had two main counts: (1) Koch was scapegoating blacks and being unfair to the poor in his policies; (2) he had ceded too much authority, and too many patronage jobs to Democratic Party bosses Meade Esposito, Stanley Friedman, and Donald Manes.

We argued that in 1977 Koch made a Faustian deal with the patronage clubhouse operators, to whom he promised commissionerships, in order to win the run-off for mayor against Mario Cuomo. And these patronage bosses gained even more power when they agreed to back Koch for governor in 1982 in the primary against Cuomo, who eventually won. They were free to place their bid riggers and contract fixers on the city payroll.

In 1986 and 1987 our assertions would be vindicated by a massive corruption scandal that would lead to Friedman's imprisonment, Manes's suicide, Esposito's conviction in two separate trials, the conviction of three Esposito-picked city commissioners, and the admission by Manes-sponsored Geoffrey Lindenaur that he had been a bagman and fixer while a deputy city commissioner.

But back in 1984 ours were just crank voices in the wilderness. Koch had a 60 percent approval rating, and the *Voice* was publishing critical articles about him almost weekly. Koch had a stated public policy of refusing to answer any questions from any *Voice* reporter. He called the *Voice* "a porno rag."

As the 1985 mayoral election neared, Koch's closest friends—instigated by ex-*Voice* writer Howard Blum—made an attempt to buy the *Voice* and get rid of me, Barrett, Conason and editor David Schneiderman. This would have been the local equivalent of Richard Nixon's friend Bebe Rebozzo buying the *Washington Post* at the start of its Watergate reporting, in order to fire Woodward and Bernstein. We did not find out about this effort until it was over. The accounts of this attempted purchase first surfaced in the *Washington Post* and *New York Times.*

In June of 1988 I got an offer from Arthur Browne, the city editor of the *New York Daily News*, to come work for him. I had been on the *Voice* for twenty-four years, and leaving was not easy. Hentoff, Barrett, Conason, and Jim Ridgeway were still at the paper and friends. I admired the work of James Hamilton, the photographer, and J. Hoberman, the film critic, and Garry Giddens, the jazz critic. But it was time to go.

For one thing, I had become distressed by the trend toward a dreary kind of political correctness. When I began one of my "Free Bobby McLaughlin" articles with an epigraph from the Bob Dylan song, "I Shall be Released," a copyeditor tried to convince me I should not quote Dylan because he was "a wife beater."

During this time, I was feeling distanced from the *Voice* emotionally and was depressed about Paul Cowan, my closest friend at the paper, who was dying of leukemia. I loved Paul Cowan the way I loved Paul DuBrul, although they were exact opposites. Paul Cowan loved everybody, including his political enemies. He was an exuberant optimist who would stop strangers on the street and draw them into conversations. He always saw the good in people before he saw the bad. He had been a civil rights volunteer, then a Peace Corps volunteer, and then an observant Jew in his forties.

Paul Cowan died in September of 1988. I spoke at his funeral, held in his synagogue at 100th Street and West End Avenue. After the service, the mourners stood for a long time in the middle of West End Avenue, refusing to let go of Paul, refusing to separate from each other, refusing to go back to their everyday lives.

Paul died a year after Paul DuBrul had passed away. It took me a long time to recover from losing two such close, longtime friends, both gone before they were fifty. You're not supposed to bury your best friends until you are in your seventies. Doing it at fifty is depressing. It gives you a lot of time to miss them.

The *News* offer required a yes-or-no answer. It forced me to explore my feelings and to weigh the pluses and minuses of remaining on the *Voice*. The two papers couldn't be more different. The *News* is a daily paper with a million readers, a tabloid with a working-class base. The *Voice* is a weekly that appeals to liberals. I decided to find out if I could reach this whole, diverse, fantastic city, not just readers who already agreed with me.

I wanted to have a conversation with readers who didn't agree with me. Writing for the *Daily News* was my chance to speak directly to the "working stiffs," those immortalized (okay, and maybe romanticized) in the work of Steinbeck, Guthrie, Bruce Springsteen, Mike Royko, and Breslin. I wanted the challenge of trying to communicate directly with the cops, firefighters, construction workers, nurses, waitresses, housewives, and bartenders of Brooklyn and Queens. I wanted to find out if my brand of American populist muckraking could move this constituency, at least on a few specific injustices or scandals.

I needed this change in order to keep growing. As Bob Dylan wrote, "He not busy being born, is busy dying."

And, indeed, the *Daily News* offered me a chance to do some serious muckracking. Arthur Browne said he wanted me to write one column a week and also work on big investigative projects with a team of reporters I would direct. Initially we talked about (and I eventually wrote about with Tom Robbins) exposés of state controller Ned Reagan and mob-dominated Teamster locals.

Dan Wolf died on April 11, 1996, at age eighty. When I heard the news, I was flooded with conflicting emotions. I still felt Dan had given me journalistic life. In that sense he would always be a father figure. I owed him so much. But at the same time, I had experienced his diabolical side, his hangup about money, his conspiratorial view of life, his warped comments about my wife, his betrayal of Alan Weitz. I did not attend the official memorial service for him. But when the *Voice* asked me to write 800 words commemorating Dan's passing, I complied. What I wrote did not paper over our differences, but I could not speak ill of the dead in the paper he created.

About three weeks after Dan's death, Nat Hentoff and I thought it might be cathartic to organize a reunion of Dan's *Voice* writers to talk about him. Such an evening might afford some closure. I called Susan Brownmiller, and she liked the idea. The evening would take place at her apartment on Jane Street. Susan called about fifty writers and editors from different *Voice* eras and different *Voice* factions.

Voice people came for an evening of free-form therapy that had both the generous feeling of an end to an era, and the petty feeling of a gripe session. This was, of course, typical for the *Voice.* The unifying theme was how Dan had made us choose between a living wage and creative freedom. We saw Dan as a father figure and he infantilized us into competing siblings.

In the end, most of the writers felt nurtured and then betrayed. As Susan Brownmiller later told me, "Dan made our careers, then he exploited us."

CHAPTER 6

Crossing the Line: Robert Kennedy, Part I

Robert Kennedy was one person who never disappointed or disillusioned me. Whenever I take the Metroliner from New York to Washington, I remember that Kennedy's funeral train traveled those same tracks, through the same green countryside, past the same billboards and railroad stations, on a hot Saturday in June of 1968. I was on that train, and even decades later I cannot shake the memory of the faces, images, and emotions as we escorted Kennedy's remains from Penn Station to Arlington National Cemetery, while a million people stood vigil along the tracks.

The train was a traveling Irish wake for the now twice-orphaned veterans of Camelot. And for everyone who had rallied to Robert's cause.

We all felt we'd been deprived of our destiny, that history itself had been cheated. The 1960s were not supposed to end like this. A whole decade of tumult and sacrifice and fresh ideas seemed to have been building toward the logical climax of a Robert Kennedy presidency, not his burial.

On that lonesome eight-hour train ride, I remember looking into the grief-ravaged faces of John Kenneth Galbraith, Arthur Schlesinger, John Lewis, Cesar Chavez, Peter Edelman, Shirley MacLaine, John Siegenthaler, Walter Sheridan, and sixteen-year-old Joe Kennedy, who walked through every train car and shook every hand.

The faces of Robert McNamara and MacGeorge Bundy were no less a ruin, even though they were the culprits, the architects of the war in Vietnam, against which we had protested so passionately. Kennedy had touched them no less than he had touched me.

The size of the crowds amazed me. The sight of poor blacks on one side of the tracks and working-class whites on the opposite side of the tracks remains thirty-two years later. Now when I ride the Metroliner through New Jersey and look out the window, I can still effortlessly conjure up images of the construction workers in their hard hats singing the national anthem; kids in their clean white Little League uniforms, hands over their hearts; housewives in curlers waving good-bye; sad-eyed blacks singing "We Shall Overcome"; cops saluting at attention; long-haired college kids wearing RFK campaign buttons.

The train reached Baltimore about six hours late, but when it arrived there must have been twenty thousand people in and around the station. The crowd, mostly black, still in shock from the loss of Martin Luther King eight weeks earlier, was singing "The Battle Hymn of the Republic." A brass band accompanied this choir of lost souls. Outside of Baltimore I remember four white people holding up a homemade sign that said simply "The Gelber family is sad."

All these years later I am still sad. What was it about Robert Kennedy that made so many people, the famous and the anonymous, those close to him and those far removed, trust him so much? What is it about his death that hurts just as much now as it did in 1968?

Part of it, I realize, is how much he influenced me. Another element is that he died young, before his potential could be fulfilled, before his ideas could be tested in power. History, especially the arts, is filled with early deaths that create tragic myths that keep growing. John Keats, Jean Harlow, Janis Joplin, John Lennon, Marilyn Monroe, James Dean, Jimi Hendrix, Dylan Thomas, Buddy Holly, Hank Williams, Bruce Lee, Charlie Parker, Montgomery Clift, Bob Marley, Robert Johnson, Tupac Shakur,

Kurt Cobain, and Bix Beiderbecke. We remember them all for the unfulfilled potential of their gifted youth. We will never see them fat and past their prime like Brando and Elvis. They are forever young, on television, in films, in our memory. So too for RFK.

Part of it is also that I knew him so well and liked him so much. With his self-mocking sense of humor, his hesitant vulnerabilities. He was at forty-two still growing, still a work in progress, still becoming a great national leader.

When he was seventy-five, jazz drummer Max Roach remarked that he still missed his collaborator, trumpeter Clifford Brown, every day. Brown had died in a car accident in 1956. "I never got over it," Max told Pete Hamill.

A lot of us feel that way about RFK.

Another element of it was captured in something Cesar Chavez said to me in 1976: "Bob crossed a line no other politician has ever crossed." Cesar was referring to how deeply, and personally, Kennedy felt about life's injustices and casualties. He had an intensity that went beyond what all other politicians felt. And part of this intensity was an anger that could be monumental. It was not just for show. He took it home.

In April of 1967, Kennedy made a life-changing tour of hunger and poverty through the Mississippi delta, arranged by Marian Wright. She saw Kennedy hug a starving little black girl in a shack and begin to sob, not aware that anyone was watching him through the back door. That night Kennedy arrived home in the middle of dinner and made a speech to his children about what he had just witnessed and how they must do something about it. Thirty years later two of his children, Kerry and Robert Jr., told me this story. Both and said it was one of the most vivid memories of their childhood, because of their father's intensity.

This is what Cesar meant about "crossing a line." Kennedy was more passionately angry about inequality than any other modern American leader. That's why in a season of riot and alienation the poor trusted him when they trusted no other public official. And that was why they lined the tracks to watch his funeral train pass.

I did not always admire Robert Kennedy. The first time I saw him in the flesh, in June of 1963, I was picketing in front of the Justice Department in Washington. The demonstration, organized by CORE and SNCC, consisted of perhaps 350 people. June of 1963 was a turning point in the civil rights movement. Over 1,000 black schoolchildren had been put in jail in Birmingham along with Martin Luther King. The Birmingham police dogs and fire hoses were on national television every night, symbols of violent repression and unyielding segregation.

Pressure was mounting on President Kennedy to introduce legislation for civil rights and voting rights. A few days after our small protest, JFK would go on national television and declare his support for new legislation and for the first time say civil rights was a moral issue. That was the same night Medgar Evers was assassinated in Jackson, Mississippi.

My feelings about Robert Kennedy that warm June afternoon was that he was not doing enough to help the movement. As attorney general he had nominated Harold Cox, James Eastland's college roommate, to be federal judge in Mississippi, where he would call black defendants "chimpanzees" from the bench. Kennedy administration judicial appointments in the South were generally less sympathetic to integration than Eisenhower's appointees had been, due to Eastland's power. Attorney General Kennedy had indicted nine civil rights workers in Albany, Georgia, on conspiracy charges, while whites who assaulted civil rights workers and burned down black churches went unpunished. I had friends in SNCC who had been stomped and urinated upon, while Justice Department lawyers took notes and did nothing.

In June of 1963, Robert Kennedy was starting to change on civil rights, but history was changing faster. He was still trying to slow down and manage the civil rights movement instead of joining it. That's why I was picketing him. Much to my surprise, in the middle of our protest, Kennedy himself emerged from the building jacketless, his tie askew, he talked to us through a hand-held bullhorn. I was impressed that he had come out and confronted us, but found what he said halfhearted and defensive.

"We haven't seen too many Negroes come out of this building!" a voice shouted out of the crowd.

Kennedy responded by telling us how many blacks he had hired at the Justice Department. "Individuals will be hired according to their ability, not their color." The bullhorn distortion made his voice sound squeaky and strident. His eyes were cold and intense, and his crewcut made him look a little like a marine in boot camp.

Over the next few months the velocity of events would sweep Kennedy up. He brokered a peace in Birmingham and, through Harry Belafonte, raised over $100,000 in cash to help bail the black students out of the jail in Birmingham. Years later Belafonte told me how the late Mike Quill, the leader of the transit workers' union, messengered over a canvas bag containing $50,000, which was called, in the union's records, a belated "speaking fee" for Dr. King. Kennedy had personally asked Harry to raise the bail money, quickly and discreetly.

The March on Washington at which King delivered his timeless oration took place on August 28. That was the day Robert Kennedy pulled John Lewis of SNCC aside and told him, "Now I understand. The students have opened my eyes. Thank you. I'm with you now."

In 1964 Kennedy ran for the Senate in New York against grandfatherly Republican incumbent Kenneth Keating. Some prominent liberals and intellectuals endorsed Keating simply out of hatred of Kennedy. Among them were elders I had looked up to, like I. F. Stone; Carey McWilliams, the editor of the *Nation* magazine; James Baldwin; and my friend, Nat Hentoff of the *Village Voice.* Other members of "Democrats for Keating" included actor Paul Newman, historians Richard Hofstadter and Barbara Tuchman, and novelist Gore Vidal. The *New York Times* also endorsed Keating, saying in their editorial that Kennedy aroused "an uneasiness that is no less real because it is elusive and difficult to define."

I wrote a supportive article about Kennedy for the *Village Voice*, which I had just started to work for, describing a night of his campaigning in Greenwich Village. I admit that his celebrity status excited me—enough to call him "the fifth Beatle." His rally remarks did not make much of an impression for their content, and indeed I was still not a Kennedy enthusiast in the fall of 1964. What persuaded me to vote for him was an essay Norman Mailer wrote endorsing him in the *Village Voice.* It said in part:

> I think Bobby Kennedy may be the only liberal about early or late, who could be a popular general in a defense against the future powers of the Right Win . . . So we must vote for one candidate because he is a neutron, or must vote for the other because he is an active principle who will grow and change and become—odds are—a leader of the Left or the Right . . .
>
> I think something came into Kennedy with the death of his brother. I think Bobby Kennedy has come a pilgrim's distance from that punk who used to play Junior DA for Joe McCarthy, and grabbed headlines by riding Jimmy Hoffa's back . . .
>
> Something compassionate, something witty, had come into his face. Something of sinew . . .
>
> Consider: six years of Ken Keating with Brussels sprouts, or six years with Bobby K. and some red snapper.

I had a friend named Roberta Gratz, a young reporter on the *New York Post*, who was also a believer in Kennedy. Her enthusiasm helped me overcome the doubts planted by Hentoff, Baldwin, and Izzy Stone. She helped convince me that they were objecting to an old skin that Kennedy had already shed. Kennedy defeated Keating, but he ran far behind Johnson-Humphrey ticket in New York.

In January of 1966 I completed my first book, which was about the emerging student radicalism. Shortly after that, my editor proposed a second book project to me—a biography of New York's newly elected liberal Republican mayor, John Lindsay. I thought about it. I liked Lindsay. He had personal decency and courage and was good on civil rights and civil liberties. I felt he had a future in national politics and had attracted some young progressive urbanists to join his new government, which had taken on the aura of a municipal Camelot.

Yet Lindsay did not interest me enough to devote three years of my life, which was how long I imagined it would take me to write a biography. He had the fortunate face and idealistic intentions of a potential hero. But there didn't seem to be any "back story" to him—no tragedy, no hidden demons, no deep secrets, nothing that gave birth to great surprise (although he did become a Democrat five years later). I thought he lacked depth and what I can only call vulnerability.

Lindsay proved to be a fine mayor who got the big things right—his popularity among the black community saved New York from the kind of riots convulsing Detroit, Newark, Chicago, and Los Angeles—but I just had no clue to any emotional truth about this tall figure of WASP rectitude. So I went back to my editor and said I had a better idea: a biography of Robert Kennedy, then starting his second year as the junior senator from New York. By the spring I had a contract and a small advance to write that book.

For a few months I read everything I could about him and covered him occasionally for the *Voice.* As it turns out, my research coincided with the series of adventures that would propel Kennedy across the line Cesar Chavez said no other American politician had crossed. In June he made his historic visit to segregated South Africa. The speech he gave at Capetown on June 10, 1966—in which he asked, "What if God is Black?"—electrified the younger generation. It was a challenge to the system of apartheid, given during the second year of Nelson Mandela's twenty-seven-year incarceration. He visited the shanty slum of Soweto and was engulfed in adulation.

When he came back to New York he led a winning reform campaign against Tammany Hall and helped get Sam Silverman elected the surrogate judge for Manhattan. The office had been a traditional vending machine of clubhouse patronage. This impressed me. Here was a guy who would take on apartheid and Tammany Hall in the same month—when he didn't have to, when it wasn't part of his job as junior senator from New York.

Kennedy was in New York frequently during the summer and fall of 1966, trying to elect a Democrat against Governor Nelson Rockefeller. Through the intercession of Kennedy staffers Peter Edelman, Tom Johnston, and Carter Burden, I was able to have a lunch with him. We clicked immediately. We made each other laugh. We talked about music, sports, movies, writers, the antiwar movement, pot smoking, the *Village Voice*, and my growing up in Bed-Stuy, which fascinated Kennedy, who grew up an American prince of privilege.

Kennedy, as I learned, was often drawn to people with working-class backgrounds. He favored the work of Hamill and Breslin. He admired José Torres and Cesar Chavez. His oldest friend was David Hackett, one of the few lower-class kids he'd known at Milton Academy. He seemed to think working-class origins gave people more passion—and he liked people who felt things passionately.

He asked me more questions than I asked him. This was a good start for a friendship, but not so good for an aspiring twenty-eight-year-old biographer.

In November of 1966 I was invited to spend a day riding with Kennedy around the city as he campaigned for Frank O'Connor, the Democratic candidate against Rockefeller, who was behind in the polls and was being outspent 20 to 1. Kennedy looked completely different than he had the day I was picketing the Justice Department. Rather than being cut short, military-style, his graying ginger hair now lapped over his earlobes in the shaggy style of the alienated young. His blue eyes were more sad than cold, more haunted than hostile. The freshly carved furrows of sorrow around his eyes and his brow made him look ten years older, not three.

In Brooklyn, Kennedy was shaking hands when a little girl in a crowd caught his attention. The girl was about ten years old and wearing glasses. Kennedy reacted to faces. He often talked about the character in the face of Andrei Voznesenski, the Russian poet. He saw something in this girl's face—shyness, sadness, sensitivity. He knelt to speak to the girl, who was holding her mother's hand. "You know something?" Kennedy said, sounding like a peer, not a senator. "My little girl wears glasses just like yours. And I love my little girl very much." Then he squeezed the back of the girl's neck because he was better at expressing feelings through action than through words. The girl's mother whispered, "Thank you so much."

Then Kennedy was back to the crowd, shaking hands, doing his best to help the candidate he knew was not going to win.

For a while I wondered if that extraordinary moment had been staged just for my benefit. But again and again I would see Kennedy relating that way with children or with anyone who looked like they had a hidden hurt.

At about 5 P.M. the sixth rally of the day ended on the Lower East Side. O'Connor told Kennedy he was tired and cold and was going to cancel the two remaining rallies back in Brooklyn. Kennedy's face showed he felt this was a sign of softness, of defeatism. Kennedy was not wearing an overcoat, and he was not the candidate, but he was ready to keep going.

After O'Connor went home, Kennedy saw two nurses from Albany who had been volunteers in his 1964 campaign and who showed up at the airport whenever he went to the state capital. They explained they were spending their vacations in New York to see him campaign. He invited them to join us in his apartment at 870 UN Plaza. At the apartment Kennedy juggled three parallel conversations. He asked the nurses about their jobs, their families, their boyfriends. He talked to his aides about the campaign and the next day's schedule. He talked to me about local New York politicians, a species he considered low on the food chain. "In Massachusetts they steal, in California they feud, and here in New York they lie," he said about the various local breeds of hack.

When the nurses left, Kennedy suddenly turned to me and asked, "Do you like poetry?" I said I liked William Butler Yeats and Hart Crane. "Can I read you some poetry by a poet I like very much?" Kennedy asked.

He disappeared into the bedroom for a minute. I expected him to return with Shakespeare, whom he often quoted. Or perhaps, if he was going to charm a writer for the *Village Voice*, he might return with Allen Ginsberg's "Howl."

Instead he emerged from the bedroom with a thin, dog-eared, underlined, jacketless volume of poetry by Ralph Waldo Emerson, whose poetry was then categorized as "minor" and unfashionable by the academic and literary establishments but who was gaining relevancy among campus rebels.

Kennedy stood in the center of his own living room, silhouetted against the neon Pepsi-Cola sign across the river in Queens, and started to read, in a monotone that was at the same time intense in its buried feelings, a poem that he must have associated with his assassinated brother.

He pays too high a price
For knowledge and for fame
Who sells his sinews to be wise,
His teeth and bones to buy fame,
and crawls through life a paralytic
to earn the praise of bard and critic

Were it not better done,
to dine and sleep through forty years;
Be loved by few; be feared by none;
Laugh life away, have win for tears;
And take the mortal leap undaunted,
Content that all we asked was
granted?

But Fate will not permit
The seeds of gods to die,
Nor suffer sense to win from wit,
Its guerdon in the sky,
Nor let us hide, whate'er our pleasure,
The world's light underneath a
measure

Go then, sad youth, and shine,
Go, sacrifice to Fame;
Put youth, joy, health upon the shrine,
And life to fan the flame;
Being for Seeming bravely barter,
And to die to Fame a happy martyr.

The last stanza he seemed to know from memory. His eyes were focused on the middle distance as he recited it.

"Do you want to hear one more?" he asked.

I said yes. He began to read an Emerson poem about Mexico that seemed to be a metaphor for Vietnam.

Though loath to grieve
The evil time's sole patriot,
I cannot leave
My honied thought
For the priest's cant,
Or the salesman's rant

If I refuse
My study for their politique,
Which at best is trick,
The angry Muse
Puts confusion in my brain.

But who is he that prates
Of the culture of mankind,
Of better arts and life?
Go, blindworm, go,
Behold the famous States,
Harrying Mexico
With rifle and with knife!

I could see there were caves and rivers and volcanoes in this man that other politicians just did not possess. This is what Mailer sensed in him—the potential to touch souls and lead armies.

Kennedy was three weeks short of his forty-first birthday the night he read me Emerson's poems. He would be dead in nineteen months.

Robert Kennedy let me into his life, without ground rules. Most days he spent in New York City, I was allowed to tag along. When he flew upstate on the sixteen-seat *Caroline*, as the family plane was called, I often was invited. When he was going to hold a particularly interesting public hearing or give a major address on the Senate floor, his press secretary, Frank Mankiewicz, would give me a heads-up call. Sometimes these long days would end with an invitation to dinner with other guests who ranged from poet Robert Lowell, to John Frankenheimer, the director of film *The Manchurian Candidate.*

I was the fly on the wall who took notes under the table. Kennedy knew I was working on a book about him to be published in the distant future. But I also wrote sporadic *Village Voice* articles about him and would tell him what quotes I wanted to put on the record. He never quibbled or tried to improve what he had said.

Some of these *Voice* articles were critical. I rebuked him for his silences over the Vietnam War and in one article written in late 1967 for not running for president.

My days and nights with Robert Kennedy were a decisive part of my political and personal education. He undoubtedly had a deeper influence on me than I ever had on him, although some exaggerated accounts suggest the reverse was the case. He taught me to see children as a special category of casualty in any situation because of their innocence and powerlessness. Kennedy opened my eyes to whole areas I had never given much thought to—labor racketeering, the history of the Teamsters' union, organized crime as a parasite feeding off the poor because of drugs and other rackets, the central role of law enforcement in a democratic society, and why public corruption is so subversive in a democracy. His emphasis on public integrity pushed me into doing more investigative journalism.

But perhaps the most important gift he gave me was his patriotism. My emotions about America were confused in 1967 because of the war. Kennedy helped me work through this alienation. His love for America changed my thinking. Along with jazz and baseball, it helped to inoculate me against the virus of anti-Americanism rampant on the New Left.

Kennedy cherished America's founding documents, and its natural beauty and abundance; its history of progress and freedom; its story of immigrant hope and assimilation; and its military dominance.

He often quoted the line from Camus: "I want to be able to love my country, and justice too." This is not quite the same thing as "My country, right or wrong." He moved me toward a realistic patriotic populism.

Kennedy also knew more than almost anyone about America's dark side—the government wiretapping, the mob, the CIA, the Teamsters, the

FBI, and twilight titans like Howard Hughes, J. Edgar Hoover, Jimmy Hoffa, Roy Cohn, and the CIA's William Harvey, whom Kennedy detested.

He never shared any of these secrets with me. But he sometimes made tantalizing references, and dropped suggestions, that made me become much more curious and aware of these forces and institutions. In an indirect way, his hints led me to cowrite a PBS documentary for *Frontline* in 1992 that made a case for the mob—specifically Carlos Marcello and Santos Trafficante—being behind the assassination of John Kennedy.

Kennedy did share some of his private thoughts with Walter Sheridan, an ex-FBI agent, who went to work for Robert in 1957 on the Teamsters probe by the McLellan Committee—the Senate committee investigating labor racketeering, named for Senator John McClellan of Arkansas. Walter remained to monitor both Jim Garrison's fraudulent assassination probe and Marcello's New Orleans mob empire. He was the keeper of confidences, the sphinx of secrets. I begged Walter to go on camera for my 1992 documentary, but he declined. After the show aired, and before his death in 1996, Walter did mutter his agreement with the mob theory of a conspiracy to me. But he granted no specifics, no details. His attitude, I think, was the same as Kennedy's—the only way ever to have unraveled any of these mysteries would have been had RFK become president. Talk and speculation were both too painful and a waste of time.

When I first met Kennedy, my life experience was limited. I only really knew about a few areas—civil rights, the culture of jazz, campus radicalism, journalism, and local politics. And I had my passions, which some highbrow friends thought were anti-intellectual—baseball, boxing, and rock 'n' roll.

Kennedy repeatedly urged me to read Shakespeare. He thought it would make me a better writer. (He even gave me a record of Shakespeare's plays that he said he listened to every morning while shaving.) He had an intellect that synthesized history, literature, and political science, and was an astute reading of character, although he put little faith in Freud or unconscious motivations.

He once told to me that he was "willing to be judged by the enemies I have made." When I asked who they were, he ticked off Jimmy Hoffa,

George Wallace, Roy Cohn, and J. Edgar Hoover. When I asked who was the worst of this quartet, he said Hoffa, but then he corrected himself: "Probably Hoover because he was in power so damn long."

Kennedy thought Hoover was a "twisted individual."* He also called the FBI director a "menace to democracy" and "a habitual blackmailer." Most historians and former Kennedy advisers believe that Hoover blackmailed the Kennedys.

Kennedy told me a story—"that you can never use," he added—to illustrate how "sick" Hoover was. Kennedy said Hoover had once sent him a copy of a tape transcript the FBI had purportedly made—apparently illegally and without a court authorization—on Martin Luther King in 1964. A motel room bug planted by FBI agents was operating while King and Ralph Abernathy were watching a TV rerun of John Kennedy's funeral. Part of the rerun included the moment when Jacqueline Kennedy knelt prayerfully with her children at the dead president's flag-draped casket.

All Kennedy would say to me is that the tape captured King making "a vulgar remark about President Kennedy and Jacqueline" that Hoover knew would always taint Robert's feelings toward King.

Taylor Branch, in his 1998 book *Pillar of Fire*, the second volume of his monumental biography of Dr. King, quoted the statement. It was more shocking than I imagined. FBI agents monitoring the bug reported they heard King say, "Look at her. Sucking him off one last time."

Hoover sent Kennedy this vulgar nugget from snooping in March of 1964, in a top-secret report that began with the warning that disclosure would jeopardize vital national security interest—meaning the illegal motel room bug. Branch wrote: "Hoover, professing to be sickened by what headquarters called 'vilification of the late President and his wife,' safely skewered three nemeses at once. Using King's unguarded rage . . . Hoover aimed a dart for the eye of the surviving brother, the Attorney General, who returned the memo to [FBI official Courtney] Evans with a terse, vacant comment that it was very helpful."

In retrospect, this dirty trick by Hoover makes Robert Kennedy's now-famous spontaneous eloquence on the night King was assassinated, in April of 1968, even more poignant and complex.

---

*Arthur Schlesinger wrote in *Robert Kennedy and His Time* that Hoover's top deputy and personal

"Who is the smartest person you ever met?" I once asked Kennedy.

"The smartest person I ever met—that you probably never heard of—is Sidney Korshak," he answered, referring to the powerful Hollywood lawyer and mob intermediary. He described Korshak as "Roy Cohn on a national level." Kennedy said he had questioned Korshak once under oath before the McClellan Committee in 1957, adding "I couldn't lay a glove on the guy. He outsmarted me at every turn." (Kennedy was chief counsel to the committee; JFK, then the Senator from Massachusetts, served on the committee.) Korshak had become legitimate, even beloved, in Hollywood by 1967. But Kennedy felt he was still the only person in corporations, unions, politics, the mob, and Las Vegas who could "reach"—meaning "fix"—a whole class of people either through past favors given or owed, or through fear of Sidney's friends. Korshak was the brains of the mega-mob.

The greatest secret of all, of course, involved what happened on November 22, 1963. To many of his friends and confidants, it was clear that if Bob never recovered from his brother's assassination, it was partly because he felt guilty about it. Yet there were very few people to whom he could express this guilt. I never discussed it directly with Kennedy, but for years afterward I did talk about it to some of his closest friends.

As I've mentioned, Kennedy suspected either the CIA or the Mafia could be involved in his brother's murder. On the day of his brother's assassination, according to a conversation I had with Walter Sheridan, Kennedy asked his labor racketeering experts to find out what Chicago mob boss Sam Giancana was doing that day. He also asked CIA director John McCone directly if the agency had any involvement in what happened in Dallas. There had to have been some basis for RFK to ask these questions. Something had provoked his immediate suspicious, despite his shock and grief.

By 1967 Bob began to express more openly his suspicions to Walter Sheridan, Richard Goodwin, and Arthur Schlesinger that organized crime, mostly likely New Orleans Mafia don Carlos Marcello, may have

companion, Clyde Tolson, said in 1968 about RFK, "I hope that someone shoots and kills the son of a bitch." Schlesinger's source was the FBI's number-three official, William Sullivan, who overheard Tolson say this a few months before Kennedy was killed.

been behind the assassination. In these conversations he was typically indirect. He referred to Marcello as "that guy in New Orleans" with both Goodwin and Sheridan, who was an expert on Marcello's mob empire.

"I don't believe Bob ever read the *Warren Commission Report* himself," Goodwin told me. He had Nick Katzenbach read it for him. I told him once, in 1967, that I felt the *Warren Report* was far from conclusive. He just leaned over and said, 'I can't focus on it. I can't focus on it,' meaning it was too painful for him, even four years later. Then he said to me, 'If anyone had anything to do with it, it had to be organized crime."

As attorney general, Kennedy ordered criminal and tax investigations into Marcello, Santos Trafficante, and Sam Giancana as part of his "Top Hoodlum" program. He did everything possible to indict them, including wiretapping, surveillances, harassment, and deportation proceedings. Wiretaps show that Giancana thought he had some kind of immunity from prosecution through his friendship with Frank Sinatra and his political support for JFK in 1960. He felt double-crossed by RFK's all-out campaign to prosecute him. More important, Giancana, Marcello, and Trafficante all participated in—or pretended to go along with—the CIA's insane plots to assassinate Fidel Castro. They mistakenly assumed this "patriotic" work would protect them from RFK's mission to eradicate organized crime.

Moreover, there is no doubt that Kennedy pressured various government agencies and officials to overthrow Castro through a program called Operation Mongoose. But the preponderance of the historical testimony and evidence is that he did *not* know about—and did not approve—this secret CIA-mob alliance to kill Castro. That alliance had been formed in August of 1960, five months before JFK became president. It seems illogical that Kennedy would choose the same three gangster chieftains he was most determined to prosecute—Giancana, Marcello, and Trafficante—to assassinate a foreign leader. He hated these guys.*

---

*While preparing the 1998 documentary on RFK that I coproduced with Charles Stuart, we discovered in the UCLA film archive footage of RFK questioning Giancana before the McLellan committee in 1959. Kennedy is taunting the Chicago killer in front of the cameras. When Giancana giggles while taking the Fifth Amendment, RFK tells him, "I thought only little girls giggled." We used this chilling moment in the documentary.

Tampa-based mob lawyer Frank Ragano has said he was "the messenger" among clients Marcello, Trafficante, and Jimmy Hoffa in early 1963. But I do not believe that Hoffa played any real role in planning or executing the assassination. He was a much subservient figure to Trafficante, Marcello, and Giancana. He was probably more of a cheerleader, or instigator, than a conspirator. On our PBS documentary Ragano, who successfully represented Trafficante in criminal trials for thirty years, said that his client made a "deathbed confession" to him that he had been involved in JFK's murder. According to Ragano, Trafficante had said to him, in Sicilian, on March 13, 1987, four days before he died, "We shouldn't have killed John. We should have killed Bobby instead."

Ragano also told us on camera—backed up by his wife—that he had had dinner with Trafficante the night of JFK's assassination. Trafficante was "the happiest I ever saw him," he recalled. "He was making toasts to the murder. He was saying now we can go back and run casinos in Cuba. He knew that Lyndon Johnson hated Bobby, and Bobby now had no more power."

Las Vegas operator Ed Becker also appeared on our documentary. He said that Marcello told him during a 1962 meeting in Louisiana that he was going to arrange JFK's murder to remove RFK as attorney general. Becker told me that Marcello told him, "If you cut off the tail, the dog will keep bitting. If you cut off the head, the dog will die."

I consider it a 90 percent probability that Marcello, Trafficante, and Giancana were behind it. Notre Dame law school professor Robert Blakey was a young prosecutor in the Kennedy Justice Department in 1962–63, working on organized crime cases. He later became chief counsel to the special House committee that investigated President Kennedy's assassination in 1978. That committee's final report stated that Marcello, Trafficante, and Giancana had "means, motive, and opportunity" to assassinate President Kennedy. In a series of interviews I conducted for our documentary, Blakey told me he was "almost positive" these three Mafia bosses had arranged the assassination, "using right-wing Cuban exiles posing as left-wing Cubans to draw Oswald in as a patsy."

Robert Kennedy may have suspected that the gangsters he had tried so aggressively—and yet unsuccessfully—to convict had conspired to murder his brother in order to remove him as attorney general. Were that true, it would explain the permanent melancholy into which he sank after November 22, 1963. It could only have been made worse by knowing that his father—mute from a stroke by 1963—had tried to steer him away from investigating the mob.

In September 1967 Kennedy invited me to accompany him on a flight to Rochester to visit a migrant labor camp. The visit would dramatize two essential truths about him. One is something Senator Jacob Javits would say in his eulogy: "Bob endured personal torture. He literally shook with indignation at the sight of starving children."

The other is something Kennedy said more than once: "Courage is the most important human quality. It makes all the other positive qualities possible." He himself was drawn to physical danger and risk. He shot the rapids, took chances skiing, climbed Mount Kennedy, and refused to use armed bodyguards. Many of the people Kennedy most admired displayed physical courage in diverse arenas—bullfighter El Cordobes, mountain climber Jim Whitaker, army general Maxwell Taylor, astronaut John Glenn, fighter José Torres, John Lewis, the civil rights organizer who faced down beatings and death threats in the South.

On that day in September of 1967, a group of us visited a farmworker camp just outside of Rochester. As we approached the camp, we found a sign that read "Anyone entering or trespassing without permission will be shot if caught." Everyone in our group stopped in their tracks, except Kennedy. He kept walking, head down, determined. He walked right into an abandoned bus that had been converted into primitive living quarters for three migrant families. We ran to catch up.

Inside the stench-filled bus were six children, all less than ten years old. Their undernourished bodies were covered with unhealed scabs and flies. Most of them had running noses. They were all black. Kennedy's face suddenly regained the stricken, haunted look it had in the months following his brother's assassination; a combination of anger, pain, empathy, and grief mingled and flattened his features. An old, stooped woman wandered into the bus. Kennedy asked her how much she earned. She said she made $1 an hour picking celery. He shook his head.

He went out and looked into the next dilapidated bus, which was empty except for one child, sitting on a filthy mattress. The broken windows were filled with torn cardboard. There was no running water and no stove. As he looked down at this lone child—who might have been in Africa or India, but was here in his America—Kennedy's hand trembled in rage. He seemed like a man experiencing an exorcism.

He walked out and confronted the owner of the migrant camp, Jay DeBadts. "You had no right to go in there," DeBadts shouted. He pointed at his sign that said interlopers would be shot. "You're just a do-gooder trying to make some headlines."

Kennedy looked at him, still struggling to control his emotions. He almost whispered, "You are something out of the nineteenth century. I wouldn't put an animal in those buses."

"It's like camping out" was DeBadts's rejoinder.

I was scared that DeBadts had a gun. He and Kennedy were glaring at each other. The rest of us were a few steps behind. Kennedy had no security or bodyguards. He also had no fear.

Finally Kennedy turned and left, and we followed him off the property. The memory of this confrontation and the children's condition of excruciating squalor stayed with him. He talked about it again and again in other places. He wrote a letter to Governor Rockefeller asking for an investigation into health conditions in migrant camps in New York. He wrote letters to union leaders urging them to organize migrant workers. He proposed legislation to give migrant farmworkers the right of collective bargaining and workmen's compensation protection.

A few weeks later he asked me if I could really imagine what it was like to live in a bus and pick celery for $1 an hour, and have no hope for a better future. He was thinking about it from the point of view of a child, not a senator. He experienced that day the way John Steinbeck or Walker Evans would have.

Magnify this day by a hundred and you have some idea of what Kennedy was going through during his growth spurt of 1966 and 1967. He had the same kind of emotional reaction when he visited the Mississippi Delta, the hollows of Appalachia, Watts, East Los Angeles, the Pine Ridge Indian reservation, Eskimos in Alaska, working-class whites in Southie and Gary, Indiana. And the Bedford-Stuyvesant community in Brooklyn.

We spent several days together in Bed-Stuy because that was where Kennedy was building a community development project to create jobs and renovate housing. I showed Kennedy the schools I attended, the library in Tompkins Park where I fell in love with reading, the basketball court in the Marcy projects where I accepted I wasn't an athlete, and the house I lived in on Vernon Avenue.

Kennedy said he "envied" my lower-class origins. They made him feel sheltered and deprived of something. Once, standing in front of my old house, I asked him what would have happened to him if he had grown up on this block of jobless men drinking beer on stoops at noon. "I would have become either a juvenile delinquent or a revolutionary," he answered. Then he looked at all the unemployed men loitering on the corner, looking depressed or lost in a haze of drink, drugs, and self-pity. "I hate welfare, I hate the dole," he said. "Jobs are everything. 'Jobs' is the most important word in the political vocabulary. Self-respect is the ball game. You can only get that from work."

What outsiders found hard to understand about Kennedy is that he secretly viewed himself as an outsider. He felt like an outsider in his own family, the seventh of nine children, sandwiched between his three sisters in the birth order, the smallest male, unable to complete with his older brothers, Joe and Jack. He was a lonely adolescent with few close friends. He was shy, awkward, and a little different, certainly more religious and introspective than his peers or siblings. In his twenties, he was perceived as ruthless and arrogant, as a "punk," as Mailer wrote.

After his brother was assassinated, a melancholy fatalism invaded his bones and never left him. The assassination was a wound that never healed. As Robert Lowell wrote in an elegy to him, "Doom was woven into your nerves." "John Kennedy was a pragmatist disguised as a romantic," Arthur Schlesinger once said. "Robert Kennedy was a romantic disguised as a pragmatist."

During the period I knew Robert Kennedy, he seemed resigned to being misunderstood. He'd acquired a tragic sense of life. He'd become a crusader of constant sorrow.

Although I couldn't change that melancholy or even touch it, there were three areas where I did try to influence Robert Kennedy's thinking: the popular culture of the 1960s, opposing the Vietnam War more vigorously, and challenging Lyndon Johnson for the presidential nomination in 1968.

I was friends with protest folksong writer-performers Phil Ochs, Tom Paxton, and Eric Anderson. I gave Kennedy their records and he enjoyed them, especially the satiric antiwar songs written by Ochs and Paxton. I also kept telling Kennedy that Bob Dylan was a genius, and passed along Dylan's records, which were becoming increasingly symbolic, hallucinatory, and poetic. He did not find it easy to relate to Dylan, although he was deeply curious about his popularity and his ability to write anthems for his generation.

Kennedy was put off by Dylan's "whining voice." In those days he preferred more mellow, mainstream singers like Andy Williams and Neil Diamond. But I kept telling him what an original Dylan was, and Kennedy kept reading about him. He once told me he had read a review of the cinema verité documentary on Dylan *Don't Look Back*. "Is that his philosophy?" he asked. "I think it's mine."

When I finally introduced Phil Ochs to Kennedy in March of 1967, he quizzed Ochs intensely about what Dylan was really like.

Then, one night during the 1968 California primary, Kennedy told me he now could appreciate the words to Dylan's songs. Bobby Darin had performed at a few campaign rallies that day and had sung "Blowin' in the Wind" for the crowds. Listening to Darin sing Dylan's words was the filter Kennedy needed to make them accessible. Dylan's own voice had been an impediment to appreciation.

Darin had started out as a brash rock-and-roller with "Splish Splash," then had gone through a phase as a finger-snapping Sinatra sound-alike, but by 1968 he had become a radical hippie, singing at Kennedy campaign events in dungarees and T-shirt.

Darin, who had grown up working-class Italian in the Bronx and briefly attended Hunter College, went a little nuts when Kennedy was killed. The night of the funeral Darin was seen sleeping near the fresh gravesite in Arlington National Cemetery. He was another who never quite got over the loss of Robert Kennedy. He died in 1973 at the age of thirty-seven.

I never got to tell Darin that it was his musical interpretation that allowed Kennedy to *hear* Dylan's words. "I really liked that Dylan line,"

Kennedy said to me. " 'How many years can some people exist, before they're allowed to be free?' " We then got into a discussion of Woody Guthrie's influence on the early Dylan and what a great song "This Land Is Your Land" was, especially the suppressed verse about the unemployed and the relief office. "This Land Is Your Land" had become Kennedy's semiofficial campaign song in California, with some new lyrics written to fit him. At every stop in the Mexican-American areas, there was a mariachi band playing it, Mexican style, to stir up the crowd.

That night Kennedy asked me what was the minimum I expected him to actually accomplish if he were elected president. "End the Vietnam War and make 'This Land Is Your Land' the new national anthem," I replied.

"That's all? I can do that." Kennedy laughed.

Then I scrawled a contract on a restaurant napkin with these two promises in writing. Kennedy signed it and even made the symbol of a notary on the napkin.

The issue of Vietnam would not be solved so easily. In February of 1966, Kennedy had proposed setting up a coalition government in Vietnam as a solution to the escalating war. He was immediately denounced by most large newspapers and by Vice President Humphrey, who famously said that would be like "putting the fox in the chicken house."

Kennedy, on the defensive, was invited to go on *Meet the Press* and explain his views more fully on Vietnam. In preparation for the appearance, he asked his advisers Arthur Schlesinger and Fred Dutton to impersonate hostile reporters and ask him sharp questions in a practice rehearsal. Schlesinger asked him to assess John Kennedy's responsibility for the trouble we were now in in Vietnam.

"Well, I don't know what would be best," Bob began. "To say that he didn't spend much time thinking about Vietnam, or to say that he did and messed it up." Then he thrust his hand up to the sky and asked, "Which, brother? Which?"

Kennedy told me he had "never had a serious discussion" with his brother about Vietnam. Cuba, civil rights, and Berlin had been the front-burner items between them. JFK had sent 16,000 "advisers" to Vietnam, but there had been no bombing and no escalation. There had been no secret plan for the future. There was no policy paper or remembered counsel that he could now use as a foundation for his own response to the rising troop shipments and casualty lists.

When I started my occasional debates/conversations with Kennedy about Vietnam at the end of 1966, I could see that the ambiguity of his brother's intentions were a huge barrier to any firm clarity in his own thinking.

Let me be clear, however. He knew much more about the history of Vietnam and Southeast Asia than I did. He had read books by Bernard Fall, Jean Lacoutre, and Theodore Draper. He had thought about questions like: What was the real nature of the National Liberation Front? How can real negotiations get started? Would a pause in the bombing produce an opening for negotiations? Was this a war of national liberation? What would China do if American involvement deepened? Was a "military solution" possible? Was victory the real goal of the Johnson administration? What did the divisions within the Johnson administration mean? Was there a "third way" between escalation and withdrawal?

I was twenty-eight years old. He was a senator who was holding private conversations with McNamara, Harriman, Bundy, Ball, and General Taylor; reading confidential cables and memos; and meeting with with world figures like de Gaulle. But I was on fire in my simple belief that the war was morally wrong; that it was a mistaken policy that was dividing the country; that it was diverting funds from the burning cities; and that it was was a needless intervention, since I was certain the "domino theory" was a hoax and a fraud. I felt like I was representing all the antiwar protesters and marchers and doomed soldiers in these conversations. Certitude and passion were my only weapons—besides Kennedy's own doubts about what his brother had intended to do, had he been reelected in 1964.

In his talks with me, one of the things weighing on his mind was whether his criticisms of the policy would have "a boomerang effect on Johnson." He knew from Robert McNamara, Richard Goodwin, and Bill Moyers that Johnson had become paranoid about him. He worried that if he spoke out against the war, it might drive Johnson into deeper involvement, out of spite.

I was far from the only person urging him to voice his opposition against the war more forcefully and frequently. His Senate aide, Adam Walinsky, was sending him memos and writing drafts of possible speeches—and inserting copies of I. F. Stone's newsletter into his night reading folder. (In October 1966 Stone wrote a newsletter essay entitled "While Others Dodge the Draft, Bobby Dodges the War.") "Bobby" always seemed to be used in a negative context. George McGovern, the senator Kennedy most admired, was telling him to oppose the war more aggressively. So were Schlesinger, Goodwin, and John Kenneth Galbraith, all three of whom published pamphletlike books against the war late in 1966. He was also getting this advice to be bolder from most of his staff, from senators Mike Mansfield, William Fullbright, and George McGovern, as well as from the free-floating activist Allard Lowenstein.

In one conversation, probably in early 1967, I asked Kennedy why he did not visit Vietnam himself and use his investigative skills to probe the real nature of the war, pacification, troop morale, corruption in Saigon, and the effectiveness of the bombing campaign. "I'm afraid that if I went," Kennedy replied, "I would see dead American boys. I might get so emotional about that, I could lose my perspective. Seeing a lot of dead boys might cause me to stop questioning the war. So I haven't gone."

Then he added: "I think I know myself. I visited a veterans hospital with Al Lowenstein and spent the morning with soldiers just returned from Vietnam with horrible wounds. I could barely handle it. I cried. I couldn't talk. If I went to Vietnam and saw such suffering and heroism, I know it would affect my judgment."

In February of 1967, with less than 30 percent of the country opposing the Vietnam War or the bombing, Kennedy told me he had decided to make a speech on the Senate floor that would detail his disagreements with Johnson's Vietnam policy. "I'm ready to cross the Rubicon," he said. What finally pushed him over the edge was an apparently brutal face-to-face meeting he had with the president on February 6. It convinced Kennedy that it didn't matter whether he spoke out or held back—he would have no influence on Johnson's Vietnam decisions. The confrontation persuaded him that the president was irrational, possibly unstable, and fatally deluded about how the war was going and the prospects for a "military solution."

When I asked Kennedy about the meeting, he gave me this account:

> It wasn't very pleasant. Johnson was mean. He didn't believe my quotes in *Newsweek* about my role in a "peace feeler" from the Vietnamese in Paris. He said I was lying. He was very abusive. He was shouting and seemed very unstable. I kept thinking that if he explodes like that with me, how could he ever negotiate with Hanoi, or De Gaulle, or Mao.
>
> He said a lot of unpleasant things, like I was responsible for prolonging the war, and for American soldiers dying in Vietnam, and that doves like me didn't have much of a political future. I didn't say much except that I planned to make a speech on the war soon that would propose a halt in the bombing.
>
> At the end of the meeting he told me he never wanted to hear my views about Vietnam again. What I learned from the meeting is that government felt the war was going so well in the battlefield, they didn't really want to negotiate now.

For the next month Kennedy went through an intense round of meetings with Vietnam critics and experts, trying to make sure his speech made the right points and had the right tone. He met with Al Lowenstein and George McGovern; reread Theodore Draper's book *The Abuse of Power*, which he said was "one of the best, but not too kind to me and my friends." Kennedy could be objective about himself. He also listened to public attacks from Johnson's allies and heard private pleas from close friends not to give the speech.

His friend columnist Joseph Alsop wrote that if Kennedy gave a speech against the bombing, he would never become president. The only thing he would be leader of was a fringe cult. Former Postmaster General James Farley—an old friend of his father's—gave a speech accusing Kennedy of "imperiling the safety of the nation" and "undermining the president."

Kennedy felt that both the hostile public attacks and the friendly visits urging silence were being choreographed in a panicked White House.

On February 13, as part of his intense preparations, Kennedy asked me to set up a private meeting for him later that day with radical antiwar critics Tom Hayden and Staughton Lynd, both of whom had illegally visited North Vietnam in 1965 and written a book about it, *The Other Side*. Kennedy knew that Hayden was a friend of mine and I had suggested that Kennedy meet with him—not about Vietnam but about Hayden's organizing efforts in the slums of Newark. He stressed that I not mention the meeting to anyone, fearing that Johnson or J. Edgar Hoover would find out and start denounce him as a dupe of the New Left or a pawn of pro–Viet Cong sympathizers.

The meeting, held at Kennedy's United Nations Plaza apartment, was low key and informative. Hayden and Lynd never said they believed in unilateral withdrawal, and Kennedy peppered them with questions.

In the middle of the meeting Kennedy looked out of the window and noticed a thick black cloud of pollution drifting up the East River from a Consolidated Edison power plant at Fourteenth Street. He stopped the conversation, went to the phone, and called Con Ed to complain about its polluting the air. He did not identify himself.

Lynd stressed the political differences between the National Liberation Front and Hanoi and the need for a unilateral cessation of the bombings without requiring any reciprocal act by Hanoi. Kennedy said he would ultimately "settle" for a "Laos-type" solution in Vietnam. But he added, "There has to be some guarantees by the other side that the border to Thailand would be sealed to infiltrators. I am concerned that we don't just end up by moving the whole damn thing over one country."

When the meeting ended, Kennedy invited us to join him for dinner with Schlesinger and Galbraith. Hayden and Lynd declined, saying they both had to speak at antiwar rallies that night. I left with them, to get their impressions and type up what I could recall about the meeting.

"He seems very fair-minded," Lynd said. "Sort of detached, not authoritarian at all. But still very much a liberal." Hayden thought he was "kind of European. He reminds me more of [French premier] Mendes-France than any American liberal."

A few days later I asked Kennedy what he made of them. "They're decent, bright fellows," he replied. "But I didn't think they told me everything they felt about immediate withdrawal." Kennedy's radar could always detect bullshit, even polite bullshit for a good cause. He wanted to hear the truth.

On March 1 Frank Mankiewicz, Kenndy's Press Secretary, called me to say Kennedy would give his Senate speech on Vietnam the next day, and I should take an early shuttle to Washington to be there. An hour after I got this tip, I was walking in the Village and ran into Phil Ochs. I impulsively invited Phil to fly down with me to Washington to hear the speech. Phil was a wonderful songwriter with a fixation about pop culture heroes like Elvis Presley, John Kennedy, and James Dean. He saw this Kennedy as evolving into something like them. He was also a passionate critic of the war, who had sung for free at dozens of protest rallies and written several exceptional antiwar and antidraft songs, including "I Ain't Marching Any More" and "The War Is Over." But he was also a patriot, in his fashion, who wrote "The Power and the Glory," a Woody Guthrie–inspired tribute to America's beauty. And he was a political satirist who composed the still-funny "Love Me, I'm a Liberal." He immediately agreed to come with me.

Kennedy had been up till 3:30 A.M. that morning, finishing the carpentry on the speech with Walinsky, Mankiewicz, and Goodwin. Phil and I were already sitting in Peter Edelman's office when Kennedy arrived. "Well, am I a big enough dove for you now?" he asked. "No, not quite." Peter smiled at him. "Well, that makes me feel a little better," Kennedy replied, smiling.

Phil and I just tried to stay out of everyone's way as reporters, TV camera crews, and three generations of Kennedy advisers flowed in and out of the cramped offices. The atmosphere was both tense and exuberant. Phil and I were both making notes.

When the speech began, Mankiewicz got us front-row seats in the Senate press gallery, next to Mary McGrory of the *Washington Post* and Martin Nolan of the *Boston Globe*, two of Kennedy's favorite journalists, though they were both independent enough to needle him in print when they thought he needed it.

Kennedy began by accepting, for himself and his brother, part of the blame for past Vietnam mistakes. "Three presidents have taken action in Vietnam," he began. "As one who was involved in those decisions, I can testify that if fault is to be found, or responsibility assessed, there is enough to go round for all—including myself."

Then Kennedy turned to his own existential preoccupations—the "pain," the "anguish," the "children," and the "responsibility." "Let us reflect for a moment . . . on the horror. All we say and do must be informed by our awareness that this horror is partly our responsibility. It is our chemicals that scorch the children and our bombs that level villages. We are all participants . . . we must also feel as men the anguish of what it is we are doing."

Sitting in the packed, hushed Senate chamber, listening to these words with their echoes of Camus, I felt history was being made and changed.

Then came the heart of the speech:

> I propose that we test the sincerity of the statements by [Soviet] Premier Kosygin and others asserting that if the bombardment of the North is halted, negotiations would begin, by halting the bombardment and saying we are ready to negotiate within the week.
>
> An international group should be asked to inspect the borders and ports to report any further escalation. And under the direction of the United Nations, and with an international presence gradually replacing American forces, we should move towards a final settlement, which allows all major political elements in South Vietnam to participate in the choice in leadership, and shape their future direction as a people.

That evening Phil and I flew back to New York on the shuttle with Kennedy. Before I left for the airport I was given a photo of a man named Frank Chavez, a Teamster organizer and enforcer. I was told he was stalking Kennedy and was trying to kill him because Jimmy Hoffa was about to begin his federal prison sentence. In the back of the half-empty shuttle Kennedy began to ask Phil what he thought of the day and what songs he was writing. He asked Phil to sing one of his new songs.

I suggested "Crucifixion" because I thought it was Phil's best song. I doubt if I consciously understood the effect this song would have on this day, at this hour. Phil had written "Crucifixion" as a metaphor for the assassinations of John Kennedy and Jesus Christ, as a song about the inevitable ritual sacrifice of great heroes. This was the day Robert Kennedy had finally come to terms with the war in Vietnam and his brother's contributions to America's original involvement. This was the day Robert Kennedy knew a potential assassin might be stalking him. This was the day he broke with Lyndon Johnson, the man his brother had chosen to be his vice president.

Without a guitar, his voice raspy and dry, Phil began to sing in the darkness of the plane.

As the night comes again to the circle studded sky
The stars settle slowly, in loneliness they die
Till the universe explodes as a falling star is raised
The planets are paralyzed, the mountains are amazed
But they all glow brighter from the brilliance of the blaze
Then, with the speed of insanity, he dies.

In the green fields of turning a baby is born
His cries crease the wind and mingle with the morn
As assault upon the order, the changing of the guard
Chosen for a challenge that's hopelessly hard
And the only single sign is the sighing of the stars
But to the silence of the distance, they're sworn.

Then came the two verses about the assassination of John Kennedy. I was looking right into Kennedy's eyes, and the gradual recognition of the song's meaning caused him to wince in pain. His County Wexford, potato-famine face was bereavement itself.

Images of innocence charge him to go on
But the decadence of history is looking for a pawn
To a nightmare of knowledge he opens up the gate
A blinding revelation is served upon his plate
That beneath the greatest love is a hurricane of hate
And God help the critic of the dawn.

They say we can't believe it, it's a sacrilegious shame
Now who would want to hurt such a hero of the game
But you know I predicted it, I knew he had to fall
How did it happen, I hope his suffering was small
Tell me every detail, I have to know it all
And do you have a picture of the pain?

Kennedy's eyes were watery. He squeezed Phil's knee. Nobody spoke a word the rest of the flight.

When we landed at LaGuardia, a New York City detective met Kennedy at the gate and asked me if I had a photo of Frank Chavez.

CHAPTER 7

Touching the Extremes: Robert Kennedy, Part II

Allard Lowenstein was a troubled and talented loner who toppled the Washington Monument: He dumped Lyndon Johnson from the Democratic ticket. The president who had mastered the inside power game of Washington better than anybody could not see what was happening in America in late 1967 and early 1968.

While the president was counting the votes in the Senate and among the Joint Chiefs, Al Lowenstein was counting the coffins from Vietnam being unloaded in Maryland and the scrubbed, moderate student body presidents, fearful about the draft, who were turning against the war that threatened their futures, a war that lacked a rationale. That was how Al Lowenstein started the "Dump Johnson Movement" that everyone in the establishment laughed at—at first. But this campus-based, unfunded insurgency ended up forcing Lyndon Johnson out of the election in 1968. It propelled Senator Eugene McCarthy into the arena and then compelled Robert Kennedy to join him. It was the classic case of one man making a difference.

In April of 1967 I ran into Lowenstein at a party. The week before, I had published an article in the *Village Voice* about Johnson and Vietnam that had ended "At Auschwitz a child who knew he was about to die screamed at a German guard, 'You won't be forgiven anything.' This is me saying the same thing to Lyndon Johnson. He is not my president. This is not my war."

In the same article I wrote with a prescience that I must have borrowed from Lowenstein and Kennedy: "There is a real possibility that the president will withdraw from the race . . . My perception of LBJ is that, like Sonny Liston, he is a bully with a quitter's heart, that he will not run if he thinks he cannot win."

Al complimented me on the prose (which echoed his) and told me he was going to spend the remainder of 1967 organizing a national, grassroots movement to deny the sitting president renomination by his own party—something that had never happened before. "Will you help us?" Al asked with his tentative, boyish enthusiasm. "You're the voice of the Village. You reach the people I want to reach."

"I'll do anything," I replied. I shared Al's belief that the best way to stop the war was to stop Johnson inside the Democratic Party.

Al invited me to meet him the next night for coffee at his family's restaurant, Granson's, at Forty-ninth Street and Lexington Avenue, to have a longer conversation about this titanic task. There Al made it clear that his ultimate objective was to draw Robert Kennedy into challenging Johnson for the nomination. Al predicted that he could mobilize moderate student opinion on the campuses and energize reform politicians, and that by the end of the year "some senator or congressman" would step up and become "the intermediate candidate" who would expose how weak Johnson was in the country.

When I pressed Al on who that "intermediate candidate" might be, he threw out several names, including those of George McGovern, Lee Metcalf, Frank Church, and Eugene McCarthy. He stressed that the endgame was Kennedy and that he wanted me to start talking to Kennedy about running. His own contacts with Kennedy would have to remain secret and back-channel until the movement got off the ground.

Al and Kennedy knew and liked each other. Al had contributed to Kennedy's famous speech to 15,000 students in Capetown, South Africa, in June of 1966 although most of it had been composed by Adam Walinsky, including its most inspiring passage:

> Each of us can work to change a small portion of events and in the total of those acts will be written the history of this generation . . . Each time a man stands up for an ideal, or acts to improve the lot of others, he sends forth a tiny ripple of hope, and crossing each other from a million different centers of energy and daring, these ripples build a current that can sweep down the mightiest walls of oppression and resistance.

Kennedy's words were a trumpet sounding against apartheid. But they also expressed what Lowenstein was planning to do that year in America—start the ripple that would grow into the wave that would sweep away LBJ's financial support and union support, stranding him without the endorsement of one senator or congressman or mayor.

My own relationship with Al Lowenstein had its up and downs over the years. I both respected and mistrusted him. I had seen him perform heroic acts and despicable acts. He was a brave visionary and a manipulative control freak. He was a liberal who kept placing himself in radical situations.

I saw this most clearly during the civil rights movement in Mississippi. Al, a charismatic campus speaker and organizer, had recruited hundreds of students from Yale, Harvard, Stanford, and other elite colleges for the summer project of 1964, led by Bob Moses. When Al realized he could not control the politics of the project and could not control Bob, he turned against the movement and tried to destroy it. He told me that Bob, whom I admired without reservation, was a "communist" and "an agent of China." I was furious at Al for this and didn't speak to him for more than a year. We had reconciled by the time he tried to win the Democratic nomination for Congress in Manhattan in 1966. He lost by a narrow margin.

When you were friends with Al, you were also friends with fifty other people. Al always traveled with an entourage of political protégés, a talented group that included Barney Frank, who became a congressman;

Greg Craig, who became Bill Clinton's impeachment lawyer and the lawyer for Élian Gonzalez; Harold Ickes, who became a top adviser to both Bill and Hillary Clinton; and a young man named Dennis Sweeny. Al also had a group of older mentors, such as Norman Thomas; Frank Graham, the southern liberal who had been president of the University of North Carolina; and, until her death, Eleanor Roosevelt. He did not seem to have any close friends his own age. (He was thirty-five in 1965.) They were either twenty-two-year-old groupies or seventy-two-year-old icons. He was devoted to the icons and expected his groupies to remain devoted protégés.

My closest friend during this period was Paul Cowan, whom I met through Lowenstein in early 1965. Al wanted Paul and me to meet, and arranged that we would all go see a movie together one night—the still-wonderful and underrated *Nothing but a Man* that featured Abbey Lincoln, the jazz singer and actress. We were to meet in front of the theater a half hour before the movie started. But Al never showed up. I saw the movie with Paul and his wife-to-be, Rachael, and we went out for coffee afterward. It was a typical Lowenstein experience—he was a catalyst, but also a little eccentric.

That evening I learned that Paul had been a full-time volunteer in Mississippi during the summer of 1964 and, like me, deeply admired Bob Moses. I had just published a long profile of Bob in the *Voice*, and Paul had read it. We talked for a couple of hours about Moses and Lowenstein, their falling out, and the future of the civil rights movement.

As we became friends, Paul and I used to speculate freely about Al's mysteriousness. Where did he get the money that permitted him to travel all over the world when had neither a job nor a steady source of income? Was he allied with the CIA? Was he gay or bisexual?

Al always traveled with young men, always very WASP-y, very handsome, and usually monied. These protégés often became disenchanted with Al and drifted away from him. There was always something impersonal about Al's friendships; there was very little intimacy in our conversations. Whenever I saw Al, he was with ten other people whom I didn't know or knew only slightly. His agenda was always the topic of the conversation. He was the only common denominator at the table.

After Al's death his sexual identity was debated in several books and magazine articles. He liked to sleep in the same bed with young men and engage in hugging, cuddling, and fondling. His closest friends still wonder whether he ever had any full sexual experiences with men and whether it is accurate to call him bisexual, since he married and had two wonderful children before getting divorced. Still, it became clear that Al was repressed, confused, and tormented. He had needs that he did not understand and was afraid to act on. He was terrified of exposure during a homophobic time. That he accomplished everything that he did while wrestling with these demons helps me understand him better and admire him even more for what he achieved.

There he was in 1967 watched by FBI agents, traveling from campus to campus, scared that LBJ or Hoover might be able to kill the cause he fought for if they found out about his secret life.

Talented young people joined the Dump Johnson movement early, including Greg Craig from Harvard, Steven Cohen from Amherst, Clint Deveaux from the State University of New York (SUNY), and Curtis Gans from the Americans for Democratic Action (ADA). By September of 1967 Lowenstein had gotten two hundred college student body presidents to sign a letter to Dean Rusk opposing the war. This followed a meeting between Rusk and a group of student leaders, during which Rusk expressed no concern over the prospect that escalation could lead to nuclear war. Rusk just said, "Well, somebody's going to get hurt," nothing more.

Lowenstein rallied students with his combination of energy and moderation. He was able to get everyone involved—not just campus activists but fraternity leaders, conservative students, athletes, professors, and business majors. He was a rumpled Che Guevara of the center, rallying moderates who had no use for SDS and the New Left. His argument was: Use the democratic process. Don't blame society. Don't destroy all the institutions. The cause of this war's escalation is Lyndon Johnson, so let's defeat him by through democratic means.

I was simultaneously covering the growing political resistance to the president; working on a book about Robert Kennedy; hanging out with Lowenstein; and an activist in the Dump LBJ movement. I could balance these rather obvious conflicts of interest only because I was working for a paper like the *Voice*, which specialized in personal advocacy reporting and made no pretense of objectivity. It defined itself as a corrective to the mainstream media and a forum for personal experiences, honestly described.

I had gone to Dan Wolf, the editor of the *Voice*, and asked what I should do. Dan said I should just keep him, and the readers, informed with full disclosure and get as many stories as possible from being on the inside with Kennedy and Lowenstein. Paul Cowan, whom I'd helped get a job at the *Voice*, and I also shared our tangled thoughts about Lowenstein with Wolf.*

I don't know if Dan ever met Lowenstein. I would doubt it. The one time I brought Kennedy to the *Voice* to meet him, Dan hid in his office and ducked the meeting. He was a passive observer who avoided direct experiences.

In the fall of 1967, Lowenstein seemed to call me every day from a different campus or airport. "All the information operators in Boston, Manhattan, Berkeley, Madison, Palo Alto, Raleigh, and New Haven know me by name," he bragged.

"Being friends with you is like spending eternity on a hold button," I replied.

Al wanted me to know about every step of progress, every good omen, every breakthrough, so I could pass the news along to Kennedy. The umbrella group of liberal Democrats in California—called the California Democratic Council—voted to give Al $1,000 for travel expenses and promised to support the movement. Donald Peterson, an important Democratic Party official in Wisconsin, signed up for the duration. Actor Robert Vaughn pledged support and donated some money. A state legislator in Minnesota enlisted in the cause. Above all, the audience response was positive at every stop he spoke.

Whenever I saw Kennedy, I gave him news of Al's progress. Kennedy absorbed it all but wanted bigger fish to join—the leader of a state leg-

---

*Paul eventually included a chapter on Lowenstein in his book, *The Making of an Un-American*, published in 1969. His portrait of Al was harsh, penetrating, accurate, and balanced with the good he did. Although long out of print, this was one of the best books on the 1960s. The only thing I didn't like about it was the title. Paul was about as American as you could get. His writing had the loving, common-man quality of James Agee, Robert Coles, and Studs Terkel. It was hard for him to criticize Lowenstein, but he felt the writer's commitment to the truth required it.

islature like Jesse Unruh in California, a congressman like Mo Udall, a senator like Harold Hughes or McGovern. But even this early in the game, I could sense that Kennedy wanted to run. Most of his advisers thought the idea preposterous, and even most elders of the liberal establishment thought it a romantic fantasy that would end up helping to elect Richard Nixon. "The people are ahead of the politicians," Al kept telling me in these late night phone calls. "Something is happening in America. *I can feel it.*"

Years later David Halberstam told me that Al's great contribution in 1967 and 1968 was in making people feel they were not alone. "The radical students thought they were the only ones who hated the war. Then Al mobilized the moderate students to join them. Then he told the middle-class housewives in the suburbs about the students. Then he brought in some clergy. Then the liberals in the professions. And suddenly nobody felt alone any more. They all became part of a movement Al created."

It is one of those ironies of life that while he was making others feel less alone, Al himself was feeling most alone. His constant traveling, his bewilderment about his own sexual identity, and his many estrangements from former disciples took their toll. But he kept going, convinced he was bending history his way.

On Saturday, September 23, 1967, Kennedy invited Lowenstein and me to drop by his home in McLean, Virginia, to talk about the Dump Johnson movement and what he should do. When Lowenstein and I arrived—at about 10:30 P.M.—we were greeted by a relaxed Bob, dressed in bright-green slacks and a green sweater. To our surprise, Arthur Schlesinger was also there, as was James Loeb, JFK's ambassador to Peru and the publisher of an upstate New York newspaper.

What ensued was a friendly debate. Lowenstein and I argued that Kennedy should challenge Johnson, and Schlesinger and Loeb argued that running against Johnson was hopeless and that Kennedy should wait till 1972. Kennedy listened good-naturedly to this discussion about his own fate, as if we were lawyers and he was the judge.

Al had kicked off his shoes and was sitting cross-legged on a an easy chair, college bull-session style. He carried about 75 percent of the case for our side. He made the immorality of the war the fulcrum of his position, not the small tactics of primary politics, but did suggest that LBJ might not run, or might pull out, if the insurgents won an early primary in New Hampshire—or, more likely, Wisconsin, a liberal, anti-war state.

At that point Kennedy spoke up for the first time. "I think Al may be right," he said. "I think Johnson might quit the night before the convention opens. I think he is a coward."

Schlesinger suggested drafting a peace plank to the platform and making that the rallying point for antiwar activists. I reminded him that there had been a strong peace plank in the 1964 Democratic Party platform, but Johnson had ignored it and kept escalating the war.

Kennedy intervened again. "How do you run on a plank, Arthur? When was the last time a million people rallied behind a plank? If I was Lyndon, I would be much angrier at Jack and Al than at you, Arthur."

At one point, Ambassador Loeb, who seemed pro-LBJ to me and not opposed to the war, asked, "Do you think his [LBJ's] people will ask him not to run if he loses some early primaries?"

Kennedy said jovially, "I'd like to see the first person who goes in there alone and says 'Please, Mr. President, don't run.' " Schlesinger stressed that no one was going to run against Johnson. Lowenstein and I argued that the war was becoming so unpopular that someone would inevitably be tempted into jumping into the race, out of either moral conviction or opportunism.

After about an hour and a half of amiable dispute, Kennedy spoke. In a deliberate, serious voice, he said, "I would have a problem if I ran first against Johnson. People would say I was splitting the party out of ambition and envy. No one would believe I was doing it because of how I felt about Vietnam and poor people. I think Al is doing the right thing, but I think that someone else will have to be the first one to run. It can't be me because of my relationship with Johnson. And his feeling toward me has more to do with my brother than me."

On this last point, the opposite was equally true. Kennedy's feelings toward Johnson also had a lot to do with his brother.

The evening was tremendous encouragement to Lowenstein and me. Kennedy was telling us that he would run if another candidate got in first and made the conflict about the war, not personalities, and unmasked the president's political weakness in a primary or two. In reading the mood of the country, Kennedy was far ahead of his best advisers.

In his generous account of this meeting in his own book, Schlesinger wrote, "Lowenstein and Newfield told Kennedy he must run. Older, cautious, and wrong, Loeb and I argued that Kennedy was too precious a commodity to be expended in a doomed effort."

On November 3, 1967, six weeks after our little tag-team debate, Schlesinger sent Kennedy a private memorandum, changing his position and suggesting he run: "I think you could beat LBJ in the primaries."

On October 11, 1967, I drove to Philadelphia with Lowenstein and Harold Ickes to be the guests on Jack McKinney's late-night radio call-in show. I had arranged the appearance with McKinney, who was part of my boxing–Irish nationalism–Hamill–Breslin network. Jack had been one of Sonny Liston's close friends and sometime sparring partner.

For the first half of the show, Jack let the three of us filibuster our case against both the war and Johnson. Then the phone calls started coming in. Caller after caller said the same thing: I agree with you guys about the war and Johnson, but unless you have a candidate to run against Johnson in the primaries, you're wasting your time. *Who is your candidate?*

Toward the end of the program I noticed Lowenstein, while answering a question, was sketching an intricate doodle. He was creating a newspaper headline that read: McCarthy Wins Wisc. Primary; Beats LBJ with 60 percent of Vote.

As Ickes drove us back to Manhattan at 3 A.M. on the misty New Jersey Turnpike—at 90 miles an hour—Al told us in confidence that he had met with McCarthy and that the Minnesota senator was willing, even eager, to run. He wanted to show up Kennedy as a coward and embarrass Vice President Humphrey, his old Minnesota friendly rival.

When I told Kennedy that McCarthy was going to run, he replied, "I don't believe it. He is not that sort of fellow. And if he does run, it will be to increase his lecture fees." Kennedy's brother-in-law Stephen Smith added, "There are only two things you need to know to understand McCarthy. His mother was German, and he quit the seminary." While neither liked McCarthy, they also understood that his running could create the opening for Robert to run later on, just as Kennedy suggested would be necessary.

About a week after the radio show, a group of us announced the formation of a citizens' Dump Johnson organization in New York. Before we announced this at a press conference, I went with Ronnie Eldridge, a West Side district leader close to Kennedy, and a few other local insurgents to see Frank Rossetti, the old-style political boss of Tammany Hall, to tell him what we were going to do. Kennedy had advised us to this. Rossetti would eventually support him, he felt, because he would have to back the senator from New York.

Rossetti was rough and uneducated, a former boxing manager out of East Harlem. He had also been the driver for Carmine DeSapio, the Tammany Hall boss who later went to prison. In the mob, being the driver is the second most trusted job in the party organization. Rossetti promised us that he would not attack or criticize the formation of our anti-LBJ group if reporters called him for comment.

But when our group was unveiled, Rossetti was quoted in a newspaper as saying we were "immature." I called him up and complained, "I thought you old-line political bosses at least kept your word, if nothing else."

"I'm sorry," he explained. "I meant to say your group was *premature.* But the wrong word popped out. I didn't mean to say 'immature.' Tell Bobby I'm sorry."

By Christmas of 1967, McCarthy had announced his candidacy. Richard Goodwin and Lowenstein were organizing his campaign. Pressure was mounting on Kennedy to do something or at least decide something. Among the minority urging him to run were his wife and sisters, Jean Kennedy Smith and Patricia Lawford; his staff members Mankewicz, Walinsky, Edelman, and Joe Dolan; writers like Pete Hamill; and from inside the McCarthy campaign, Al Lowenstein.

I decided to write an essay for the *Voice* that, as we used to say, let all my feelings hang out. The war was getting worse. I had studied McCarthy's voting record, and it was so conservative on domestic matters of race, labor, and poverty that I could not honestly tell people he would make a fine president.

> If Kennedy does not run in 1968, the best side of his character will die. He will kill it every time he butchers his conscience and makes a speech for Johnson next autumn. It will die every time a kid asks him, if he is so much against the Vietnam War, how come he is putting party above principle?
>
> It will die every time a stranger quotes his own words back to him on the value of courage as a human quality.
>
> Kennedy's best quality is his ability to be himself, to be authentic in the existential sense. This is the quality the young identify with so instinctively in Kennedy. And it is this quality Kennedy will lose if he doesn't make his stand now against Johnson. He will become a robot mouthing dishonest rhetoric like all the other politicians.

This was rough stuff. Kennedy had a right to be angry with me for putting it in print, particularly since it was the sort of thing I could have told him in private.

Instead, when I saw him about a week after this essay was published, he said, "My wife cut out your attack on me. She shows it to everybody." I asked Kennedy to tell me what he felt when he read it.

"I understand it," he began. "It was discerning. On some days I even agree with it. I just have to decide now whether my running can accomplish anything. I don't want to run only as a gesture. I don't want it to drive Johnson into doing something really crazy. I don't want it to hurt the doves in the Senate who are up for reelection [in 1968]. I don't want it to be interpreted in the press as just part of a personal vendetta or feud with Johnson. It's all so complicated. I just don't know what to do."

What happened next is recorded history. The Viet Cong's Tet offensive, which began on February 1, 1968, shattered American illusions, proving the war was not being won. McCarthy did well in the New Hampshire primary on March 12. And Robert Kennedy announced he was running for president on March 16, in the same Senate room where his brother had announced his candidacy in 1960. Fifteen days later, Johnson quit the race, just as Kennedy—and Al and I—anticipated.

The day Kennedy announced, I later discovered, was the same day of the My Lai massacre of women and children by Lieutenant William Calley's troops. I've always dreamed about writing a play about that one day in history, with the two parallel events unfolding one in Washington and the other in Vietnam, on a split stage.

For most of the eighty-one days of that campaign I traveled with Kennedy, his staff, and a press corps, all of us bonded by hope and idealism. None of us will ever forget it, because none of us has ever seen anything like it since. Robert Kennedy touched something in the American soul. The raw intensity of those eighty-one days was scary, partly because he had no Secret Service protection to keep the crowds away from him. The emotions that his name and his message ignited were so volcanic that from the beginning some, especially Pete Hamill, feared that something violent was going to happen. American society could not absorb such frenzy. Something had to explode.

Now, after decades of dull, low-turnout elections, I can see just how historic and singular that spring of hope was. In the intervening years I have covered many campaigns—from Nelson Rockefeller's to the two Clintons—but none has matched that intensity. Mario Cuomo connected with liberals and Italian American immigrants because of the poetry of his oratory and his background. Jesse Jackson connected with the young and poor blacks.

But Kennedy had it all—a bond with blacks, Hispanics, Native Americans, working-class whites, students, Catholics, Irish, women, and veterans. He evoked a universality rooted in both hope and memory.

When he announced, I wrote a piece in the *Voice* endorsing him and went on several radio and TV shows to argue his case. Mine was not a popular position with *Voice* readers or among liberal intellectuals, most of whom were for McCarthy. They saw Kennedy's belated entry as proof of his ruthlessness. Young people stopped me on the street and insulted me for backing Kennedy. I got hate calls at home from strangers. My hero, Murray Kempton, told me he could never forgive my craven judgment. My friend Nat Hentoff thought I had ruined my career. I was a distinct minority in the inbred world of Manhattan liberals.

I did have some comforting company—Hamill, Breslin, Norman Mailer, and Mike Harrington, for example. I tried to salve my wounds by noting that most of those writers who were backing Kennedy had working-class origins.

But that did not really ease the humiliation of getting spit at by McCarthy admirers who shouted "Sell-out" at me in Washington Square Park. "How much are they paying you to write that shit?" Or of getting approached by a stranger in a restaurant who announced, "I've been waiting fifteen years for your boy to finally come out against McCarthy. Now he's done it. But it's the wrong McCarthy!"

Still, I never doubted that I was right in choosing Kennedy over McCarthy. I knew he would make a good president, perhaps even a great one. I believed he could change history. And felt McCarthy was essentially a one-issue candidate with no special feeling of kinship with minorities or the white working class. Eventually hatred of Kennedy—and of me—subsided. He kept winning the black vote across the country by huge percentages. It became clear that he could win the nomination and that McCarthy could not.

The first speech of the campaign took place on Monday, March 18, in the basketball fieldhouse at Kansas State University, located in Manhattan, Kansas, a place as close to middle America as you can get. I did not see a single black face among the fourteen thousand corn-bred, farm-raised, wholesome-looking college kids who packed the building. At first the crowd was friendly but reserved. Kennedy started out with his usual tentativeness, stammering a few times. His right leg shook behind the lectern. Toward the end of his fifty-minute speech, which was all about Vietnam, his voice grew more emotional, his nervousness subsided, and he started coming out of his shell.

"I am willing to bear my share of responsibility," he said, "before history and my fellow citizens. But past error is no excuse for its own perpetuation. Tragedy is a tool for the living to gain wisdom, not a guide by which to live. Now, as ever, we do ourselves best justice when we measure ourselves against ancient test, as in the *Antigone* of Sophocles: 'All men make mistakes, but a good man yields when he knows his course is wrong, and repairs the evil. The only sin is pride.' "

His hair was flopping over his forehead. He jabbed the air with his clenched fist, a gesture that hauntingly suggested his brother. I could see

Adam Walinsky, who wrote the speech, crouched under the platform, invisible to the crowd, mouthing the words as Kennedy said them.

> So I come here today, to this great university, to ask your help; not for me, but for your country, and for the people of Vietnam . . . I urge you to learn the harsh facts that lurk behind the mask of official illusion with which we have concealed our true circumstances, even from ourselves . . .
>
> There is a contest on, not for the rule of America, but for the heart of America. In these next eight months we are going to decide what this country will stand for—and what kind of men we are. So I ask for your help, in the cities and homes of this state, in the towns and farms . . . so that we might have a new light to guide us. And I pledge to you, if you will give me your help, if you will give me your hand, I will work for you and we will have a new America.

Suddenly this crowd of students, students who had never protested and never rioted, made a noise that sounded like Niagara Falls, like a thousand amplifiers exploding from too much pressure. Stanley Tretick, the photographer from *Look* magazine, who was a special favorite of Kennedy's, looked at the hysteria and enthusiasm and shouted in my ear, "This is Kansas, fucking Kansas! He's going all the fucking way!"

As Kennedy brushed the hair out of his eyes and waved to the crowd, hundreds of students came rushing toward the platform, creating a haze of dust from the dirt floor. They surrounded him, screamed his name, tried to pull his cuff links off, scratched his hands. One girl held up a copy of John Kennedy's book *Profiles in Courage*. Kennedy saw his dead brother's face on the cover of the paperback and froze. Then he signed the book and squeezed the girl's hand, holding it an extra moment.

Flying back to Washington that night, Jimmy Breslin asked Kennedy if he could see the faces from the platform while he spoke. "I saw every face in the building," Kennedy answered.

This was how it went in most places during the first two weeks of the campaign. One exception was the University of Alabama, where Kennedy was greeted with only polite applause. In 1963, as attorney general,

Kennedy had ordered racial integration in Alabama over George Wallace's schoolhouse-door defiance. After his speech Kennedy took questions. One student asked if he would accept "second place on a ticket with Lyndon Johnson." "You don't understand," he quipped. "I said I was for a coalition government in Saigon, not here." The kids cheered his wit.

On Saturday, March 23, the campaign plane took off for California, where the reception was so enthusiastic that for the first time it began to made me think he would actually win the nomination. When we got to Sacramento, a crowd of about fifteen thousand people—mostly white and middle class—cheered his attacks on the war in a shopping center mall in the middle of a hot afternoon. In San Jose, a big crowd of mostly Mexican Americans went wild with joy and mobbed him when the speech was over. I went back with a television crew that had lost some sound equipment in the crush. All we found were five shoes, none of which matched.

"Our brave young men are dying in the swamps of Southeast Asia," Kennedy said, using Pete Hamill's stirring language. "Which of them might have written a poem? Which of them might have cured cancer? Which of them might have played in a World Series, or given us the gift of laughter from the stage, or helped build a bridge or a university? Which of them could have taught a child to read? It is our responsibility to let these men live . . . It is indecent if they die because of the empty vanity of their country."

The next day there was a rally in Monterey, which was supposed to be a Republican enclave of the affluent. Five thousand people were at the airport to greet him. A highway patrolman told me, "The road from here to Salinas is one big parking lot. Five thousand more are still trying to get here. I've never seen anything like it."

Then Los Angeles. The motorcade left the airport without police escort, so hundreds of cars, and some motorcycles, just fell in and joined it. For a while I rode in Kennedy's open car and was able to see the faces of people at the curbside as they reached out to touch him. The faces were so joyful they made Kennedy exuberant, almost giddy. At one point a long-haired hippie ran alongside the car and handed him his draft card to sign, which Kennedy did, laughing. A woman in a bathrobe and her hair in curlers ran out of her house, almost hyperventilating, hugged Kennedy, and begged for his autograph. When we got to the Mexican American section in East Los Angeles, it was complete bedlam. Music, sombreros, dancing, kissing, hugging. This went way beyond politics. It was spiritual salvation.

About a week later Kennedy invited Jimmy Breslin and me to join him on a one-day trip to some Indian reservations in New Mexico and Arizona. Those states did not have primaries, but Kennedy wanted to be with Native Americans for whom he felt such deep affection and for whose cause he crusaded in the Senate. At each reservation, Kennedy spoke about jobs, education, alcoholism, and the suicide rate among Indians, which was triple that of any other racial or ethnic group of Americans. He told them he knew it was a sign of depression caused by poverty, hopelessness, and abandonment by Washington.

On the helicopter flight back to Los Angeles, Kennedy asked Breslin if he had learned anything from this day. "Yeah," Jimmy replied. "The way you talked the only reason that Jim Thorpe won the Olympic gold medals is that the rope broke." Kennedy seemed taken aback by Jimmy's gruff cynicism, not sure if it was intended as a putdown or an example of black Irish wit.

"Jimmy," he said, "I used to think that growing up poor was good for your character. But then I got to know you, and now I'm not so sure anymore."

"Fuck you, Senator," Breslin replied, still offering no clue whether he was serious. Jimmy always had bad taste in what he said and superb taste in what he wrote.

During the time I knew him, Kennedy was going through staggering growth and equally staggering change. One major cause was the assassination of Martin Luther King on April 4, 1968. King's murder came five days after Lyndon Johnson had withdrawn from the election and announced that he was starting peace talks to end the war. This made the war less of a campaign issue and LBJ less of a political target. Kennedy needed another crusade, and in the days following King's murder and the worst rioting America had experienced in years, his focus shifted from Vietnam to race and poverty. While this shift may have started as a tactical necessity, it was swiftly internalized.

The night of King's funeral, Kennedy held a profane and therapeutic meeting with King's closest disciples. Some who were there, such as the Reverend James Bevel, vented their grief by cursing at Kennedy, questioning his commitment, demanding he provide details about what he proposed to do. Kennedy absorbed their anger and was moved by it. Later he told me that the meeting was "helpful to me . . . they had to get it out of their system."

Kennedy also walked behind King's casket during the funeral procession and was deeply affected by what people said to him along the route through the hot Atlanta streets, by seeing firsthand what a void King's death had left in the hearts of the poor.

King's death changed the way Kennedy thought about himself. He felt he now had an obligation to pick up King's fallen standard, of trying to unify blacks and low-income whites. It was a role he knew he was the only person who might be able to fill it. In many ways, it was ironic that King's murder should have such an impact on him. He had never been close to King and, from what I heard him say, did not particularly like him. Kennedy had never had a working relationship with King, the way he had with Harry Belafonte, John Lewis, Charles Evers, and Cesar Chavez. And I don't think Kennedy ever got over that revolting tape transcript that J. Edgar Hoover had given him in 1964. "King is not as pure or high-minded as you think he is," Kennedy once said to me.

Kennedy knew that LBJ would leak the fact that as attorney general, Kennedy had signed a wiretap order on King's home. This was one of the most indefensible things Kennedy ever did. Johnson finally did leak the story to columnist Drew Pearson in late May of 1968, just before the Oregon primary. But Pearson's column confused "bugging" with "wiretapping," and Kennedy's defenders were able to muddy the issue.

Despite this tangled relationship with King, Kennedy managed to give his now-famous speech in the Indianapolis ghetto the night of King's murder. Rejecting the warning from the local police not to attend the rally, he not only showed up, he broke the news that King had been shot and died in the past hour to a crowd of about five thousand who had been waiting for him to arrive from the airport. The crowd gasped and fell silent when Kennedy, standing on a flatbed truck, bathed in television lights, told them what had happened.

Kennedy's remarks have been quoted many times, so I will not quote them again here at any length. What was most extraordinary is that he spoke without notes. He had the capacity to improvise wisdom and poetry in this moment of national crisis.

King had been assassinated in a broad daylight, killed by a bullet to the brain from a rifle. Of course it made Kennedy think about his brother.

And indeed, Kennedy's remarks contain the only public reference I'm aware of that he ever made to Lee Harvey Oswald, although it was curiously impersonal and indirect, reminiscent of his referring to Carlos Marcello as "that guy in New Orleans."

"I had a member of my family killed, and he was killed by a white man," Kennedy told the shocked crowd. He ended his remarks, in the chilly darkness that night, this way:

> As the writer Aeschylus wrote, "Even in our sleep, pain which can't forget, falls drop by drop upon the heart, until in our own despair, against our will, comes wisdom, through the awful grace of God."
>
> So let's dedicate ourselves to what the Greeks wrote so many years ago. Contain the savageness of man and make gentler the life of the world. Let us dedicate ourselves to that. And say a prayer for our country and our people.

Thirty years later I spoke to Georgia congressman John Lewis, who had organized that campaign rally in Indianapolis, while working as a volunteer. I asked what he felt that night. "I never saw anyone speak from the depths of his soul like Bob did that night. I was devastated because I loved Dr. King so much. But as we left the rally site for the hotel, I was thinking to myself, at least we still have Senator Kennedy."

And yet, as enormous as the impact of King's death was on Kennedy, this final change did not come in one blinding religious revelation. It came bit by bit, day by day, as he traveled among blacks and low-income whites in Indiana, Nebraska, and California during the last eight weeks of his life. As with most of Kennedy's growth spurts, it was mostly experiential—from touching, seeing, feeling, listening. In his last weeks, he came to understand that his ambition and career were no longer the private property of the Kennedy family. They belonged to those who were giving, investing him with their hopes and their votes. Robert Kennedy and the poor passionately discovered each other, for one moment in time.

I spent the last two weeks of the Indiana primary—Kennedy's first test with the voters—traveling with him. On April 26 he spoke to a hostile crowd of careerist medical students at the Indiana University Medical Center. At the end of his prepared remarks, a black custodian shouted out from the balcony, "We want Kennedy." Dozens of white medical students started chanting "No we don't" from the front rows.

One student asked Kennedy, "How can you say health services are inferior in the slums when everyone knows Negroes don't make use of the facilities that already exist?" Then another jumped up to ask, "Where are we going to get the money to pay for all these new programs you're proposing?" "From you," Kennedy shot back.

Then, setting aside all polite political conventions, as almost no politicians do these days, and addressing his antagonistic audience honestly and directly, Kennedy said:

> Let me say something about the tone of these questions. I look around this room and I don't see many black faces who will become doctors. Part of civilized society is to let people go to medical school who come from the ghettos. I don't see many people coming here from the slums, or off the Indian reservations. You are the privileged ones here.
>
> It's easy for you to sit back and say it's the fault of the federal government. But it's our responsibility, too . . . It's the poor who carry the major burden of the struggle in Vietnam. You sit here as white medical students, while black people carry the burden of the fighting in Vietnam.

Some of the students began to hiss and boo. Kennedy glared back at them with total contempt in his cold blue eyes.

May 6 was the day before the Indiana primary. The official schedule called for the campaign to leave the Evansville airport at 10:55 A.M. and to end the day with a hotel reception in Indianapolis at 1 A.M. on May 7.

The scene I will never forget from that long day was the motorcade through the streets of Gary, Whiting, and East Chicago. As attorney general, Kennedy had sent the mayor of Gary and several of his cronies to prison on corruption charges, and now this faction was working hard to defeat Kennedy. The Kennedy family's political apparatus had helped elect thirty-four-year-old Richard Hatcher as the first black mayor of a city roiled by bitter racial polarization.

Right before the motorcade reached Gary, two men climbed into Kennedy's open car. One was Hatcher. The other was Tony Zale, who had come out of Gary's steel mills in the 1940s to twice win the middleweight boxing championship. Zale was a hero to the city's Slavic and East European population that had been the core of the anti-Hatcher resistance. The three of them, Kennedy, Hatcher, and Zale, standing and waving from the open car, went through the Polish neighborhoods, and the Italian neighborhoods, and the black neighborhoods. They received a positive reception in the white ethnic areas, a tumultuous reception in the black areas. There the crowds were five deep on the street. I remember ragtag, ad-hoc bands playing on street corners and rooftops as we passed by.

That image of the open-car motorcade with Kennedy, a militant black mayor, and a Polish boxing hero has endured in my memory as a symbol of inclusion and equality, of what people can accomplish with goodwill. It is like the baseball I have, the one signed by all the 1949 Brooklyn Dodgers.

For a portion of the motorcade Kennedy invited me to ride on the trunk of his car with the photographers. He wanted me to see the expressions on the faces he was seeing. He wanted me to hear what the teenagers were shouting as they ran alongside his car, for block after block, and what the older black women were whispering in his ear as they ran out of their homes and bars and beauty parlors to greet him.

Sitting on the trunk of the car, I got a chance to ask Zale about his famous 1946 fight with Rocky Graziano at Yankee Stadium. Graziano had gone down in the first round, Zale had gone down in the second round, and Zale finally won by a knockout in the sixth, although he was losing on points at the time. "How did you manage to get up in that second round?" I asked Zale. "I was thinking I would rather get hit some more by Rocky than lose and have to go back to work in a steel mill again," he replied.

At the end of this exhilarating and exhausting day, Kennedy invited a group of us to join him for a 1:30 A.M. dinner at the only restaurant in Indianapolis open then, a place called Sam's Attic. The group included David Halberstam, who was also writing a book on RFK; John Douglas, who had worked under Kennedy in the Justice Department; Loudon Wainright of *Life* magazine; and photographers Stanley Tretick and Bert Glynn. Kennedy looked the way Zale must have looked after the Graziano fight. His hands were cut and swollen and sore from all the people he had touched, some of whom tried had to drag him out of the car. Fatigue slowed his speech and blotched his skin. His eyes were hollow and pushed back into their sockets. But he was also feeling relief that the Indiana campaign was over. When Halberstam and I prodded him to tell us what he felt about the state, he became reflective.

"I like Indiana," he began. "The people here were fair to me. They listened to me. I could see this face, way back in the crowd, and he was listening to me, really listening to me." He continued, "The people here are not so neurotic and hypocritical as in Washington and New York. They're more direct. I like rural people, who work hard with their hands. There is something healthy about them. I gave it everything I had here, and if I lose, then, well, I'm just out of tune with the rest of the country . . . I loved the faces here in Indiana, on the farmers, on the steelworkers, on the black kids . . ."

He stopped for a moment, and it looked like he was falling asleep, right at the table in the restaurant. Then he came out of his reverie and suddenly said, "Do you know that when black children drew a picture of a house, they almost never drew in the sun? I saw that once in a study of drawings made by white and black schoolchildren."

On election day Kennedy called my room and invited Breslin and me to join him in his private suite at 6 P.M. to await the results. I knocked on the door at the appointed hour, and the writer Theodore H. White opened it a crack. Every four years White wrote an insider book called

The Making of the President. His first one, about JFK's 1960 campaign, had been a best-seller. He felt exclusive access was his entitlement. "No press allowed," he declared through the crack, and then tried to slam the door on me. "Fuck you!" I screamed, charging at the door with my shoulder and almost knocking White over. Kennedy, coming out of the shower and wearing only a towel, started laughing at the generational conflict over access to him. Later he whispered to me, "Do or die, Bed-Stuy, that's you, Jack."

At about 7:15 P.M. Peter Edelman called from Washington, D.C., to say Kennedy would win by a two-to-one margin over Humphrey. Then Larry O'Brien emerged from the bedroom with the first raw numbers from some weathervane Indiana precincts. In one poor Polish precinct in South Bend, Kennedy got 241 votes, McCarthy got 86, and Indiana Government Branigan, the stand-in for Hubert Humphrey, 62. An all-black precinct in Gary reported 697 for Kennedy, 52 for McCarthy, 16 for Governor Branigan. When those numbers were announced, Ethel Kennedy blurted out, "Don't you just wish that everyone was black?"

In the end 42 percent of the vote went for Kennedy, to 31 percent for Branigan and, 27 percent for McCarthy. Kennedy had carried an astonishing 85 percent of the black vote in a three-way race. He also won the seven white backlash counties that George Wallace had won in 1964.

After his victory speech Kennedy asked me to tag along with a group that was going out for dinner—at the airport restaurant. As we walked through the almost-empty airport lobby, Kennedy noticed two college volunteers wearing McCarthy buttons and straw campaign hats. They were sitting on their luggage, looking both dejected and yet somehow defiant when they saw Kennedy. One of them, a young woman named Pat Sylvester, was from the University of Massachusetts. The other, a young man was named Taylor Branch, was from the University of North Carolina. Branch would later win the Pulitzer Prize for his magisterial biography of Martin Luther King.

"You had such cruddy canvassers, and you still won," Pat said.

Kennedy clearly admired her fire and determination. "How does everybody feel about tonight?" he asked.

"We're going to stay with McCarthy," she replied firmly.

"I don't know what happened," Branch said. "I canvassed black neighborhoods, and they wouldn't listen to me for five seconds."

"That wasn't your fault," Kennedy said. "Why wasn't McCarthy effective for you in those areas?"

"But you're a Kennedy," the girl shot back. "It sounds like a newspaper rehash, but it's still right. You have the name."

"Look, I agree that I have a tremendous advantage because of my last name," Kennedy responded. "But let me ask you, why can't McCarthy go into the ghetto? Can you tell me he's been involved in those areas? Why did he vote against the minimum wage for farm workers? Why did he vote to exclude a large proportion of people from the Minimum Wage Act?" Kennedy said all this quietly, puffing on a small cigar.

The conversation ended with the two students reaffirming their support for McCarthy. Kennedy told them, "You're dedicated to what you believe, and I think that's terrific." Then he told them he would drive them back to the city and find them a hotel room, so they would not have to sit up all night at the airport, waiting for their early-morning flight.

The next morning there was a victory breakfast of champagne and scrambled eggs on the plane back to New York City. Kennedy sat down next to me and started to complain about the *New York Times*'s interpretation of his Indiana victory. Tom Wicker had written a news analysis piece that said the real significance of the election was that "McCarthy, the man who first challenged President Johnson, had done the most to advance his own cause." "He finished last!" Kennedy exclaimed after reading me this sentence. A *Times* editorial, titled "Kennedy's Inconclusive Victory," was mostly an attack on what they called Kennedy's "conservative" campaign in Indiana. I certainly did not think it was "conservative" for Kennedy to talk about law enforcement, to condemn rioting, or to advocate decentralized government.

"Let me tell you something about the *Times*," Kennedy said in exasperation. "When I was announced as President Kennedy's campaign manager in 1960, the *Times* said I was too immature and inexperienced to do the job. When I was appointed attorney general, they said I was too young and inexperienced, even though I had done a nice job as campaign manager. When I ran for the senate in New York against Keating, the *Times* endorsed Keating, but said I had done a fine job as attorney general. Now I'm running for president, and they criticize me on the editorial page, and in the analysis pieces, although they still mention I'm a good senator. They always admit I was effective in every job I've ever had, but that never affects their judgment, and each time they say I'm not qualified for the next job."

The primary season came down to California on June 4. McCarthy had won the Oregon primary the week before and had the momentum. Nonetheless, Kennedy was drawing phenomenal crowds, and the polls had the election about even. He saw Hubert Humphrey as his real competition for the nomination, and Humphrey was nailing down large delegate commitments in states without primaries, while Kennedy and McCarthy were facing the voters. Kennedy believed he had to win the California primary, then needed some immediate and important defections from the McCarthy camp before the New York primary on June 18.

A majority of the Hollywood A-list of liberal movie stars were for McCarthy, led by the widely respected Paul Newman, and including Barbra Streisand. Kennedy's California A-list supporters were limited to Lauren Bacall, Warren Beatty, and his sister, Shirley MacLaine.

One of the people on RFK's list of calls to make as soon as the California results were known was Al Lowenstein. Al was still offically supporting McCarthy but was telling friends privately that he wanted to switch to Kennedy. But Al was also going to run for Congress on Long Island, where McCarthy had pockets of support, so a switch was tricky.

I had a close friend and an acquaintance who were working in the McCarthy campaign as speechwriters—Paul Gorman and Jeremy Larner. Throughout the primary season we needled each other when our paths crossed. They would shout "ruthless and opportunist" to me, in reference to the negative qualities critics saw in Kennedy. And I would shout "vain and lazy" to them in airports and TV studios. Those were, I thought, McCarthy's most irritating personal qualities.

By the time of the California primary our debate had become unequal. Both Gorman and Larner had become disillusioned with their candidate. Larner later wrote a fine memoir of his disenchantment called *Nobody Knows.* And Gorman told me how disturbed he was by McCarthy's refusal to campaign among blacks and Mexican Americans and by a remark McCarthy had made in white suburban Oregon. McCarthy has told an audience in Corvalis—a college town—that Kennedy was running best, "among the less intelligent and less educated people in America. I don't mean to fault them for voting for him, but I think that you ought to bear that in mind as you go to the polls here on Tuesday."

Gorman and Larner immediately protested that remark to their candidate. "Was that unfair?" McCarthy asked. "I think it was," Gorman replied. "But it's true," said McCarthy. Gorman and Larner then asked what he meant by the remark. "Nothing," McCarthy replied, and laughed.

The night before the California primary I met with Gorman to try to persuade him to defect to the Kennedy campaign should McCarthy lose. The conversation became almost comical when Paul started to quantify what size of a margin of Kennedy victory might be big enough to justify his defection. Just a majority? A win by four percentage points? By eight points? My friend was clearly troubled by McCarthy and struggling to figure out what was the right thing to do. He had been sympathetic to Kennedy at the start of the year and went to work for McCarthy—originally as his press secretary during the Wisconsin primary—only because Kennedy had not run.

Paul was more alienated from McCarthy than Larner, but also felt a loyalty to the idealistic antiwar students who supported McCarthy and did not want to be disloyal to them. He also did not want to work against Kennedy during the upcoming New York primary. I reinterviewed Paul for this memoir about his divided feelings on that night before the California primary. He recalls being angry at McCarthy for giving a speech that he, Paul, had written, that was drafted as an even-handed criticism of both Kennedy and Humphrey on Vietnam but delivered as an attack on Kennedy. In his delivery McCarthy had truncated the anti-Humphrey sections.

Paul still believes that McCarthy "hated Kennedy so much that he preferred Humphrey to be the nominee," despite their differences over Vietnam. He also says that he believed Kennedy's coalition with the poor was much more appealing than McCarthy's narrower and whiter constituency. Paul's recollection is that our meeting ended with an agreement that he, Larner, and possibly Sam Brown would meet with Kennedy for breakfast the morning after the primary, *if* Kennedy won. I was supposed to set up this meeting.

Before the sun rose on June 4, I started to drive around Los Angeles with a couple of Kennedy campaign workers. I didn't even know what I was looking for, but what I found was one of the most moving sights I have ever seen in American politics. We drove around Watts and East Los Angeles, and I saw lines of blacks and Mexican Americans waiting to vote even before the polls opened. All my life I had heard the cliché "blacks don't vote, Hispanics don't vote." Now I was seeing living refutation of this assumption about sloth or ignorance or lack of civic patriotism. I was seeing evidence that if they had someone to vote for, someone they believed would make a difference in their lives, they would wait in line to vote. In the Mexican American areas a sound truck was blaring the message "Today is the day that Cesar Chavez asks you to vote for Robert Kennedy." When this day was over, the turnout in these poor minority neighborhoods would be higher than in affluent Beverly Hills. And Kennedy would win 90 percent of the Mexican vote and 85 percent of the black vote.

By 7 P.M. we were all gathered on the fifth floor of the Ambassador Hotel. Kennedy and his family and a few advisers were in room 511. Friends, celebrities, and favored writers were in room 516 across the hall. At about 8 P.M. Kennedy, grinning puckishly, poked his head into room 516 and asked, "Do you want to hear about the Indians?" He announced that one Indian precinct on a reservation in South Dakota had voted 878 for him, 9 for Humphrey, and 2 for McCarthy. A few minutes later he reported that he would easily win the primary held that day in South Dakota, the state in which Humphrey was born, before he moved to Minnesota.

By about 8:30, some of us had been invited into Kennedy's suite. The atmosphere was tense. NBC's sample precincts and exit polling were projecting McCarthy as the winner, while CBS was reporting Kennedy would win. Kennedy, who was being funneled private projections by Pierre Salinger and Larry O'Brien, knew he was slightly ahead, but not by as much as CBS was projecting. When Kennedy wanted to have a private conversation with Steve Smith, or Goodwin, or Walinsky, or Sorenson, or Fred Dutton, he would retreat into the bathroom and close the door. His brother Ted and John Siegenthaler were running the headquarters in San Francisco.

By 10:30 the raw votes from the black and Mexican areas had come in much bigger than NBC's computer experts had anticipated, and now Kennedy was ahead in the actual vote count. He was being projected as the winner by all three networks.

In the notebook I was writing in that night I jotted down the word "liberated." That's how Kennedy seemed to be that last night. He was relaxed, funny, in control, happy, optimistic. Dick Goodwin saw, for the first time, "An easy grace, a strength that was unafraid of softness." He had accomplished something on his own. When I wrote down the word "liberated," I think I also meant liberated from the shadow of his brother.

Kennedy did network interviews with Roger Mudd and Sander Vanocur and was playful and teasing with both of them. By coming back from defeat in Oregon and winning California, Kennedy seemed, at last, at peace with himself. He had done it right, and done it on his own.

At some point he phoned Mayor Richard Daley in Chicago and spoke for a few minutes. No one knew the exact words spoken, or if they were meant sincerely, but afterward Kennedy said that Daley had "hinted" he would support him at the convention in August. Daley was sick of the war, and had always had a deep and sentimental affiliation with the Kennedy family. If Illinois, a nonprimary state controlled by the Daley machine, would shift to Kennedy, the nomination was winnable.

At about 11:30 Kennedy returned to the suite from the TV interviews and sat down on the floor next to me, Budd Schulberg, and Hamill. He lit up a small victory cigar, savoring every puff as he watched more returns on the TV. "What should I say in my speech?" Kennedy asked Schulberg. "Well, of course, you know who won this election for you," Budd replied. Kennedy said he knew it was the blacks and the Mexicans.

Then he began to ask Schulberg a series of questions about the Watts Writers' Workshop and the Frederick Douglass Community Theater that Budd had founded after the 1965 riots. "I think you've touched a nerve," Kennedy said to him. "We need so many new ideas . . . I think that workshop idea of yours is a kind of throwback to the Federal Theater and the Writers' Project of the New Deal. We have to encourage not just mechanical skills and jobs in those areas, but creative talent. I saw in Watts, at the Douglass House, so much more talent to be channeled, strong self-expression. I'd like to see it on a national scale, with federal help. I'll do everything I can . . ."

Jesse Unruh interrupted to say it was time for Kennedy to go downstairs to the ballroom and claim his victory. The last conversation I ever had with Kennedy was about a promise of federal help for the arts in black communities.

I started to watch Kennedy's victory speech on the television with a happy group of about twenty supporters in room 516. I saw him thank Steve Smith, Cesar Chavez, Ethel, Freckles his dog, Delores Huerta and Bert Carona of the farmworkers' union, "my friends in the black community, Rafer Johnson and Rosey Grier." Carol Welch, Kennedy's campaign secretary, who once worked in the Johnson White House with Bill Moyers, tapped me on the shoulder. "Jack, the senator is going to leave for The Factory [a disco] right from his press conference. You ought to go down now so that you don't miss him."

Bob Scheer and I went down in the elevator together and reached the main ballroom just as Kennedy was finishing his remarks. Suddenly we saw some agitation near the podium. Something was happening. Then I heard an awful sound spread across the packed, celebrating ballroom. It sounded like a collective moan. Some horrible news was being passed along.

People started running and screaming. A girl in a red party dress, sobbing uncontrollably, rushed by, screaming "No, God, no! It's happened again!" That sound I thought was a moan became a wail of grief. The ballroom sounded like a hospital that had been bombed. It was the sound of the twice wounded.

Scheer and I started desperately to look for a TV set. We wandered into another ballroom and into a celebration for Max Rafferty, who had just won the Republican primary for the Senate nomination. There was no panic, no tears here. Steve Smith appeared on the TV screen to ask, very calmly, for a doctor. That's when it clicked in my numbed brain—Kennedy had been shot leaving the ballroom.

I ran back into the Kennedy ballroom and into complete hysteria. Girls in campaign hats and buttons were on their knees, praying and weeping at the same time. A college kid with an RFK peace button was shouting, "Fuck this country!" again and again. A large black man was punching the wall, screaming out of control, "Why, God, why?"

In a daze I returned to room 516, where the victory party had become a death vigil. George Plimpton, who had helped subdue the assassin, rushed in. "Is he still alive?" Plimpton asked the stunned room of Kennedy's closest friends and supporters. Stan Tretick was on the couch hugging and comforting his wife. John Lewis was sitting on the floor, mumbling to himself, "Why him? Why, why, why?" I sat down and hugged John and we cried in each other's arms.

The phone kept ringing and I picked up once. It was a hysterical McCarthy volunteer promising she would "switch to Bobby, if he lives."

At about 5:30 A.M. somebody asked Bob Scheer and me to pick up Ed Guthman at the Hospital of the Good Samaritan and bring him back to the Ambassador Hotel.

When we got to the hospital I noticed Charles Evers, the brother of the assassinated Medgar Evers, sitting on the steps of the hospital alone, away from the crowd that had gathered. Evers embraced me and croaked, "God, they kill our leaders, and they kill our friends." Then we drove Guthman back to the Ambassador Hotel in silence, except for one remark Guthman made.

"You know," he said, "there were a hundred people in that hotel who would have gladly taken that bullet for Bob."

I went back up to the fifth floor and saw Fred Dutton, the tough old pro who had worked for JFK, sag into his room alone and shut the door. His sobbing soon filled the hallway. That's when I knew Bob would not live.

I flew back to New York. On Thursday night I had a somber dinner with my four closest friends—my future wife Janie Eisenberg, Paul Gorman, Geoff Cowan—Paul Cowan's brother, who was working for McCarthy in Connecticut—and Tom Hayden, who had backed neither Kennedy nor McCarthy and was already organizing a protest at the Chicago convention against the Democratic Party and the war. Tom had been ambivalent about Kennedy. Former SDS president Todd Gitlin told me that Tom had called Kennedy "a little fascist" in a conversation with him that same week.

We were a tight group of old friends, grieving all through the dinner, when somebody suggested we go up to St. Patrick's Cathedral, where Kennedy's body was, and try to talk our way in, even though the public was not going to be admitted until 5:30 the next morning.

We were standing on the steps of the cathedral when two old Kennedy friends noticed us—Ronnie Eldridge and Bill Hadded. They invited us inside, past the heavy security detail. They told us that other "Kennedy people" had been coming by out of some spontaneous mourning instinct, and they were improvising an honor guard through the night around his casket.

As I waited my turn to stand vigil, I noticed Tom walk away from us and slump back in the shadows. As he sat alone in an empty pew, tears began to form in his eyes.

Here was a man who had not voted for Kennedy in California, who was an apostate Catholic, weeping in this grand church. I wondered whether he was weeping for Robert Kennedy or for America. It was, I decided, the same thing.

At dinner Tom had shown us a green cap he had recently gotten from a Cuban revolutionary in Havana. I could see that symbol of Castroism sticking out of his pants pocket while his sobs echoed in the cavernous cathedral.

When it was my turn to stand vigil at Bob's coffin, I found myself between Robert Vaughn, the actor who had befriended Lowenstein and the Dump Johnson movement, and popular late-night radio personality Barry Gray, who was fighting back his tears.

I could see Paul Gorman, the half-Catholic, half-Jewish McCarthy speechwriter, lighting a candle. He was weeping, too. I could also see Joe Crangle, the old-line Irish political boss from Buffalo, who looked a little like Bobby Darin, off in the shadows by himself. He was also crying.

I wept all through my vigil at the coffin while a priest intoned a prayer in Latin. And I thought again of the quotation from Pascal that Camus invokes at the start of *Resistance, Rebellion, and Death*: "A man does not show his greatness by being at one extremity, but rather by touching both at once."

Later this same night George McGovern saw Mayor Daley of Chicago standing vigil at the casket. Daley, his head bowed, was sobbing uncontrollably, the cords of his neck bulging out. A mere ten weeks later, of course, Tom Hayden and Richard Daley would be leading opposing armies of protesters and police in a violent battle in the streets of Chicago.

Only Robert Kennedy could have united both Hayden and Daley in tears, in that church, on that night.

Had Kennedy lived, Daley and Hayden might have been on the same side in Chicago. Without him, they went to war with each other.

That is the meaning of Pascal's aphorism.

CHAPTER 8

The Space Left by King

For almost forty years I have been trying to make sense of the 1960s, trying to understand how the pure contagious idealism of 1960 to 1965 deteriorated into violence and stupidity, how the movement cracked up so fast. I certainly don't claim academic detachment about this decade, which has been the subject of hundreds of books and college courses and endless debate. Some of the key players of the 1960s, like Tom Hayden and Phil Ochs, were close friends, and others, like Irving Howe and Jerry Rubin, were acquaintances. I put my hopes and dreams on the line and left them as puddles on the ground.

As an activist and as a writer, I was part of some of the defining moments of the decade. I was one face in the crowd of 250,000 when Martin Luther King, Jr., gave his unforgettable "I Have a Dream" speech in Washington in 1963. It is still the greatest speech I ever heard, although I know now that King was stringing together bits and pieces of other sermons and riffs that hot day to conjure his magic spell. King's warm-up act that afternoon was the twenty-two-year-old Bob Dylan, fresh from

Greenwood, Mississippi, singing "Pawn in their Game," his new song about the sniper who had killed Medgar Evers two months earlier.

I spent 1965 doing reporting for a book about the origins of the New Left that was published in 1966. It was dedicated to the memory of Andy Goodman, James Chaney, and Michael Schwerner, the three civil rights activists murdered in Mississippi in 1964, and began with an epigraph from Ignazio Silone: "A society is renewed when its humblest element acquires a value."

I marched on the Pentagon in 1967, realizing that the middle class was shifting against the war and that this meant votes.

I was on the campus at Columbia University in April of 1968 when police were invited onto the campus by university president Grayson Kirk and beat up hundreds of students—and some faculty—in a traumatizing night of brutality and class warfare that reduced Professor Daniel Bell to tears.

I was present when Robert Kennedy was assassinated.

I was tear-gassed by the police in Chicago during the 1968 Democratic convention; bailed Tom Hayden out of jail one night; and covered the first antiwar protest by active-duty GIs in 1968, organized by Fred Gardner at Fort Jackson in South Carolina. I spoke at the University of North Carolina and at Duke University, on the first day of the first nationwide campus moratorium against the Vietnam War in October of 1969.

I voted for Dick Gregory instead of Hubert Humphrey for president in 1968, then regretted it as soon as I found out that Nixon had defeated Humphrey by less than 1 percent of the vote. (I atoned for this act of defiant bad judgment thirty-two years later by voting for Al Gore and Joe Lieberman. I thought those who voted for Ralph Nader were self-indulgent dilettantes, just as I had been in 1968.)

What happened in this country between 1960 and 1969 is personal to me, not an old newsreel or a class in sociology or history. I was witness to events in which I also participated intensely. For years I have had deep conversations with movement friends about the turning points of this era, about how things might have turned out differently had certain events not happened.

What if the Democratic Party liberals and Roy Wilkins and Bayard Rustin had insisted the Mississippi Freedom Democrats get more than two symbolic seats at the 1964 Atlantic City presidential convention? Did their capitulation to LBJ make the turn toward antiwhite, antiliberal separatism inevitable? What if the leadership of SNCC hadn't asked the white staff to resign in 1965, and SNCC had not abandoned its founding mission of being an interracial movement, creating an interracial society? Why did so many smart people succumb to anti-Semitism and Israel-bashing at the 1967 New Politics convention in Chicago?

What if Grayson Kirk had not asked the NYPD to invade the Columbia campus and forcibly remove students from the occupied buildings? Did this violence lead to the formation of the Weathermen? What if Martin Luther King and Robert Kennedy had not been assassinated?

All these questions. But now, at least, there are a few certainties.

I can now recognize that Martin Luther King, Jr., was possibly the greatest American of the twentieth century, or at least the equal of Franklin Roosevelt. King was America's Gandhi. He was what Plutarch meant when he said "virtue in action" should be the standard for measuring great leaders and heroic lives. King held no office higher than Citizen, but he made two presidents bend toward civil rights and voting rights. He transformed the South, ended legal segregation, and empowered millions of blacks through nonviolence. When King was alive, even his closest colleagues took him for granted and patronized him a little. My friends in SNCC mocked him as "de Lawd." Andrew Kopkind, the talented radical journalist, assured me King was "passé" after urban riots during the summer of 1967. White radicals, drunk on the cheap wine of Eldridge Cleaver, started dismissing King as an "Uncle Tom." Some of these same imbeciles were also calling Ralph Ellison, Louis Armstrong, and Joe Frazier "Uncle Toms," too.

King was a very formal man, not easy to know. My brief encounters with him across the South yielded no great insights into his private character. I shared only one meal with him, three weeks before his death, when I was working on a profile of him for *Life* magazine.

King's greatness was founded on his unshakable commitment to nonviolence, democracy, egalitarianism, individual rights, an interracial society, and his refusal to give into the temptations of apocalypse all around him after 1965. Other movement leaders I knew surrendered to the furies of violence, capitulating to a blind hatred of America because of the war, or deluding themselves that the country was in some revolutionary condition because of the urban riots. Some thought looting a liquor store was revolutionary. SNCC put itself out of existence by abandoning integration, nonviolence, and the liberal ethic.

No one had more stress on him than King in these years; nobody felt more lonely, betrayed, abandoned, and melancholy than King did.

J. Edgar Hoover was using all of the FBI's resources to destroy him. The Klan wanted him dead. Other black leaders were informing on him to the FBI. He was under pressure to break all contact with his trusted friend and adviser, Stanley Levinson, whom the FBI and the Kennedy administration wrongly kept insisting was a paid Russian spy. And, as I've said, when he came out against the Vietnam War in April 1967, he was rebuked by the *New York Times*, Ralph Bunche, Jackie Robinson, and the NAACP.

King, rooted in his religion, inspired by scripture, never wavered on his principles, even when they seemed bypassed by fashion. His faith allowed him to believe that politics could be an expression of love and redemption. Some of his disciples, like James Bevel, went off the deep end. Stokely Carmichael became a Black Power separatist. Rap Brown became an armed robber. Bayard Rustin drifted into support for the Vietnam War. But King never wavered. He never stopped growing, never stopped expanding his goals from integrating the Montgomery public transportation system in 1955, to winning blacks the right to vote in the South, to trying to desegregate housing in Mayor Daley's Chicago, to opposing the Vietnam War, to mobilizing an interracial movement of the poor, to defending the rights of labor in a strike by garbage collectors in Memphis, where he died at age thirty-nine. As the Reverend Jesse Jackson says, "Martin was not killed because he was a *dreamer*. He was killed for doing."

My dinner with King took place on March 10, 1968, after he had spoken at Hunter College to a membership rally of Local 1199—the hospital worker's union in New York City. He felt a deep kinship with that union because of its leaders, Leon Davis and Moe Foner; he called himself "a fellow 1199-er" in his remarks, having supported the union's strikes for recognition and collective bargaining in 1959 and 1962.

King took as his text that night Mike Harrington's book *The Other*

America as he spoke about his Poor People's Campaign and about the alliance of civil rights and unions.

At dinner, King was visibly depressed and fatigued. He spoke for several minutes about the rejections he had suffered, especially not being invited to attend the funeral of President Kennedy. He also talked about how Lyndon Johnson had avoided meeting with him and how J. Edgar Hoover had tried to pressure the city of Atlanta into canceling a dinner in his honor after he had won the Nobel Peace Prize. He seemed like a man on a losing streak, trying to change his luck.

What struck me most about King that night was his goodness, his sense of sacrifice. He certainly had an extraordinary intellect and a supple sense of strategy and people, but you could immediately sense his love of humankind, the depth of his faith in nonviolence, his sense of himself as "doing God's will," and his capacity to be spiritual in a violent and materialistic world. Twice that evening King insisted, according to my notes, "Love always conquers hate."

Taking our farewells that night, I knew he was a great man, but I don't think I understood exactly how great.

It has taken the perspective of time, the echo of his eloquence, to understand the wisdom of his judgments and the enormity of his courage. It has also taken the work of his biographers—particularly Taylor Branch—to make his story both biblical and personal, to show all that he accomplished despite loneliness, despite the constant harassment and illegal surveillance by the FBI, despite his compulsive womanizing, and despite his acceptance of an early and sudden death. You can perform great deeds without being a perfect human being.

Over time King has grown in my imagination, and in the process expanded my understanding of American history. If I see footage of him at the Lincoln Memorial, or in Selma preaching for voting rights, or giving his sermon about excellence—"and if you are just a humble street-sweeper then be the best street-sweeper you can be"—or opposing the Vietnam War at Riverside Church, or delivering his Nobel Prize speech in Oslo, or telling us that "The arc of the moral universe is long, but it bends towards justice," the timbre and cadence of his voice still stir my deepest emotions.

King combined thought and action at the highest level. He combined strength and sweetness in just the right balance. At the risk of sounding maudlin, he was just too good for the fevered America of 1968, when hate was out of its cage and running wild.

In the spring of 1965 two moments foreshadowed the split between liberalism and radicalism. The first took place on April 17, at the SDS March on Washington against the Vietnam War. More than twenty thousand students converged on Washington for this protest, which surprised everyone by its size. Bob Moses told us, "Don't use Mississippi as a moral lightning rod. Use it as a looking glass. Look into it and see what it tells you about all of America."

Paul Potter, the twenty-four-year-old president of SDS, declared, "If the people of this country are going to end the war in Vietnam and to change the institutions which create it, then the people of this country must create a massive social movement—and if that can be built around the issue of Vietnam, then that is what we must do."

Joan Baez sang Bob Dylan's sardonic song "With God on Our Side." And my friend Phil Ochs performed his satiric song "Love Me, I'm a Liberal." One reason Phil sang that song was because the day of the march, the liberal *New York Post* had run an editorial by James Wechsler (my friend, too) red-baiting this SDS march in a particularly baseless fashion. Phil sang—and the crowd loved it:

> *I cried when they shot Medgar Evers,*
> *tears ran down my spine*
> *And I cried when they shot Mister Kennedy*
> *As though I'd lost a father of mine*
> *But Malcolm X got what was coming,*
> *He got what he asked for this time,*
> *So love me, love me, love me,*
> *I'm a Liberal*
>
> *Sure, once I was young and impulsive*
> *I wore every conceivable pin*
> *Even went to Socialist meetings,*

Learned all the old union hymns,
Ah, but I've grown older and wiser,
And that's why I'm turning you in,
So love me, love me, love me,
I'm a Liberal.

The rally speaker following Phil's song was the journalist I. F. Stone, the independent radical pamphleteer I had started reading in college. His mere presence gave the march both gravity and credibility. When Stone, then in his sixties, reached the microphone, he began to criticize Phil and his song. "I've seen snot-nosed Marxists come and go," Izzy said. "I don't like to see all liberals lumped together and attacked like this. Please, don't make this mistake. There are good liberals, and there are bad liberals. Senators Wayne Morse and Ernest Gruening are good liberals, opposing this God damn war. Liberalism is not our enemy." Like the SDS presidents between 1963 and 1965—Todd Gitlin, Paul Potter, and Carl Ogelsby—he made a distinction between humanist and imperialist liberals.

I thought of Izzy as more of a radical than a liberal, but after the march he explained to me that he believed deeply in the "liberal ethic of tolerance, reason, free speech, and civility." He was speaking against the war on campuses and already sensing antiliberal and anti-intellectual tendencies among some of the students who came to cheer his feisty, learned remarks. I also thought Phil's song was a work of art, not an attack on tolerance or civil liberties, but I respected Izzy so much that I took his defense of "the liberal ethic" to heart.

Phil himself laughed off the whole episode. He enjoyed controversy, he looked up to Stone, and he loved performing.

The second episode was not so good-natured—or so quickly forgotten by the personalities involved. In May of 1965, in Greenwich Village, a debate took place between Tom Hayden of SDS and Irving Howe, the democratic socialist intellectual. I wrote about it for both the *Village Voice* and the *Nation*, carefully taking a neutral view, trying to be balanced. The debate was fierce, personal, and left scars on both men. Hayden was my friend and Howe a figure I admired from a distance. But each simply didn't like the scent of the other. "I said things to spite him," Tom later told me, "There was just an unhealthy dynamic between us."

At the time of the debate Tom was a community organizer living in the Newark ghetto, focused on rats and stoplights near schools. He was totally opposed to the war in Vietnam. Howe was critical of the war, but he wanted even-handed denunciations of both sides. He was also known as a brutal debater. As a professor at Brandeis in the 1950s, he had destroyed the communist writer Howard Fast in a debate that was so one-sided it almost created sympathy for the morally bankrupt Fast, who renounced communism a few weeks later.

Irving made an opening statement that was based on his forthcoming *Dissent* article, "New Styles in Leftism." I reluctantly agreed with more than half of what Irving said about the New Left's romanticism about Castroism and other forms of Third World authoritarianism. I also reluctantly came to agree with his critique of participatory democracy as another fuzzy romantic idea and certainly not a notion superior to representative, elective democracy of one person/one vote. Howe also spotted "an extreme, sometimes unwarranted hostility toward liberalism" that was destructive.

Howe's own style of leftism was overbearing, smug, prosecutorial. He had an urge to tell free-thinkers what to think. At one point he started to demand that Hayden say whether a series of communist and Third World tyrannies were authoritarian. "What about China, Tom? What about Cuba? How about Albania?" Howe was right intellectually but offensive socially. And Tom should have had no problem calling these regimes by their rightful name. Instead, he got up and walked out of the debate and left the small, packed hall on University Place.

Years later Howe expressed regret about his performance that night. He told me he had wanted so badly to save the New Left from being taken over by authoritarians that he couldn't help himself. He said what had been on his mind, and in the only way he knew how: as a former working-class Bronx Trotskyite educated at City College, class of 1940. There was no real communist influence in SDS in 1965, no takeover commissars, certainly nothing like what had happened the 1930s or 1950s. The League for Industrial Democracy's assault on SDS in 1962 and the *New York Post*'s editorial of April 17 warning that the SDS march might become "a pro-Communist production" were not rooted in reality.

Howe now strikes me as a towering but temperamentally flawed figure. He was one of the New York intellectuals who was right about most of the big issues of his time—the Cold War, Stalinism, McCarthyism, Israel, Eichmann, civil rights, Vietnam. But his strident public platform style made others deaf to his brilliance. He had no talent for friendship with people he disagreed with, the way Murray Kempton and Mike Harrington did. Early in the 1950s, he was very close to C. Wright Mills. Then they disagreed in print over Mills's 1958 pamphlet, "The Causes of World War II," and the two friends never spoke again.

In *Dissent* magazine in 1963, Irving published an embarrassing and condescending attack on Ralph Ellison for not being angry enough, for not being enough like Richard Wright. This was a misreading of the erudite and universal Ellison, who retaliated by demolishing Howe in two essays in the *New Leader* magazine. They can be read together in *The Collected Essays of Ralph Ellison*, The Modern Library edition, published in 1996, under the title "The World and the Jug." I read every word of the exchange. It was the only time I ever saw Irving lose a debate, and lose badly to the writer I came to think of as both lethal and dignified, an economical Joe Louis of letters.

Howe wrote that Ellison's great novel, *The Invisible Man*, was inferior to Wright's *Native Son* because it wasn't about the "ideological and emotional penalties suffered by Negroes in this country." Of course it was partially about black victimization! It still amazes me that Howe, who was primarily a literary critic of the first rank, could not see this. And how he could try to categorize Ellison in a little shoebox labeled "black writers." Ellison's influences were as universal as Faulkner, Freud, T. S. Eliot, Hemingway, and Malraux. In his elegant, patient rebuttal, Ellison wrote: "I tried to the best of my ability to transform these elements into art. My goal was not to escape, or hold back, but to work through; to transcend, as the blues transcended the painful conditions with which they deal."

After reading "The World and the Jug," Ellison became a pervasive influence on my thinking. I read all his essays. I read everything about him. I felt for him when black nationalists and Black Panthers slandered him as an Uncle Tom during the late 1960s. Ellison's essay writing style was rational and scholarly, but those who knew him, like my friend Stanley Crouch, told me he was a volcano inside. James Baldwin once said Ellison was "almost too angry to live." The spectacle of Howe lecturing Ellison on what to think about race was a window into the paternalistic and monolithic side of Irving's thinking. Irving just liked to pick intellectual fights and couldn't stop himself from personalizing differences.

But this was not Irving's fault alone. This style of rigid rancor was adopted by most of the so-called New York intellectuals. For example, long friendship between Irving Kristol and Lionel Trilling was ruptured in 1972, when Kristol could not convince Trilling to sign a "Democrats for Nixon" newspaper ad. Norman Podhoretz, even more cantankerous than Howe, stopped speaking to many old friends who remained Democrats and then attacked them in his books for bad faith and lost nerve. And the feud between Mary McCarthy and Lillian Hellman ended up in a lawsuit.

Had Irving Howe not told others what to write about, had he developed a lighter touch in his public debating style, he might have gotten some of the New Left to hear his perceptive admonitions. I think Irving knew this and deeply wished he had a different temperament, one that was more generous and forgiving, more like those of his friends Daniel Bell, Nathan Glazer, and the intellectual he most admired, the historian Richard Hofstadter. Hofstadter became Howe's role model "of what the scholar-intellectual ought to be." He said that Hofstadter had "the mystery of goodness" and a "liberalism of the spirit."

In his wonderful memoir, *A Margin of Hope*, published in 1982, Irving wrote of Hofstadter, "He was wonderfully free of that grating aggression which is so frequently declared the spring of American success. Modest and humane, but above all without the need to impose himself, which seems a special curse of intellectuals . . . He had reached a security of being I could only envy."

My own views during this 1965 to 1968 period straddled several camps. I felt comfortable with the first-generation SDS views about using activism and moral protest in the struggle for egalitarianism. I felt a growing sense of hope that Robert Kennedy and the liberal wing of the Democratic Party would end the war. I admired the democratic clarity of purpose and historical perspective of Mike Harrington and Irving Howe. And Martin Luther King, more and more, seemed to represent everything I most admired—a commitment to nonviolence, personal courage, and a synthesis of thought and action.

I did not try to reconcile or clarify the inherent contradictions. I did not have Irving Howe's almost compulsive contentiousness, the need to define every distinction, dispute every point. Each tendency, each approach had merit. They didn't have to be perfect. RFK and King didn't have to like each other. It was a movement, not a conspiracy.

What was unambiguous about my thinking was that I didn't like what was developing farther Left. I did not like violence, or blaming America for everything wrong in the world, or calling cops "pigs," or denying free speech to political opponents, or defending dictatorships like Cuba, or unfairly attacking Israel and Zionism. In 1968 I was invited on a junket to Cuba. But when I met with a high-ranking diplomat from the Cuban mission, we got into an argument about democracy, Russian interventionism, and free speech for Cuban dissidents. The invitation was withdrawn before I could say I didn't want to go.

I also developed a strong and reciprocated antagonism to Jerry Rubin, the cofounder with Abbie Hoffman and Paul Krassner of the Yippie movement. I found Rubin egomaniacal, antidemocratic, nasty, self-promoting, liberal-baiting, intolerant, and anti-intellectual. He seemed a buffoon pretending to lead a revolution. Once we debated on a college campus and I read a pasage from his book *Do It!* in which he advocated that readers do things like "Dynamite the toll booths . . . Blow up Howard Johnson's on the turnpike—the universal oppressor of everybody." "Since you haven't done any of these things yourself, Jerry," I said to Rubin, "but you urge impressionable kids to do them, you should have called the book *YOU Do It.*"

Rubin and I also competed for influence over Phil Ochs, who was friends with both of us. Like me, Phil was ecumenical and nonideological in his radicalism. He even liked John Wayne. He simply wanted to stop the war and not get stuck with a choice between Humphrey and Nixon in 1968.

In April or May 1968, Phil asked me to join him and Rubin for dinner, so he could referee while we debated the politics of that season. Phil had already performed at a McCarthy rally and seemed ready to switch his allegiance to Kennedy. But he also was excited about the plans for a big protest at the Democratic convention in Chicago that Rubin was already organizing with Tom Hayden, Abbie Hoffman, Rennie Davis of SDS, and David Dellinger, an older pacifist.

The dinner proved both revealing and unpleasant. Rubin kept denouncing Kennedy as the worst of all the possible alternatives, as the purest form of evil, as part of an imperialist system that was destroying the poor and the young.

I told Rubin that he was just afraid that Kennedy might get nominated and ruin the fun of his Chicago demonstration, that Kennedy was a threat to his base and to the existence of all his planning for Chicago. "Your pal Bobby is just a rich bastard," was Rubin's rejoinder. "We'll have a hundred thousand kids in the streets kicking his ass. He's not really against the war. Bobby, Johnson, and Humphrey are the same person."

Phil was irritated by Rubin's cartoonish point of view, and the evening ended with Phil saying he was for both Kennedy and McCarthy. Deep down, Phil was really a patriot who loathed violence. He didn't buy into Rubin's shtick that the whole system was rotten and only a revolution—led by youth—was the solution. He had gone to military school as a teenager and composed "The Power and the Glory," a patriotic hymn to America, which he called "a beautiful shipwreck." He wanted to save the system from itself.

On May 30, 1968, Phil and I flew to California a few days before the climactic primary showdown between Kennedy and McCarthy. During the five-hour flight, Phil promised me he would switch his public support to Kennedy if Kennedy won the California primary. I think RFK's loss to McCarthy in Oregon made Kennedy seem both more attractive and more vulnerable to Phil.

After RFK was murdered, Phil gave a concert at Carnegie Hall and dedicated his encore song to Kennedy's memory. At that point Rubin jumped on stage, shouting that Sirhan was "a freedom fighter." But Phil was undeterred. He was profoundly affected by Kennedy's assassination. He tried to write a song about it, but never finished it. His notebooks contained the draft of a long eulogy to RFK that he hoped to rework into a *Village Voice* article.

But by the end of 1968, following the convention violence, the disappointing turnout during the protests, and then Nixon's election, Phil began his long, slow slide into depression and creative silence.

The far more resilient Rubin began his transition from Yippie revolutionary to yuppie salesman and materialist. By the time of Ronald Reagan's inauguration in 1981, he went to work at a Wall Street brokerage house and then became famous for hosting "networking parties" for two thousand upwardly mobile singles at the Palladium nightclub on Fourteenth Street. He died in 1994, struck by a car while jaywalking in Los Angeles. At the time he was marketing a line of bee pollen and ginseng drinks.

Like a lot of other reporters, I was on the campus of Columbia University at 2 A.M. on April 30, 1968. I could see a brigade of a thousand police officers—some on horses, some in plainclothes—slowly begin to advance on the five buildings occupied by students protesting the war, racism, and the impersonality of a large campus. We could all smell blood in the air.

About five minutes before the assault began, I found myself standing next to the city's (black) human rights commissioner, William Booth, who would later become a judge.

"What are your thoughts at this moment?" I asked Booth.

"That the publisher of the *New York Times* and the District Attorney of Manhattan [Frank Hogan] are both trustees of Columbia," was Booth's answer.

Booth's comment was part of the lead of the *Village Voice* article I published the following week. That article, critical of the coverage by the *Times* and particularly by assistant managing editor Abe Rosenthal, became a point of public contention and debate for over thirty years.

Let me explain why it was so critical and controversial. About an hour before my exchange with Commissioner Booth, I was walking across the campus with Jules Feiffer when we saw Abe Rosenthal emerge from what seemed to have been a closed meeting of the top police brass. I went up to Rosenthal and asked if a police raid was imminent. He claimed he had "no idea" but seemed embarrassed at having been seen being part of a police strategy meeting.

Over the next hour I spoke to several *Times* reporters who were on the campus, including John Kifner, Steve Roberts, and Robert Thomas (who would end up bloodied and in the hospital that night, despite his having prominently displayed a police card identifying him as a working reporter).

These reporters told me in bits and pieces an amazing story of the *Times* getting preferential insider treatment all day from the NYPD. They didn't know all the details, but they thought that sometime earlier in the day, *Times* city editor Arthur Gelb had been tipped off about the timing of the raid and even been given a piece of paper with the logistical details, down to the minute of the entry of the mounted police on the campus. *Times* reporters considered "reliable" were given copies of this internal NYPD memo, but others, like Richard Reeves, the reporters told me, were excluded. Some of the paper's top editors feared Reeves might tip off the students.

By itself, this preferential treatment was not a big deal. I would not have written 1,500 words about it. What made it news, a story, was how biased and distorted the *Times*-published coverage of the police bust turned out to be. Besides the trustee connection, there appeared to be a quid pro quo for the access.

There was a lot of police brutality and excessive use of force. Over a hundred students were treated at two hospitals. Everyone on the campus could see the police were beating students up. Yet Rosenthal's column maintained that many of the cops actually seemed "almost fond, in a professional way, of the students."

The next day, May 1, the *Times* published one lead story on the police raid and eight sidebar stories. The lead story, under the byline of Sylan Fox, did not even mention police brutality until the twenty-third paragraph. Moreover, Rosenthal himself wrote a front-page column that day.

It also did not mention a single incident of police violence. Instead it was all about the anguish of President Kirk and the students' vandalism of his office. (The student leaders were obnoxious and unwilling to negotiate, especially their obtuse leader, Mark Rudd.)

The *Times* did have a reporter—John Kifner—who was actually inside an occupied building when the police attacked. He offered to write a first-person account of what happened, but his editors were not interested. They assigned Kifner to write a story about student vandalism.

The day my *Voice* article appeared, I received a phone call from a very angry Abe Rosenthal. "Everything you wrote is a lie," Rosenthal began. "You have intentionally attempted to harm the credibility of the *Times*. You are an assassin. You will never work for this paper as long as you live, and you will never write for this paper as long as you live. There was no police brutality. You're a little guttersnipe."

I certainly was "little" compared to Rosenthal. I was but a thirty-year-old reporter for a left-wing weekly paper with 140,000 readers. He was a Pulitzer Prize winner and one of the top editors on the best paper on the planet—then and now. But I trusted my own eyes. I felt Rosenthal was overly sympathetic to the police and to the university administration. I also felt there was an inherent conflict of interest, in that the *Times* publisher was also a university trustee. And I trusted what the younger *Times* reporters had told me about the inner workings of that great paper on that particular bad day.

Over the years my reporting about that violent night has been confirmed many times over, both in an official report and in an official history of the *Times*. A few months after the event, a special commission issued a report of what happened at Columbia. Chaired by Archibald Cox, then best known as the former solicitor general under Robert Kennedy but soon to gain fame as the Watergate prosecutor fired by Richard Nixon, the commission came to this conclusion: "The police engaged in acts of individual and group brutality for which the layman can see no justification . . . Dean Platt testified that when he pointed out to two police officers the brutal charge of the plainclothesmen in front of Furnald Hall, the officers replied they could see no policemen . . . Some students attacked the police and otherwise provoked the retaliation. Their fault was in no way commensurate with the brutality of the police, and for the most part, was its consequence. There was no substantial vandalism in Low Library," the Cox report ended, a direct contradiction of Rosenthal's page-one column.

The release of the Cox Commission study inspired Murray Kempton to revisit Rosenthal's column in his own *New York Post* column of October 11, 1968. Kempton took aim at Rosenthal's passage describing a police officer standing among the ruins of President Kirk's office. Choosing a sentence from Rosenthal's column—"A policeman picked up a book on the floor and said, 'The whole world is in these books; how could they do this to these books?"—Kempton tweaked Rosenthal's credibility. "I recall thinking at the time that Rosenthal's sense of theatre had led him over the brink with that last touch; the dramatist has to be careful in the assignment of the appropriate sentiment to the appropriate character."

In his telephone call to me, Rosenthal had insisted that he had had no privileged access, that the *Times* had had no privileged access, and that Arthur Gelb had had no inside information. He kept repeating that the *Times* was objective and that I was biased, "making up a story out of whole cloth to damage the *Times*." But in 1999 an official history of the *Times*, written by Susan Tifft and Alex Jones, was published. The book was written with the cooperation of the Ochs and Sulzberger families, although the paper's proprietors had no control over the content. It contained three pages on Rosenthal and the Columbia bust.

The book establishes that Arthur Gelb was given an exclusive advance tip about the bust, and that

> at 10 P.M. [Gelb] dispatched to Columbia every reporter he could lay his hands on.
>
> When he tracked down Abe Rosenthal at a Broadway theater where he was watching "Hair," Rosenthal said he wanted to see the action for himself. With Nat Goldstein, the *Times*' circulation director, he hitched a ride *with the police* [emphasis added] up to Columbia—a decision he later admitted was "not the most brilliant in the world" . . .
>
> In an unusual move for a top editor, Rosenthal had written a passionate eyewitness account . . . Within New York journalism circles,

there was talk he had purposely assigned himself the Columbia story because Punch [*Times* publisher Punch Sulzberger] was a university trustee.

Rosenthal denied having any political agenda, and when Jack Newfield attacked him in the *Village Voice* for one-sided coverage, he angrily responded that Newfield was trying to "damage the major asset of the *New York Times*—its reputation for integrity."

Officially, the *Times* has never admitted any error, but privately the paper was embarrassed.

Abe Rosenthal's lifetime blacklist of me at the *Times* proved to be more of a graylist. In the eighteen months prior to my article, I had been assigned six book reviews for the *Times*, and they were all published. To this day I have never been asked to review another book. But in 1971 and 1972 I did publish two op-ed columns in the *Times*, both assigned—courageously—by David Schneiderman, who later became editor and then publisher of the *Voice*. One was about lead poisoning in slum children and the other about the massacre of inmates at Attica, published on the first anniversary of the carnage.

Ever since I met him in late 1961, when he wrote a piece for *New America*, I considered Tom Hayden the most original thinker and perhaps the best radical writer of his generation. By the summer of 1963, we had become close friends. During 1965 and 1966 I wrote several admiring articles about his organizing efforts in Newark. He was a major figure in my first book, *A Prophetic Minority*.

But in the months leading up to the 1968 Democratic convention in Chicago, I started noticing some changes in Tom. He was becoming more angry, more hostile to the liberal ethic, more like Abbie Hoffman and Jerry Rubin, who were his intellectual inferiors.

In May of 1968, in the course of writing a long *Voice* profile of Norman Mailer, I spent a few hours with Norman and Tom. They had an exchange that I included in my *Voice* article.

"I'm supporting Robert Kennedy because I'm not sure I want a revolution," Mailer said. "Some of those kids are awfully dumb." Tom replied that he was a revolutionary and that a vote for George Wallace "would further my objective more than a vote for Robert Kennedy."

In San Francisco, during the weekend before the California primary, a large group of us were having dinner in a Chinese restaurant. The group included, among others, me, Paul Gorman, and Jeremy Larner—who were both working for Eugene McCarthy—and Tom. At the start of the evening, Tom greeted Jeremy with the question, "Why are you a whore for McCarthy?" Jeremy said something that Tom disagreed with, and Tom suddenly lunged at Jeremy with chopsticks, trying to gouge his eyes out. We grabbed Tom and a fistfight was averted, but the incident was ugly enough to cast a pall on the good cheer among old friends.

In the weeks leading up to the Chicago convention, I saw a lot of Tom and thought he was on some apocalyptic, hallucinatory trip. He kept assuring me that 200,000, maybe 400,000 demonstrators would come and that this would be the showdown of the century. Now it was all about "disruption and resistance," not nonviolent civil disobedience. He was repeating Malcolm X's phrase "by any means necessary." He was quoting Huey Newton. And he was rooting for George Wallace. With King and Kennedy both dead, it was the time to regroup, to begin the long process of working through existing institutions. Tom, like so many others, was swept up in a fantasy of revolution. He was rushing to the barricades. But instead of being behind him, the working class was against him. By the summer of 1968, the tactics of the New Left—the burning of American flags, Rap Brown urging blacks to "shoot honkies," turning the police into the enemy, waving Viet Cong flags and pictures of Che Guevara—had outraged blue-collar America, the unions, the middle class, and the suburbs. Just as the *New York Times* editorial board and significant parts of the establishment were turning against the Vietnam War, the New Left was turning against America.

To this day, my memory of the 1968 Democratic convention begins with the smell of tear gas. After three days of no sleep, my clothes reeked of it. I was probably gassed once a day while attempting to cover the decentralized demonstrations and hang out with Hayden, who wore a football helmet and a fake nose, and keep up with the events inside the convention hall through my McCarthy and Kennedy contacts.

The biggest story about Chicago—after police brutality—was how few protestors actually showed up. Rather than 400,000, the total number was more like 10,000 or 15,000. The threats of violence by the Yippies had kept kids away. The confusion over whether the city would grant any permits also kept kids away. By 1960s' standards, the protest was a failure.

I wrote two articles in four days. On the Monday night of the convention, Paul Cowan and I collaborated on an article written between 4 and 6 A.M. and phoned into the *Voice* office at 8 A.M. for the next day's edition. I wrote a second article on Wednesday after the worst of the carnage was over, the peace plank had been defeated, and Humphrey had been nominated. That article tried to describe the police riot on Wednesday evening, outside the Hilton Hotel, in spare, apolitical, Mailer-esque narrative detail:

> The light gray smoke from the exploding tear gas canisters was the first omen of violence. The burning, suffocating tear gas curled lazily up towards the upper floors of the Hilton and Blackstone hotels. The young demonstrators began choking, covering their faces with handkerchiefs and jackets, and grudgingly retreated. Then the blue-helmeted police charged into the coughing, tearing people, swinging indiscriminately at Yippies, pedestrians, priests, photographers, girls, doctors, and middle-aged women.
>
> At the southwest entrance to the Hilton, a skinny long-haired kid of about 17 skidded down on the sidewalk, and four overweight cops leaped on him, bringing their long black nightsticks down in short, chopping strokes on his head. His hair flew from the force of the blows. A dozen small rivulets of blood began to cascade down the kid's temple and onto the sidewalk. He was not crying or screaming, but crawling in a stupor towards the gutter. When he saw a photographer taking his picture, he made a V-sign with his fingers.
>
> A doctor in a Red Cross arm band and a white uniform began to run towards the kid, but two other cops caught him from behind and knocked him down. One of them jammed his knee into the doctor's

throat and began clubbing his rib cage. The doctor squirmed away, but the cops followed him, swinging hard, sometimes missing.

A few feet away a phalanx of police charged into a group of women, reporters, and young McCarthy activists standing idly against the window of the Hilton Hotel's Haymarket Bar. The terrified people began to go down under the unexpected police charge, when the plate glass window of the bar shattered, and the people tumbled backwards through the glass. The police then climbed through the broken window and began to beat the people, some of whom had been drinking quietly in the hotel bar.

At the side entrance of the Hilton Hotel, the police were chasing one frightened kid of about 17. Suddenly Fred Dutton, a former aide to Robert Kennedy, moved out from under the marquee, and interposed his body between the kid and the police.

"He's my guest in this hotel," Dutton told the police.

The police started to club the kid.

Dutton screamed for the first cop's name and badge number.

The cop grabbed Dutton and began to arrest him, until a *Washington Post* reporter identified Dutton as a former RFK aide . . .

A pretty girl, a campaign worker for Senator McGovern, began to cross the narrow street between the Blackstone and Hilton hotels. She was on an errand for the senator. Without warning, two plainclothesmen ran into her, knocked her down, and then kneed her in the neck.

Upstairs on the fifteenth floor, the girls who worked for Senator McCarthy were treating the bloody and the sick. They were ripping up Conrad Hilton's bedsheets and using them as gauze and bandages. Jerome Grossman, a bureaucrat in the McCarthy campaign, asked them not to destroy hotel property, but nobody paid attention to him. A lot of the girls had bloodstains on their dresses, legs, and arms.

Richard Goodwin, the ashen nub of a cigar sticking out of his fatigued face, mumbled, "This is just the beginning. There will be four years of this."

I saw Phil Ochs every day of the convention, and he was alternatively manic and depressed. He was in his usual conflicted limbo politically: staying in a room inside the Hilton Hotel as a guest of the McCarthy campaign and, at the same time, out in the street with Rubin, Hoffman, and the Yippies. He was with them when they held a press conference nominating their pig for president, and together we listened to Rubin tell reporters that the Yippies had poisoned the city's water supply with LSD, a dangerous prank in an already paranoid city. Phil bounced between the McCarthy staff and the students in Lincoln Park on Monday. I heard both Hoffman and Rubin tell him that he couldn't be in both camps at the same time.

But Phil said he could. He would not be bound by ideological restrictions. He kept telling reporters that he believed McCarthy could still win the nomination, although he admitted to me that he realized the convention was too tightly controlled to be affected by the kids in the parks. He was also disappointed by the turnout, having believed the predictions that hundreds of thousands would come. He would later write a funny song about a protestor who, frightened by all the predictions of violence in Chicago, went to Detroit to feel safe.

On Wednesday afternoon the protestors split into two factions. Phil was distraught to see such disunity in his own community.

There were about twelve thousand kids in Grant Park, near the bandshell, with a permit from the city, surrounded by about a thousand Chicago police in riot gear. I walked up to these cops and saw that some of them were wearing skin-fitting black leather gloves that I was later told were loaded with birdshot. They had taken their name plates off. Suddenly one kid (or maybe an agent provocateur) climbed the flagpole and took down the American flag, to the cheers of the protestors. This gave the police their excuse. They charged directly at Rennie Davis—the protest's organizing leader—chanting "Kill Davis, kill Davis." They beat him unconscious in a few seconds with their sticks and loaded gloves.

With Rennie knocked out, panic began to spread. Dave Dellinger took the microphone and pleaded for peace, calm, and nonviolence.

But Tom Hayden grabbed the microphone away from Dellinger and gave the crowd counterinstructions. He urged them to use guerrilla tactics, to disperse throughout the city in small bands. Shaken by the beating of his friend Rennie, caught up in the drama, Tom wanted confrontation. I remember Tom shouting, "I'll see you in the streets."

At some point—I can't remember exactly when—Tom gave me, Paul

Gorman, and Paul Cowan a cassette tape. He asked us to play the tape through a megaphone from inside the Hilton Hotel to the crowds massed outside, when they were starting to nominate Humphrey. Paul Cowan put the tape in his pocket.

And then Tom, in his disguise, led about a thousand hippie/Yippie/guerrilla wannabes into the streets.

Phil did not follow Tom. He sat down on the grass in Grant Park with Allen Ginsberg and Ed Sanders and began to chant "*Ommmmm.*" At the moment of truth, at the hour of anarchy and violence, Phil sided with the poets, pacifists, and Buddhist meditators.

The night before—Tuesday, August 27—was LBJ's birthday. So the Yippies had picked that night for their big event of the week, a concert and rally at the Chicago Coliseum. They billed it as an "anti–birthday party" for the president. There were speeches by William Burroughs, Jean Genet, Abbie Hoffman, Dick Gregory, and Paul Krassner. But the emotional peak of the whole night took place when Phil sang "I Ain't Marching Any More." It is a sensational song, and in the context of Chicago on that night, it had the power of an anthem.

Early in Phil's performance of the song, a young man jumped up on the stage and burned his draft card. The crowd roared, and then, across the jammed arena, one could see flickering yellow lights from lighters and matches burning draft cards. It was a mass spiritual exorcism of the war and the draft. When Phil left the stage, the crowd cheered for at least three minutes. He later called that night "the greatest moment of my career."

But the next day—Wednesday—Phil was in front of the Hilton, trying to talk a group of National Guardsmen into laying down their weapons. As I've mentioned, Phil had gone to military school. He loved this country for the freedom it gave him to write his songs. He was trying to win over an adversary with logic and love. He thought he could convince one or two guardsmen to step out of their assigned roles and make a historic gesture for peace. One guardsman stepped toward Phil and told him that he was a fan, that when he was in college he had bought Phil's records and had taken a date to one of his concerts. But after seeing Phil in Chicago, he would never buy another of Phil's records again or attend any of his concerts.

Phil was devastated. His fantasy of conversion had turned into rejection.

At about 5:30 or 6 P.M. on that Wednesday, I reconnected with Cowan and Gorman on the McCarthy floor of the Hilton Hotel. (Gorman was still working on McCarthy's campaign staff as a speechwriter.) By then the peace plank had been defeated—1,567 to 1,041. The Democratic Party had formally ratified the war.

Humphrey's inevitable nomination was a few hours away. There were jeeps, tanks, and troops massed around the hotel. There were five or six thousand students directly across the street, taunting the troops.

We had Tom's tape. One of us got the bright idea that maybe we had better listen to the tape before playing it to the kids outside. I remember sitting in Gorman's fifteenth floor hotel room and listening to Tom's words: "This is Tom Hayden. I got past the pigs, I'm inside the Hilton. Join me. Join me."

All three of us were horrified. We respected Tom and were all his close friends. We understood the stress he was under—followed by the police, arrested, marked for a beating by the police, trying to lead a faction of protestors, trying to stop the war, locked out of the hotels. But we also knew that we could not play this tape. It was a lie. Tom was not inside the hotel. The tape was summoning kids to walk into tanks and guns. It was a trick invitation to a massacre. "This is off the wall. It's manipulative," Gorman said.

A few months later Tom, Abbie, Jerry, Rennie, Dellinger, Bobby Seale, and two peripheral academics were indicted for conspiracy. That's when it dawned on me. Had we played the tape, Tom and the others would have faced even more serious felony charges. The tape could have provided the prosecution with a smoking gun. The tape would have been subpoenaed. (I have no idea where it ended up at the end of that awful night.) Gorman, Cowan, and I would have been subpoenaed and probably indicted.

Like Gorman and Cowan—until his death—I have remained friends with Tom. He lived with Janie and me for nine months in 1971 after getting expelled from the Red Family commune in San Francisco. Tom was then rediscovering his Irish roots, calling himself Emmett Garrity. I introduced him to Jimmy Breslin, Pete Hamill, and Paul O'Dwyer.

So far as I know, the Chicago Tape incident has only been written about twice. In the early 1970s, Fred Gardner reported the story accurately in the San Francisco city magazine. Fred had been in Chicago with *Rampart's* magazine, and we told him about it at the time. An inaccurate version of the tape story is included in one of David Horowitz's books. In this telling, Horowitz confuses Paul Cowan with his younger brother Geoff. Geoff told Horowitz that he got it wrong, but Horowitz has never corrected his version, in which he has Geoff convincing Tom not to play the tape. Geoff, now the dean of the Annenberg School of Communications at USC, was with us in Chicago, and his brother, Paul, immediately told him about how we refused to play the tape. He never heard the tape himself.

I still admire Tom Hayden as a political thinker. What he wanted me to do in Chicago was dangerous and crazy. But it is not the whole life of Tom Hayden. I was under much less stress than Tom that week, but I threw a typewriter out the window of the Hilton Hotel, at the police, when I saw kids getting beaten. None of us is perfect; Chicago in 1968 was an extreme experience.

I include the tape episode here because it is true, and it would have been dishonest to leave it out. If I had left it out, it would have been because Tom was my friend for 40 years, and I wanted to cover for him. Tom was not his better self during the 1968 convention, or during the months leading up to the convention. He had some revolutionary fever. So did a lot of people.

I told Tom years ago that he should never have become a politician. He should have been a writer and professor. Now Tom is out of office, after losing a City Council race in Los Angeles by a few hundred votes last year. I hope to see more of his writing and thinking now that he is liberated from the rat race of politics. The lunacy of the tape is outweighed by all the good Tom has done.

After Chicago I was more stressed out than at any other time in my life. I like to eat and I wasn't eating. I like to sleep and I wasn't sleeping. I had spent the previous five months witnessing the hate running loose in the country.

The murders of Kennedy and King, the police brutality at Columbia University, the blood and brutality in Chicago, and the failure of the antiwar movement to make any impact on the Democratic Party—these were a cumulative shock to the nervous system.

That September a group of us went to Martha's Vineyard for two weeks of rest and recovery. The family of Paul and Rachael Cowan owned a home in Menemsha. Janie and I, and Paul Gorman and Enid, rented houses nearby. We played ball on the beach, ate lobster, read books, soaked up the sun, smoked a little dope, and listened to the new record by The Band called *Big Pink*.

It was a time for cementing lifelong friendships, a time for getting the political horrors of the year out of my mind. During these two weeks I also learned how to take a vacation. The view from Lucy Vincent Beach was breathtaking—the breaking waves, the rocks, the sun, the expanse of ocean, the dunes. Each night the sunsets at Menemsha beach drew a crowd. We clapped for the sun, respectfully, at the moment it sank below the horizon of the ocean and made the water orange in its glow.

Since then Janie and I have returned to the Vineyard many times. But none of those summers could match that first visit to this paradise, when the beauty of this place helped me to heal.

Those two weeks of casual, daily socializing also helped give me an enduring appreciation for Rachael Cowan. It was easy to overlook Rachael because Paul was so exuberant, optimistic, unpredictable, funny, talented, and well known. But she often made the most sense in a room full of hyperintellectual, self-absorbed men.

The product of a Protestant heritage in Massachusetts, Rachael converted to Judaism. After Paul died of leukemia in 1988, Rachael went to rabbinical school and became an ordained Reform rabbi. She had already been a civil rights worker, author, photographer, and mother of two.

When my mother died at ninety-two in 1991, I asked Rachael to officiate at her small funeral. She had met my mother only once, at my wedding to Janie. The night before the funeral Rachael got me to talk about my mother's life of hardship and sacrifice. From it she wove into a beautiful, psychologically sensitive eulogy that left me sobbing on my thirteen-year-old daughter's shoulder.

We drifted away from the Vineyard after Paul's death, partly because Jane and I both found ourselves looking for his silhouette jogging on the misty Menemsha roads.

Back in Manhattan, after these idyllic two weeks, I spent a lot of time with Phil Ochs. Chicago took something out of Phil's soul. He slipped into a depression that he never emerged from. He felt defeated. The movement was over, and he had drawn his inspiration from the movement. The intensity and violence of 1968 created many emotional casualties. Phil was just one of the more talented and well-known victims.

I remember one long night, sitting up till dawn with Phil and Paul Cowan. Phil poured out his existential despair while he drank. It was not over the state of his career but over the state of the country, over the state of the movement. He was still grieving over Kennedy's death. He was sickened by the Nixon-Humphrey choice in the election. He felt Chicago was a flop. He had become disillusioned with Rubin and Hoffman—not as friends but as "leaders" who didn't know what they were doing, who didn't understand power, who came to Chicago unprepared. As he got drunker, Phil kept repeating Norman Mailer's immortal line, "The shits are killing us."

At the end of the depressing but emotionally bonding night, Phil autographed a copy of his songbook and gave it to me. It is a gift that I still treasure. His typically ideologically diverse inscription said: "To Jack Newfield, the Malraux, Camus, Fanon and Lippmann of this or any other generation. Phil Ochs."

Phil began to remind me of the two great artists of the Jazz Age whose Muse stopped functioning once that age was over—Scott Fitzgerald and Bix Beiderbecke. They both descended into alcoholism, and so did Phil.

About eight months after Chicago, Phil, then twenty-seven years old, recorded a new album, which he called *Rehearsals for Retirement.*

The cover photo was Phil's tombstone. The marker read:

PHIL OCHS
(American)
Born: EL PASO, TEXAS 1940
Died: CHICAGO, ILLINOIS 1968

The record is a cry of pain, filled with great topical songs that expressed his emotions of defeat, exhaustion, and revulsion with society's injustices—the same feelings Phil had poured out to me and Paul Cowan a few months earlier. The final song—a creative valedictory—is "No More Songs," written early in 1969. Sung to a funeral dirge melody, the lyrics say:

Hello, hello, hello
Is there anybody home?
I only called to say I'm sorry,
The drums are in the dawn
And all the voices are gone.
And it seems that there are
No more songs
Once I knew a sage
Who sang upon the stage
He told about the world
His lover.
A ghost without a name
Stands ragged in the rain,
And it seems that there are
No more songs.

In addition to "No More Songs," Phil's requiem for a troubadour, *Rehearsals for Retirement* contains a song about the Chicago cops, "I Kill, Therefore I Am," as well as "William Butler Yeats Visits Lincoln Park" and "The Scorpion Departs but Never Returns."

In the 1960s, Phil wrote at least a dozen songs I think of as classics: "I Ain't Marching Anymore," "Crucifixion," "There but for Fortune," "Changes," "Love Me," "I'm a Liberal," "When I'm Gone," "The War Is Over," "The Party," "Chords of Fame," "Pleasures of the Harbor," "Outside of a Small Circle of Friends," and "I'm Going to Say It Now." Phil did write a few more songs, and he filled dozens of notebooks with partial songs and fragments of never-published articles. But the cover photo on *Rehearsals* was symbolically true. He did die in Chicago in 1968, at least spiritually.

By 1975 Phil was a tormented ruin, an alcoholic sleeping in parks and doorways, stinking from vomit. He kept talking about suicide and tried it once, but failed. He developed another personality he called John Train. When he was John Train, he talked about the Mafia being after him, about the assassinations of the Kennedys and King, and about Sonny Liston. He told me the assassins who killed Liston were stalking him now. I wanted to intervene, but I didn't know how. I pleaded with Phil to get professional help, to check into a clinic or psychiatric hospital, but he didn't take me seriously. I talked to his friend, folksinger Eric Anderson, and to his former manager, Arthur Gorson, about doing something, but we were all helpless. We didn't know how to save him. I felt like a failure, an inadequate friend, a hopeless liberal afraid to invade Phil's privacy.

Phil opened a club called Che but made a mess of it. He performed at Folk City but rambled about conspiracies. That night he talked to me about how he had gotten mugged in Tanzania, and it had ruined his vocal chords. He was reluctant to perform in public after that.

Phil was now two people. When he was John Train, he was violent and hostile. The man who chanted with the pacifists in Chicago started fights, attacked people, kept a hammer in his belt. He was arrested several times for violent acts. When he was Phil Ochs, he felt guilty, depressed, begging to atone for last night's drunken atrocity. I don't know if modern medication or extended hospitalization might have stabilized or salvaged Phil. It was never really tried.

Phil committed suicide by hanging in April of 1976. He was thirty-five years old.

There are a lot of people who believe that the 1960s ended in December of 1969, at the Altamont Speedway, where the Hell's Angels killed a black man as the Rolling Stones sang "Sympathy for the Devil." Or that the 1960s ended in March of 1970, when three middle-class, well-educated former SDS members killed themselves in the townhouse explosion on West Eleventh Street in Manhattan, as they manufactured a terrorist bomb. Or that the 1960s ended when the four students were killed by National Guardsmen at Kent State University on May 4, 1970. Or that the 1960s really ended when Jimi Hendrix and Janis Joplin died of drug overdoses in 1970. But these were aftershocks, death rattles.

The 1960s ended the night Richard Nixon was elected president in

November of 1968. Nixon changed the values, direction, and culture of the nation.

Janie and I were invited to watch the election returns that night at the home of Steve and Jean Smith, the sister and brother-in-law of Robert Kennedy. The evening began with dinner and then assembling in front of the television. By about 3 A.M., only six or seven guests remained. The outcome was still in doubt, with three states still "too close to call," including Illinois. This last group of guests consisted of hardcore Nixon haters—except for Murray Kempton, who didn't hate anybody. Finally, at about 3:30, Murray told me he was going home.

"Nixon is going to win," Kempton said.

"How do you know?" I asked.

"I know Mayor Daley," Kempton replied. "He is not the sort of man who would steal the presidency from the same guy twice."

Steve Smith, who was there in 1960, almost fell down laughing.

What I knew by the time the sun rose the next day was that Nixon was the new president and everything I had worked for since 1958 was defeated.

I came face-to-face with Richard Nixon only once in my life, and it stands as one of my proudest moments. It occurred in 1985, long after his disgrace, and in the middle of a rehabilitation that would culminate with President Clinton crying at his funeral. I was on the shuttle flying to Washington to see Lena Horne perform at an ASCAP awards ceremony organized by my friend Ken Sunshine. Walking up the aisle, I suddenly found myself looking into Nixon's face, as he was taking his jacket off and about to take his seat. Out of some deep, visceral, primitive instinct, the words came out of me. "Oh, when did you get out of the can?"

I gazed into his cold, dead eyes and saw a racketeer who had committed impeachable offenses; who violated the rule of law; who fired Archibald Cox to try to keep his incriminating tapes secret; who selected the bribe taker Agnew as vice president; who sabotaged the Vietnam peace talks in April of 1968 to win the election, using Anna Chennault and John Mitchell to commit treason; who authorized the payment of hush money to conceal his crimes; who corrupted the FBI and the IRS; who authorized the hiring of Teamster goons to beat up peace demonstrators ("Yeah, they've got guys who'll go in and knock their heads off"); who propped up the Greek junta; who engineered the overthrow of the democratically elected Allende government of Chile.

I consider my timely quip an inspired improvisation, but far from adequate payback from what Richard Nixon did to my country.

Looking back on the 1960s now, as I've said, I find myself thinking more and more about the loss of Martin Luther King, Jr. He was just thirty-nine when he was buried. How much more might he have achieved, and how much more he would have grown, had he lived the span of years the Bible promised.

Looking back now on the movement, I think the turning point came when the extremists broke off and attacked the liberal ethic and the idea of an interracial society; it died when violence, anti-Americanism, and negative rhetoric infected it.

King had been the bulwark against this decay. He had been the personification of nonviolence and integration. He had loved America—and all humankind—in spite of imperfections. And his public vocabulary had reflected this patriotism. It was derived from the spirit of Lincoln, Jefferson, and the promises of the Constitution. I feel now more keenly than ever that I was privileged just to know King, to have been present at his great speeches in 1959 and 1963 in Washington; in 1965 in Montgomery; in 1967 at Riverside Church in New York City, when he came out against war in Vietnam; in March of 1968 at the hospital workers' union rally where he spoke about his poor people's campaign. I feel now, keenly, that I was privileged to have walked behind him while marching on a muddy road from Selma to Montgomery. This led directly to the Voting Rights Act of 1965—the greatest achievement of the 1960s.

Sometimes you can't really understand greatness until after it is gone. You can't see how much space it occupied until after it has left us. King's space has remained vacant for more than thirty years. This helps us see how irreplaceable he was, how uncommon such "virtue in action" is in the cycles of history. He was a precious gift from God that America did not know how to treasure.

CHAPTER 9

The Neighborhood Code Gets Tested

My first day of work at the *Daily News* was Tuesday, June 28, 1988. I started on a Tuesday because Gil Spencer, the editor, gave me permission to go to Atlantic City on Monday, June 27, to see the Mike Tyson–Michael Spinks fight. Gil was a patrician boss with a taste for the low-rent sporting life.

I arrived at the *News* at a time the paper was on the upswing. Gil had been named the editor in 1984 and started making changes. Lars-Erik Nelson was writing a trend-setting column out of Washington. Bob Herbert and Juan Gonzales were up-front columnists, Gil having hired Juan late in 1987 out of Philadelphia, where Juan had worked for him. Marcia Kramer was covering City Hall, Jerry Capeci was covering organized crime, Marilyn Thompson and Kevin McCoy were doing investigative stories, and Gail Collins was writing a witty column. Arthur Browne was running the city desk and was in charge of editing the major investigative projects. Gil had put him there in one of his instinctive judgments.

This was a rising, happening newspaper.

I worked for Gil at the *News* for fifteen months, and it was one of the joyful periods of my career. It lasted only fifteen months because Gil suddenly quit in September of 1989, following a fight with the publisher over the endorsement for mayor and because Gil believed that the executives of the Chicago-based Tribune Company, which owned the *News*, were determined to break all the unions at the paper. Gil was a union man. He didn't want to be there to watch the damage that a strike would cause to families, friendships, and his own conscience.

But for those fifteen months, I followed every lead and tip. Morale was high, loyalty was intense, and the paper was getting even better. I wrote one column a week, plus a series of long-term investigative projects with Tom Robbins that probed entrenched power. Gil always played them on the front page. With the *News* circulation at over 1 million, these stories had an impact. Gil was protective, enthusiastic, and smart. He appreciated what we were doing because he was an editor who resented authority, mistrusted most politicians, and had once been a reporter himself. He never said no to any proposed subject or target of an inquiry. He had no sacred cows in the establishment. And he had the relaxed confidence of someone who came from money and liked underdogs.

Gil also bought the serial rights to the book I wrote with Wayne Barrett—*City for Sale*—about corruption in the Koch administration. The *News* ran it over several days in December of 1988 with splashy layouts and large photos. This caused Koch to write a letter complaining about me to the *News*' publisher, James Hoge, but Gil defended me to his boss. "Once we got you in the door, they can't kick you out," Gil reassured me.

I recently asked Gil why he hired me. He said:

> I hired people who were like me. I hired people on instinct, who swung for the fences, people who cared, had a sense of humor, had an urge to break big stories, and were a little bit crazy. I tried to hire reporters who were a little bit dangerous, and could write like hell. That was my philosophy.
>
> I had learned to hire nut balls and screwballs like Pete Dexter in Philadelphia, because the bigger papers wouldn't hire away my best writers if they were a little cuckoo.

> I hired you and Juan [Gonzales] because you were like me. But columnists like you and Juan are also dangerous for editors like me. You rub powerful people the wrong way, and then they call me up. But deep down I enjoyed that you could make big shots come crying to me.

Gil was sixty-two and at the peak of his powers when I arrived at the *News.* Like Dan Wolf he had never gone to college. He also didn't know how to work the computer system, and loved horses like Seattle Slew and Sunday Silence. Gil had an aristocratic manner combined with a vernacular wit. The son of a "society lawyer," he had gone to Groton but fallen in love with the racetrack before he graduated. He took his college courses at Garden State and Delaware Park racetracks. When I asked him about his early life, Gil summed it up this way: "I resisted my family's pressures to attend college, my mother kicked me out of the house until I found a job, then I joined the navy, chased girls, became a copyboy, led a newspaper strike in Chester, Pennsylvania, and eventually became the editor of the *Trentonian* at a time every politician in New Jersey was going to prison."

Gil won the Pulitzer Prize in 1974 for his editorial commentary on these scandals in New Jersey. He was officially nominated for the honor in a letter written by assistant U.S. Attorney Johnathan Goldstein, but the idea came from Herb Stern, the fabled prosecutor who put all those corrupt politicians away and had become a federal judge. In 1987, when the time came for Gil to write his letter to the Pulitzer Committee nominating Jimmy Breslin, he went back to his roots. In his letter, Gil compared Breslin to the great racehorse Sea Biscuit. Jimmy won the Pulitzer that year for his coverage of the political corruption during the Koch administration.

The first investigative project Tom Robbins and I worked on at the News was a four-day, 10,000-word series on the state controller, Edward Regan. It was given a tremendous amount of space and daily summaries of the previous installments.

While Tom and I were still at the *Voice* together, I had received a series of anonymous typed letters from a member of Regan's staff. These letters alleged that Regan was concentrating his political fund raising on

Wall Street firms that did business with his office and that, as the sole trustee of the state's then $38 billion pension fund, he was rewarding his biggest donors with favors from this pool of money. This included law firms, bond houses, banks, securities underwriters, and real estate developers.

Then my anonymous pen pal (whom I never met) sent me a copy of a memo written by Regan's well-paid special assistant, Joe Palumbo. The Palumbo memo said that the financial houses that seek to do business with Regan should be given a straightforward message—"those who give will get." The memo, which was widely circulated in Regan's office, suggested that the controller's office let Wall Street executives understand that if they agreed to be "responsible for raising a sizable amount of money" for Regan, "they, or their firm, would make a sizable amount of money. While still not the most subtle approach," it added, "it would send a clear message."

Tom and I spent the summer of 1988 researching all of Regan's contributions and correlating them with contracts and loans granted by his office, including pension fund mortgages and selections to be part of profitable underwriting syndicates to sell the state's paper debt. In some cases we found that Regan's office denied contracts to executives who refused to play the give-to-get game. Our research showed that between 1985 and 1988, Regan had raised $4.6 million, and that 90 percent of this money came from individuals and financial companies that did business with his office.

Tom and I were on a timetable to start publishing this series after Labor Day. But on the night of Monday, August 29, I got a phone call at home from one of my old friends at the *Village Voice.* He told me that the *Voice* was planning to run a "short, nothing knockoff" of our Regan series in Wednesday's paper, to punish Tom and me for leaving. My three friends at the *Voice*—Wayne Barrett, Joe Conason, and Bill Bastone—then faxed me this squib of a story, which contained no original reporting. Written by Rick Hornung, it had been hidden in a secret computer file, but Bastone—a computer whiz—found it and sounded the alarm.

Wayne remembers that he even talked to *Voice* editor Martin Gottlieb that night and urged him not to run the piece. "I told Marty," Wayne recalled recently, "that you had worked here for twenty-four years and had left without even a pension. I told him this Regan tip was your pension, and he shouldn't try to spoil it. I told him I had warned you it was coming, but I didn't tell him we had faxed you a copy . . . Me, Joe, and Bill were put on probation because of what we did. There was a whole witch-hunt . . . I thought one of us could get fired over this. But the inquisition ended after a few months, and we were taken off probation without anyone squealing."

I can't remember which of them actually placed the call to me, but whoever it was, I thanked him profusely. It doesn't matter who it was. The call was a collective act of loyalty. I then phoned Tom Robbins and Arthur Browne to say that we had to write the Regan series the next day, that it had to start running on Wednesday, because of the *Voice* effort to spoil our scoop.

Starting at 8:30 A.M. the next morning, Tom and I worked nonstop for fourteen hours to get the first article written and a draft of day 2 into the computer. I found making the transition from the leisurely structure of *Voice* articles to the formatted hard-news style of the *News* a little difficult. Arthur Browne had us rewrite the "nut graf"—the summary essence of the story—all day long until we got it just right.

At about 9 P.M., the *News*' libel lawyer and his junior assistant showed up to vet the story for defamation. The more senior lawyer was inebriated, so the junior partner—Kevin Goering—got to shine, and because of his performance on this hectic deadline night he soon became the regular libel counsel for the *News*. Fortunately, we had already conducted our face-to-face interview with Regan, so we had his quotes to incorporate into the story. He had called the Palumbo memo "bizarre" and "incredible" after we had handed him a copy and he had read it, very slowly, in front of us.

At the end of the day, with the "nut graf" published, it was time to compose "the wood"—the front page. That's when I first got to work with the legendary Joe Kovach, who was in charge of the front page. Joe had supervised the writing of the most famous *News* headline of modern times—FORD TO CITY: DROP DEAD—during New York City's fiscal crisis in October 1975.

Jimmy Breslin had left the *News* for *Newsday* before I started, but he gave one aria of advice the first week I was there. "There's just three human beings worth even speaking to left at the *News*," Jimmy said. "Bill Gallo is a lovely gentleman, Spanish not Italian, really shy, and a genius of a sports cartoonist . . . Just listen to Joe Kovach. The paper comes out because of him. If you ever have a problem, go to Kovach. He's a leader. Everyone else is a herd of sheep. And find Stu Marques. He's a real quiet guy on rewrite. Not too social. He did some time in the joint in New Jersey, and he put it right on his job application. I asked Dick Oliver why he hired Marques, and Dick told me he thought every paper should have at least one reporter who can pick a lock." Jimmy's three character references hit the trifecta.

One day I overheard the barrel-chested, thick-armed, rough-tongued Kovach making a subtle point about Truman Capote's prose. (It reminded me of the time I found an underlined, dog-eared copy of Montaigne's essays hidden in a drawer in Breslin's desk when he was at the *News*—buried under copies of *Ring* magazine and the *Racing Form.*) Joe had had a hard life of family tragedies. His first child had died in premature birth. His daughter, Libby, had injured her spine in a freak home accident and died at thirteen. His son, Glenn, accidentally hanged himself at home, playing with a Venetian blind. After he buried three of his children, he found out his wife was an alcoholic. Joe's friend the novelist Pat Conroy once told the *Los Angeles Times*, "There's great pain in Joe's eyes. It looks like *King Lear* has been played across his face several times."

Like others of his tabloid breed, Joe was a workaholic, dedicated to the job. At the end of this long day of crashing the Regan story he was demanding a catchy headline to dress up our exclusive exposé. An editor scrawled a proposed headline on a memo and handed it to Joe. "I don't want no pussy headline on this story!" he bellowed. "These boys have kicked ass. They deserve a kick-ass wood."

With time running out, we agreed on "CASH, CLOUT & CONRACTS." And in smaller type: "Those who give will get." And below that: "Aide's memo sparks *News*' probe of state controller Regan." It was all on page 1, along with a photo of Regan looking confused.

I will always treasure working with Joe on the Regan series. He was the real deal. He knew what was going to be important the next day and he wanted to make it accessible to the reader. He could trim a story with the precision of a brain surgeon. He could pump energy into a newsroom at deadline time with the force of a nuclear generator. And he was the institutional memory of tabloid journalism.

Joe retired a few months after we worked together on the Regan series. He didn't like the new trends in the business. He didn't like all the celebrity and gossip stories. He didn't like soft stories generated by market research. He didn't like all the political correctness that was making conversation dull and repressed—although he was pro gay and pro–equal rights in his politics, and he was a self-taught intellectual who read widely. Joe Kovach was never deferential to time-study consultants with clipboards or to marketing gurus who talked about demographics and niche markets. He didn't want a paper with puffy profiles of celebrities tied to movie openings set up by press agents. He just wanted to grab the truth by the throat and display it to the world.

Joe's farewell party at a bar near the *News* lasted all night. Survivors still talk about it. Several people recalled the time Joe screamed at a short copyeditor, "I'd like to punch the crap out of you, but you're too God-damned small. Maybe I'll piss on you. But then you would drown."

I saw Joe again for a few weeks in 1993. Pete Hamill drafted him out of retirement to work a few days a week at the *Post.* This was during a staff mutiny against our owners, which I'll discuss in the next chapter. Joe loved that atmosphere of rebellion, watching kids half his age do crazy things to keep a tabloid newspaper alive.

The morning after day 1 of the Regan series hit the newsstands, Tom and I were in demand. TV and radio shows wanted us. The *Bond Buyer* interviewed us. Our coworkers trooped by our desks to congratulate us. At one point Gil wandered by and told us that Regan had called him. "He was whimpering like a baby. I hope you're going to hit him even harder in tomorrow's installment." Nobody seemed to notice the knock-off squib in the *Voice.*

I can't claim that the series on Controller Regan opened my eyes to need for campaign finance reform, because I had been writing about the issue long before Joe Palumbo's smoking-gun memo arrived in the mail one fine day. But the Regan money project did intensify my focus on the nefarious ways politicians raise money and the debts to vested economic interests they accrue along the way. Over the last ten years I have written many columns arguing that campaign finance reform may be the most important reform, because until it is accomplished all other efforts at equity will be harder to accomplish. The gun lobby's contributions will continue to block further limits on access to handguns—even though 70 percent of Americans favor tougher gun control. The insurance and pharmaceutical industries will continue to block legislative attempts to make HMOs more responsive to patients than to accountants. Oil and gas interests will have an advantage over environmentalists through their ability to make large donations. Money tilts the playing field of democracy. The more I have written about "soft money" abuses and conflicts of interest arising from campaign money, the higher my opinion has grown of Senators John McCain and Russ Feingold, who have led this reform fight in Washington for years.

On September 23, 1988, Regan was subpoenaed to testify in public under oath before a state ethics committee known as the Feerick Commission. The commission made Regan look like a fool. It confronted him with dozens of memos sent to him by staff members, showing he was directly involved in fund-raising from companies his office regulated and conferred benefits on. He repeatedly claimed he had not actually read those memos, which were addressed to him. Regan appeared well coached on how to avoid perjury and was willing to act dumb and inept to dodge this criminal pitfall. He was willing to make a bad impression in order to survive in office. The strategy worked, and he was never prosecuted, although his reputation evolved into a crass quid-pro-quo fund raiser. Regan eventually resigned and was recently appointed to be the president of Baruch College, the business school of the City University system.

Two investigative stories Tom and I wrote ended up with people getting murdered by the mob—Jimmy Bishop and Fred Weiss. They tried to go halfway with the Mafia while still talking to us and trying to appear legitimate to respectable society. It didn't work.

Jimmy Bishop was a colorful rascal, an ex-marine who won the Bronze Star in Korea and who got his start in the painting business dangling from ropes while painting high bridges. This balancing act was a metaphor for Bishop's life. He rose to become the secretary-treasurer of the painters' union and a Democratic Party district leader in Queens. For years he met secretly with gangsters and shared payoffs for "labor peace" with them. But in 1989 he was ordered to quit his union job by a younger mob faction that wanted bigger profits and more control. For over a year Bishop was telling a mixture of truth and fiction to me and to the Manhattan District Attorney's office. He was still trying to dangle in air above water that was over his head.

I stumbled onto the painters' union story one day in 1989 when I accompanied my wife to the wake for the father of her friend filmmaker Christine Noschese in Brooklyn. At the wake I noticed little caucuses of gangsters in different corners of the room where the body was lying in an open casket. I overheard people whispering that Jimmy Bishop wasn't coming to the wake because his life had been threatened. He had to "get out of the union." Christine's father had been an officer of the painters' union but was hostile to the mob and had not been involved in the systemic graft. He was a self-described anarchist out of the immigrant school of Sacco and Vanzetti.

After a month of digging, Tom and I went to see our sources in the labor racketeering section in the Manhattan District Attorney's office. They turned white. It seemed they had just started a long-term undercover operation inside the painters' union. They were planning to install a hidden camera in the office of the union's corrupt new leader, Paul Kamen. They begged us to wait three months before we wrote anything. Then they asked us to wait another three months. Then yet another three months.

At that point Arthur Browne and I met with district attorney Robert Morgenthau and negotiated a deal—information for delay. We finally agreed to hold our story back until February of 1990, to give the investigation time to collect evidence, install a hidden camera, and try to "flip" a few witnesses. This is standard newspaper practice. We were trying to balance being good citizens and giving the DA enough time to take down the union leadership with the desire to get an exclusive story. A year is a long time to wait, but I felt it was the right decision in terms of the public interest and in terms of all the honest members of the union who, if there was a solid criminal case, would eventually be liberated from the thugs and grafters. The risk we took by holding back for a year was that another paper would hear about the sting and scoop us.

As we worked on the story, I made contact with Jimmy Bishop, who gave me his home phone number and agreed to talk to me "on background" for our story. Bishop confirmed that he had resigned his job running the union because his life had been threatened "seven or nine times, I can't remember exactly." He said the people making the threats were "killers at the top of the Luchese crime family." He said he was frightened enough to "put my six grandchildren in hiding."

Bishop also claimed, "I'm an honest union leader. I have no connections to organized crime." But in the same conversation he described how his first death threat arrived. "My friend [whom Bishop would not identify] rang my doorbell in the middle of the night. He had been coming home from the trotters when five guys in two cars forced him off the road. They spread-eagled him over the hood of his car and stuck a pistol in his mouth. They ordered him to come right to my house with their message to resign. My friend was so scared I thought he would puke on my rug."

When I asked who he thought was behind the threats, Bishop gave a one-word answer: "Gaspipe." (Antony "Gaspipe" Casso was the underboss of the Luchese family in 1988.)

Our front-page story ran on February 12, 1990. It told of a long history of organized crime controlling the six-thousand-member painters' union. We also revealed that the prosecutors had video- and audiotapes, "including a scene in which a top union official counts and divides $15,000 in cash among several of his business agents." We named the mobsters who controlled the union and its pension and insurance funds—Victor (Little Vic) Amuso, the boss of the Luchese family, and his partner, Gaspipe Casso. We recounted how these racketeers forced Bishop to resign and installed Paul Kamen two weeks later. The third paragraph made clear where our sympathies lay. The union, it read, was "rife with schemes that line the pockets of mobsters, union officials, and corrupt painting contractors—while severely shortchanging the union's rank and file."

I didn't want anyone to think I was against unions only against the parasites at the top who strangle union democracy and collaborate both with management and mobsters. In typical fashion, the corrupt business agents in the painters' union also discriminated against their own minority members in hiring practices. In follow-up columns to the page-1 exposé, I told the stories of black and Latino members of the painter's union who suffered discrimination in hiring by the union they were paying dues to. Very little of the original information in our story had been provided by Bishop, but he had confirmed some details in his sly fashion, while still implausibly denying he had done anything illegal or partnered with the mob. Bishop, who had a minor talent for blarney, thought he could con all of us—me, the mob, and the DA.

Three months after our article appeared, Jimmy Bishop was shot eight times and killed outside a Queens apartment complex while waiting to meet his mistress. I wrote a personal reminiscence about our conversations for the next day's paper. Ultimately Bishop's killer was arrested and became a federal informant after the mob tried to kill him, too. Paul Kamen and many of the business agents of the painters' union were convicted and jailed, based on the videotape evidence.

Fred Weiss was a white-collar version of Jimmy Bishop—more of a salesman than a marine. A former city editor of the *Staten Island Advance*, Weiss became a successful real estate developer, even publishing his own vanity press book on converting land into money. He liked talking to reporters, always offering gossip and rumors about Staten Island politicians and mob figures.

In February of 1989 Tom and I were working on an exposé of a cartel of carting companies that was illegally dumping toxic chemical and medical waste in Staten Island. Our law-enforcement sources had shown us surveillance pictures of a bubbling thirty-five-foot-deep pit, filled with infectious red-bag medical waste, asbestos, and tons of raw, rotting garbage. The site was located just off the Staten Island Expressway, in a community named Arlington. The evidence showed that more than forty mob-connected carting companies were dumping poisoned trash at this site, in the predawn hours, without the proper licenses. The neighbors in the working-class area were complaining of eye irritations and nausea from the noxious odors rising from the pit.

We knew that Weiss was a partner in this landfill, but he had ducked us for several weeks. Then one day he called and asked to come into the *News* city room and meet with Tom and me. "The only illegal trash at our site," he swore to me, was "one half-eaten cheese sandwich."

A few days later Weiss showed up for our interview. Perhaps to intimidate us, he brought along the two small-time mobsters who were his partners in the toxic dump. Angelo Paccione and Anthony Vulpis were wearing jeans, zipper jackets, baseball caps, and John Gotti sneers. "These guys got nothing to hide," Weiss said. "They are legitimate businessmen. Ask them anything you want."

"Do you know Jimmy Brown?" Tom asked, referring to the alias of James Failla, the Gambino capo who controlled the family's carting interests.

"I think we gotta be somewhere else," Vulpis suddenly declared, and walked out of the news room with Paccione. Weiss remained behind to make pleasant small talk.

I next saw Vulpis and Paccione in federal court a few months later, during their trial for running the illegal dump, for which they would be convicted. Weiss had been indicted with them but was not sitting with them at the defense table. The rumor was that he was cooperating with federal prosecutors.

On September 11, 1989, Fred Weiss was executed mob style. He was shot in the head and found in his car outside his Staten Island condo.

I never felt any guilt over or responsibility for the deaths of Weiss and Bishop. I was just doing my job. They were killed because they were criminals, cohorts of organized crime, who got caught by law enforcement and then were the considered risks to become informers by the mob. They chose a way of life outside the law and they paid the price.

Charles Brumback, sixty-two in 1990, an accountant from Toledo and an avid reader of Ayn Rand's novels, was the CEO of the Chicago Tribune Company, which owned the *Daily News*. Starting in March of 1989—a year before the union contracts expired—Brumback began planning to end unionization of the *News*. He was a man on a mission, telling a few *News* executives that he was in a "win-win" situation. Either he would break all the unions or sell the paper. There was no room for compromise or separate deals with the "good unions." That was the message Brumback gave James Hoge, the publisher of the paper.

Brumback had already broken the unions at the *Chicago Tribune*. He had built the nonunion *Orlando Sentinel* into one of the most profitable papers in the country, although the *Sentinel* had the built-in advantage of a booming population center and the most modern printing plant in America at the time.

A book about the strike at the *Daily News* by Richard Vigilante, published four years after it was over, contains a portrait of Brumback that is intended to be sympathetic, since Vigilante generally approves of Brumback's tough corporate strategy. Vigilante describes Brumback as "utterly immune to the working-class romanticism that is so crucial to union solidarity as well as union P.R. And political power, in Catholic and Jewish New York. He is that most terrifying of persons, the man with a clear conscience."

Since I was a management employee at the *News*, I was invited to a series of meetings with the paper's top executives to prepare for a strike. By the summer of 1989, because of these indoctrination sessions, I was learning about the enemy from behind their lines. I listened intently and kept notes.

Brumback hired Nashville lawyer Robert Ballow, the country's leading hired gun in busting unions. The *News* paid Ballow a huge fee, and he started his offensive. He gave militant speeches against the vices of unions. He saw reporters, editors, photographers, drivers, and pressmen as an enemy to be destroyed, not as a working people with wives, children, mortgages, and tuitions, to be negotiated with over wages and benefits.

Brumback and Ballow had become a tight team after defeating the unions in the 1985 *Chicago Tribune* strike. They had won by using scabs. That strike was their paradigm for New York. They studied it the way a football coach studies the films of the opponent's last few games, or the way a general studies satellite photos of potential bombing targets.

Brumback was convinced that there was no reason why he couldn't duplicate the Chicago trick in New York. He started hiring a small army of security guards and built a secret strike newsroom in an abandoned Sears plant in New Jersey. The building was surrounded by barbed-wire fences. Later, dogs would be used to patrol its perimeter. A security company, run by the city's former corrections commissioner, was also retained.

I didn't understand the fury coming out of Brumback and Ballow. The Chicago Tribune Corporation had reported net profits of $242.4 million in 1989, on gross revenue of $2.5 billion. The company owned seven newspapers, six television stations, four radio stations, a TV production company, a newsprint manufacturing business, a TV syndication company, and the Chicago Cubs baseball team. Brumback was making $833,000 a year, plus deferred bonuses and "incentive compensation." Ballow was earning perhaps even more. What was behind their vehemence? What abstract theories were making them clench their fists?

After the union contracts expired in March of 1990, the *News* management got more and more aggressive, trying to provoke a strike. They advertised for "replacement workers"—scabs—in the *News* itself. A few days later I saw a line of applicants two blocks long; two thousand people were willing to cross picket lines, thinking about their own financial problems and career prospects. Later in the year, the *News* drivers—a rough, mobbed-up bunch—were ordered to take their potential replacements with them on a shift, to show them their routes. Most of them complied. They had been told by the union leadership to resist all provocations to strike.

As part of my management indoctrination, I was given a tour of the *News'* printing plants and given a lot of labor contract material to read. I also talked to some members of the craft unions. It was undeniably true that there was an extravagant amount of featherbedding, waste, and thievery of papers going on and that it was costing the *News* millions of dollars every year. The scruples of the drivers' and pressmen's two unions were not all that different from those of the painters' union and Controller Regan. There were 36,000 hours of mandated overtime in the union contract that were not even worked. The pressmen were mostly Irish and the drivers mostly Italian and Jewish. There were very few blacks or Latinos in those two unions. And it was clear to anyone who looked closely that the drivers' union was influenced by the mob, mostly by John Gotti's Gambino family.

At one meeting I attended, Jim Hoge said that "work rule reforms" would save the paper between $70 and $100 million a year. On my tour of the antiquated Brooklyn plant I saw crews of thirteen pressmen running presses that only needed crews of six or seven. I could also see that there was a lot of open drinking on the job in this dungeon of a workplace. Hoge explained that almost 15 percent of the paper's total expenses went to overstaffing and fake overtime payments. He promised the executive staff that once "management controlled the workplace," the *News* would invest all the savings in building a new printing plant with color presses. In 1982 the unions had accepted the elimination of 1,340 jobs—saving the *News* $50 million a year—in exchange for a promise of new color presses. But this promise had never been kept, and left the taste of bad faith in the mouth of labor. Still, my own eyes and ears confirmed the accuracy of most of what Hoge was saying about union inefficiency.

Such moral complexity was made almost irrelevant by what was actually going on. Brumback's "win-win strategy" was to go to war with all ten unions, not just the pressmen and the drivers. He had no interest in trying to negotiate a separate peace with the honest Newspaper Guild and its seven hundred white-collar editorial employees. In Brumback's thinking, a new contract with the Guild would only make the paper harder to sell or more costly to close. He would either crush all ten unions in one year or sell the paper, rejecting all suggestions he try to accomplish his goal over two contracts.

Brumback had no emotional attachment to the paper or its people. The *News* was just another property to him, just another product. He was an accountant, a number-cruncher. As far as he was concerned, we could be manufacturing widgets or slaughtering hogs. He looked only at the bottom line and saw unions as the root source of red ink.

Brumback and Hoge both insisted, as an article of faith, that the *News* was losing money and that this was the rationale for breaking the unions. But after the strike started, a group of striking financial writers formed a research committee. Their analysis claimed that the *News* was only losing money on paper. And because the company had spent $27 million on strike preparations, including fees to Ballow. The strike planning was still in the background in late August of 1989, a cloud on the horizon. I didn't want to think about it. I didn't want to face it. I was having too much fun working for Gil Spencer. As long as Gil was in editor's chair, I deluded myself that things would somehow work out.

Then on the Friday before Labor Day weekend, somebody in the newsroom (I can't remember who) told me that the *News* was going to endorse Ed Koch rather than David Dinkins in the Democratic primary for mayor, then two weeks away. I was shown the Koch endorsement in the computer system, ready to go. I felt sick and scared. The *News* had been exposing Koch throughout his third term. Breslin had won his Pulitzer mostly because of his columns about the corruption under Koch. The paper had serialized the anti-Koch book I had written with Wayne Barrett. All the paper's columnists, including me, were for Dinkins. A Koch endorsement was just illogical. It would make the paper look incoherent. It had to be an arrangement.

Most of the columnists made a pact that we would all write columns supporting Dinkins, in response to the paper's formal endorsement of Koch. There was a steady flow of disappointed people going into Gil's office all day. But the game was being played over our heads, in Hoge's eighth-floor office. I saw Gil talking in the hallway with Michael Pakenham, the editorial page editor and his loyal friend. I could sense that a high-stakes corporate struggle was going on, but I didn't know what was happening. I could see the trees shake and the waters splash, but I couldn't tell who was winning.

At the end of the day I saw Gil for a moment. All he said was "It's stopped for now. It's just a goddamned shame."

What that cryptic lamentation was meant to convey I didn't know.

A few days later the *News* endorsed Richard Ravitch for mayor. Ravitch, a fringe candidate favored by a small elite that knew he was a good manager, got 4 percent of the vote. Dinkins won the primary. On September 14 Gil resigned as the editor.

In December of 2000 I had dinner with Gil, just after he celebrated his seventy-fifth birthday, and asked him to tell me what happened back in September of 1989 and why he had quit so suddenly.

"I was talking to Pakenham one day," Gil began, "when Hoge poked his head into the doorway of my office. I told him we were going to endorse Dinkins for mayor. And he said no we weren't. We were endorsing Koch. There had been no discussion, no conversation. Gil told Hoge that if they endorsed Koch they would all look like fools.

"I just flashed," Gil remembered. "He said 'Koch,' and I said 'Fuck you.' "

Hoge told him that he would lose his stock options. After Hoge left, Gil called his wife and asked her what his stock options were worth. His wife told him $350,000. But Gil's mind was made up. He would leave. A few hours later Pakenham came into Gil's office and informed him, "You won! We're endorsing Ravitch instead."

This transparent dodge seemed absurd to most of us.

A day or two later Gil met with Hoge. Gil recalls telling his boss the company was making a great mistake in trying to break the unions. He detested Ballow and everything he stood for, saying that Ballow was "making money out of misery." Gil quit a few days later. Hoge let him keep all the stock options. "Ballow broke it for me," Gil said. "He was evil."

I pushed Gil to solve the underlying mystery. Why had Hoge pushed so hard for the Koch endorsement? "Look, I can't exactly prove this, but here is what I think," Gil replied. "It was all tied to the strike. I believe that people higher up than I felt we had some understanding with Koch that City Hall and the police would favor the paper and not the unions when the strike came."

Two historical forces, the Tribune Company's strike planning and the primary for mayor, both involving a lot of money, collided in September of 1989. They trampled on me, on Gil, on Dinkins, and on the *News* as an institution. Could we have done anything to make things come out any different? I wondered. "No," Gil replied. "The big boys were playing." I suspect this is what he had in mind that day when he lamented. In 1989, "It's just a God-damned shame."

There was a brief crisis at the *News* the final weekend of the David Dinkins–Rudy Giuliani general election for mayor in 1989. The Giuliani campaign had gotten custody of fifty-four pages of "love letters" sent to Dinkins from eight different girlfriends scattered around the country. These letters—plus seventeen photographs—had been stolen by a disgruntled former Dinkins staffer out of his office files, where they were stored in an act of stupidity. The sister of the former Dinkins staffer who took them worked in the Giuliani campaign, which is how they came into play during the last days of the election. The letters had originally been given to Fred Dicker of the *Post*. But the *Post* wouldn't print the story. One or two editors at the *News* were considering doing a story about the letters, and the *Post's* possession of the letters, as a way to get the story out.*

At about noon on the Saturday before the election, I was in the city room and saw Adam Nagourney starting to write some kind of story about the letters. He seemed uncomfortable about the assignment and didn't want to talk about it. Adam did not have copies of the letters, and I suspect he was feeling used by the Giuliani campaign.

I pleaded with several editors at the *News* that it would be both morally wrong and racially inflammatory to publish any story about these salacious letters so close to the election.

Some were afraid of being scooped by the *Post*. They didn't know whether the *Post* was doing the story on the letters. Also, the Giuliani campaign was spreading rumors in the press corps that some publication was going to do a letters story before the election. The idea was to create enough uncertainty, enough fear of getting scooped, to force the *News* to publish the story.

My arguments against doing the story were based on both privacy rights and racial fairness. But the debate was taking place as the rules of the game were changing. The year before—1988—the media had exposed Gary Hart's infidelity with Donna Rice, and it had ended his presidential campaign. The genie was out of the privacy bottle. But in 1989 editors and reporters didn't know what the new ground rules were. They

---

*My account of the love letters saga is relatively brief and limited to what I actually saw and know. This is because the account in Wayne Barrett's biography of Rudy Giuliani (*Rudy! An Investigative Biography*) is so extensive and accurate.

were not codified in any newsroom. Reporters and editors were groping for some guidelines.

I had never written about any politician's sex life and I hoped I never would. I had declined several opportunities to write about Mayor Koch's private life, believing it was not relevant and not news. In the future I would reject an opportunity to write about Mayor Giuliani's private life. I knew from my friends inside the Dinkins campaign, who had been shown copies of them by Fred Dicker, that these "love letters" were authentic (Dinkins was still denying their authenticity to most of his own campaign staff). I was still uncomfortable with this kind of privacy invasion by the media. None of these women were on the city payroll, and the affairs these letters seemed to establish did not have any effect on Dinkins's performance of his public duties. The pre–Gary Hart standard was that journalists did not write about a politician's private life unless they could prove that it had a direct, negative effect on his public performance. The Dinkins letters didn't meet this old test for what was news.

The letters helped redefine and clarify my views about character as a measure of leadership and fitness for high office. I believe character is an important measure, but I think character should be defined much more broadly than just sex.

Character is somebody's essence as a person, how they behave when they think nobody is watching them. As a measure of character, adultery is less important a measure than financial integrity, for example, or being truthful, or being free from prejudice, or, having a moral sense like Lincoln's. Having the courage to stick to unpopular beliefs is a far better measure for judging someone's fitness for public leadership.

Richard Nixon was probably faithful to his wife, but he raped the Constitution. Thomas Jefferson almost certainly fathered an illegitimate child with his slave Sally Hemmings, but that did not make him any less of a thinker, writer, and president. Franklin Roosevelt and Martin Luther King may have been the two greatest American leaders of the twentieth century—and they both committed adultery.

Later on that same Saturday afternoon, I watched Andrew Cuomo save Dinkins's election by helping to talk the *News* out of printing the love-letters story. For three hours. I sat in Andrew's East Thirty-third Street office at HELP (the nonprofit group he founded to build housing for the homeless) and listened as he worked the phones. Andrew was only a volunteer in the Dinkins campaign, but this delicate assignment fell to him because nobody else wanted to talk to the candidate about such intimate matters. Andrew made the case for bedroom privacy rights, employing arguments both legal, ethical, and personal.

In the end, no paper disclosed the existence of the love letters. Dinkins won the election by a small margin. He turned out to be a weak mayor and a disappointment to me, but I still feel I was right to argue against publishing the story.

There cannot be a different standard for exposing the private life of a black politician than for a white politician. The *Daily News* had not written about the sexual misconduct of any white politician without the rationale of a woman speaking on the record or a lawsuit being filed in a public court. There was no equivalent of Paula Jones or Gennifer Flowers on Monica Lewinsky in the Dinkins story, no sexual partner willing to be quoted. And there was no firsthand proof, as there had been with the Gary Hart–Donna Rice assignation, when reporters for the *Miami Herald* staked out an apartment and saw Hart arrive and depart. Had the *News* published this story two days before the election, and had the story cost Dinkins the election, it would have generated justifiable bitterness, even despair in the black communities of New York City.

Some think my views conservative, overly cautious behavior in the competitive tabloid world. But I believe newspapers are part of a larger community and need to be responsible. We journalists can't simply do whatever we want and then hide behind the First Amendment when our fairness or judgment is questioned. The First Amendment is too sacred to be exploited for a low purpose. The Bill of Rights contains other liberties and protections in addition to freedom of the press. We should take into account all the liberties guaranteed by the Constitution. The rights of a free press come with responsibilities, and the privileged status granted to us by the First Amendment ultimately needs the support of the greater community. We jeopardize that support whenever we are reckless, whenever we use our rights to violate another individual's rights. Remembering that can sometimes save us from making mistakes.

One result of the *Daily News* strike—one of the greatest shames, as far as I was concerned—was that it chased away professionals like Stuart Marques. In October of 1988, I got a chance to act on Breslin's advice and get to know Marques when we worked together for a week on a big, three-full-page Sunday takeout on the Mike Tyson–Robin Givens breakup.

A team of five of us, including Mike McAlary and Mark Kriegel, did the reporting. Stuart was the rewrite specialist who combined and synthesized our various sections and raw notes into a consistent, coherent story that sang with one voice. Stuart had all the qualities of the master rewriter—speed, focus, and intelligence. He could weave disparate parts into a whole, seamless tapestry. When I asked Stuart what made him so good, he speculated that it might be because he suffered from attention deficit disorder (ADD). He thought it actually enhanced his ability to "shut out the rest of the world and just concentrate on writing, structure, length, and deadline."

Even with Stuart's skills, things didn't always go smoothly. At one point McAlary claimed one anecdote in my section "never happened," disputing my description of how Robin Givens had tried to cash a $581,000 check she had written to herself from a Mike Tyson Enterprises checkbook, writing "reimbursement for expenses" on the stub. I had written that the check had bounced because Don King had changed all of the Tyson-Givens joint accounts to Tyson's name alone. I knew this was true from several sources, including Tyson's manager, Bill Cayton, and Cayton's lawyer, Tom Puccio, a close friend. I made my case to Stuart, Mike made his, and then Stuart went with my version. A week later the *Post* published a copy of the actual $581,000 check, and McAlary was quick to apologize to both Stuart and me.

Stuart reminded me of my other loyal friend with a rap sheet—boxing trainer Teddy Atlas: The more vulnerable and needy you were, the more generous and sensitive they became. Stuart had been arrested twelve times between the ages of fourteen and twenty-two, and he spent three and a half years in prison, serving one stretch as a juvenile, another as an adult in Bordentown Prison. He had adult convictions for larceny and burglary. His last arrest came when he was on parole and innocently happened to be in the wrong apartment when it was raided by the police because the occupant was a marijuana dealer. With the tough-love intervention of his uncle Hy, Stuart went straight after this experience. He liked to read in prison, realized he had an interest in journalism, and was hired by the daily in Passaic, New Jersey in 1974. It was the birth of a natural.

Stu was hired at the *News* in 1980, and put on the rewrite desk. He watched the first-rate editors on the city desk—and learned. Years later Stuart ended up as my boss at the *New York Post,* where he was city editor, and is then managing editor for news.

When the strike began in October of 1990, Stuart had been married to *News* reporter Joanne Wasserman for only three months, and Joanne was pregnant with their son, Sam. "We went from two paychecks to none in one day," Stuart remembered. "I needed a job right away with a baby on the way." He got a job at Fox television's *A Current Affair,* the pioneering tabloid TV magazine show, and began his transition from rewriter to editor and manager. In 1993 Ken Chandler became the new boss of the show. A month later Ken became the editor of the *Post,* and Stu went with him, reuniting us. Because of his own background, Stuart would make the *Post* into what some of us came to call "the Church of the Second Chance," a haven for redemption of all troubled souls. He hired people who had talent and a past, and they all flourished.

For example, he hired Maggie Haberman as a copykid at twenty-one. Maggie had just emerged from a troubled adolescence and needed a break. Stuart asked me to mentor her, and we worked together on a series of investigative projects involving union corruption, judicial patronage, and an installment of New York's ten worst judges. Maggie is now a reporting star.

Stuart also took a chance and hired a young relative of columnist Doug Montero as a copykid. The young man was on parole for armed robbery. He did well and is now in college.

Stuart also hired my son, Joey, though he has no criminal record I'm aware of, first as a summer intern when he was eighteen and then as a staff photographer at nineteen, after Joey showed promise and a quick lens at the back exit to the courthouse and outside a police station for a perp walk.

When I asked Stuart where he acquired his management style, he replied that his models were the editors back at the *News* in the early 1980s. "They were good human beings," Stuart said. "They were straight shooters. They didn't play games. They tried to help you as a human being if you had a problem. Their philosophy was, 'If I can count on you, you can count on me.' They didn't believe the job was only about business."

Stuart Marques must have been a lousy thief, judging from the number of times he was arrested. But he became a natural Tab Man, first on rewrite and now as an editor with a sixth sense for judging how big a story is going to be, how to cover it, and how to play it in the paper. I can still see him on Friday night in 1988, writing that 110-inch Tyson story, moving his fingers on the computer terminal as fast as Tyson moved his hands in the ring, organizing all the material and story lines against the deadline, hyperfocused on the computer screen. It was like watching Duke Ellington convert chaos into a concerto.

The *News* strike finally began on the evening of October 25, 1990. The trigger was a driver named Gary Kalinch, who refused an order to stand up at the Brooklyn plant while putting cover sheets on stacks of newspapers coming off a conveyor belt. He said he was sitting down because he had a sore knee. The drivers' supervisor insisted he do the job standing or he would be suspended. This dispute started the strike. It may or may not have been a setup by management, which had been planning for the strike for sixteen months and trying to provoke it since March, when the union contracts expired. I agonized for the four days about what to do. I didn't work, and I didn't write.

The strike forced me to confront myself, testing my own integrity, my willingness to live by the words I wrote. Could I exhibit the sacrifice and courage that I preached? Could I live up to the old neighborhood code, which was "never cross a picket line"? In my heart I knew I had to resign and join the picket line of my peers. But doing it was not so easy. I would have to surrender a job that I loved, to support unions that were not perfect. But the Tribune Company had napalmed the middle ground. There was no space for a morally nuanced intellectual position. People would remember what I did—not what I thought.

I compared myself, in the privacy of my imagination, to Elliot Richardson, the attorney general Richard Nixon ordered to fire Archibald Cox as the special Watergate prosecutor. Richardson chose to resign. Solicitor General Robert Bork, on the other hand, fired Cox and kept his own job and career. Nobody remembers what legal arguments Richardson and Bork made that day. We remember what they did.

I listened over and over to some of my favorite music—John Lennon's "Working Class Hero," Sam Cooke's "A Change Is Gonna Come," and Springsteen's "The River" and "My Hometown." I also listened again and again to Miles Davis's "Sketches of Spain," with its haunting flamenco-flavored trumpet solos. And to Billie Holiday singing songs like "Solitude" and "Fine and Mellow." Ever since I first heard it in the 1950s, her voice has conveyed to me—and to so many others—the loneliness of the human condition.

I knew what Robert Kennedy and Martin Luther King would have done in my shoes with their values. King always chose conscience, and RFK believed courage was the paramount human virtue.

As usual, Janie was wise and to the point. She told me I had no choice. Forget about the loss of income, she said. When I whined about how other striking *News* writers were already getting job offers from television and other papers and I wasn't, she gave me confidence to believe that I was good enough to to get another daily newspaper job—and another healthcare plan that covered our kids. She said that even if it took a while, we could handle it.

Then I called some of my journalistic role models. "You ought to resign soon," Murray Kempton counseled. Pete Hamill told me, "You should do whatever will make you feel good about yourself when you have to explain all this to your children in ten years."

Jimmy Breslin, who had resented the newspaper craft unions ever since the *Herald Tribune* folded under him, gave me the opposite advice. "Why would you throw away your career to help out a bum like John Gotti?" Jimmy asked, referring to gangster he believed ran the drivers' union. "You have a job. Go to work tomorrow. A J-O-B is the most important thing in the world. Don't throw yours away."

The truth was that I was afraid. I was afraid I would never get another job on a daily paper again. But now I was able to talk about it, acknowledge it for what it was. "Facing your fear" is something I had heard Teddy Atlas and Cus D'Amato tell their gym fighters. Boxing taught me that it was not unmanly to feel fear. Feeling it was human. Admitting it was no shame. The only cowardly thing was to surrender to fear.

On Sunday night Juan Gonzales called me and said matter-of-factly that it would help the strike a lot if I resigned. Juan didn't put any pressure on me. I told him I would probably do it and would let him know by Monday evening.

I had enormous respect for Juan. He had grown up in desolate East New York, in the Cyprus Hills housing project, and gone to Franklin K. Lane, a public high school with low reading scores and a high dropout rate. But Juan got straight A's and was accepted by Columbia University, which was where I first met him. He was one of the few mature and thoughtful leaders of the 1968 student occupation of the campus. I met him again in 1969, when he was one of the leaders of the Young Lords, the radical Puerto Rican group patterned on the Black Panthers. I covered the Lords in East Harlem, where they agitated for better sanitation and the testing of children for lead poisoning by the city's health department. Juan then went into the newspaper business and worked for Gil Spencer at the *Philadelphia Daily News*. In December of 1987, Gil hired Juan to be a columnist for the *New York Daily News*.

On the third day of the strike, Juan was drafted to be the chair of the rank-and-file strike committee. The national leaders of the Newspaper Guild remembered Juan's leadership role during a six-week 1985 newspaper strike in Philadelphia—a strike Juan led against Gil Spencer. This only increased Gil's respect for Juan. Juan's father had advised him always to attend union meetings and listen. And Juan had attended every Guild meeting at the News, even when there were only three or four people present from the editorial staff. He already knew all the issues. He had even been present for a ritualistic strike authorization vote months earlier. Juan was our Tom Paine—a writer and a radical who knew what he was doing.

As soon as he became chair of the strike committee, Juan met with his friend Dennis Rivera, the leader of the hospital workers' union. Dennis threw himself into the strike, even though his union did not collect dues from a single *News* employee. Juan and Dennis would lead the strike together, and they would also be the reasons the strike would be won. Dennis convinced John Cardinal O'Connor to back the strike and to condemn scabs, and this became a major factor in gaining popular support for the strike. (Dennis is Catholic and half Irish.) Dennis donated $55,000 from his Union's Treasury to start a strike fund, after some other, bigger unions, balked at making a contribution.

On Monday afternoon I reached Juan and told him I was ready to quit. "I love you" was his reply, in a voice choked with emotion. Then I sat down and wrote, and rewrote, my letter of resignation to Jim Willse, who had replaced Gil as the editor.

> *Dear Jim,*
>
> *Working at the* Daily News *was the best job I ever had. I loved it. I loved the people, the audience, the life of a columnist/reporter.*
>
> *Resigning is one of the hardest things I have ever had to do. Not just because I loved what I do. The issues here are hard. I know there are real abuses by some of the unions. I know what you have to do is no fun. The whole situation is tragic, and neither you nor I caused it to happen.*
>
> *But my conscience and self-respect just can't allow me to ratify the breaking of unions with my labor and my name. I tried to find rationalizations and hiding places, but there are none.*
>
> *I would just be miserable working for a paper that locked out its unions, and sitting next to scabs at desks once occupied by my friends.*
>
> *The paper has forced me to choose between my job and my conscience. I have to choose my conscience in order to live with myself, and be able to explain my life to my children.*

On Wednesday morning I went into the *News* office, cleaned out my desk, collected as many files as I could carry, and handed my letter to Jim. We did not make eye contact or speak, but he gave me a pat on the back as I turned away from him. Richard Rosen, the Sunday editor, gave me a warm embrace on the way to the elevator.

Feeling depressed and sorry for myself, I walked out of the *News* building. And there, waiting to cheer me up, were five hundred members of the hospital workers' union, a loud band, and Dennis Rivera, my compadre and the president of this mostly black and Latino union. As Dennis hugged me, a crush of cameras, reporters, and pickets engulfed us. (Dennis later gave me an inscribed photo of this moment. It hangs in my living room to this day.) Striking columnist Gail Collins gave me a kiss. Barry Lipton, the president of the union, gave me a hug.

The next morning *Newsday* ran a three-column photo of me, Dennis, Gail, and Lipton. The headline next to the photo said: "NEWFIELD QUITS; 100 COME BACK." My resignation was news because I was management; no other management employee would quit. My resignation occurred the same day most of the photography staff and half the sports department crossed the picket line and went back to work. When I was in the newsroom packing up my files I saw "replacement workers" and some Guild members working. I won't name them, but I hope Dorothy Parker's quip is true: "Time wounds all heels."

I also saw the Yeats-quoting John Scanlon, the *Tribune*'s public relations consultant, exulting "We've won! The unions are finished!" John's father had been a militant member of Mike Quill's transport workers' union, but John would work for union busters like the *Tribune* and Frank Lorenzo of Eastern Airlines. When I noticed Scanlon, who died last year, celebrating a premature victory, I was doubly glad that I had done what I did. A few weeks later Murray Kempton wrote the most savage column I had ever seen him write about Scanlon. Thankfully, Murray violated his own gentleman's rule against writing about people he hated. He turned his loathing into prose that would tarnish Scanlon's reputation.

> When Roy Cohn was alive, there were occasions when somebody would pull at trick so repellent that he dared not confess its authorship. In such cases, you could always count on Cohn to clear the mystery by assigning himself the unearned discredit. Roy Cohn's wandering spirit has found its reincarnation in Scanlon.

In the early evening of the day I quit the *News*, I spent an hour on the boisterous picket line, where I was welcomed with more hugs from the rank-and-file strike leaders—Gonzales, Robbins, and Capeci. Juan told me that my quitting had shifted the momentum of the strike back to the unions after a bad two days. As the November wind swirled around, I picketed and sang the old union hymns with some of the most professional reporters in the business.

When I got home, I called one of the senior editors at the *News*, who was supervising the production of the scab paper. He was still my friend, even from the other side of the barricade. "It's really strange in here," he told me. "All the people we hate are crossing the line and coming back to work."

The significance of what I had done did not fully register until the day after I had quit, when I was invited to say a few words to a vast labor rally in the middle of East Forty-second Street, organized by Local 3 of the Electrical Workers. Fifteen thousand union members were massed in front of the *News* building, filling most of the block with signs, union banners, and drums. It seemed like the entire union leadership of the city was on the platform.

I received a hero's introduction from Local 3 president Tommy Van Arsdale, and the fifteen thousand blue-collar workers cheered the mention of my name. The cheers echoed in the canyon of Forty-second Street, up to the windows of the newsroom on the seventh floor, where the scabs could hear it. The drums in the crowd beat out a rhythm. The colorful banners from different local unions were hoisted up and down in the darkness. The bright lights of the television cameras blinded me for a second as I walked to the microphone.

This was a fantasy of working-class unity come true. This was like Ebbets Field. This was like the Robert Kennedy–Tony Zale–Richard Hatcher motorcade through Gary, Indiana, in 1968. This was like a Bruce Springsteen concert in New Jersey.

I mumbled a few sentences of optimistic militancy, and waved, and retreated to the back of the platform, where my man Jim Bell of the UAW swallowed me up in his powerful arms. I looked out over this crowd of electrical workers, carpenters, truck drivers, and thought, "These were the people who were beating up the antiwar demonstrators twenty years ago."

For one night I felt like the working-class hero that John Lennon sang about and that I wanted to be. I felt that I would always owe the priceless memory of this night, of fifteen thousand blue-collar workers cheering my name, to Charley Brumback and Robert Ballow, and to their intransigent antagonism to craft unions and working stiffs. Both the irony and the solidarity made this a sweet moment.

CHAPTER 10

The *Post* Mutiny

The Monday after I had quit the *Daily News*, I started writing for the weekly *New York Observer*. It was for half the pay, but emotionally this poor boy from Brooklyn still needed the security of a steady job. I felt like I couldn't miss work for even a week. The *Observer* had a small circulation in Manhattan. "You're not read anymore," my friend Bill Lynch teased me. "You're just faxed around by fixers."

But a group of my friends, led by Andrew Cuomo and public relations consultant Marty McLaughlin, began a campaign to get me hired by the *New York Post*. They quickly enlisted Eric Breindel in this cause. Eric was then the editorial page editor of the *Post*. He agreed to lobby for me with the *Post*'s pubisher, Peter Kalikow.

I knew persuading Kalikow to hire me wouldn't be easy. In 1986, in a *Village Voice* cover story, I had named Kalikow, a major real estate developer, one of New York's "ten worst landlords." Then in 1988 Tom Robbins and I wrote a front page story in the *Daily News* revealing that Kalikow initially had been blacklisted from the state pension fund by

Ned Regan. But five months after Kalikow made a $25,000 campaign contribution to Regan, he was granted a $6 million loan from that pension fund. The loan helped Kalikow build an office complex at 101 Park Avenue.

After Breindel and McLaughlin, who did PR for Kalikow, did a lot of pleading and lobbying in my behalf, I had a lunch with Kalikow. I found him funny, smart, gossipy, down-to-earth, and, perhaps most entertaining of all, a Brooklyn Dodger nostalgia buff. After reluctantly acknowledging that every fact I wrote about his mortgage deal with the state was accurate, he offered me a job writing one column a week, starting in November of 1991. I was thrilled. The *Post* was the paper in whose pages I had first read Kempton and Cannon as a teenager; it felt like a homecoming. "But there is one caveat to my offer," Kalikow said with a straight face. "Your first article for the *Post* must be 'the ten worst tenants.' " "How about the nine worst landlords?" I countered. Kalikow laughed. We had a deal.

In the course of this lunch Kalikow told me that being the publisher of the *Post* had cost him some good friends who had been tweaked or needled in the paper. They had expected the publisher to protect them. "It got to the point that I stopped having the first edition delivered to me at 10:30 at night. I didn't want to know which of my friends was mentioned unfavorably until the presses had stopped rolling and the last edition was delivered. So when people, big shots, would call me at home at 11 P.M., when they heard what the first edition said about them, I could honestly say I didn't know what they were talking about." Then he added, "Al D'Amato is my best friend. If you ever attack him, you better be right."

From my first day in the newsroom I could tell that working at the *Post* was going to be fun. It was a rowdy but happy ship of nonconformists who didn't fit in anywhere else. I felt I had joined Robin Hood's band of merry men.

I asked Pete Hamill how to log onto the computer system, so I could start writing my first column. Pete (then not as totally computer literate as he is now) took an index card with written instructions out of his wallet, and we followed them together. I was very tentatively touching computer keys to log on when reporter Jim Nolan, one of Pete's many younger-brother protégés, starting laughing at us. "You two guys look like you come from the bomb squad," he quipped.

After gingerly writing my column, I asked Charley Carillo, then a humor columnist (and a future novelist), to tell me about the editor, Jerry Nachman.

"I've never had a real conversation with him," Carillo said.

How could that be?

"My mother brought me up right," Charley deadpanned, "and she taught me never to talk to anybody while they have food in their mouth. Jerry is always eating."

He pointed to Nachman, sitting in his darkened office alone, silhouetted against the magnificent Brooklyn Bridge eating take-out Chinese food.

At the end of that first day I had a cup of coffee with Nolan at the South Street Diner, next to the *Post.* Nolan is now a reporter on *The Philadelphia Daily News.*

"We are the crash-test dummies of American journalism," Jim explained. "The *Post* reporters do everything that's crazy and dangerous first. If we don't die, then the other tabloids and television copy it, because they know it's not fatal."

Little did Jim and I know that we would eventually survive one of the biggest, craziest car wrecks in the history of American journalism.

It began in January of 1993 with rumors. Kalikow was going broke. The bank was going to pull the plug on Kalikow's line of credit. Our salaries were going to be cut. The paper couldn't meet payroll. There was no money to buy newsprint.

Nobody knew anything for sure, but it felt like the *Post* might fold any day.

Then on the afternoon of Friday, January 22, the editor, Lou Colasuonno, who had replaced Nachman in 1992, called a meeting in the newsroom and made the rumors official. Lou announced that Bankers Trust had cut off all of Kalikow's credit. He said *if* there was a paper on Monday, the price would go up from 35 to 50 cents. All salaries were being cut by 20 percent effective immediately.

Lou also confirmed that Kalikow had stopped making his contributions to the employees' 401(K) pension plan and was no longer making

FICA payments to the federal government. The unpaid federal tax bill was now $4.3 million. I liked Kalikow, but not enough to like being cheated, or like the paper becoming part of a criminal indictment.

The buzz in the office was that the *Post* would be dead in forty-eight hours. I saw reporters rush into the library and take their own byline clip files and start to write résumés for job applications.

That night New York's governor, Mario Cuomo, called me at home and said he was working on finding a buyer for the *Post* and that I shouldn't worry.

Allow me to freeze the narrative of the *Post* mutiny for a moment here to properly introduce Cuomo into this memoir.

Mario looms large in my life. Son of an illiterate immigrant ditchdigger, he could have run for president in 1988 or 1992 and should have accepted an appointment to the Supreme Court in 1993. He is a man of great complexity. A brilliant appellate lawyer, and therefore a brilliant critic of anyone else's arguments and ideas, he is a lethal counterpuncher, with a question for every answer. In political particulars we differed enough to make for a lively and contentious friendship.

Mario is hard to get to know, and I would never claim to understand him. He is guarded, solitary, and trusts very few people outside of his family. In this way he is similar to four other Italian sons-of-immigrant icons of his generation—Joe DiMaggio, Dean Martin, Frank Sinatra, and Rocky Marciano. Mario once confided to me that he is most happy when he is alone, writing in his diary, early in the morning. The great orator prefers solitude.

Cuomo first became a friend in 1970, when I went out to Corona, Queens, to write a story for the *Village Voice* defending sixty-nine Italian American homeowners whose houses were about to be torn down by the city to make way for an athletic field for Forest Hills high school.

Cuomo was then an unknown, pro-bono lawyer for the community writing legal briefs that tied up the lawyers for New York City in court. Cuomo was impressed with my article and surprised by the fact that a writer for a radical Manhattan weekly would go up against the liberal mayor and his Ivy League lawyers to defend a bunch of working-class conservative Italians from Queens, almost all of whom had voted for either John Marchi or Mario Priccacino against Lindsay the year before.

In 1977, when Mario ran for mayor and lost to Ed Koch, my wife, Janie, worked as a volunteer in his campaign and sometimes drove Mario around to night meetings. One night Mario got into a heated argument with the conservative activist Mike Long outside a parochial school in Brooklyn. Mario felt Long had insulted him, so the future governor decked Long with one quick punch. In his youth Mario had boxed at the Beaver Gym in South Jamaica, and he knew how to pivot and get leverage behind his right hand.

Mario jumped into my wife's car and they drove two blocks before he got an attack of conscience. He asked my wife to drive back and make sure Long was not hurt.

Long was woozy but standing and not injured when my wife and Mario returned. But the incident would become a running joke between Mario, Janie, and me. Mario always maintained that Long had "slipped." His powers of speech were so magical that he almost convinced my wife that she had not seen what she had seen.

Between my coming to the defense of the Italian American homeowners in Queens, my giving Mario some of his first newspaper publicity (along with Jimmy Breslin in *New York* magazine), his fondness for my wife, and my observing the code of *omerta*, (silence) when it came to revealing that he had punched out Mike Long, Mario and I became close friends. But being Mario's friend is a little like being Rocky Marciano's favorite sparring partner.

Our bond has survived some strong disagreements, such as: over whether to build a highway on the West Side of Manhattan instead of trading in the funds for mass transit; Mario's vigorous support for Jimmy Carter over Ted Kennedy for the presidential nomination in 1980; and his selection of Republican Sol Wachtler over Milton Mollen to be the chief judge of New York State during Mario's first term as governor. I admired Sol enormously—and Sol credited Janie's late father, Joe, for mentoring his start in Republican politics—but I thought Mollen was probably the most impressive and impartial judge and public conscience in New York in my lifetime.

Mollen, now eighty-one, has a practical intellect. He either worked for, or with, the last six mayors of New York. I once asked him who among them—Robert Wagner, John Lindsay, Abe Beame, Ed Koch, David Dinkins, and Rudy Giuliani—he thought was the best. "That's easy," Milton replied. "Wagner. Because he never took anything personally. He never made a decision in anger. He never personalized differences."

I assumed that at least part of the reason for the governor's extraordinary intervention efforts to save the seven-hundred jobs at the *Post* was his desire to save my job in particular, a kindness I will always appreciate. In the end, Mario did as much to save the paper as Pete Hamill and Marc Kalech.

To resume the *Post* mutiny. At 6 P.M. on the Sunday after Colasuanno's near-death announcement about the *Post*, about twenty-five editors and columnists were summoned to Peter Kalikow's sixth-floor office. Kalikow began the session by telling Cindy Adams, the gossip columnist, "Don't worry, we ain't dead yet." Behind him, the television news was already reporting that after 192 years of publishing, the *Post* was closing. Cindy was more than just a gossip columnist. She was an important behind-the-scenes player, along with Eric Breindel, in trying to find a new buyer for the bankrupt paper or putting together a syndicate of new investors. Cindy had a lot of people's unlisted phone numbers.

Kalikow, wearing jeans and boots, said he was going to suspend publication immediately, while a new source of capital was being scouted. He did not mention severance pay for his workers. It felt like a death sentence.

There was one morbidly funny moment that broke the tension. A local TV station was doing an obit on the *Post* and columnist Mike McAlary came on screen in an interview he had taped a few hours earlier. "We have to find a new owner," Mike was saying. "Kalikow is dead in the water with Maxwell." This was a harsh reference to Robert Maxwell, the poststrike owner of the *Daily News* for a brief period, who had drowned mysteriously two months earlier in the Canary Islands while a financial scandal was engulfing him.

McAlary was standing right next to Kalikow when his pronouncement of appeared on television. But the good-natured owner just made a playful fist and cocked it under his columnist's jaw. Mike quickly recovered, telling Kalikow he was really referring to "Cornbread Maxwell of the Boston Celtics."

Suddenly the phones started ringing. Breindel, who looked like he hadn't slept for a week, began talking intensely. He started to smile. When he hung up, Eric told the group, "I don't want to raise hopes needlessly, but we just got an expression of interest." We were in a Frank Capra movie. A reprieve for the free press at the last minute! All jobs are saved in the last scene! Kalikow gave me a hug and whispered, "I hate bankers. I think I am a Democrat again."

The name of our savior began to filter out over the next hour. "Hoffenberger?" "Hoffman?" Steven Hoffenberg! That was the name. I had never heard of him. Nobody in Kalikow's office seemed to know who he was—except Cindy Adams. She said he was a friend of the limo mogul William Fugazy. As my colleagues celebrated our survival, I was getting a queasy feeling in my stomach just from the mention of Fugazy. I went down to the *Post* morgue and pulled the clips on Steve Hoffenberg.

There were only a few. One involved a partnership between Hoffenberg and the disgraced former Attorney General John Mitchell. Another mentioned the Teamsters' union pension fund. A third referred to a lawsuit brought by retirees in Louisiana against Hoffenberg. I am normally an optimist, but these clips made me apprehensive. Who was this guy my friend the governor sent to rescue us?

At about 10 P.M. Kalikow, looking weary but relieved, came into the city room and said, "The deal is done. We will publish tomorrow. Don't send the pressmen home." Editors asked Kalikow who Hoffenberg was. Kalikow replied that he had no idea. "I never heard of him," the publisher said. "But I love him."

I shared my unease with a few reporters who knew how to work the computers to get LEXIS and NEXIS research on Hoffenberg printed out.

For the next two hours, the bad news about Hoffenberg spewed out of the fax machines. Frauds. Lawsuits in twenty states. SEC investigations. Citizens saying he cheated them. No assets in his own name to pay creditors and court judgments. Karen Phillips (who would become one of the heroines of the mutiny) and I started to develop a gallows humor as we read each other excerpts from the information pouring out of these machines about our new owner and employer. Hoffenberg was infamous in Florida and Louisiana. He was a man who cheated widows and orphans. The SEC said that he had taken in $215 million by selling notes while he dishonestly inflated the income and net worth of his company, Towers Financial Corp. He owed more than $1 million in court judgments. He had been found guilty in 1982 of fraudulently diverting the assets of a Manhattan hardware business. He was a scam artist, a con man.

If Hoffenberg couldn't pay creditors, how could he keep the *Post* afloat? At the end of this up-and-down night the editors were sitting around trying to write the wood announcing our resurrection. "How about 'Hoodlum Saves Child from Fire' "? I suggested. Everyone laughed, but the wood shouted the next morning: "NEVER SAY DIE! LAST MINUTE DEAL SAVES *POST*."

The next day I called Cuomo, whom the *Post* reported had sent a state trooper to locate Hoffenberg on Sunday.

"We needed Sonny, and you sent us Fredo," I began, knowing the governor's secret fondness for the *Godfather* movies.

"I think I screwed up," Mario allowed. "It's a big misunderstanding." He then explained that he never intended Hoffenberg to become the buyer. "It was supposed to be a guy from West Palm Beach named Abe Gossman, a wealthy, pro-Israel philanthropist who owns some medical facilities. I don't know this guy Hoffenberg. It's a misunderstanding.

"Somebody, I can't tell you who, called me up and said there was a very rich guy who owns nursing homes and is ready to buy the *Post*. What did I think? I thought this guy was referring to Abe Gossman. I got the two guys confused. So I gave a ringing endorsement to Hoffenberg, thinking I was talking about Gossman. I thought I was saving the *Post*, but I did it with the wrong guy.

"Tell Janie not to worry," Mario added. "We'll make everything come out right in the end. A governor knows a lot of rich people."

Hoffenberg did have a loose affiliation with what Cuomo called "medical facilities." His company, Towers Financial, bought up debt owed to hospitals and nursing homes at a discount and then sold securities based on projected future earnings from the receivables. All those pieces of paper that came out of the fax machine reported that the SEC believed Hoffenberg misrepresented the value of the receivables. This was the way he defrauded the investors.

From the first day, I developed the habit of calling Hoffenberg "Bugsy" in conversations with other *Post* staff members. Others took to referring to him as either "Lepke" or "Meyer." It was all a comic code for "Jewish gangster." We employed the names interchangeably. In a meeting with Hoffenberg, Mike McAlary and Colasuanno asked him, "Are we working for gangsters?"

"I'm not a wise guy," Hoffenberg told them, "I'm a tough, aggressive businessman."

His first week as the temporary publisher, I was invited to dinner with Hoffenberg and the *Post*'s publicist, Howard Rubenstein.

"Bugsy" was not much of a listener. Rubenstein told him I had won an Emmy for an investigative television documentary on Don King. "Don King is a great guy, one of my best friends," my new boss responded. In the course of the evening I found Hoffenberg to be a salesman/hustler, publicity-crazed, and to know entirely too many mobsters. He proudly wore his new press card around his neck all through dinner, as if he were a cub reporter covering a fire.

Hoffenberg spent part of the evening pestering Rubenstein to get him on television, to get him a profile in *New York* magazine, to get him as much publicity as possible. Howard knows more about media and image-making than anyone else in New York. He knew that any publicity would be bad publicity. Howard gently tried to suggest this unpleasant realism to Hoffenberg. But the would-be publisher was focused on making himself famous overnight. He seemed to think publicity was a bulletproof vest against prosecutors, when it was actually a neon sign.

I had arrived at this dinner perplexed as to why Hoffenberg was trying to buy the *Post*, given all of his legal problems, and knowing from the governor that he was just a case of mistaken identity. By the end of the evening I reached the conclusion that Hoffenberg's crazy idea was to take the *Post* hostage, use it as a shield against the SEC and the FBI. His thinking was that as long as he was impersonating the civic patriot, "rescuing" the seven hundred jobs at the *Post*, they wouldn't put him in jail.

On most days the *Daily News* published well-researched stories about the various investigations into Hoffenberg. At the same time, the *News* was starting to make offers to lure away *Post* staffers, who were understandably thinking there was no job security at the *Post.* They were looking to Colasuanno for assurance and stability. But Lou was in an impossible position. He knew exactly who our new owner was, and he had to try to pump up staff morale, armed only with his own likable, blue-collar personality. At one meeting with the nervous résumé-writing staff, Lou declared, "I'm the canary in the coal mine. As long as I'm still breathing, you're okay."

Six days the canary flew out of the mine. Then Lou made a $300,000-a-year-deal with publisher Mort Zuckerman to become the new editor of the *Daily News.* Mike McAlary, with his own $300,000 contract, flew the coop with Lou, the canary. So did makeup editor Jim Lynch, columnist Amy Pagnozzi, and city editor Richard Gooding. The *News* hired the whole pack of defectors, intending it to be the final punch that killed the *Post*. They were hired more to injure us than to improve the *News.* And none of them are there today. (McAlary died of colon cancer in 1999 when he was in the middle of doing some of his best work.)

One of the few experienced editors left behind was Marc Kalech, Colasuanno's closest friend since they were copyboys together. Marc was periodically overlooked and underestimated. On February 1, the morning after the Big Defection, I came in and saw Marc sitting glumly behind his desk. In a possibly insensitive attempt at humor, I said, "You look like the last Japanese soldier they left behind on Iwo Jima."

Marc explained that the group of defectors was put together by McAlary. "Nobody asked me to join it. I didn't know anything about it. But I was a little suspicious yesterday, when I saw [Richard] Gooding wearing a suit. It was a fucking Sunday, and I had never seen him wear a suit before in twenty years." (Richard was having his job interview with *News* owner Mort Zuckerman.)

A few hours later Hoffenberg named Gerard Bray the new editor, Steve Cuozzo the managing editor, and Kalech the city editor. He told the staff that "Castellano" had jumped to the *News.*

Bray was a gruff fussbudget. He was comfortable with authority and decision making, having been the business and financial editor for the previous decade. He was a good office politician with a reputation for being a dangerous poker player. But his experience was narrow. He didn't know much about crime and cops—the staple of a tabloid. He had limited knowledge of government, politics, youth culture, and pop celebrities. And he didn't seem to have much in common with the paper's young, informal, nonconforming staff of crash-test dummies.

My first interaction with Bray came when he walked up to me in the newsroom and told me that I had to begin wearing a suit and tie every day to work. I thought his priorities were a little out of order, worrying about a dress code when there was no cash flow for payroll; no money for paper or newsprint; when we were owned by a public scoundrel on the cusp of being handcuffed; and when our editor had just defected to the competition that was trying to put us out of business. Kalech told me to ignore the new dress-code policy and just go out and dig up stories that would "make the wood."

As that eventful day came to a close, I looked around the newsroom. The abandoned desks made me feel as if I was in Saigon a week before its fall.

That night I decided the best way, and maybe the only way, to save the *Post* was to draft Pete Hamill to become the editor. Bray just did not have the hard-news background or leadership skills to do the job. Pete had been my compadre since the 1960s. If I knew anything in this world, I knew that Pete would make a great editor, even if he had no "management experience." I knew he was a natural teacher of young columnists and reporters. Every time I had written something I was unsure about, that I knew needed fixing in some way, I asked Pete to read the manuscript. He could see immediately what needed revision or deletion. He knew as much as any scholar or academic about the history of New York, was deeply knowledgeable about photography, art, immigration, architecture, film, jazz, race relations, Hispanic culture, and sports. And I knew that as the eldest of seven siblings, he was a natural leader. I believed Pete was born to edit a New York tabloid. I gave my idea to Mario Cuomo, Eric Breindel, and Howard Rubenstein. They all loved it and said they would try to get Hoffenberg to think it was his own. The hard part was getting Pete to take the job, if it was ever offered.

On Saturday, February 6, Pete and I walked from the *Post* on South Street to Benito's Restaurant on Mulberry Street. In the course of the half-hour walk I attempted to make the case he should become the editor of the *Post.*

Five years earlier Pete had had a serious cancer scare. A heavy smoker, he was told he had lung cancer. But when they opened him up on the operating table, the surgeons discovered the dark spot on the X ray was only a dormant tuberculosis, from when Pete worked at the Brooklyn Navy Yard as a teenager. The cancer diagnosis gave him a strong sense of his own mortality. He wanted to write books that mattered before his time ran out. Editing the *Post* might seem like a risky distraction for a man now fifty-eight, with a memoir and novels and film scripts to write. He would be setting aside his own agenda to join a sinking ship. Pete had also just gotten an offer from Mort Zuckerman to become the "Sunday editor" of the *News.*

Pete felt that accepting a job from a man like Hoffenberg could be a kind of moral corruption. As we ate our pasta, he said, "Do you realize you're proposing I go to work for a hoodlum? Would Kempton or I. F. Stone take this job working for Lepke? What artist has ever voluntarily gone to work for a hoodlum? Name me one."

"Ray Robinson boxed for Frankie Carbo," I said.

"That's one. Name me another."

At that point the owner of the restaurant recognized us and offered us a bottle of wine and sat down at the table. I summarized the state of the debate for him.

"Mr. Hamill," he said, "you should take this job. In America everyone is a little bit crooked."

By the end of our walk to my house in Greenwich Village, Pete had relented, at least to the point of letting his lawyer, Richard Emery, meet with "Lepke." As we parted, I told Pete we should have a new masthead motto—"Drop the gun, keep the cannoli."

I'm not sure how the idea of making Pete the editor traveled to Hoffenberg, but he jumped at it. Bray, who wanted power, tried to scuttle it, but Cuozzo and Kalech embraced the move, sensing the possibility of both credibility and salvation.

One Thursday night in mid-February the deal was made in Emery's law office, with Kalech, Cuozzo, Bray, and Hoffenberg all present. I was in the newsroom waiting for the call confirming that Pete was going to be the new editor, so that I could write a column about him for the next day's edition. An exuberant Kalech called night editor Mike Hechtman at 10:45 P.M., just in time to get the Hamill announcement into the second edition.

"We have to replate," Kalech said, using newsroom jargon for "make changes." "Pete is going to be the new editor! Give me somebody on rewrite and I'll dictate a story," he said with some urgency.

"Can you call back later?" Hechtman replied. "I have a big fire in Brooklyn."

"Forget the fire, just give me rewrite," Kalech shouted.

As Pete was signing the multiple contracts, Lepke was asking him, "How hot was Jackie Kennedy?"

As part of his contract, Pete received three commitments from Hoffenberg in writing. First, Pete would be given absolute editorial independence and autonomy. Second, Hoffenberg would immediately restore the 20 percent pay cut the staff took on the day Kalikow was within an hour of shutting the paper. Third, editorial budget would be expanded so that Pete could replace those who were fleeing to the better-financed *News.*

I think sentiment had something to do with Pete taking the job. He had started his career at the *Post* in 1960, at age twenty-four. He got the job by writing a combative letter to editor James Wechsler, expressing his youthful Brooklyn/Catholic/working-class reactions to Wechsler's book *Reflections of an Angry Middle-Aged Editor.*

"The *New York Post* gave me my life," I heard Pete say on more than one occasion. And now he felt some obligation to give the *Post* life.

When Pete's appointment was announced, Edwin Diamond wrote a glowing profile in *New York* magazine but also observed, "Hamill seems to be a man reason has fled, agreeing to ship on as captain of the Titanic after it hit the iceberg." But Pete told me, "When I got my *Post* try-out back in June of 1960, everyone told me the paper was about to fold. The *Post* is always about to die, but never does."

Pete was the editor of the *New York Post* from February 22 till March 28. Short a tenure as this was, it was filled with bigger and bigger distractions and circuses. He worked at least thirteen hours during most of those dramatic days. But even with all his hard work, he was never able to apply his full talents to the task, mostly because, also on February 22, a mad mogul named Abe Hirschfeld became Hoffenberg's 50 percent "partner," in exchange for a cash infusion of $3 million.

Hoffenberg knew Hirschfeld because he had dated Hirschfeld's daughter, but from the outset these two unstable sleazoids fought each other for legal control of the paper. Hechtman said, "They should both be in the Hebrew Home for the "Criminally Insane." That was the day Hoffenberg chased Abe down the hall.

Despite the anarchy all around him, Pete quickly made a series of hiring and promotion decisions that sent a message of inclusion to women and minorities and to the city. Pete is a universal humanist in his affections, and the instinct goes deeper than just Jackie Robinson–Brooklyn Dodger romanticism. In 1945, when Pete was ten years old, his mother took him to a movie theater in Park Slope to watch the first newsreels about the liberation of the Nazi concentration camps in Germany. His mother told him to "remember these films." These were victims of hate and anti-Semitism, of theories of racial supremacy. Pete shared this childhood memory at his mom's funeral service in 1998. He traced many of his convictions to this experience. His mother gave him the gift of tolerance.

One of the first things Pete did was to name Joe Nicholson to be a columnist, making Joe the first openly gay daily columnist in New York and maybe in the country. Then Pete assigned Karen Phillips to be his new baseball columnist and sent her to Florida to report from spring training. Karen had been covering the courts and was a leader of the Newspaper Guild chapter at the paper. She was already a kind of folk heroine in the city room because she had slapped McAlary in the face at McFadden's Bar a few days after he had defected to the *News* and been quoted predicting that the *Post* would be dead in forty-eight hours. The day after the slap Mike sent a gracious computer message to everyone at the *Post*, apologizing for what he had said and predicting he would soon return to the paper.

Karen's baseball columns were spectacular. Before she left for Florida, Pete had told her he wanted someone to cover baseball as an outsider, as a human-interest story. There were enough statistics junkies and trade gossips on the beat. Karen was a baseball fan and a member of the *Post*'s *fantasy* baseball league. But she was a professional reporter with a good eye and a sharp mind first.

She proved Pete's instinct about her was right. I was amazed no other paper hired her. Karen should have become a star, if the newspaper business was based on merit.

Pete promoted education reporter Andrea Peyser to columnist. He gave Mark Kriegel, a sports columnist and one of his protégés, a cityside column in the front of the paper. He appointed Tommy Ko to be deputy managing editor for layout and design. Tommy had been born in China, grew up in Hong Kong, and had started at the *Post* as a copyboy in 1972. He appointed Maralyn Matlick to be the associate metro editor. Maralyn had started as a copygirl in 1976. She was the first woman to be part of the city desk decision making. She was promoted to Sunday editor in 2001.

He promoted investigative reporter Murray Weiss to be an associate metro editor. In the summer of 1993, Murray edited my series on the Crown Heights riots that won the Golden Typewriter Award from the New York Press Club.

Pete also hired four black reporters, ending years of city room apartheid in one week. For years *Post* editors had claimed they had wanted to hire blacks to cover a city that was becoming more than 30 percent black but couldn't find any who were "qualified." Pete found them, with no trouble, on a tiny budget, and got them to join a paper with poor survival prospects. All that was ever needed was a strong will based more on journalistic common sense than any liberal social engineering. All that was needed was the absence of stereotype and prejudice.

Pete also appointed me to be the "investigations editor" and asked me to start preparing a "ten worst judges" project with Jim Nolan. Pete intended the judges project to be part of a new Sunday magazine he was planning to start. By the time it ran, Pete was gone. But the new editor, Ken Chandler, did run "NY's 10 Worst Judges," with the biggest front-page headline of bold type in years.

During the thirty-five days Pete had as editor, he also hired Willie Neuman and Larry Celona as reporters, and both remain to this day.

Willie speaks fluent Spanish. Larry got hired as a police reporter when he came to bring me his résumé after he was foolishly fired by the *News*. Larry had a two-day growth of beard and was wearing a hooded, stained gray sweatshirt. Pete noticed him to talking to me in the newsroom and immediately invited Larry into his office and hired him on the spot, even though he looked like a mob hitman on a stakeout.

These new hires helped offset the raids by the *Daily News*. Colassuano, now running the *News*, was orchestrating them. Lou once told me how much he had "looked up to Pete" and that as a *Post* copyboy, he would get a thrill just picking up Pete's copy at his home or the Lion's Head bar—in the age before fax machines and modems and in the age before Pete stopped drinking. Pete called Colassuano up. "Cut this shit out!" he told him. Colassuano's poaching stopped.

The remaining staff of younger reporters, yet to earn their reputations, seemed inspired just to be working for Pete. They started coming in early and leaving late. Many seemed motivated by a rising fury against the "traitors" who jumped to the *News*. They wanted to put out a paper better than the one being put out by all the big names who had defected for huge salaries and long-term contracts.

One of those *Post* reporters who rose to the occasion was celebrity writer Bill Hoffman. One morning he was telling me how he was taking pills to settle his nervous stomach and how his mother was calling him every day, worried that the paper would die and her son would be jobless. Two hours later Hoffman was in Pete's office, describing a terrific and exclusive story. There was a confirmed case of food poisoning at the posh Plaza Hotel, owned by Donald Trump. Soon Trump's posse of publicists were on the phone trying to kill the story, claiming it was a case of "stomach flu" unrelated to the Plaza's kitchen.

Pete and Kalech said, "Print the story." We were really going to be a paper that stood up to the powerful, worshipped no sacred cows, and tried to see the city through the eyes of the subway riders, hardhats, and working stiffs. Under Kalikow, Senator D'Amato and City Council President Andrew Stein had been protected. Now everyone was fair game if the facts were there.

Hirschfeld was a meddling pest on most days. He pressured Pete to print his wife's awful poetry on page 3. He also pressured Pete to assign a negative story on Stanley Stahl, a business partner Abe was having conflicts with. Pete refused to assign such a story. Seven years later Abe went to prison for trying to hire a hit man to murder Stahl.

For his part, "Lepke" was pressing Pete to place large photos of topless women on page 3, the way the British tabs did. "Boobs" were the only thing these two boobs could agree on. Hoffenberg also wanted to see an exposé of the SEC in the *Post*. This would have looked completely self-serving, since the SEC had just frozen Hoffenberg's assets, blocking the emergency transfusion of $500,000 of his personal funds into the paper.

Early one Friday morning Pete called me up and said, "My last two paychecks bounced. Lepke gave me a spaldeen. I might have to quit if he doesn't make them good today." "I'll deal with it," I said. "But should I go see Lepke or Abe? Who is really in control?" We decided I would go to see Lepke, since he was the one who had hired Pete and the rubber checks came from his Towers Financial Company. He also seemed marginally less vindictive and less crazy than Hirschfeld.

So I took the F train to the *Post*, planning what I would say to Lepke. I also was adjusting to my new role as debt collector and bagman for Hamill. I believed that Pete would walk away from the *Post* if I came back empty-handed. He was fed up fending off the daily lunatic requests from both our owners.

When I arrived at the *Post*, I called Hoffenberg's assistant, explained who I was, what I wanted, and said I was on my way up to the sixth floor. There were goons and bodyguards with earpieces and walkie-talkies everywhere. I couldn't tell which thugs worked for which wacko. I told Lepke's gatekeeper, "Look, Pete is from Park Slope. I'm from Bed-Stuy. Hoffenberg is from Bensonhurst. We are all Brooklyn boys, so let's work this out nice and quiet, so there won't be any bad publicity. I'm a debt collector like Hoffenberg. Pete is owed $10,500, and I'm owed $2,000, and I need to leave this office with the money that is owed for honest labor."

This got me into Hoffenberg's office. Peter Faris, the only professional manager left in the building, was at a desk, heroically negotiating for newsprint on credit for the next week. I repeated my little speech to Hoffenberg, calling myself a "receivables collector" instead of the more colloquial "debt collector." He offered me partial payment in cash from a stash in his desk. "I would prefer checks, but I'll take cash as a last resort," I heard myself say. I imagined somebody in the future asking me if I took any notes during this period and replying "No, just cash." "Cut the checks for Mr. Newfield," Lepke shouted to an assistant. Then, to me he said, "You have to wait until Charley from uptown gets here to sign them."

It was then noon. I waited and waited. I began to suspect I was being stalled till the banks closed. "Waiting for Charley from Uptown," I thought, would make a good title for a play about the *Post*, like *Waiting for Godot* or *Waiting for Lefty*.

As I waited, I could hear phone conversations that sounded so dire I feared the paper might expire while I was waiting in Lepke's office. There was no toilet paper in the bathrooms, no chemicals to print photos, no paper for the copying machines. Faris was pleading for time with creditors, begging for newsprint from the *Boston Herald American*, a Murdoch-owned paper. I began to wonder if Murdoch might ride to the rescue and save us yet.

At about 3 P.M. Lepke reappeared and said, "Would Pete wire the money to California, where the banks are still open, so the check would not have time to bounce in New York?" I didn't understand this scam transaction and called Pete. He said, "Just bring me the money."

It was 5 P.M. There was still no sign of Charley from uptown. I was using this wait productively, making friends with the chiefs of security, ex-FBI agent Bill Kelly and his deputy, ex-cop Al Sheppard. They would turn out to be crucial back-channel allies in the mutiny phase of the opera.

Finally I was notified that Charley was in the building. "Just wait a little while longer." I heard Lepke calling Rubenstein to set up more radio and television interviews for him. In came Charley, who was dressed like a Hollywood hoodlum. He wore a pinky ring and ear stud, and had the upper body of a weight lifter.

"What's the number on Hamill's check that bounced?" he asked. I explained it was not a number I had committed to memory, like Ty Cobb's lifetime batting average.

"Call Hamill," he said. "Ask him to look and see if the bounced checks have holes punched in them. If there are no holes, he should try to redeposit them again."

I finally lost my patience. "This is it!" I told Charley. "I've been sitting here all day. If I don't have the checks in five minutes, I'm leaving. I'm tired of being jerked around. There's going to be a mutiny if I don't get them now."

Five minutes later I was handed two checks. Pete got $8,500 out of the $10,500 owed to him. I got half of the $2,000 owed to me. I put the checks in my pocket. Draping my arm around Lepke's thick, strong neck, I whispered, "I know you're a gangster, but thanks anyway."

Lepke laughed. "Nah, I'm no gangster, I'm just a shylock."

But it turned out that I was a total failure as a collector of receivables. When Pete tried to deposit his check the following Monday, it bounced. My check bounced, too. I should have taken the cash.

On March 12 the *Post* carnival as I refer to it now began in earnest. For two weeks I felt I was living in a washing machine, getting thrown topsy-turvy every minute.

That Friday began with a hearing in federal bankruptcy court, in a building named for Alexander Hamilton—the founder of the *Post*—before a visiting substitute judge from Vermont named Francis Conrad. Judge Conrad cared little about New York or newspapers. He even put his indifference to the future of the people on the *Post* on the record, with his cramped, technical, procedural point of view of the estate case before him that day. "My concern is the estate," he declared.

Looking down at all the anxious *Post* staffers filling the courtroom, he continued, "The reporters before me are not really before me in court, not my jurisdiction. What is before me is stock—an asset of Mr. Kalikow."

Kalikow wanted Hirschfeld rather than Hoffenberg to control the paper with an option to buy, and that is what the judge ruled. Hirschfeld and Kalikow had an agreement that Hirschfeld would bail out all of Kalikow's tax obligations, but Hirschfeld was only committed to fund the *Post* for a few weeks.

Sitting in that courtroom, I felt the verdict was a death sentence for the *Post*. Hirschfeld was unstable, nasty, and only in it for some short-term personal publicity or maybe for the real estate. He had no knowledge of the newspaper business and no interest in learning about it. He was seventy-three and had amassed a fortune building open-air parking garages but knew nothing about printing, distribution, design, or—least of all—reporting.

Back at the paper, Kalech gave me some new information confirming that Hirschfeld's control really was a death sentence. He told me Hirschfeld planned to fire Pete in a few minutes and make Gerard Bray the new editor. "Gerard, Cuozzo, and myself," Marc said, "have taken a blood oath that none of us will take the editor's job if Pete is fired, but I have my doubts that Gerard will live up to our handshake." This blood-brother pact had been sealed with a handshake in the men's room in the courthouse an hour earlier.

At 5 P.M. that same day, Bray came into Kalech's office and said, "Pete's been fired. I'm the new editor."

"Fuck you, Gerard" was Marc's angry response to the betrayal. Cuozzo went nuts and started cursing Bray.

Bray did not respond directly, but turned to Pete. "Abe wants you out of the building by midnight."

I watched Pete call Abe, reaching him in his car. "You didn't have the balls to fire me yourself, you coward! You wouldn't do it to my face, you little prick!" Pete hung up and then started to pack up his pictures of Paul Sann, the Brooklyn Dodgers, and Ray Robinson. He placed them gently into a bag.

Jim Nolan helped me round up about thirty reporters, photographers, and editors for an emergency meeting in the (foodless) cafeteria. Now was the time to act.

Nolan and I pleaded for some drastic protest against Pete's firing. A Newspaper Guild member disagreed, saying Pete was management and that his firing had nothing to do with the union contract. I argued that this was bigger than the union contract. The survival of the paper was at stake. Labor and management were "all in the same concentration camp now." This was about the free press, the First Amendment, and the life of the city—not the Guild contract. By the end of the meeting, mostly thanks to Nolan's skills as a speaker (which were a lot better than mine), most of the staff seemed ready to close ranks and rumble, once we had a coherent strategy, which we didn't yet have.

All day weather forecasters were predicting a monster snowstorm was about to hit the city, and as I walked out of the building, the first flakes were starting to fall. It snowed all day Saturday. Early Sunday several *Post* staffers called me at home and said I better come to the paper immediately. They said Abe was planning a 2 P.M. press conference and that there was a strong rumor he was going to appoint Bill Tatum to be the new editor.

Bill Tatum and I had once been friends. We had marched side by side from Selma to Montgomery in 1965. But once he gained control of the *Amsterdam News*, he began writing editorials that struck me as antiwhite, anti-Jewish, and needlessly inflammatory—in an effort to sell papers. He was a racial arsonist in a city parched by tension. Tatum supported the feral teenagers who brutally beat and gang-raped the young woman who became known as the Central Park Jogger. Tatum alone published her name and called her attackers "young black martyrs," even after they were convicted. He defended City College Professor Leonard Jeffries's version of black supremacy and white inferiority. He tried to rally support for Tawana Brawley's claim of rape, even after the state attorney general and the courts found it to be a hoax. He praised Louis Farrakhan often. In 2000 Tatum would cause a national stir when his editorial condemned Al Gore for selecting Joseph Lieberman to be his running mate. Tatum wrote that Gore picked the Jewish senator "for the money." "Jews from all over the world," Tatum wrote, "especially in Europe, Africa, Israel, and South America, will be sending bundles of money. America is being sold to the highest bidder."

I knew I could not work for Tatum and Hirschfeld, even for a day.

I had come to believe that part of the secret of life involves what I call "peace through fiction." I knew it was necessary to forget my occasional disappointments in the people with whom I worked. Paul O'Dwyer and Murray Kempton had taught me to stop personalizing honest differences with others. I had learned to swallow small slights and not to hold on tightly to every grudge. I learned how to pretend to get along, how to be more tolerant of weakness. I learned how to let go of old resentments for the sake of the larger group or the larger objective. But Tatum was beyond the pale of decency. I could not overlook his attacks on Jews or his journalistic record of ignoring what was true. He was not a professional. I was ready either to resign or to resist Tatum. Fighting every form of prejudice was my identity, my code. There could be no peace with anti-Semitism.

I rode the subway to the East Broadway station and then trudged through the snowbanks to the *Post.* The streets were serene and beautiful, but my mind was a tumult of anger and apprehension.

How could Tatum edit the *Post,* a job once occupied by the poet William Cullen Bryant? What tradition did he share with *Post* writers like Walt Whitman, Washington Irving, Joseph Lash, Murray Kempton, Jimmy Cannon, Max Lerner, and Jimmy Wechsler?

When I got to the city room, Kalech told me that Bray had just resigned as the editor. Abe had demanded he fire 275 unionized workers, 72 of them in editorial. Bray knew the paper could not function with such a skeleton staff. And firing members of the Guild and other unions without cause, and without a due process hearing, was illegal under the existing contracts.

At 2 P.M. everyone who was in the newroom ran up to the sixth floor to witness the Hirschfeld press conference. We were all in a rage before we entered the room. When we got there, Hirschfeld and Tatum, and their wives, were seated at a table in front of microphones. Photographers from other papers and television news crews were in position to record the event. Hirschfeld began to ramble in his semicoherent fashion. He variously explained that Tatum was the new editor, the copublisher, and his partner. "I speak to you as a friend," Abe said as he announced he would fire 275 employees later that day.

"Don't call yourself our friend," copy chief Barry Goss shouted. "Why did you fire Hamill?" he asked, his usual self-effacing manner gone.

All Barry knew about Tatum was that he had published the name of the raped jogger. This infuriated Barry. He lived near the jogger, and as copy chief, he enforced the rules about not naming rape victims in print. "I knew her address, I felt close to her," Barry told me later.

"I did not fire Hamill," Hirschfeld insisted. "He resigned, I never fired him."

"You LIAR, you COWARD," Barry screamed back. "Where is your decency?"

"I was in the room when you fired him," Marc shouted. "You're a liar, Mr. Hirschfeld." That "mister" was the last sign of respect Marc would ever show Hirschfeld.

I found myself advancing toward Hirschfeld and Tatum until I was about twelve inches away from them. I knew I was losing control of my emotions. I was screaming the word "dog" at them again and again. And then: "You rotten fucking scumbags!"

"I'd rather nobody own the paper than you two," somebody shouted.

The still photographers were clicking their shutters furiously. The TV camera crew from NY1, the all-news cable station, was capturing all this raw emotion on videotape, and would run it all day and all night. The next morning the *New York Times* published a four-column photo of Marc and Steve pointing at Hirschfeld, their fingers extended and their mouths open in midinvective. I was standing just behind them, a scowl on my face. The shot had been taken a split second before I lost control and started screaming the word "dog" in their faces.

The press conference ended with Hirschfeld and Tatum backing out of the room, looking frazzled. I felt empowered, part of a spontaneous mutiny. I sensed the courage of people who felt they had nothing left to lose, of people who had been pushed too far. We knew we were putting our jobs on the line, and we felt no fear.

Back down in the newsroom, a new dynamic began to develop. With Pete gone, people started looking to Marc Kalech for leadership. In the organizational chart, Cuozzo was higher, but authority began to flow toward Marc. People gathered in his office, asking him what to do next. Marc started to make decisions, and people liked those judgments. Had Marc been invited to join the group defection to the *News*, the *Post* might have disintegrated.

That Sunday afternoon, with the camera crews milling around the newsroom and the lobby, Marc decided the *Post* would not publish on Monday. Breindel, who was also a lawyer, advised Marc about the legalities of not publishing, suggesting plausible reasons to give the other papers, like the press conference disruption, the snowstorm, and accidental computer system problems. "Just make clear," Eric said, "that we are going to make a good-faith effort to publish tonight . . . Make sure the Guild does not walk out, because that would play into Abe's hands. Remember, there are legal implications for everything we say and do now."

"The shutdown liabilities," he added, "for Hirschfeld would be washed away if the Guild struck. He pro bably wants to provoke a strike."

Marc followed Eric's legal advice when he briefed reporters in the conference room. He created a false paper trail of layouts, dummies, lists of articles, but he quietly instructed the technical computer staff to crash the system.

On the 10 P.M. TV news, Hirschfeld was saying, "They're printing the paper now." But the March 15 *Post* was never printed or distributed.

Late in the evening Steve Bumbaca, the controller, came down to the newsroom. He said that Hirschfeld and Tatum had drawn up a list of 175 employees to be fired. He told me I was high on the list. Tatum had insisted I be among the first to be fired.

On Monday morning I began organizing the "Save the *Post* Rally," set for 5 P.M. on Thursday. We needed to reach out to the city, to show that our readers cared about our fate, that seven hundred jobs mattered, that a free press mattered, that we were revolting against our demented owner. We needed to create a constituency.

The truth was I didn't know what we were doing. I was over my head, pretending to be Joe Hill. I may have activist instincts, but I am not a professional organizer. Jim kept saying, "You were a leader of SDS. You must know what to do next." I really didn't. But I was able to fake it from the memory of watching others do it. So Jim and I made phone calls all morning, ignoring the fact we had both been on the list of those fired.

The first person I called was my friend Ken Sunshine, who had worked for Mayor Dinkins and who was just starting his own public relations business. Ken put his new clients on hold to help us. He agreed to get Mayor Dinkins to speak at the rally. He also started asking TV assignment editors to cover the rally. NY1 ended up doing it live, and so did NBC.

I called Dennis Rivera, the president of the hospital workers' union, and asked him if he would donate a sound system and flatbed truck for the rally. "Where do you want it delivered and what time?" was all he asked. I called some of Pete's close friends, and every one of them said yes, they would come and speak: Norman Mailer, playwright Herb Gardner, actor Danny Aiello, former *Post* columnist and boxing champion José Torres, TV interviewer Charley Rose, and musician Willie Colon.

We called the union leaders, and they all said yes: Sandy Feldman of the teachers', Barry Feinstein from the Teamsters', Phil Caruso from the police union. And the politicians all said yes, too: Rudy Giuliani, Alan Hevesi, Ruth Messinger, Andrew Stein, Peter Vallone, Mark Green, and Brooklyn DA Charles Hynes. Two of the new black reporters Pete had hired—Carolyn Butts and Gracien Mack—agreed to speak.

I asked Nolan to be the master of ceremonies. He was better on his feet, and more articulate, than I was. I have a talent for funny one-liners, and they sometimes catch the essence of something, but that I am not good at improvising or pumping up a crowd over an extended period of time. In fact, that same day a TV crew stopped me outside the *Post* and asked me to say something about the succession of owners we had gone through in a month. "We've gone from snakes, to rats, to worms," I said. But I lacked the confidence to command a rally or stir a crowd. It was a paradox of public performance that helped me understand how some political candidates could be effective in one format and robotic in another.

At about 1 P.M. Kalech asked me to stop organizing the rally and come into his office. He told me he had decided that the whole news hole—the first twenty-two pages—in the next day's paper would be devoted to stories and columns trashing Hirschfeld and Tatum. Did I want to contribute something? I told him I did. I had a long history with Hirschfeld. Marc said I had until 5 P.M. to write the column. Then he stressed the whole project was top secret. Hirschfeld and Tatum were on the sixth floor. If they knew what we were doing, they would prevent the paper from coming out. The security guards were covertly keeping us informed about their movements.

The entire staff was now working on the mutinous edition. Everyone was making calls, gathering information, and writing stories.

The idea to publish a mutiny paper came to Kalech in the shower that morning. We would go out, guns blazing, he thought. Maybe it would force Abe to sell the paper. The visual accompaniment occurred to him while he was waiting at the toll plaza of the Queens Midtown Tunnel. It was to have a drawing of Alexander Hamilton with a tear coming out of his eye on the front page. "It would be a cry for help from our founder," recalls Marc, "something totally different."

It wasn't till early afternoon that Marc shared his vision with the layout editors, Tommy Ko and David Ng, photo editor Vern Shibla, and artist Dennis Wickman. Wickman went to his computer and designed Hamilton with a solitary tear as big as a bathtub bubble. Marc looked at it and said it should cover the whole front page. He got a call and went off to bankruptcy court for another hearing before Judge Conrad.

Then another shock. Fifty of the fifty-one Guild members fired that morning had been rehired by Hirschfeld. Only Frank DiGiacomo of page 6 remained fired—for "insubordination." Breindel, Dicker, Seifman, and I were still off the payroll because we were not in the Guild. As Cuozzo left for the courthouse, he told me we would put out a normal paper—"Plan B"—if the judge restored Hoffenberg as the owner. Otherwise it was the still secret "Plan A."

By 5 P.M. I had finished my column on Hirschfeld. It began:

> We are living through the Marx Brothers version of the Hitler-Stalin pact here at South Street. Only this time the *Post* is Poland.
>
> Fifteen years ago I named Abe Hirschfeld one of the ten worst landlords of New York. While I was preparing the article he offered me a bribe of a free apartment if I left him out. I put him in.
>
> The next time I saw him was in 1990, on TV, spitting in the face of a Hispanic woman reporter in Miami. The wild spray of saliva perfectly symbolized Hirschfeld's attitude towards working reporters.

My column, written with white-heat intensity, ended this way:

> Hamill is our Yeltsin standing on a typewriter.
>
> The arrangement that made Hirschfeld the temporary operator of the *Post* raises questions. The decision was made by a visiting Bankruptcy Court judge from Vermont, who did not know Hirschfeld's history as slumlord-spitter-screwball. He had not presided over any of the previous court proceedings involving the *Post.*

> The problem with bankruptcy court is that it has a metal detector in the lobby, but not a CAT-scan. There should be a sanity test to get into a courtroom there.
>
> Honest Abe would never have gotten in.

At 5:30 P.M. Kalech called Tommy Ko from the courthouse. "Plan A," he said. "Hoffenberg lost."

How our secret held I don't know. Why Hirschfeld and Tatum never entered the fourth-floor newsroom remains a mystery. Emotions were running so high they probably feared a personal assault. The tension became unbearable as the clock ticked toward 10 P.M. when the presses would begin to roll. I still feared something would stop this mutinous *Post* edition from reaching our readers. Hirschfeld and Tatum had the computer capacity in their offices to see what was in tomorrow's paper and to shut off the electricity. But they never learned how to use the equipment.

Marc began to alert the TV stations and other papers to what we were doing. He scheduled live interviews as the paper was rolling off the presses. That would start the stampede to the newsstands in the morning. He even got a copy of the front page to the *News,* which ran it in Tuesday's editions.

I didn't know how the city was going to react to this mutiny paper. Had we gone too far? Would it seem like a high school prank? Would it create a sympathy backlash for Hirschfeld and Tatum? Would this be the final edition of the *Post* ever to come out?

At about 9 P.M. I went down to the loading dock and talked to some of the leaders of the drivers' union and the pressmen's union. I told them about the Thursday rally and how we needed a big turnout from the blue-collar unions as part of our coalition. One of the beefy drivers told me, "Your plan better fuckin' work, because I'm broke and too old to go back to mugging." Another said, "I've been watching you on television for years and telling people you're nothing but a nigger lover. Then I watched you on TV this week, and you're just like George Brett. You're a fucking psycho, just like me." I knew that Hirschfeld had left the building at 8 P.M., and I told some drivers that nothing could stop the mutiny edition they were about to start delivering. They seemed to love the audacity of it, the cowboy outlawness of it.

The drivers, the pressmen, and the security guards were essential to the coalition we were trying to organize. So was Phil Caruso of the Policeman's Benevolent Association and the leaders of the other unions joining our rally. I had learned from the *Daily News* strike how to create this big-tent alliance between the white-collar reporters and the blue-collar craft unions. Without this unity, we would look like pampered elitists play-acting the 1960s. We could not have organized this mutiny without the men with big hands, and ink-smudged aprons, union cards, and zipper jackets, who printed and distributed the paper. These men did not know Pete personally. But they sensed a kinship with his working-class roots.

I went back up to the news room to watch Kalech get interviewed on television. Marc was holding up a copy of the Hamilton front page for the camera. A pressman brought up a bunch of papers to the newsroom and there was exultation. We got away with it! Reporters were reading the headlines out loud to each other.':

> "WHO IS THIS NUT?" "HONEST ABE DOESN'T KNOW SPIT ABOUT JOURNALISM" (my column); "HATE TWINS' PLANS FOR NEWS ARE NOOSE TO US" (Kriegel's column); "TATUM'S PAPER FANS RACE HATRED."

Every article in the news hole was a direct attack on our two bosses. A large photo on page 3, shot from videotape, showed Abe spitting on the woman reporter in Miami. The cartoon by Sean Delonis depicted Abe in a straitjacket in a padded prison cell. Debby Orin did a story, based on a report by the Anti-Defamation League, that documented Tatum's bigotry against Jews and whites. It quoted his headline in the *Amsterdam News* after blacks rioted against Jews in Crown Heights—"MANY BLACKS, NO JEWS ARRESTED IN CROWN HEIGHTS." The mutiny paper was actually tougher on Tatum than Hirschfeld, I thought. It's worse to be called a bigot than be called a nut.

I went back outside onto South Street and watched the delivery trucks depart the loading dock and disappear into the dark. Some of the drivers were whooping it up. I was thinking this would make a great ending to a sequel to Richard Brooks's film *Deadline USA,* the one I saw when I was seventeen and made me think journalism was such a romantic occupation.

The Hamilton edition was a sensation. All 425,000 copies were sold off the newsstands by noon. It was an instant collector's item. The *Post* city room was flooded with faxed messages and phone calls of solidarity from newspapers all over the country. How could we have doubted what we were doing?

The following day the *New York Times* published an editorial cheering us. It said, "The *Post* hit the streets yesterday with a pungent, brassy issue that illustrated just what the city would lose if the paper shuts down . . . Only the *New York Post* would publish an issue skewering its own boss . . . Here's a cheer for that rowdy, raucous crowd on South Street. Given what a series of buyers have done to your newspaper, your rage is well placed."

Early in the morning Pete called me and said he was going into the paper to start to edit it again, even if he was fired. Reading the Hamilton edition, he felt he had to do something. I called Kalech to tell him Pete was coming back, but he already knew. He told me that it was his forty-fifth birthday and that Pete's return was the best birthday gift he could possibly receive.

By 10:30 A.M. the newsroom was packed. There were dozens of television news crews with cameras. There were reporters and columnists from the other papers, including Murray Kempton, wearing a happy smile. There was a big birthday cake for Marc. Most people assumed it was a welcoming cake for Pete. Abe Leibenwhol, the owner of the Second Avenue Deli, had sent over a huge platter of cold cuts.

Pete walked briskly into the city room at 11 A.M. to wild cheering. Flashbulbs went off. Television news crews turned on their lights and jockeyed for position in the crush. It felt like a game-winning, walk-off-home-run celebration in the World Series. Pete spoke briefly. "I saw the paper last night and I almost started weeping myself," he said. "That front page was an act of journalistic courage unprecedented in this country. I saw my name listed in the masthead as the editor-in-chief . . ." He paused, composed himself, and then added, "So I better come in and edit the paper." The chant of "Pete, Pete, Pete" filled the city room.

I caught Pete's eye and he rushed over and gave me a hug. The next day our embrace took up a half page, across five columns, in the *Post.* A smiling Charley Carillo is pictured next to us applauding, and Bill Hoffman's upraised fists frame my head on one side and Pete's on the other. Pete is grinning from ear to ear.

The next thing I knew Al Walker asked me to introduce him to Murray Kempton. Al Walker's real name was Alfred Embarrato. He was a capo in the Bonnano crime family. He was also a delivery foreman for the *Post.* He controlled the loading dock and all the gambling and loan-sharking along South Street. He had his own executive parking space. He had just pled guilty to extortion, in a scheme to steal 10,000 papers every night, for ten years, for a black market he controlled. Even after his guilty plea, nobody considered firing him—or taking away his private parking spot. Walker was not just some old white-collar criminal. He had two prior convictions for selling heroin, serving four years in the 1930s. When he was arrested again in 1955, the FBI described him as a "major interstate trafficker in drugs."

But now, in the midst of this joyous chaos, I guided Walker over to Murray Kempton. "I'm pleased to meet you, Mr. Kempton," I heard him say.

Murray immediately recognized Walker. "You once made me a loan during the 1962 newspaper strike when I was out of work and in debt. As I recall, it was at very favorable terms. Thank you, fellow worker."

Everybody looked up to Murray. He had the capacity to make people behave a little more civilized than they really were. The next day Murray published his column in *Newsday.* It began:

> The besieged *New York Post* staff, depleted in numbers, pillaged by marauders, and captained at the breach by the last romantic, who is Pete Hamill, has turned desperately at bay, loaded all guns from its diminishing stock of newsprint, and volleyed defiance of Abe Hirschfeld and Wilbert Tatum, the latest pretenders to its capture and gutting.

> Wilbert Tatum is a busy baiter of whites, and, to an excessively unappetizing extent of Jews, and scarcely a useful coadjutor for any publisher intent upon plausible appeal to a cosmopolitan city.
>
> Tatum is too cynical not to adjust his views to readers of minimal sensibility; but he has earned a repute noisome enough to almost guarantee the *Post*'s extinction, and that may explain his attraction to Hirschfeld.

Murray's column ended within an exquisite crescendo of hope and memory:

> On the fourth floor the beleaguered gave loud tongue to Pete Hamill's return to lead their resistance; and he himself was so cheerful as to stir in one visitor the fugitive hope that when he whom a dream has possessed might indeed survive all odds.
>
> But then the *Post* still shines with the illusions of that visitor's youth. Had it not been for it, he could never have known Martin Luther King, been graced with the company of Duke Ellington, burned with Bobby Kennedy, and laughed with his brother the president, and watched Ernest Green take his diploma as the first graduate of color at Central High School in Little Rock.
>
> It remains the youth of those who cheered Pete Hamill yesterday; and may God be good to them and find them a savior.

The afternoon of Pete's triumphant, if unauthorized, return to the editor's office, Mario Cuomo called me at the paper with a back-channel briefing on the state of play. "We have two chances here," Mario said. "I have put together a group of rich guys to save the paper. Ken Lipper and Ron Lauder and the Fisher brothers are the core of it. They are talking about putting up forty million to keep the paper going for a while and to get rid of Hirschfeld. Their basic motive is to keep alive a strong voice for Israel. It may work and it may not work. There's also a long shot hope that Murdoch will emerge. I'm trying to pave the way for him to get a waiver in Washington, which he would need to own both the *Post* and Fox television in New York. You guys just keep doing what you're doing. The Hamilton edition was sensational. It's the only thing people are talking about. Do something like that again for tomorrow."

Thursday, March 18, was an especially dizzying day inside the washing machine of the *Post.* Ups and downs came so fast you could get whiplash.

Our rally was scheduled for 5 P.M. Mayor Dinkins was wavering on whether to participate. The temperature was supposed to be about 40 degrees, with a biting wind coming off the East River. The local TV news shows intended to go on live at the start of the rally. The politicians were calling me, asking to speak first, or early, to get on TV. I had a final list of forty-three speakers, including *Post* writers Mark Kriegel, Andrea Peyser, and Breindel. Pete was scheduled to be the second speaker at 5:15 P.M.

Early in the afternoon a subpoena was served on Pete by Hirschfeld to appear at an emergency hearing in bankruptcy court at 5 P.M. This was obviously designed to prevent Pete's appearance at the rally. Richard Emery, Pete's lawyer, called and said that Judge Conrad had signed an order keeping Pete out of the *Post* building. Richard said Pete had to appear in court and could not speak at the rally. Kalech decided we would keep the news of Pete's banishment from the rally a secret. He told Nolan and me to look for a signal from him and then introduce him to the crowd instead of Pete. He would inform the crowd what happened and that Pete was in danger of going to jail—a dramatic exaggeration.

Before the rally began I got some more bad news. The big-money group of investors Cuomo had put together to replace Hirschfeld had fallen apart. Some would not accept Pete as the editor, feeling he was "too liberal." The main investor who opposed Pete was financier Thomas Rhodes, the president of the *National Review.* Ken Lipper, on the other hand, wanted Pete, and Breindel was trying to reassure the conservatives that he and Pete had a good working alliance and that Pete was pro-Israel. But this ideological infighting caused Larry and Zachery Fisher, multimillionaire realtors, to withdraw.

Just before the rally was to begin, Dinkins called me and said he would come—if he could speak first. I told the mayor that was fine with me. His participation was important because it separated the mayor from Tatum and integrated our support.

About eight hundred rowdy people assembled for the rally. The drivers and pressmen carried "Save the *Post*" rally posters and waved T-shirts with the "Never Say Die!" front page on them. Members of Local 6 of the hotel and restaurant workers' union came with a huge banner. A *Post* delivery truck was parked in front of the building with a bunch of drivers—and Cindy Adams—sitting on top of it. South Street was closed to traffic. Reporter Bill Hoffman arranged for three strippers from a topless club to arrive in a limo. They made the vibe fun and funky.

Mayor Dinkins began his opening remarks with a jibe against Breindel's editorials, which I thought was petty. Then he promised to do "everything possible to save the jobs at the *Post.*" (A few months later, when Dinkins was asked to write a letter to the FCC supporting Murdoch's waiver request, he refused to do it. This broken pledge was one reason the *Post* endorsed Rudy Giuliani that November rather than George Marlin, the Conservative Party candidate, whose endorsement was already in the computer system.)

After Dinkins spoke I got the signal from Kalech. He took the microphone, a desperate look in his eye, and informed the crowd that Pete would not be able to address them because Hirschfeld had moved to "throw Pete out of the city room and into jail . . . If he's sent to jail, we'll take over this place for good . . . The bastards are up against the wall and they're scared . . . Pete will go to jail over our dead bodies!"

Norman Mailer spoke next. "I've loved it, hated it, and sworn at it," he began, "but it's the paper I tend to read first every morning, because you can argue with it. It's alive!" Then Mailer added, "The key thing about the paper is that every reporter should be allowed to tell his own lies, rather than the lies his owner imposes."

Phil Caruso, the president of the PBA, picked up on Kalech's theme. "This is one cop," Phil said, "who will never lock up Pete Hamill, tonight, or ever. I'd go to jail before I'd ever lock up Pete Hamill or anybody else from this newspaper."

During the rally NY1 reporter Sharon Dizenhuz shouted up to me on the platform asking if I would come down and do a live interview. Almost all the daily print and TV reporters were sympathetic to our mutiny, but Sharon had been among the most supportive. I gave Nolan the handwritten order of the speakers and climbed down to answer questions and to reprise my best one-liners.

I thought the rally had been a success, but when I got back up to the city room at about 7:30 Kalech and Cuozzo seemed sunk in a depression. The collapse of the group of new investors was a crushing blow. The judge's order banning Pete from the building was another setback. And they did not have a front page for Friday's paper. In the background Hirschfeld was being interviewed on CNN's *Crossfire* show. He was bloviating about rehiring Pete as a columnist. "The most important thing," Abe was saying, "is for me to meet Pete Hamill anywhere, anytime. He is a great reporter and columnist. He knows how to write columns, and I know how to write checks."

The gloom in newsroom was so deep that Marc and Steve began to brief the staffers in small groups, saying "The next twenty-four hours will look terrible, but then things will start to look better. We will be fine in the end."

"I was making it up," Marc says today. "I was at the end of my rope that evening. I was exhausted and had run out of ideas. I was just trying to keep hope alive, while I didn't know what to do next." That's when he called Governor Cuomo.

"I'm thinking of writing an open letter to Judge Conrad and putting it on the front page of tomorrow's paper," Marc told Mario.

Then there was a long silence.

"I could hear Mario thinking," Marc says now. "He was silent for about forty seconds, but it felt like an hour."

Then Mario started dictating what the open letter might say. ("It was the voice of God," Marc recalls.) "No one has more respect for the law than we do," Mario began. "After all, the First Amendment to the Constitution is the very foundation of our existence and our freedom. We understand when a judge, sitting on the bench in the courtroom, says he must make his ruling strictly on the basis of the letter of the law."

Marc was writing furiously. Over the next few minutes he edited the governor's dictation, mixing in some of his own tabloid colloquialisms, like calling Hirschfeld a "madman." The key sentence—Cuomo's—was "We question laws whose strict interpretation will kill this paper."

To that plea for flexibility and for big-picture common sense, Marc added, "You might think that what has happened here in one week has no bearing on what you must decide, but you can't really believe that."

The penultimate section—pegged to a penultimate court hearing on Friday—was a collaborative effort between Marc and Mario:

> There are people in our community who are coming forward to save us. We know who they are. So do you. You must allow them time to assemble the paperwork your laws require them to have.
>
> You must not allow a disastrous ruling to stand, simply because the letter of the law says you are allowed to consider only one person. That person does not care what happens to us. He's only looking to protect himself.
>
> Judge Conrad, the people are watching what you do.

This text, surrounded by white space, ran on page 1, under the minimalist headline: "AN OPEN LETTER TO THE JUDGE DECIDING OUR FATE."

The layout set it in the form of a sober, judicious memo from "The employees of the *New York Post.*"

The lawyers for Hamill, the creditors, and Murdoch all say that this open letter had a decisive effect on Judge Conrad. One of them told me, "All morning he was making rulings for Hirschfeld. Suddenly he shifted after lunch and started making all his rulings against Hirschfeld. The only possible explanation for such a 180-degree shift is that he read the front page of the *Post* during the lunch break."

During the morning session Judge Conrad had declared the *Post*'s sale to Hirschfeld a "done deal." But in the afternoon Jan Constantine, a lawyer for Murdoch's News Corporation, got up to speak. She reminded the court that Murdoch had a right of first refusal (from his 1988 sale of the paper to Kalikow) and that he was refusing to waive this right.

"Rupert Murdoch is not going to buy the *New York Post* again," Judge Conrad declared with ignorant finality from the bench.

"It is not beyond the realm of possibility," Jan responded. A few in the courtroom audibly exhaled at her words.

At about 3 P.M. Friday, while this hearing was still going on, Bill Kelly's security staff alerted us that Tatum was planning to enter the newsroom for the first time, occupy Hamill's vacant office, and start acting as the editor. A group of us in the newsroom were prepared to block Tatum's path to Pete's office. I don't know why Tatum never set foot in the newsroom during the entire siege.

About 4 P.M. Kalech got a phone call from Roger Wood, who had been editor of the Post under Murdoch during the 1980s. Marc put the call on the speaker phone.

"There is hope," I heard Roger say.

Cuozzo said, "We are out of stunts, please tell us what you know."

"Dear boy," Roger replied, "the white steeds are being saddled all over town as we speak."

This meant Murdoch was going to be the savior Murray Kempton had asked God to send us. He was already working with Cuomo on the earthly waiver.

After this thrilling phone call, a group of *Post* reporters arrived with shopping carts piled high with groceries. They moved into Pete's empty office and declared they would sleep there for a week to stop Tatum from moving in. I felt like I was back at Columbia University in 1968, among the sit-in militants waiting for the police to bust in.

Then came another revolution of the washing machine I was living in. A breathless Kalech came back from Judge Conrad's courtroom at about 6 P.M. and shouted, "The judge restored Pete!"

Judge Conrad ordered Pete and Abe to try to work together for two weeks, during which no firings or hiring could be executed. Then there would be a "final" *Post* hearing on April 2—before another judge, Burton Lifland—who came from New York. Outside the courthouse Abe kissed a horrified and surprised Hamill on the cheek, in a photo that would become famous for the look of disgust on Pete's scruffy, grimacing face.

I recently asked Marc Kalech how he felt now about his week of inspired improvisation. "I felt back then, while it was happening, that this was the most important thing I would ever do in my professional life. I felt my whole life was going to be measured by how I performed that week.

"I don't know how much of a factor it was that my forty-fifth birthday occurred during that week. But I felt what I did that week would make me a man."

Over the weekend I was able to catch up and see some of the television coverage Janie had taped for me and read some of the national papers.

Our mutiny was all over network television, and all the coverage was sympathetic to our cause. Television was playing it as a Frank Capra movie, the working stiffs revolting against the rich, lunatic owner and trying to fire their boss.

In the *Washington Post*, Richard Cohen wrote, "The takeover of the New York Post by its staff is so wonderful that mere WOIDS cannot do it justice. It should be a musical, the journalist version of 'Les Miserables.' "

In *Newsday*, Pulitzer Prize–winning cartoonist Tom Darcy depicted the *Post* staff in the same pose as the marines raising the flag on Iwo Jima, except he had us sticking the flag into Hirschfeld. "Stick it, you can't fire us, we've got a paper to print," read the flag.

Our mutiny had seized the imagination of our profession and of New York City. We were leading the TV news every night for a week. Wherever I went that weekend, I was recognized. *Post* truck drivers honked their horn at me. Ordinary people stopped me on the street to voice their support. Cops and firefighters wished me luck.

I couldn't understand why Hirschfeld wanted to own the *Post*. He was a landlord and parking lot mogul, not a newspaper man. A clue as to why came in an article in the *Boston Globe*. In an interview with by Tom Mashberg, Abe said, "I came to buy this building, but I got stuck with the *Post*. My choice would be to own the building, and close the paper." That was the answer. He wanted the real estate. He was thinking condos, location. Kempton's intuition, that Hirschfeld had bought in Tatum to kill the paper, made more sense than any other explanation.

On Saturday night Cuomo called me to say he had spent the day smoothing the way for Murdoch to get a waiver from the ban on cross-ownership of media within a single market. He had spoken to Ted Kennedy, who sponsored the waiver, and said Ted was going to be "helpful." Mario also told me he had been talking to Michigan congressman John Dingell, who was then chairman of the House committee with oversight of the FCC. This was the kind of intrigue that Mario excelled at. That he was doing it to assist Murdoch, who had opposed him in every election, gave Mario a kind of perverse pleasure. He knew that saving the *Post* that would not produce any editorial favors for him.

On Sunday morning Mario called again to alert me that Hirschfeld was going to ban me, Eric Breindel, David Seifman, and Fred Dicker from entering the building on Monday morning and that he was determined never to restore the four of us to the payroll. Mario wouldn't tell me how he knew this, but Bill Kelly, the chief of security, confirmed to me that he was on Hirschfeld's "direct orders" to stop us from getting in to 210 South Street. He also said that by Thursday he thought I would be able to sneak into the building through a back door. Until then I was exiled.

On Sunday evening I talked with Pete, who told me he was going to edit the paper on Monday out of the South Street Diner, adjacent to the *Post*, as a gesture of protest against the "South Street Four" being banned from the building. He said we should all meet him at 9 A.M. at the diner. From there we would all go to the *Post* office for our symbolic rejection at the door, so that with the TV cameras could cover it.

When I got to the diner, Pete was seated in a booth with two cell phones, a laptop computer, and his lawyer, Richard Emery. Reporters, photographers, and television news crews were already present to memorialize our banishment.

All four of us had stories or editorials to write for that day's paper. I was going to write a column based on an exclusive interview with Sol Wachtler, the chief judge of New York who had been indicted for threatening a former mistress. I thought Watchtler was not being treated fairly. He was mentally ill with bipolar illness and did not belong in prison. I would write my column at City Hall and send it by computer to the paper, where a hard copy would be printed out and walked down to Pete, who would edit it in the diner. All four of us got a ride to City Hall in the back of a *Post* delivery truck.

Though united in our banishment, we "South Street Four" were all different. Seifman was a reporter and City Hall bureau chief with no discernible political point of view. Dicker had been a Maoist in his youth, but now he was conservative and Cuomo's leading tormentor in Albany, where he was bureau chief. Breindel was a brilliant conservative ideologue who had been a liberal in college at Harvard, where he roomed with Robert Kennedy, Jr., and dated Caroline Kennedy. Until he had been arrested for heroin possession, Breindel had also worked for Senator Moynihan. He had helped me get hired at the *Post*, and, despite our philosophical differences, we were in the process of becoming close friends. I had always admired men of the Left like Arthur Schlesinger and Murray Kempton who had been able to form warm friendships with men of the Right, like William Buckley, and I was pleased that I was starting to do that with Eric. When he died at age forty-two, in 1998, I was an usher at his funeral, where his eulogists included Henry Kissinger, Rupert Murdoch, Norman Podhoretz, and Mayor Rudy Giuliani.

At the appointed hour we all went to the door of the *Post* and were politely barred from entry by Bill Kelly, our secret ally.

We went back to the diner. Reporters began to pepper us with questions. Eric and Fred were blunt. They pointed out that all four of us were Jews, all four of us had been fired by Tatum, and all four of us had criticized various black leaders who were friends of Tatum. Seifman had exposed Hazel Dukes, the director of the city's off-track betting corporation. Dicker had been the first reporter to reveal the anti-Semitic speech made by City College Professor Leonard Jeffries, in which Jeffries argued that "rich Jews" had been responsible for the African slave trade and that "Russian Jewry in Hollywood" sought the destruction of black people. And Eric had written a prize-winning series of editorials in 1991 that alerted the city to the racism directed against the Koreans during the boycott of a deli in Brooklyn, led by Sonny Carson, who once bragged, "I don't hate just Jews. I hate all white people." Eric's editorials were rightly tough on Mayor Dinkins's refusal to break the boycott, or settle it, for eight months. And I had been writing investigative articles about Tatum's friend Don King for years and describing Tatum's pal Al Sharpton as a hustler and con artist.

Pete agreed that our reporting was the reason behind our being banned and fired and that the *Amsterdam News* had been anti-Semitic under Tatum's reign as editor and publisher. He told the reporters that he had warned Hirschfeld on Sunday, "In the context of Tatum, firing four Jews looks like hell."

When I was asked how long I was prepared to work without being paid, I replied, "I'll work for free for Pete until Hirschfeld leaves and allows a professional publisher to buy the paper."

"We're all on work release," Pete chimed in.

Another reporter asked me, "How does it feel getting fired by Hirschfeld and Tatum?"

"It's an honor, like making Nixon's enemies' list," I answered.

Then I heard Pete yell out to a waiter, "Bring me some copy, hold the cholesterol." We all laughed.

Sitting in the diner that day with Pete, surrounded by the New York media, I felt that our mutiny was perfectly consistent with the moral code of the old neighborhood I had grown up with: Be loyal to your friends. Don't be afraid of bullies. Never give up. Most important was the Jackie Robinson rule—intolerance won't wash.

At one point the deposed Hoffenberg showed up at the diner with a folder of documents. When Pete saw him, he went for a walk until he was informed that Hoffenberg had left. Later that day Hoffenberg issued a press release announcing that he had formed a new partnership with Al Walker, the gangster and loading dock foreman, and Gerard Bray, who had been editor for twenty-four hours. The press release, which used Walker's real name, Al Embarrato, read, "Al Embarrato will assist the partnership in enlisting *Post* employees as partners and owners of New York Post Publishing Incorporated. Under the expansion plan, employees who become partners/owners would acquire equity interest in exchange for a temporary, voluntary reductions of their salary."

This was Hoffenberg's last scam. No legitimate investor was going to go near Embarrato. Pete had been right to flee the diner. He told me he ran out because there were photographers around and he didn't want to be caught in another embarrassing pose, as he had been when Hirschfeld caught him by surprise and kissed him. "The single most ignominious moment of my life," he called the kiss.

The next day Judge Conrad, who was by then back in Vermont, held a hearing on our status. He ruled that, as editor, Hamill had the right to publish our articles and columns and that, as the temporary publisher, Hirschfeld had the right not to pay us and to bar us from entering the building. I was satisfied with the ruling, feeling that it was more important to be in the paper than to be in the building. And I could see anyone I wanted to in the South Street Diner. By Tuesday evening, though, the diner was so crowded with reporters it was impossible actually to do any writing or editing there.

On Tuesday Hirschfeld went on television and said that the "South Street Four" were all "animals." That gave Cuomo a chance to rise to our defense. In an interview he said that we made up "much of the heart of the *Post*," and that Hirschfeld had "made a mistake" in firing us, in terms of devaluing the asset of the *Post*. "Fred Dicker spends about 40 percent of his time figuring out how to slander me—with great success, incidentally—but who is very good at what he does," Mario said. "Eric Breindel, the award-winning editorial writer, writes a lot of brilliant editorials that I disagree with," he added. His comment about me was less barbed. "Jack Newfield is one of the great columnists in the country."

Thursday, March 25, was my last day inside the washing machine. Bill Kelly let me into the building in the morning. "If anybody asks," he told me, "just say you're packing up your files. That should take you about a week. Don't rush." Although I hadn't been paid with a legitimate check for about two months, I went right to work with Jim Nolan on our ten-worst-judges article. I made calls all morning about Judge Lorraine Backal. She made the final list and was eventually barred from the bench and disbarred for life because she had been paid for hiding drug money while a judge.

Late in the morning Cuomo called me and said that Murdoch's entry now depended on Judge Conrad and that there was going to be a telephone conference call from Vermont at 5 P.M. Ted Kennedy was issuing a public statement saying he would not oppose a waiver for Murdoch if the FCC granted him one. Senator Fritz Hollings of South Carolina would also not do anything to prevent Murdoch from becoming the buyer of last resort of the *Post*. Hollings and Kennedy had originally sponsored the prohibition against cross-ownership. "Judge Conrad is the ball game now," Mario said.

It was now clear that something had to happen fast. Hirschfeld was becoming increasingly unstable and sending signals he would not let

Murdoch into the picture. Two days earlier, at a press conference, Abe had been asked by a reporter if he would sell the *Post* to Murdoch. "I heard of two other interested parties," Abe responded. "Two homeless people in the Bowery." Would there be changes in the masthead? "Rome wasn't burnt in a day," Abe answered. We might have felt like characters in a Frank Capra movie, but Abe had become a character in a Mel Brooks burlesque.

The climactic conference call was a surreal scene. With Pete inside his glass-walled office were Breindel, Kalech, and Richard Emery. Like most of the staff, I pressed my face against the glass, trying to read facial expressions and body language. On the phone were lawyers for Kalikow, *Post* employees, the creditors, Murdoch, Hirschfeld, and Judge Conrad. The call lasted two hours. It began with the disclosure that Hirschfeld had not paid his FICA taxes to the government and had not put as much money into the *Post* as he had promised. This did not please the lawyer for the creditors. Then somebody said that Hirschfeld had stopped paying the twenty-three security guards on the *Post*'s payroll. Abe conceded that was true. "I only need three, not twenty-three," he said.

The judge then asked Bill Kelly, who had spent twenty years with the FBI, to join the conference call and identify himself. Kelly told the judge that Abe had ordered him to fire all twenty-three security guards and to swear it had been Kelly's decision, not Abe's.

"In all my thirty years of being employed," Kelly told Judge Conrad, "I have never disobeyed a direct order from a superior. But when Mr. Hirschfeld told me to lie, I could not do that, sir." Kelly's forthrightness was the turning point. Even Judge Conrad now understood that Abe was a vindictive crank who would destroy the value of the *Post* for everyone involved, including the creditors, and Kalikow, and all seven hundred employees.

Then Robert Miller, one of the lawyers representing *Post* management employees, told Judge Conrad that there existed an alternative to Hirschfeld's ownership, and asked that Rupert Murdoch's representative announce himself.

A voice replied, "Your honor, my name is Arthur Siskind. I am the general counsel of News Corporation. Mr. Murdoch is willing to run the

Post for sixty days. During that period he will try to obtain the waiver from the FCC. We have received sufficient assurance about the waiver to make this offer today."

At that moment, my face still pressed against the glass, I could see Marc, Eric, and Emery punch the air in joy. Pete only smiled, knowing Murdoch's ownership meant he would probably not remain on as editor.

Judge Conrad agreed to give controller Steve Bumbaca bill-paying authority to vendors, employees, and creditors during the sixty-day period Murdoch was nailing down the waiver that Cuomo had prenegotiated for him in Washington.

"If your honor wants Mr. Bumbaca to disturb my money," Abe interjected, "I would rather withdraw from the *Post.* I will leave. I don't want to be a part of it anymore."

"You have to deposit the four hundred thousand dollars you promised to invest in the *Post,*" the judge told Abe.

"Put me in jail," Abe croaked.

"Mr. Hirschfeld, I don't have the authority to do that," Judge Conrad replied.

More fists pumped the air behind the glass. Abe had self-destructed.

When the call ended and Pete, Marc, and Eric emerged, there was kissing and hugging and tears all around. I found Bill Kelly and told him I thought he was a great man.

The next morning Steve Bumbaca went into Abe's office and tried to go over a list of checks that needed to issued for the paper to continue to publish over the next three days. Abe ignored him. When Bumbaca pressed the issue, reminding Abe about depositing the $400,000 ordered by the court, Abe got up and walked out of the room. Bumbaca and his lawyer called Judge Conrad in Vermont.

In the afternoon there was a forty-five-minute emergency telephone conference with the judge. Abe wasn't making any sense now, saying that Murdoch's company was "little" and that his was "big." "There are people with real needs who are being hurt by what is going on," the judge told Abe.

At the end of the hearing Judge Conrad ordered Abe to allow $364,000 in checks to be paid "to keep the paper operating."

"I can't take it any more," Abe replied. "I'm getting sick. I'll get a heart attack."

Judge Conrad said he would "void" Abe's management contract to run the *Post* on Monday and award one to Murdoch.

On Friday night Governor Cuomo called the *Post* city desk with a message for the staff. "Don't worry, Murdoch's deal will go through on Monday. The only person with anything to worry about tonight is Mort Zuckerman."

On Sunday, March 28, Murdoch called Pete and invited him for a cup of coffee. Murdoch told Pete that he had asked Ken Chandler, the former managing editor, to become the *Post*'s new editor. He then offered Pete a job as "editor at large," which would include writing a column, give him an office at the *Post*, a book deal with HarperCollins, and an arrangement to appear regularly on Fox Television. Pete was pleased by the generous offer and the cordial meeting but turned the package down quickly. He already had book contracts and TV offers. He would publish five books over the next six years, two of them bestsellers—the memoir *A Drinking Life* and the novel *Snow in August.*

Pete also felt it would be unfair to Chandler to be a ghost with an office, where reporters with "the usual city room needs, desires, and ambitions might come to complain." Pete made the right choice. Chandler proved to be an excellent editor and is now the publisher.

On Monday, March 29, at 3 P.M., Rupert Murdoch entered the *Post* newsroom flanked by Ken Chandler, Eric Breindel, Howard Rubenstein, and his son Lachlan. A dozen camera crews trailed in his wake. He had not been at the *Post* since 1988, when he was forced to sell the property he so plainly loved. He stood up on a desk and addressed the happy mutineers.

"This is a great moment for me," he began. "This is a very emotional moment for me. And I realize at this moment that the real heroes are all of you. Especially Pete Hamill, and the fight he led the last few weeks . . . I am now announcing the rehiring of David Seifman, Jack Newfield, Fred Dicker, and Eric Breindel."

The *Post* was saved and I had a job again.

You never know how you will react under pressure when the time comes. You never know what you will do when you are tested by fear, by fatigue, and by long odds.

Anyone can talk like a hero, and anyone can act like a hero until the day of testing comes on somebody else's timetable, and you have to conquer fear and perform.

You never know how your friends and coworkers will react in a crisis. Who will rise to the occasion? Who will drift away and hide under the stress? Who will become a leader from the low rank and the back bench? Who will think clearly about the whole group when all seems lost? Who will act like some of the rich passengers on the *Titanic,* who paid bribes to be the first into the lifeboat?

For eight weeks I was in a foxhole with the seven hundred–member staff of the *New York Post,* including the drivers and pressmen. I discovered what I could do. And I discovered that the "crash-test dummies" of the tabloid business could perform like the marines when the bell rang.

When it was over, I felt an abiding bond with all my coworkers that I can only compare to the way members of championship sports teams describe teammates they have gone through fire and rain with, to reach a common goal, and at the end, they trust totally because they have the shared experience of jeopardy and triumph.

I have heard Mariano Rivera talk about David Cone. I have heard Willie Stargel talk about Roberto Clemente. I have heard Steve Kerr talk about Michael Jordan.

And that is the way I feel about Marc Kalech, Pete Hamill, Peter Faris, Jim Nolan, Eric Breindel, Karen Phillips, Maralyn Matlick, Barry Gross, Bill Kelly, Charley Carillo, David Seifman, Joe Nicholson, Tommy Ko, Colin Miner, Steve Cuozzo, Marsha Kranes, Mark Kriegel, and all the South Street merry mutineers.

As I write this, both Hirschfeld and Hoffenberg are in prison. Hirschfeld was convicted of criminal solicitation in the murder-for-hire scheme, and Hoffenberg was convicted of various federal financial fraud felonies.

On Friday, June 8, 2001, I was fired by the *Post*'s new editor, Col Allen, effective immediately. The reason he gave was that he wanted to take the paper in a "different direction." Our meeting lasted no more than a minute.

When I returned to the newsroom I saw Stuart Marques, the managing editor for news and the paper's pumping heart, packing up the books and mementos in his office, including his picture of Jackie Robinson stealing home.

I asked Stuart how he thought we should handle the inevitable calls from the rest of the media about what just happened.

"Don't complain, don't sound bitter," he advised. Then he repeated the jailhouse motto from his youth—"Shut up and do your time like a man."

I wandered down the hall to see if Marc Kalech was okay. Marc had been on the *Post* for thirty-five years, had helped save the paper during the Hirschfeld circus, and was now the managing editor for the arts. Marc was on the phone telling his wife, TV journalist Marcia Kramer, that he had just been fired.

All told, six people were fired, including Lisa Baird, the paper's only black editor.

I was back inside the washing machine, again feeling like a piece of cloth being flung around. I remembered all the times I heard Pete Hamill quote the warning from his mentor, Paul Sann: "Don't get used to being too happy. Newspapers will always break your fucking heart."

A little dazed, I found myself standing outside Stuart's office, accepting hugs and kisses from crying staff members. Most were young reporters I had mentored in some way. Then I walked the three blocks to the law office of Mario Cuomo. I wanted his advice. I also wanted him to read the severance agreement I had been asked to sign. My friend Ken Sunshine, the public relations consultant, rushed over to Mario's office. For two hours the three of us discussed my options. Mario agreed to represent me in the matter, insisting that he would not accept a fee.

Mario is a grand master at playing three-dimensional chess, and Ken is a wizard of spin, a skill he acquired representing Leonardo DiCaprio, Barbra Streisand, and Andrea Bocelli. I felt like I had a million dollars worth of talent for free. Ken helped me think about how I wanted to come across in the media, what to say to those covering the story of the *Post* firings.

I had already decided, with the prompting from Stuart that I would be positive in my public comments. During my life I had witnessed enough athletes and politicians accept loss with class, and I wanted to emulate them. I didn't want to whine, or complain or scapegoat. I wanted to show that I could get up from a big punch and keep going.

The only reporter I had thus far spoken with about what happened (though I had already received dozens of requests) was from *Newsday*. The next morning she quoted me, accurately, as saying "I had ten great years. I'm not angry. I'm not bitter. I am grateful for the run I had there with great people."

While meeting with Mario and Ken, I suddenly remembered that the day before I had committed myself to appear on NY1, the all-news cable channel, that night at 7, to discuss the politics of the week. My dream team of advisers urged me to cancel immediately. They didn't believe I could maintain my upbeat response under the pressure of live television and at the end of a stressful day. I thought that keeping the date was part of dealing with adversity. I assured them I could carry it off. I knew I had internalized Kempton's "losing side consciousness" well enough to impersonate a dignified loser.

I believed what I had told the *Newsday* reporter. While it was true I felt deeply sad about losing the chance to work with people like Stuart, Lisa, and all those fierce young reporters, I was grateful that the *Post* had allowed me to go after establishment sacred cows and to disagree with their editorial policy. I felt as if I had had a "good run."

I did the TV show. A friend who watched it told me I came across as diplomatic. As he put it, "You were fuckin' Averell Harriman!"

When I got home, I played back the day's phone messages and returned a few calls. Repeating the same thing to everyone—that I didn't know what I would be doing next—created a small panic attack. The knot of fear in my stomach I had felt when I quit the *News* made a return visit. It was the same fear: of never getting another column on a daily newspaper, of never returning to the glorious routine of waking up, making my morning phone calls, dropping in on the courts, or City Hall, or a source, and gradually developing my next column from information and instinct. I wondered whether I would ever again get a chance to practice this daily ritual.

Talking to Janie—solid, commonsensical, perceptive Janie—helped me grasp that my identity was not my column. My identity was me. My identity was my family, my friends, my ideas, my attitude. I would not allow the judgments of strangers to define my self-worth. I am me, and what's in my head, whether I have a column in a paper or not. When I quit the *News* and felt fear about the future, I sought solace in music and in long-gone political leaders. Now I found myself thinking about people I knew—three women whose courage in crisis was an inspiration to me.

I thought about how Janie had faced the removal of her cancerous kidney in 1997 with stoic serenity. Worrying more about how I was coping than she was about herself, she went into the operating room with a squeeze of my hand and a smile.

I thought about Joyce Wadler of the *New York Times*, who I have known for more than twenty years. My pangs of self-pity vanished when I thought about how she had vanquished cancer twice—first breast cancer and then ovarian cancer. "Kicked its ass twice!" Joyce boasted. Her sassy valor put my little anxieties into their proper perspective.

And I thought about Lisa Baird, single mother of two girls, who was fired with me. Lisa was as brave as any boxer I ever knew. Cancer was all through her body before she was fired. She limped, and was often in pain, and sometimes had to go home early, but she still edited my column with angry good humor. She treated words the way a jeweler treats diamonds: every change she made was for the better. A psychologist might categorize Lisa as "oppositional defiant." She had attitude. She recognized no authority except the truth. Lisa knew she was dying, but she kept coming to work and doing her job. I never heard her say anything that suggested self-pity. (Lisa died from cancer on October 27, 2001. She was 44.)

How could I possibly let myself get depressed over losing a column, when these three women had faced mortality with such resilient grace?

In the days that followed, whatever feelings of loss or fear I felt were pushed aside by an avalanche of love and support that poured in on me. I received more than a hundred calls, from colleagues, political figures, and old friends.

My dismissal from the *Post* created an awkward situation for my son, Joey, who now works as a photographer there. I told him to balance his loyalty to me with being a professional and continuing to perform to the best of his ability for the new editors at the paper. He was in a confusing circumstance for someone so young, but he handled it fine. His job is important to him, and the most important thing he could do was keep it. Joey covered the terrorist attack on the World Trade Center and took some amazing pictures. The next day, Pete Hamill mentioned Joey in his column, describing his professionalism as they ran for their lives, as the Towers crumbled and the cloud of black debris rushed towards them.

The Monday after my firing, old friends called with assignments to write articles for both *Playboy* and *Penthouse* magazines. Victor Navasky, the former editor of the *Nation* and a longtime friend, also called with an offer. He said that the Nation Institute would give me a grant to investigate the economics of boxing and write an article that proposed a "Bill of Rights for Boxers."

All this generosity made me feel appreciated and loved. Some friends even assured me that it was "a good career move" to get fired in a public way and to be depicted as a martyr to liberalism by the *New York Times.* Jules Feiffer told me that when he was fired by the *Village Voice*, it had revived his career. "People felt sorry for me. People gave me a lot of mercy patronage because they perceived I got a raw deal Public terminations are a splendid commercial opportunity," added this pioneering satirist and ironist.

On the Tuesday following the firings, we organized a surprise party for Stuart Marques at a restaurant in the Village. Stuart needed his own avalanche of affection from the dozens of reporters he had hired over the years, the ones he had brought into the "Church of the Second Chance." I was proud that my son, Joey, came, demonstrating his own loyalty to Stuart, who hired him.

I usually dodge speaking at events like this, feeling shy and inadequate to the occasion. But this time I managed to speak, from the heart, to a room filled with colleagues from both the *Post* and the *News*, about the ex-con, who had just told me, "Shut up and do your time like a man."

"You are a model of what it is to be a man," I began, looking directly at Stuart. "You give loyalty, and you generate loyalty. You have courage and you inspire courage in those who worked for you. Like Joe Frazier, you are a relentless truth machine. You don't let anyone lie to themselves. I would follow you anywhere—on a commando mission, or a prison break."

The end of Stuart's party was the closest I came to tears over the end of my happy run at the *Post.* I was standing in a corner with Janie and my eyes started watering. The party was over. I would never again get to work with this next generation of tabloid professionals. I knew I would sorely miss this close-knit collaborative community. This is what was almost "breaking my fucking heart."

The next morning I went to the *Post* to pack up my files. Most of them were research on the city's worst judges and landlords, the muckraking feature that I had conceived at the *Voice* in the 1970s. There were also files on the navy's bombing of Vieques, which had been my last column, and dozens of folders on the Reverend Al Sharpton, and club owner Peter Gatien.

As I struggled off the elevator in the lobby with my overloaded boxes, two security guards detained me and asked me to step into an office.

"What do you guys think I stole?" I asked.

"A computer," one replied as he searched my boxes.

"I don't even use a computer," I said. "I'm a manual typewriter kind of guy."

CODA

I can't compose some tidy summation. I have no six-point program for unraveling the mysteries of existence. I can't dash off an inspiring homily. There is no cheap grace. I have acquired too much respect for doubt along the way, too much appreciation for paradox, complexity, and for mystery itself. I am still struggling with who I am, and how I got there.

How did I know at sixteen that I wanted to become a journalist? Why did I enlist in the civil rights movement at twenty? What made Jackie Robinson, Martin Luther King, and Robert Kennedy such enduring inspirations to me, despite their mistakes and stumbles?

Where did I get the good instinct to pick out Mike Harrington, Bob Moses, and Murray Kempton as mentors? How did I know to marry the ideal mate in Janie?

What saved me from sharing the violent nihilistic fantasies of the late 1960s? How did I manage to go to a predominantly black high school and come out supportive of black equality, when others became my opposite, from similar experiences?

Why is that egalitarian, optimistic air of 1950s Brooklyn still in my lungs?

How have I managed not to lose my ancient baseball signed by Jackie Robinson, Pee Wee Reese, and most of the other 1949 Dodgers? Somehow I have been able to keep this talisman of inclusion for more than half a century, though I have lost almost everything else from my childhood.

I was shaped by being a nonobservant Jew who absorbed all the history of my tribe, by anti-Semitism, by five thousand years of persecution and intolerance, by the Holocaust, by reading Anne Frank, and by covering the Crown Heights riots of 1991, where Hasidic Jews were the victims and the police stood passive for two nights. Being a Jew is part of "losing side consciousness."

Elsewhere in this book, I quoted Bob Dylan's line "He not busy being born, is busy dying." About ten years ago I was able to apply this challenge to stretch yourself to learning how to make documentary films. I have now either written or coproduced six documentaries. Learning this new craft taught me to really see details, become more visual, think more clearly about narrative, and integrate my love of music with filmmaking. I even convinced Wynton Marsalis to compose the original music for an HBO documentary on Sugar Ray Robinson I made with Kirby Bradley in 1998. Wynton won an Emmy for the music he wrote and played, to match the images and moods of Sugar Ray on screen.

I have completed four films with Charley Stuart, who invited me into his editing room and taught me most of what I know. We shared our own Emmy for our PBS film on Don King. Learning a new craft after fifty does make you feel like you are busy being born.

As politics seemed more empty, I followed my instincts and started to write more, and with a fan's enthusiasm about the arts and popular culture. In the last two years I wrote a series of pieces celebrating the paradoxical funny and original HBO series *The Sopranos*. I published celebrations of filmmakers Spike Lee and Phil Alden Robinson; of Ken Burns's nineteen-hour meditation on the history of jazz; and of Bruce Springsteen. I discovered I liked writing positive columns more than negative ones.

I can't completely answer the questions I asked myself at the start of this coda. No one thread unifies a life and a career. At best there are only fragments and intuitions and contradictions. Life is always a puzzle with a few missing pieces.

There has been a quest for community as a substitute for the family structure I missed growing up. And a quest for mentors as a substitute for the father I never knew.

Janie, my wife of thirty-one years, and the unconditional love I feel for my children, have healed the void inflicted by growing up in a bizarre family environment. Family love is the root of fulfillment.

A few years ago, groping for some coherence to my politics, I found the Hebrew concept of *tikkun olam.* Roughly translated, it means to "heal or mend the universe," to transform the world, to make it more whole than you found it. This Hebrew concept (which I first heard the liberal Catholic Mario Cuomo talk about) is that God created the universe, but did not finish it, or make it perfect. Therefore we have an obligation toward improving the world. This is a spiritual, moral, and individual conception of justice. It is this mending mission itself that lends some meaning to our existence.

Tikkun olam is an alternative to an excess of materialism, cynicism, narcissism, and selfishness. It is probably the impulse behind Rabbi Hillel's second great question I invoked as an epigraph—"If I am only for myself, then what am I?"

Tikkun olam is the rationale for community, coalition, and collaboration. It is probably what fused my identification with Jackie Robinson. It is what led me into the civil rights movement, to Selma, and to Amite County in rural Mississippi. It is what helped me choose subjects to write about like lead poisoning in slum children, and Bobby McLaughlin's wrongful conviction for murder.

It gave me the emotions of group solidarity and connectedness that led me to quit my column at the *Daily News* and join the striking union members on the picket line.

We should believe in something more substantial than our own transient careerism and material possessions. We need a source of commitment to others. We should try to make the world a more equal place.

The two great modern, secular articulations of this idea can be found in speeches by Martin Luther King, Jr., and Robert Kennedy—a black Baptist preacher and an Irish Catholic politician. King's speech was delivered on February 4, 1968, exactly sixty days before his assassination. This is what he said:

> I don't want a long funeral. I'd like somebody to say that Martin Luther King, Jr., tried to love somebody. I want you to say I tried to be right on the war questions.
>
> Say that I was a drum major for justice. Say that I was a drum major for peace. That I was a drum major for righteousness. And all the other shallow things won't matter.
>
> I won't have any money to leave behind. I won't have the fine and luxurious things to leave behind. I just want to leave a committed life behind.

On June 10, 1966, Robert Kennedy spoke the following words to a crowd of young people in Capetown, South Africa—words from inside the wall of apartheid:

> Let no one be discouraged by the belief there is nothing one man, or one woman, can do against the enormous array of the world's ill—against misery and ignorance, injustice and violence. . . . Few will have the greatness to bend history itself; but each of us can work to change a small portion of events, and in the total of all those acts will be written the history of this generation.
>
> It is from numberless, diverse acts of courage and belief that human history is shaped. Each time a man stands up for an ideal, or strikes out against an injustice. Or acts to improve the lot of others, he sends a tiny ripple of hope, and crossing each other from a million different centers of energy and daring, those ripples build a current which can sweep down the mightiest walls of oppression and resistance.

King's notion of love and justice, and Kennedy's belief that one person can make a difference and that human courage can change history, are my best shot at political wisdom. They have universal application.

The concept of *tikkun olam* is but one way to reach these goals. Other roads go through the Sermon on the Mount, the Ten Commandments, the secular teachings of Dr. King and Abraham Lincoln.

For me, the best part of the 1960s was about repairing the universe. That's what ending segregation, stopping the Vietnam War, and enacting the 1965 Voting Rights Act were about.

Today I think of myself as a child of both 1960s activism and music, and the 1950s Brooklyn of the Dodgers, the Brooklyn of hope, inclusion, and cohesion. I feel about growing up in Brooklyn the way Nelson Algren and Mike Royko felt about Chicago, the way Eudora Welty and Willie Morris felt about Mississippi, the way James Baldwin felt about Harlem, the way Bruce Springsteen feels about the blue-collar Jersey shore towns.

A specific local place with distinctive character, can influence sense and sensibility for a lifetime. It's regional memory—like the blues and country music. I have never forgotten the values of my old Bed-Stuy neighborhood, the code of honor, unity, loyalty, fair play, and no surrender.

In retrospect, I now think growing up the way I did, raised by a single mother, was my salvation in a particular way. It gave me the proper fear of failure. It made me a scared striver, because I knew there was no margin for error, no safety net. I knew I would never have a life of soft landings. I had to make it on my own.

Growing up the way I did taught me hard work, discipline, and a belief in education, and gave me a survivalist instinct to enter the world across the Brooklyn Bridge.

After I was fired by the *Post* last June, I assembled a different kind of writing career. I started to write regularly for the *Nation* and *New York* magazine, and started working on a book about the consequences of fame. I also began work as a researcher/reporter on an HBO mini-series on the birth of rock and roll, told through the eyes of Atlantic Records. This gave me a chance to work with director Taylor Hackford (a friend who got me the gig), and immerse myself in the righteous music I grew up with—Ray Charles, Joe Turner, the Drifters, Otis Redding, LaVern Baker, Bobby Darin, and Aretha Franklin.

I'm also getting to work with Jerry Wexler, the former Atlantic executive who fused black and white, north and south, urban and rural, soul and gospel, to create this American sound. Jerry now 84 is rock and roll history. He produced Aretha's greatest soul albums, sang uncredited backup to Joe Turner on "Shake, Rattle and Roll," gave a eulogy at Otis Redding's funeral, and paid payola to Alan Freed in the Brill Building—$600 a month in cash to Freed's bagman.

I found this new, diverse, freelance career invigorating. When you are writing two columns a week against a deadline, you tend to write what you already know and think. But when you have more time to read and write you start to develop new thoughts, and acquire knowledge in new areas. You grow.

I had my newspaper dreams walking up Marcy Avenue to Boys High. I had my newspaper dreams riding the G train home late at night to the Myrtle-Willoughby station, after putting the Hunter *Arrow* to bed at the printers. I managed to live a lot of those fantasies.

More importantly, I found the fulfillment of family love and loyal friendships. These matter more than a prize plaque on the wall, or an old, framed front-page scoop.

When the soul singer Howard Tate sings, "Get it while you can," he is talking about love, not money, and not sex.

The late senator Paul Tsongas, knowing he was dying, remarked, "I hever heard of anybody on their death bed say they wished they had spent more time at the office."

Now I want to tell it—my story, my information, my perspective, my little piece of history,

I want to be a link on the chain, passing along the legacy I received form a free college education, from free Shakespeare in the park. I want to pass along the legacy Jackie Robinson and Murray Kempton gave me more than fifty years ago, in a state of mind called Brooklyn.

INDEX

Index

Index

Index

Index